Structuring Music through Markup Language:

Designs and Architectures

Jacques Steyn
Monash University, South Africa

Information Science REFERENCE

Managing Director:	Lindsay Johnston
Editorial Director:	Joel Gamon
Book Production Manager:	Jennifer Romanchak
Publishing Systems Analyst:	Adrienne Freeland
Assistant Acquisitions Editor:	Kayla Wolfe
Typesetter:	Lisandro Gonzalez
Cover Design:	Nick Newcomer

Published in the United States of America by
Information Science Reference (an imprint of IGI Global)
701 E. Chocolate Avenue
Hershey PA 17033
Tel: 717-533-8845
Fax: 717-533-8661
E-mail: cust@igi-global.com
Web site: http://www.igi-global.com

Library of Congress Cataloging-in-Publication Data

Structuring music through markup language : designs and architectures / Jacques Steyn, editor.
       p. cm.
   Includes bibliographical references and index.
   Summary: "This book offers a different approach to music by focusing on the information organization and the development of XML-based language, presenting a new set of tools for practical implementations, and a new investigation into the theory of music"--Provided by publisher.
   ISBN 978-1-4666-2497-9 (hardcover) -- ISBN 978-1-4666-2498-6 (ebook) -- ISBN 978-1-4666-2499-3 (print & perpetual access) 1. Music--Data processing. 2. XML (Document markup language) I. Steyn, Jacques.
   ML74.S77 2013
   780.285'674--dc23
                                          2012023347

British Cataloguing in Publication Data
A Cataloguing in Publication record for this book is available from the British Library.

All work contributed to this book is new, previously-unpublished material. The views expressed in this book are those of the authors, but not necessarily of the publisher.

List of Reviewers

Antoine Allombert, *Bordeaux University, France*
Sergio Canazza, *University of Padova, Italy*
Giovanni De Poli, *University of Padova, Italy*
Myriam Desainte-Catherine, *Bordeaux University, France*
Ichiro Fujinaga, *McGill University, Canada*
Michael Good, *MakeMusic, Inc., USA*
Perfecto Herrera, *Universitat Pompeu Fabra, Spain*
Alexander Refsum Jensenius, *University of Oslo, Norway*
Marc Leman, *Ghent University, Belgium*
Cory McKay, *Marianopolis College, Canada*
Jyri Pakarinen, *Aalto University, Finland*
Antonio Rodà, *University of Padova, Italy*
Gerard Roma, *Universitat Pompeu Fabra, Spain*
Wijnand Schepens, *Ghent University, Belgium*
Alvise Vidolin, *University of Padova, Italy*

Table of Contents

Detailed Table of Contents

Chapter 1
Jacques Steyn, Monash University, South Africa

Information architecture is about information structures and their relations within the information space, and in this chapter the music information space. To determine what the structures and relationships are, an ontological investigation is launched. Ontology in Information Systems has a specific meaning, and is here considered to be a methodology that results in a specific information architecture. Ontologies can apply to many levels of investigation and description, and to any of contemporary music disciplines. Music is here demarcated to a core consisting of pitch-frequency and tempo-time relationships, mapped onto music space. The roles of PitchSets ("octaves"), scales, and tuning systems within this space are explained, and proposed as the core components of the object "music." The most basic and generic markup language for music should thus start from this core. All other ontologies and markup are secondary to this object.

Chapter 2
Jyri Pakarinen, Aalto University, Finland

This chapter discusses the central physical phenomena involved in music. The aim is to provide an explanation of the related issues in an understandable level, without delving unnecessarily deep in the underlying mathematics. The chapter is divided in two main sections: musical sound sources and sound transmission to the observer. The first section starts from the definition of sound as wave motion, and then guides the reader through the vibration of strings, bars, membranes, plates, and air columns, that is, the oscillating sources that create the sound for most of the musical instruments. Resonating structures, such as instrument bodies are also reviewed, and the section ends with a discussion on the potential physical markup parameters for musical sound sources. The second section starts with an introduction to the basics of room acoustics, and then explains the acoustic effect that the human observer causes in the sound field. The end of the second section provides a discussion on which sound transmission parameters could be used in a general music markup language. Finally, a concluding section is presented.

Chapter 3

This chapter presents ACE XML, a set of file formats that are designed to meet the special representational needs of research in Music Information Retrieval (MIR) in general and automatic music classification in particular. The ACE XML formats are designed to represent a wide range of musical information clearly and simply using formally structured frameworks that are flexible and extensible. This chapter includes a critical review of existing file formats that have been used in MIR research. This is followed by a set of design priorities that are proposed for use in developing new formats and improving existing ones. The details of the ACE XML specification are then described in this context. Finally, research priorities for the future are discussed, as well as possible uses for ACE XML outside the specific domain of MIR.

Chapter 4

While representing musical processes or musical scores through Markup Languages is now well established, the authors assume that there is still the need for a format to encode musical material with which a musician can interact. The lack of such a format is especially crucial for contemporary music that involves computing processes. They propose such a formal representation for composing musical scores in which some temporal properties can be interactively modified during their execution. This allows the creation of scores that can be interpreted by a performer in the same way a musician can interpret a score of instrumental music. The formal representation comes with an XML format for encoding the scores and also interfacing the representation with other types of Markup Language musical description.

Chapter 5

Chronicle is a new universal system for representing time-related data. Although the system was developed for the representation of symbolic music, it is readily applicable to other types of data with complex time structure, such as audio, multimedia, poetry, choreography, task scheduling, and so on. Different levels of complexity are supported. The lowest level deals with a stream of events ordered in time. Subsequent higher levels add the possibility to organize the data in groups and subgroups forming a hierarchical structure, local timing, automatic layout of sequential or parallel sections, association of data with other elements, working with multiple timescales, time mappings, and more. The system is primarily concerned with the treatment of time and structure. The domain developer is free to choose the event data types; timescales and organizational constraints most suited for the application. The Chronicle system defines an XML-based encoding based on a set of level-specific DTDs, but it also offers software support in the form of classes, interfaces, libraries for reading and writing XML, tools for level reduction, etc. It is hoped that developers of new XML-encodings in different domains can use Chronicle as a powerful base layer. The software can also be useful for researchers who need an easy and flexible way to store XML-data.

Chapter 6

Gerard Roma, Universitat Pompeu Fabra, Spain
Perfecto Herrera, Universitat Pompeu Fabra, Spain

In this chapter, the authors discuss an approach to music representation that supports collaborative composition given current practices based on digital audio. A music work is represented as a directed graph that encodes sequences and layers of sound samples. The authors discuss graph grammars as a general framework for this representation. From a grammar perspective, they analyze the use of XML for storing production rules, music structures, and references to audio files. The authors describe an example implementation of this approach.

Chapter 7

Alexander Refsum Jensenius, University of Oslo, Norway

The chapter starts by discussing the importance of body movement in both music performance and perception, and argues that for future research in the field it is important to develop solutions for being able to stream and store music-related movement data alongside other types of musical information. This is followed by a suggestion for a multilayered approach to structuring movement data, where each of the layers represents a separate and consistent subset of information. Finally, examples of two prototype implementations are presented: a setup for storing GDIF-data into SDIF-files, and an example of how GDIF-based OSC streams can allow for more flexible and meaningful mapping from controller to sound engine.

Chapter 8

Sergio Canazza, University of Padova, Italy
Giovanni De Poli, University of Padova, Italy
Antonio Rodà, University of Padova, Italy
Alvise Vidolin, University of Padova, Italy

During the last decade, in the fields of both systematic musicology and cultural musicology, a lot of research effort (using methods borrowed from music informatics, psychology, and neurosciences) has been spent to connect two worlds that seemed to be very distant or even antithetic: machines and emotions. Mainly in the Sound and Music Computing framework of human-computer interaction an increasing interest grew in finding ways to allow machines communicating expressive, emotional content using a nonverbal channel. Such interest has been justified with the objective of an enhanced interaction between humans and machines exploiting communication channels that are typical of human-human communication and that can therefore be easier and less frustrating for users, and in particular for non-technically skilled users (e.g. musicians, teacher, students, common people). While on the one hand research on emotional communication found its way into more traditional fields of computer science such as Artificial Intelligence, on the other hand novel fields are focusing on such issues. The examples are studies on Affective Computing in the United States, KANSEI Information Processing in Japan, and Expressive Information Processing in Europe. This chapter presents the state of the art in the research field of a computational approach to the study of music performance. In addition, analysis methods and synthesis models of expressive content in music performance, carried out by the authors, are presented. Finally, an encoding system aiming to encode the music performance expressiveness will be detailed, using an XML-based approach.

MusicXML is a universal interchange and distribution format for common Western music notation. MusicXML's design and development began in 2000, with the purpose to be the MP3 equivalent for digital sheet music. MusicXML was developed by Recordare and can represent music from the 17th century onwards, including guitar tablature and other music notations used to notate or transcribe contemporary popular music. MusicXML is supported by over 160 applications. The development and history of MusicXML is described in this chapter.

Chapter 10

The information architecture of acoustic music instruments is described. As contemporary acoustic research has not yet covered all the possible materials, shapes, designs, and other essential properties of possible acoustic instruments, the model proposed in this chapter serves as a high-level analysis with meta-level XML-based markup elements and attributes. The ultimate design goal of the proposed model is to be able to create a software synthesis application that could recreate the acoustic sounds of music instruments faithfully, as well as the ability to create novel acoustic sounds using virtual music instruments. It is proposed that algorithms be created, which might lead to more realistically sounding instruments, as well as creating totally new sounds based on the properties of acoustic instruments, even the virtual creation of new types of acoustic instruments that would be impossible to build with real materials. It is further proposed that the properties of different components serve as modifiers on a base soundwave. Modifiers include the materials used in the construction of instruments, energy sources, dimensions of 3D acoustic cavities, and relationships between instrument components are considered. The properties of a wide range of musical instruments have been considered, ranging from ancient acoustic instruments to modern ones, as well as including the instruments of many music cultures. Following on a logical analysis and synthesis of previous research rather than acoustic lab results, a high-level generic and universal model of the information architecture of acoustic music instruments is constructed.

Preface

This book is about Music Informatics—how ICT (Information and Communication Technology) is used in the domain of music, and more specifically, using XML languages to label the semantics of the structures of the information architecture of music.

Very crudely, ICT is about data, process, and actor, where actor could be a human agent or another IT system. XML is about the data of ICT, not so much about process or actor, although the data or information about processes and actor could be expressed in XML. Structured data enables computers to find and manipulate specific data. The tables of structured data are semantically ignorant. Today, with much more powerful computing power, data searches and manipulation does not require structured data, as such processes could be performed on unstructured data. However, to give sensible results, semantics is required, at which computers are notoriously poor. Markup languages is an attempt to add semantics to unstructured data. The very method of applying markers to information imposes structure on the data, which could then be used effectively by computers. Markup languages could of course also be used to mark the information of structured data. Markup languages are good not only at structuring information, but also at clarifying relationships between such structures. This is achieved by declaring hierarchical relationships, where vertical nodes imply inheritance, while horizontal nodes imply peer relationships.

The architectural structure of a building can be used as analogy to explain information architecture. A building has important structures, such as beams, foundations, walls, doors, and windows. These could be aesthetically designed in many different ways. While building architecture is about both structure and aesthetics, information architecture is concerned only with structure. Markup languages describe information structures and their relationships, while visual information aesthetics is achieved by applying style sheet languages to the information structures.

The hierarchical relationships of information structures need to be constructed by designers. The discipline of ontology, defined not as philosophy, but as Information Systems, investigates how such relationships could be defined, while the results of such an investigation constitute a particular information architecture. Information architecture is about information structures and their relations within the information space.

This book is thus about structuring music and marking those structures so that the music data can be manipulated with ICT. As is evident from the different domains of music covered by the different authors in this book, *music,* or the components of music regarded as important to describe, contains a vast variety of possible information structures.

In the chapter, "The Information Architecture of Music," Steyn explains the relevance of ontology and information architecture to determine what should be marked. The word "music" has many different meanings, as is true of so many other words used in human language. It is possible to design an XML language to describe and mark any of the domains of meanings of music. The investigator will first need to demarcate the field that needs to be marked, and then analyze the information structural components of the field and indicate their relations. The final step is to design a particular markup language around the structures.

The chapter "The Physics of Music" by Jyri Pakarinen approaches music from the perspective of acoustics of the soundwaves of music, and regards the fundamental frequency as one of the most important parameters for the design of a music markup language. Not only the acoustics of instruments are important, but also the acoustics of the room in which the music is performed, as that is where listeners process the music. This investigation into the internal structures of music can be regarded as an analysis of the intrinsic features of music.

In "Expressing Musical Features, Class Labels, Ontologies, and Metadata Using ACE XML 2.0," Cory McKay and Ichiro Fujinaga approach music from an extrinsic point of view. Automatic retrieval of music related information is very challenging, while classification can never be absolute. The definitions of a piece of music might be arbitrary and different people might class it in different genres. Yet most classification engines restrict classification into single genres. One of the design goals of ACE XML is to address this shortcoming. The generality and modularity of ACE might also allow its functionality to be extended beyond just being a classification tool. It might also be possible to address the symbolization of intrinsic music events with this system.

Antoine Allombert and Myriam Desainte-Catherine's chapter, "Towards an Encoding of Musical Interaction," covers interactive scores. Traditional scores are passive, closed entities, and applications typically merely render this static form in yet another static form. For example, if a score is in the MIDI format, tempo variations cannot be introduced by the musician during real-time performances—only during recording. Their proposal is to allow for such static scores to follow the dynamics and tempo variations of real-time performance.

Wijnand Schepens and Marc Leman's chapter, "Chronicle: XML-Representation of Symbolic Music and Other Complex Time Structures," create a universal timeline used for synchronizing information from many different sources in addition to music related events, including poetry, choreography, and task scheduling.

The chapter "Representing Music as Work in Progress" by Gerard Roma and Perfecto Herrera is about collaborative composition over networks, specifically for the domain of social networking. By using a visual interface, networked users can compose songs jointly by selecting among audio samples.

Alexander Refsum Jensenius developed a Gesture Description Interchange Format (GDIF) to capture the body movements during performance. His chapter, "Structuring Music-Related Movements," investigates taxonomies of the different types and layers of movements, as these and not technical matters were the issues in the project.

The chapter, "Expressiveness in Music Performance: Analysis, Models, Mapping, Encoding," by Sergio Canazza, Giovanni De Poli, Antonio Rodà, and Alvise Vidolin, is about emotional expression during performance, especially when needed to be captured for machines that lack emotions. Music is presented in multiple layers at different levels of abstraction—multidimensional spaces—as music needs to be understood as an integration of many subsystems. Emotional expression is one such subsystem.

Michael Good created an XML application (MusicXML) for Common Western Music Notation (CWMN), which has been a commercial success. In his chapter, "MusicXML: The First Decade," he gives an overview of this development and some of the challenges encountered during this journey.

In the chapter "Universal Information Architecture of Acoustic Music Instruments," Jacques Steyn proposes a high-level generic description to account for the acoustic properties of musical instruments, not from the acoustic soundwave point of view, but from the point of view of the structures that play a role in the creation of the unique sounds of different acoustic music instruments.

Music is a very complex entity, consisting of many domains. The information architecture of any of these domains, and in fact, any of the subdomains of each of these domains, can be expressed in some or other form and information architecture. In the past, most XML applications of music focused on CWMN. In this book, apart from Good's historical overview of MusicXML, none of the chapters is about CWMN, but about other aspects of music. There is a vast field that awaits cultivation of information architecture descriptions, while an integrated strategy should perhaps rather be followed. Perhaps in the first phase, efforts should focus on establishing ground rules for a generic music ontology so that we know which concepts would form the core around which XML languages could be developed to better capture the semantics of the information architecture of music.

Jacques Steyn
Monash University, South Africa

Chapter 1
The Information Architecture of Music

Jacques Steyn
Monash University, South Africa

ABSTRACT

Information architecture is about information structures and their relations within the information space, and in this chapter the music information space. To determine what the structures and relationships are, an ontological investigation is launched. Ontology in Information Systems has a specific meaning, and is here considered to be a methodology that results in a specific information architecture. Ontologies can apply to many levels of investigation and description, and to any of contemporary music disciplines. Music is here demarcated to a core consisting of pitch-frequency and tempo-time relationships, mapped onto music space. The roles of PitchSets ("octaves"), scales, and tuning systems within this space are explained, and proposed as the core components of the object "music." The most basic and generic markup language for music should thus start from this core. All other ontologies and markup are secondary to this object.

INTRODUCTION

The purpose of this chapter is to briefly investigate the concept of music, and by demarcating that object offer clarity for a project to create a generic markup language for music. An information system is here constructed as representing the perceived world, and for computer systems, this representation is translated into formats that a computer can use. It is this presentational format that I will call information architecture.

From all the possible contexts in which the term "music" is used, its meaning will be determined by the design goal of the application, and the definition needs to be clearly demarcated. The design goal in this chapter is to build an application that could handle the basics of music, i.e. the essentials required for a system to create music. The contemporary context for the design goal is that of music synthesis and DAWs (Digital Audio Workstations). This is based on the assumption that universally music is about performed soundwaves, but particular cultural "normative" subsets of the potential frequency spectrum.

DOI: 10.4018/978-1-4666-2497-9.ch001

Information architecture is about the design of relationships of information that could be used sensibly for computer applications. This goal seems to be exactly that of ontology as defined in Information Systems, but for present purposes, there is distinction between ontology and information architecture. Ontology, informed by an epistemology, is about the process of analyzing and constructing entities to be used within a specific domain. The ontological process is a methodology, an investigation into the characteristics of things and how they relate to other things. In a sense, it is about knowledge design: the design of the constructs regarded to be important for some or other domain of investigation. A particular set of constructs could be created following a diversity of methods. Much of the information systems literature on ontology may be regarded as a meta-analysis of the details of ontology, about defining this and about the methods to be used to determine the structure. Ontology is about the design of a design, so to speak, and in the construction of the entities and their relationships analytical, constructivist and hermeneutic strategies are followed. Information architecture on the other hand, is a particular result from an ontological investigation. It is the result of an ontological and epistemological investigation, but based on the choosing of a particular result among many to be implemented in application design and development. Many possible sets of ontological systems might be constructed for a particular domain, each having its own information architecture. The choice for a particular set is guided by the design goal of a particular artifact. Considering the design goal, one asks: Which available ontological set is the most appropriate for the particular design goal?

Why is information architecture important for music? It analyzes music information and builds a structure of relationships as an exercise independent of chip, circuit, or synthesis design. By presenting the detailed information structure, based on this structure the design of chips, circuits and synthesis could follow any engineering route. By being comprehensive, all the minute structural details of music are presented before the engineering process commences. Such a design approach might benefit the quality of the output of an artifact. Presently engineering design of music artifacts seems to focus on using the hammer approach, tweaking algorithms until the desired result is achieved. It does not seem to be sophisticated about the details of the information structure that could be identified independently from the hardware or algorithms.

From an application development point of view, such meta-design discussions is not essential as praxis is the goal. However, when the information architecture is investigated in this manner, more efficiency could be built into applications. Ontological investigation may offer a variety of information architectures, depending on the assumptions and goals. An analogy may express this better. In the design of a building an architect certainly needs to understand the limits of materials to be used in a specific construction, but the focus is on the design of the building, the spatial relationships between structural components of the building. Information architecture is about the structural relationships between information chunks. The data structure of the information to be used by processors needs to be clarified. Structuring the data is not an objective activity, especially when semantics is attached to the data. In practice, one might get away with a very wide range of designs, although some would be more efficient than others. A poorly designed system may still work, while extracting relevant data from it might be a nightmare. Another design might have been more efficient to extract appropriate data. These are architectural issues, not ontological. A particular ontology might serve as guide for a better design, but ontology does not supply the final and ultimate model, as a "better" application is measured by how well it fits the design goal. For music, clarifying the information architecture may serve for better application design, as well as facilitate information exchange between devices and between the components of devices.

Computers are number-crunching machines, very good at data storage and retrieval, but very poor at semantics. The notion of a markup language (*Generalized Markup Language* [GML]) was invented by Goldfarb, Mosher and Lorie with the aim to add semantics to data (Goldfarb & Prescod, 1998). GML became a standard in 1986 as Standard Generalized Markup Language (SGML, ISO 8879:1986), and many descendents have since then been created. The World Wide Web was, content-wise, built on HTML, which was based on a very small set of SGML. In the late 1990s HTML was extended as a much more powerful language, called XML, which facilitates semantics, especially the management of data which is now no longer dumb data, but more sensible information. XML was in fact not a redesign of HTML itself, but of the concept, while itself also not being an applied markup language. XML is a meta-language used for creating XML-based markup languages.

Markup languages are highly hierarchical with parent and children nodes in strict architectural relationships with one another. Determining the nature of a particular markup language involves the design of systems of nodal relationships between concepts. Phenomena, artifacts, and even concepts can be analyzed to construct relationships between them. It is this constructed set of relationships that is known as information architecture. When expressed in a tree diagram, the information architecture of a description of concepts is clearly visible. In this book aspects of music are analyzed and the information architecture—that is the nodal relationship between constructed concepts—is expressed with a markup language that could be effectively used by computers, especially for information management and exchange. Identifying the particular set of concepts depends on an ontological approach to what is investigated and analyzed. The entire universe could potentially be described, which means that the object of

description needs to be properly demarcated to trim down the possible description to essentials.

Ontology and an XML Language for Music

Unlike most other created objects (such as paintings or books) that have single root instances as artifacts, the music object is not so clear. A painting (i.e. the entity or artifact with physical dimensions) is a single instance in time and space, and the manuscript of a book is so too, even if numerous copies are made. These artifacts are interpreted, but the interpretations do not change them. A music composition is more elusive. The score (as symbolic marks on some surface, such as paper or computer screen) may be a single root instance, but a score consists of a series of cues and clues that need to be interpreted during the musical performance or production, thus changing them. The music audience as receivers have the final interpretation for that performance, but their interpretation does not change the version they hear. Music can also be performed without a score, and even without a score ever been written. A score is thus not essential for music. Is music as artifact the original composition, an interpretation of it by being performed, and if the latter, whose performance? And what about jamming? Is that not performed music? Further, even the same same set of performers may not perform the same piece of music exactly the same in each instance of performance. In this sense, there are many instances of the same created object. There are even different root instances of performances of the same score, and variations or improvisations may themselves become root instances.

In the language of computer programming, the "score" (in an abstract sense, such as composition and arrangement) might be considered similar to declaring a parent class, while the aspects mentioned above inherit the properties of the parent score. However, while child nodes in a computer language inherit properties blindly, a creative human agent is involved at each node in the hierarchy of the music object, and can twist and turn the properties, even introducing new ones. Performances can vary quite significantly, and different ones may occur over many decades, even centuries. The relations between parent and child nodes are thus not clear solid lines, but dotted, with inputs from the human agent (as product of cultural knowledge and personal history) in an infinite number of ways. Described in this manner, the meaning "score" cannot be restricted to a written artifact. A jam session may develop in a totally unplanned manner, as one musician may start a new direction, followed by fellow band members. The "score" in this case is determined by conventions such as pitches acknowledged to belong to sets (scales). What exactly needs to be described with a markup language aimed at describing the object "music" becomes a very complex question.

Kania (2007) points out that discussions on the ontology of music focus on the metaphysical, attempting to find answers for the 'authentic performance,' which Ridley criticizes. Ridley's *Against Musical Ontology* (2003) is about what qualifies as a musical work, and he argues against Goodman's position that it is the musical score that defines the work. This debate is about the differences between the (supposedly) normative score, and variations of performances of that score. It is a debate about some kind of pre-determined entity. Such debates take as foundation a score, which by definition depends on some or other system of notation, while music can exist without any score, as is evident firstly from all non-scored folk music that exists. Secondly, the huge market of pop music and garage band originals that have no formal scores (in the sense of a record of the composition) also indicates that the score cannot be the foundation of music. Perhaps most importantly, the fact that writing down as a written score a piece of music a composer hears in his mind is a very difficult exercise, requiring extensive training in music notation. If "score" is to be the most fundamental aspect of music, it cannot be the written score, but some other abstraction, in which case score is perhaps not the best term to use.

Ridley's concern is further about what counts as a faithful performance, which assumes quite a bit. It assumes that the score is objective. However, no score is objective. A score is interpreted by musicians or directors, while such interpretations depend on the traditions and conventions in which the musician has been trained. Even basics such as tuning a written symbol to a particular frequency depends on tradition. Tempo and pitch variations are relative. The Latin words used for tempo variations are not mapped to clock time on printed scores. A score could at most contain guidelines proposed by a composer, while each performance is an interpretation of that score. Therefore, to attempt to judge which performance is faithful is misguided. The very assumption that it is possible to determine what the "true" score is suggests adherence to the outdated interpretation of ontology, still stuck with the ancient Greek position.

The composition or score cannot constitute the very basics of music. The basics is more likely the performance, but more specifically, the soundwaves created during the performance. These are the essentials. All other matters come after the fact—after the performance. Even the audience interpreting the music is an interpretation of the soundwaves, and a description of the audience must thus come after a description of music as soundwaves. The discipline of music has many sub-disciplines, such as music psychology and cognition (including e.g. music therapy and physiological human sound perception), music theory, analysis and composition, ethnomusicology, historical musicology, music and mathematics, music education, organology, music acoustics and psychoacoustics, sociomusicology, music management, technical music recording (in the sense of writing symbolic visual notations of the audio events), technological music sound recording (in the sense of studio technologies), metadata (such as information about music, including research on music), music appreciation and more. The domain of music is huge, and the object of music can be approached from many different angles. A markup language could be designed for any of these.

However, there is a core which is *music itself*, and around which all other themes about music revolve. None of these disciplines of music is "music"—they are *about music*, perhaps to be called meta-music. It is possible to describe any of these domains with some kind of ontological system. The focus on the information architecture in this chapter is not on any of these, but on the object of music itself. Music in this chapter will be defined as a physical-cultural artifact and phenomenon that can be described from many different angles. Physical here means the soundwaves and their acoustics that are regarded as music. A distinction could be made between the architecture of music itself and the architecture of descriptions of music.

In positivist and related traditions, what is perceived in the world is regarded as facts, and an analysis of that goes by the name ontology. The conceptual twin of ontology (which is a theory of the nature of things), is epistemology (which is a theory of knowledge). Although these terms are relatively new in the history of philosophy (ontology in the 1600s by Glocenius and epistemology in the 1800s by Ferrier), the themes of investigation have been around since the ancient Greeks. Over the past few decades, the term ontology has been used in Information Systems, but in a sense different to its use in traditional philosophy.

To the ancient Greeks what we call ontology was contemplating existence and their program was about discovering the essences of the natural state of things, which was regarded as objectively self-evident. Aristotle, for example, held that things (including events) had a true nature. Things have their own essential natures, and events have their own natural tendencies. This distinction dominated western thought until fairly recently. As Wyssusek (2004) points out, since

Immanuel Kant (1724-1804) it was known that epistemology informs ontology, and that it is far from objectively obvious what the essences or nature of things really are. Our interpretation of the being of something (ontology) depends on the knowledge (epistemology) we bring to that analysis. A particular set of knowledge is culturally instructed, with each generation of humans inheriting a stock of previous knowledge which they adopt, adapt by modifying, and add to with new knowledge. Therefore, ontology is a cultural artifact, bound by history.

In Information Systems ontology acquired, through Wand and Weber (1990, 1993), a particular meaning of the term as originally presented by Bunge. Wyssusek argues that this interpretation of ontology "...is grounded in a rather materialist-realist philosophical position that hardly finds any support in contemporary philosophy and social sciences" (2004, p. 4304). This implies that the dominant Wand-Weber view of ontology in Information Systems is biased toward this program, and that Weber's defense that it does not matter whether one approaches ontology from a subjectivist or objectivist position does not make sense, as the very notion is defined from a biased objectivist position. One cannot merely slap on some subjectivist concepts onto an idea that was in the first place constructed positivistically. In information systems, the use of the term ontology has several different meanings and the debate is still continuing with attempts to "standardize" what is meant with the term in this discipline (Wyssusek, 2004; Fonseca, 2007).

Chandrasekaran, Josephson, and Benjamin define ontology in Information Systems as follows: "Ontologies are content theories about the sorts of objects, properties of objects, and relations between objects that are possible in a specified domain of knowledge" (1999, p. 20; also see Gruber, 1992), and "Ontologies are quintessentially content theories, because their main contribution is to identify specific classes of objects and relations that exist in some domain" (1999, p. 21). In a manner of speaking, ontology involves establishing a fixed set of terminology that could apply across natural languages and similar boundaries. In their words: "First of all, ontology is a representation vocabulary, often specialized to some domain or subject matter. More precisely, it is not the vocabulary as such that qualifies as an ontology, but the conceptualizations that the terms in the vocabulary are intended to capture. Thus, translating the terms in an ontology from one language to another, for example from English to French, does not change the ontology conceptually" (1999, p. 20). The second aspect of the meaning of ontology they identify concerns the body of knowledge that describes some domain. "In other words, the representation vocabulary provides a set of terms with which to describe the facts in some domain, while the body of knowledge using that vocabulary is a collection of facts about a domain" (1999, p. 20).

Attempting to describe the concepts and relationships of a domain is really a taxonomical effort, which depends on some classification method. Put in other words, an ontological analysis of the domain of research or discussion relates to an attempt to arrive at conceptual categories, which is about the classification of identified concepts. This taxonomical formalization offers a technical vocabulary to be used. For software applications, clarification of terms facilitates information processing. Information scientists attempt to gather the basic concepts and establish nodal relationships between them. In this sense, information scientists working in the field of ontologies are now doing for the information space what the early modern scientists did in their disciplines. In the biological domain, the name of Carl Linnaeus (1707-1778) comes to mind.

A distinction can be made between formal ontology and material ontology (Zuniga, 2001). A formal ontology involves "the general investigation and description of the properties of objects in the world and the relations existing between different sorts of objects" while a material ontol-

ogy is domain specific, describing "the structure of the domain and the relations of the objects therein" (2001, p. 190). Note that neither is objective, and firstly involves the interpretation of the world, structuring it and then assigning the objects to that structure, which assumes some taxonomical method.

Ontology in information systems attempts to define domain specific factual knowledge, and typically using some formal methods to determine what the facts are. These methods are meta-theory dependent. They are based on formal predicates of the kind used in predicate calculus, such as *X is a type of Y*, or *A is a component of B*, and function in a logical positivist paradigm. Should another meta-theory be used, perhaps the results would be different. A more constructivist approach might be followed, and it would be interesting to see how different methods triangulate, although I have not come across such an exercise. The classification and clarification is done by assigning special meaning to terms, expressed as "standard" labels of which the semantics is made explicit. This is done so that exchange of information could be facilitated. An XML-based language is one method to formalize basic concepts, and to express their relationships, typically in hierarchical nodes such as *X is a type of Y*, or *X is a child of Y*.

One of the debates among the Greeks was whether the nature of things are timeless (are static), or changing (are dynamic). Heraclitus argued for changing nature, and his well-known example is that one cannot step into the same river twice. More recently, process philosophy, such as proposed by Alfred North Whitehead (1861-1947) in *Process and Reality* (1960), raised objections to the static view of *being*. If phenomena are dynamic in nature, being is not constant, but continuously changing. Any description would be a time-stopped slice in their historical development. If being is never static and stable, but dynamically changing over time, it implies that any time-slot description would be valid only for that time-slot, and not for earlier or later slots. This is not very helpful for semantics to be used by computers, as it would imply having changing descriptions for the "same" being. Computers are, unfortunately, really poor at handling semantics, and certainly cannot cope with handling changing semantics.

This problem of stasis versus change also bothered the linguist Ferdinand de Saussure (1857-1913) who distinguished between synchronic and diachronic approaches (1990). A synchronic interpretation would be a time-slot slice within historical change, while a diachronic analysis would be across historical time. Although he started out as a historical linguist, he eventually favored the synchronic approach for linguistic investigation, in which relationships between entities feature significantly. This approach introduced by Saussure lead to a major paradigm in the social sciences in the twentieth century: structuralism. The present status of computer technology cannot handle changing semantics. From a purely pragmatic point of view, a synchronic and even structuralist approach is advisable, even though one might have intense philosophical problems with that worldview.

The twentieth century also saw other challenges noted against the views of the ancients, such as that the world is not objectively given in the sense of Plato's form theory. Our brains interpret the world, as convincingly shown by cognitive psychology, and more recently neurobiology. The essences as well as knowledge about them are not given supra-historical entities, but cognitively and culturally constructed. We use our knowledge to construct essences, which means that epistemology informs ontology. The object "music" is not given, but constructed. Computers have no brains and are dumb technologies that need to be told what to do. If the purpose of a project is to design and construct computer software for music, we need to analyze what we mean with the word "music," thus demarcate the concept, and state which entities and relationship would be important for the design goal of the particular artifact. If the purpose is an envisaged design artifact, the function of the

artifact will largely be the filter for the definition determined through ontology. In addition, as artifact design is important, the guidelines of Design Science are important.

Ontology could be approached idealistically and pragmatically. The case for the idealistic definition is weak, and as a practical artifact is the goal of a Design Science approach, the position in this chapter will be pragmatic. From a pragmatic approach, the design goal of a specific artifact would guide the constructed ontological system. This implies that for an information systems artifact the design goal needs to be specified first, and then the ontology constructed that would enable the creation of the most efficient artifact to meet that goal. Design Science thus precedes ontology. Ontology certainly is important, as it offers a useful tool to clarify the concepts and relationships of the domain for which the artifact is designed. However, ontology could never be an isolated, supra-historical closed system. Ontology informs the engineering artifact (Fonseca, 2007). This pragmatic approach to ontology will be followed in this chapter, as worded by Lenci:

"The dynamics of knowledge and of the ontologies that represent it depend on its contexts of use. Knowledge is created or acquired for some purpose, i.e. to be used as a tool to achieve a certain goal or to perform a particular task. Use also changes our knowledge about entities and processes and consequently leads us to revise our ontological systems. Moreover, the employ of some body of knowledge to perform a task may produce new knowledge that has to be added to our ontologies, possibly resulting in a major revision of their structure, if some breakthrough in the knowledge system has occurred" (2010, p. 241).

Given such an approach to music ontology, it follows that there is not a single music ontology. There are several, and their boundaries depend on how the notion of music is defined, or demarcated for each. In addition, for the world of computing, it should be determined which of the possible constructed ontologies would be the most useful in the creation of computing tools, for whatever goal is to be obtained. This means further that when a design science methodology is followed, the project is defined to solve some or other practical problem or challenge that is encountered. The design solution is created and tested against the existing body of knowledge. Ideally, a prototype is built to check the validity of the proposed solution before embarking on production. For an efficient use of information by computer systems, semantics needs to be added to data, and semantics is supplied by an ontological investigation into the domain of the planned artifact. There is a typical iterative feedback loop here (a hermeneutic cycle). The artifact is roughly defined; then an ontological investigation is undertaken, of which the results feed back into refining the definition of the artifact. An ontological result, translated into a format for computer use, is an information architectural system. In addition, in typical Design Science fashion, no artifact (especially software) ever obtains its final release version. It is thus quite acceptable to in the first instance design a meta-model as outcome, which is refined over many iterative design cycles, with (hopefully) each cycle improving on the previous outcome. I say hopefully because in practice many brand-name software products become worse from a usability perspective, and often new releases are also technically inferior to previous versions, even when bloated functionality is added.

Music information architecture is a system expressing the information structures and their relationships in the music information space created through the ontological investigation of the object of investigation, which in this case is music.

Music Ontology Project

The information architecture for music proposed in this chapter differs quite extensively from a project called *Music Ontology*. According to Raimond *et al.* (2007) and Raimond and Giasson (2010) the goal of the Music Ontology project is to create a vocabulary that could be used for exchanging music-related information. This statement is very vague—music-related information means different things to different people—and requires some clarification. Raimond and Giasson define the project as follows:

"The Music Ontology Specification provides main concepts and properties for describing music (i.e. artists, albums, tracks, but also performances, arrangements, etc.) on the Semantic Web" (Raimond & Giasson, 2010).

The Music Ontology project approaches music from three different levels of expressiveness. In order of levels of complexity, they are:

- "**Level 1:** Aims at providing a vocabulary for simple editorial information (tracks/artists/releases, etc.)
- **Level 2:** Aims at providing a vocabulary for expressing the music creation workflow (composition, arrangement, performance, recording, etc.)
- **Level 3:** Aims at providing a vocabulary for complex event decomposition, to express, for example, what happened during a particular performance, what is the melody line of a particular work, etc." (Raimond & Giasson, 2010; bullet format by present author).

It is clear from this that the Music Ontology project in its present form covers only a small domain of music. It is thus one, and only one possible ontology, so the chosen name is disproportionally ambitious to what it actually describes as it seems to be restricted to listener requirements. The properties identified in the Music Ontology project clearly indicate that the interest in the project is what I call extrinsic music properties (Steyn, 2002). There is not much about the intrinsic properties of music, not about important music systems such as acoustics, instruments, musicians (such as playing techniques) and so forth. It is not about the markup of the music details within the package, such as the musical tones produced by an instrument, or instrument or musician control of the music event. Consider the categories of the Music Ontology project: Basics, Record Types, Release, Mediums, Performance Relationships, Signal Relationship, Musical Work Relationships, Musical Expression Relationships, Musical Item Trading Relationships, Record Relationships, Arrangement Relationships, Musical Expression / Manifestation Relationships, Musical Manifestation Relationships, Publication Relationships, Other Versions Relationships, Workflow Properties, Priduction Relationships, Musical Association Relationships, Affiliate Relationships, External Web document links Relationships, Get Music Relationships, Music Communities Relationships, Show/Festival Relationships. The Music Ontology project is about packaged music, and the music object as the final product.

There certainly is room for the Music Ontology project. However, the use by this project of the name *Music Ontology* is misleading. There is much more in music to be described ontologically, and as argued in this chapter, a very different core to be considered for the basics of music.

Systems of Description

Most objects in the universe can be described on several levels, each with its own ontology and information architecture. The exposition in this section of the chapter is important as some commentators of MML (e.g. Haus & Longari, 2005) have interpreted its concepts and examples as functining on the wrong level. They regard MML as a notation system, which it is not.

The design goal of this chapter is the description of the basic components of the music, but as music could be described on many different levels, some basic descriptive systems need to be distinguished. The following systems are distinguished for the purpose of this chapter:

- System of Explanation
- System of Abstract Theoretical Constructs
- System of Human Language Description
- System of Formal Symbolic Expression
- System of Markup Expressions

A markup language for music could be designed for any of these systems. It is thus important to be able to distinguish between the different meanings of the word *music* in each of these systems, as the design goal of a particular markup language for a specific application will depend on which system is used for the definition of the object to be semantically described. Debates on what should be described with a markup language for music often go around in circles as there is a lack of clarity of the distinction between how concepts function on these different levels. Most XML-based languages for music restrict the meaning of an XML language for music to music notation, while a few pay attention to other sub-domains of music, but there is still a vast field that could be explored and for which markup languages could be designed.

In the following exposition, the term "music" needs to be clarified as it could be used in the different senses of each of these systems. The following conventions will be used to distinguish between the meanings:

- /music/ System of Explanation: Theory
- |music| System of Abstract Theoretical Constructs: Concept
- {music} System of Human Language Description: Human language
- !music! System of Formal Symbolic Expression: Written format
- <music> System of Markup Expressions: e.g. XML

System of Explanation

A System of Explanation, as a particular set of theories, describes the object of investigation on a meta-level and operates within a particular philosophical framework, which is based on a set of assumptions. The notion of *systems of explanation* relates to that of *paradigm*, as introduced by Thomas Kuhn (1962). There are several systems of explanation of music as a phenomenon, ranging from the mystical *music of the spheres* notion (see e.g. James, 1993), to music as material physical soundwaves studied by acoustics.

Philosophers have contemplated on the nature of music probably since the time our ancestors, after a day of hunting and gathering food, gathered around the fireplace for evening contemplations. In a book such as the present one, contemplations about *what music is*, or supposed to be, is only important in so far as computers are dumb artifacts and the concepts we want them to handle need to be made very explicit. We need to refine the semantics of terms such as music, which in turn depends on implicit ideology and philosophical frameworks. Being explicit is what is important for computers, even if it is wrong according to some or other philosophical system. Many books and articles have been written on what music supposedly is, and it is far beyond the scope of this chapter to even attempt a summary of the different definitions. Since praxis, in the sense of a working artifact is the goal of a project such as this one, it is more productive to lay claim to a particular definition of music and get on with the job. Admittedly, given a different definition, the artifact as outcome will be different, so the design of the artifact is guided by the definition. The definition should thus receive the necessary attention.

The technical term /music/ in a System of Explanation is the function of some or other paradigmatic definition of music. In this chapter /music/ is defined as a set of culturally preferred physical sound waves (as defined by acoustics). Defined on this meta-level, music consists of a cultural element, a psychological element, as well as the sets of sound waves that are regarded to be music, which in turn is guided by sub-systems such as tuning conventions and scaling systems. Not all psycho-cultural properties apply to acoustics—only those relating to the sets of pitches, or relationships between pitches within "octaves," as defined by a particular culture. As this definition regards music as a cultural-acoustics system—that is performed—descriptions of music such as writing systems are of secondary importance. The phrase "music writing system" will be used to refer specifically to visual written symbols used for expressing the sounds of music.

The System of Explanation will not feature in the markup language described in this chapter. A markup language can be designed for this system. Here this system informs the process of demarcating the notion of music.

System of Abstract Theoretical Constructs

Within the theoretical framework of a philosophical System of Explanation, concepts are analyzed and clarified (System of Abstract Theoretical Construct). Concepts do not have objective, supra-historical meanings, but their meanings emerge through relationships to other concepts within their theoretical framework, which does not need to be a formal framework. Each individual human brain has broader frameworks—called mental models by cognitive psychologists—within which concepts obtain their meanings. So academic concepts may differ from non-academic ones, even if they represent the same thing. The term /music/ is expressed with a conceptual construct |music|, but |music| obtains its meaning through the framework of /music/—a process circular by its nature.

The abstract entity |note| may be defined as consisting of two sub-systems, namely |frequency| and |time|. This abstract entity |time|, an Abstract Theoretical Construct, may be clock-time ignorant, so the common sense definition of time does not apply. The theoretically constructed concept |time| may be expressed with a string of letters t-i-m-e, but it is due only to human communication constraints—we use language to express our thoughts. Strictly speaking Abstract Theoretical Constructs cannot be expressed in any other manner than with language, which would mean the System of Human Language Description, but it is important to note that a theoretical construct functions on a meta-level with specific formal and technical relationships to other concepts within a theoretical framework. The job of philosophy is typically to dissect such constructs, as they are often implicit, and linger in the subconscious dark corners of our brains, as our frameworks are inherited stocks of internalized knowledge. The fact that some contemporary intellectuals still cling to an ontological definition of music that dates back to the ancient Greeks indicate that frameworks are not objective.

It is on this level that ontology and information architecture function in this chapter. The markup language outcome labels the concepts constructed in this system.

System of Human Language Description

A System of Human Language Description consists of sets of human communication semiotic signs and symbols used to express the system of explanation. As this is our primary means of communication, all the other systems are also expressed by using this system. The content covered in this chapter is expressed in the English language. The conceptual construct |music| is expressed in English as {music} and in German as {musik}. The paragraphs of this chapter are in the human language of English, and express the thoughts presented about the object we call music in this language. These thoughts could be communicated in any human language—thus using different sets of linguistic and semiotic signs and symbols. In literature, this language is often called "natural language," but any such "natural" language is also based on cultural conventions and not natural in

the same sense as rocks, trees and mammals are natural. In practical terms, /music/ can be discussed over a beer without any reference to a formal descriptive system—or {music}. It is possible to discuss any music concept informally, even though this might be done sloppily. In ordinary language, concepts are often very fuzzy and used glibly as the main point is to converse, not to be conceptually clear.

System of Formal Symbolic Expression

In the System of Formal Symbolic Expression aspects of music, such as events as soundwaves, are expressed visually with specially designed symbols. These sets of symbols are conventional and several such systems have originated in different human cultures to record music events, or planned music events (e.g. scores). The word "formal" is here not used in the sense of calculus or formal logic, but for a technical conventional system that expresses music not in ordinary language, but with specifically designed symbols. For example, we could talk about a music note, which would be ordinary language, but we could also talk about the blob and stick symbol of Common Western Music Notation (CWMN), which is a technical convention. The dominant System of Formal Symbolic Expression in use today is the blobs and sticks set of symbols of CWMN. Other symbol sets are possible to express the same {music}. This means that the formal symbolic expression of {music} would be !music!, but also that {music} could be expressed symbolically by using many different kinds of !music! conventions. The sticks and blobs could also be expressed by alphabetical symbols, which are strictly speaking then not alphabetical symbols, but technically specific visual (and spoken) renderings of !notes!. Thus *A* has a very different meaning to !A!. The first is a letter used in human language, the second is a symbolic representation of some music pitch.

System of Markup Expressions

The standard set of symbols to express the terms in an XML language is derived from the Extended Backus-Naur Form, and particularly the signs <, >, and /. A description such as <music> might refer to the XML element name for the "music" of one of the other systems. As mentioned above, a markup language could be designed for anything in the universe for any level. A markup language could be designed for each of the systems above, as well as for any of their sub-systems. A markup language could be designed for /music/, |music|, {music}, and !music!.

Each of the above systems would have its own sets of ontologies, its own concepts, and relationships. There is some self-reference here. Ontology features in each system; human language is used to express the ontology, while the first three mentioned systems feed into one another in a feedback loop of self-organization. An ontology cannot be determined without considering the theoretical framework and the concepts within that framework, yet it is the job of ontology to determine what the concepts are.

THE MUSIC OBJECT

In order to choose an information architecture for music, it is essential to demarcate what "music" will mean. That meaning will be informed by ontology as method, bearing in mind that the process of investigation is iterative, and also informed by many knowledge systems.

A definition of music is quite elusive—it could function on different levels. Defining music as organized sound, or as soundwave patterns, is not sufficient, as many other phenomena, including human language, conform to this definition. Even defining music with reference to tones only is not sufficient, as many Asian languages (such as Mandarin) are tonal languages in which pitch intervals are important for distinguishing meanings of similar sound sequences (i.e. structural words), which by such a definition would make these music, not language.

There are no proper records of how music evolved through history. The oldest music instruments known from archaeological excavations are bone flutes with holes, indicating the use of several pitches at least by 35,000 years ago. The oldest known music descriptions indicate the use of only two pitches (Sachs, 2008), but this was most probably for religious purpose and most likely the purpose of such music was to get into some religious trance. The existence of instruments suggests very ancient origins for performed music. Human language writing systems are relatively new, dating from about 5000 years ago. There is no evidence that music was written down that long ago, but arguing from absence of evidence would commit the logical fallacy of *argument um ex silentio*. Despite the fear of committing this fallacy, it can be safely concluded that most probably performance is more basic than music notation. A generic music markup language should thus commence with performance elements (frequency and time) rather than the writing down of music. Historically then, music is about performance, not about writing music.

Joseph Fourier (1768-1830) was the first to show that complex soundwaves could be described in terms of simple sine waves. A complex combination of these simple waves, such as a host of tuning forks playing together, could be used to generate complex sounds such as those of whole orchestras. Fourier's analysis is the basis on how music is generated synthetically by sound synthesizers, and even by digital sound protocols, such as those used on CDs, DVDs, and MP3s. It is possible to describe those waves with a markup language. An ideal markup language for music would start by describing such soundwaves. However, that would imply element and attribute names for each of the frequency digits between 0 and 20kHz, including possible harmonics. This will not be economical. Historical developments of conventions such as octaves and scales offer extremely useful shorthands for music description and markup.

Today the soundwaves performed can be analyzed scientifically, such as spectral mapping. Soundwaves used in music do not make use of the entire available spectrum of possible human audible hearing. Cultures select from this continuum of frequencies, but by means of pitch sets, which consist of pitches in specific relationships with one another, as defined by culture specific scales. Once pitches are performed, they are realized as frequencies. In previous eras, before scientific tuning, there was not a constant mapping between a pitch and a specific frequency. For computer applications, exact frequency mapping is important.

The frequencies of performed music can always be measured. Perhaps for music writing systems frequency is not important, but the fact that performed music always, by nature, involves frequency, suggests that it should be taken as the foundation of music. Frequency is primary, while pitch (as a specific selection from the possible range of frequencies) is secondary. It is not a contestable assumption that performed music predated the recording (in the sense of writing it down) of music. It further implies that a system should be designed with frequency as basis, and that pitches are instantiated variations on a continuum of frequencies. The fact that pitches feature so prominently in musicology is due to the dominance of the written score in CWMN.

This is how "pitch" will be used in this proposed music information architecture. Given the potential spread of the sound frequency spectrum, cultures select among the possible frequencies, but this selection is not arbitrary. A subset is selected, while it is not actual frequencies that are selected, but given some or other base, cyclical individual pitches in relational patterns. It is more the cultural relationships between pitches, expressed as intervals, that are important than frequency. Yet, at the instance of a performance, the base pitch

is mapped to a frequency, which in effect fixes the frequencies of the remainder of pitches—although it must be admitted that many performers, especially in folk music, float around and do not necessarily stick to the exact ratios expected by the formal PitchSets of their cultures. Pitch will here mean the potential value of a base frequency. A pitch in CWMN may be expressed as *E*, but the value of the frequency of *E* is unknown until realized through performance. Pitches are concepts before the processes of tuning and performance. At the instance of performance, pitch as concept is fixed to frequency. Any software system requires this formality, as the software itself cannot decide to which frequencies pitches must relate. The fact that contemporary software systems, DAWs and synthesizers seem to do that is because they are informed of the convention by designers of the systems.

Tuning must have been problematic before the use of external technologies to serve as objective reference point. It is only as recent as the 1800s that Heinrich Hertz (1857-1894) objectified the measurement of frequency. Before the external fixing of pitches to frequency, the relationship between a pitch and frequency was arbitrary, except for the intervals between pitches within an instrument. Pitches were tuned in relationship to one another based on some or other interval, typically a conventional scale, which is culturally determined. It is only as recently as around 1917 that pitches were formally fixed to frequencies in western music. Before then the relationship was arbitrary.

A software system could be designed in which pitches are arbitrarily related to frequencies. Users would need to fix the relationships. But users are typically musicians who would like to get on with the job of making music, and not so much on spending times to get the ratio's to a satisfactorily level. This is demonstrated by the popularity of the pre-determined construction of music instruments by manufacturers. On string instruments bridges are often fixed by the manufacturers, and for wind instruments holes are fabricated according to specific tuning systems. Users (musicians) need not worry about such detail.

For a generic markup system then, the starting point should be the human audible spectrum of frequencies onto which other systems are mapped. In the first instance the PitchSet and scale systems should be mapped, and then the relevant tuning system. Scales define relationships between pitches, while tuning fixes the pitches to frequencies. Other systems, such as symbolic representation systems map on top of these, and are thus secondary.

RECORDED MUSIC: NOTATION

For many centuries and in different cultures music compositions have been recorded in some or other system of writing. These systems are visual displays of soundwaves, which are audio events. It was only after the advent of recording sound with specialized audio capturing technologies that a different medium could be used for recording music. The word "recording" has two different meanings: audio recording, and visual recording of audio events. Recording music serves two purposes: to keep a historical record, on one hand, and on the other, for a composer to present guidelines how musicians should perform the composition. Notation is a symbolic written system—i.e. !music!—used by composers or transcribers to record music events. Such visual recording systems have been around probably for several millennia. Before the advent of sound recording technologies in the late 1800s, recording was visual, using symbolic representation systems such as the blobs and sticks of CWMN. One of the earliest uses of soundwave recordings in ethnomusicology was performed by Walter Fewkes in 1890, who recorded songs of the Passamaquoddy and Zuni Indians using the phonograph (Sachs, 2008). Recording sound is thus relatively newer, while recording symbols

that express sound is much older. Note that recording symbols is not about the symbols, but about capturing music sound. If by some historical quirk sound recording technologies developed before written recording, perhaps music would never have developed music notation systems.

One of the earliest western writing systems specifically designed for music was the neume system developed by the Christian Byzantine Church perhaps earlier than 800 CE. This system can also be regarded as a Cartesian grid, even though the grid system was only introduced conceptually many centuries later by René Descartes (1596-1650) in his *La Géométrie*, published in 1637. In the neume system, relative frequencies were indicated on four horizontal lines, which served as cues for the human eyes to determine whether a note rises or lowers in frequency in relation to the previous note. This system was developed as a memory aid for chanting. Guido d'Arezzo (991/992 – died after 1033) extended the functionality of the neume system by adding some features such as another line (resulting in five horizontal lines), which developed into what is today known as Common Western Music Notation.

Ingram (2004) summarizes a tremendous range of different styles of music scores (as well as some dance movement scores) and from many different cultures in use over the past thousand year. Most could be mapped onto a music space coordinate system. Exceptions are, for example, Korean zither notation which uses box divisions for rhythm, but which could nevertheless be mapped onto music space if additional descriptors are developed.

Compared to written recording, the recording of soundwaves is today perhaps the most frequent use of recorded music, as demonstrated by the billion-dollar music recording and distribution industry. In this context, it is the final music product that is distributed. Users of these products access this music through technological playback devices that allow users to control several events, such as to start a song, pause, and stop it, and do searches (such as the mechanical reverse and forward). Markup languages have been developed to control such products. SMIL, for example, is a language developed to control the playback of music, specifically on the Web. Such languages describe music extrinsically, as the control is of the final packaged music performance, not the details within the performance.

Markup languages for describing the events within a composition or performance have focused predominantly on the score, and particularly on scores written in CWMN. Recorded music in either sense of symbolic notation or recorded soundwaves is not essential music. They are processes performed on music, which means something else must be more basic. There is need for a more abstract system that would describe the core properties of music, and which would allow any possible notation systems to map onto this basic system.

ESSENTIAL MUSIC

This section summarizes the object of music as demarcated from an ontological investigation, with the purpose of establishing an information architecture for music that could apply generically to any music application. For the Greeks an ontological investigation was about determining the natural essences of something, a view I do not share. Essences are not self-evident, but we construct them, depending on our ideologies and conceptual frameworks. To deconstruct the object of music, logic is used (which is also not self-evident) which is informed by many disciplines in the domain of music.

The basic assumption for this discussion is that music is about making music, creating soundwaves, by using a variety of methods. The most essential "instrument" is the human voice, while artifacts created especially for making music are commonly used. In the distant past perhaps natural objects were used—rocks, sticks, etc., but at least

by 35,000 years ago some cultures have had the ability to create music instruments using tools.

Making music does not necessarily require an audience. The lonely shepherd may while away time by playing on some or other instrument; and a lonely woman may mumble or chant some favorite tunes while cooking. The lonely musician is his or her own audience.

Formal knowledge of cultural music systems is not a requirement to make music. The shepherd may just jam away not following any formal norms. The shepherd only requires knowledge such as that it is possible to make music, about the music instrument itself (skills such as that a flute must be blown) developed over many generations. A younger generation acquires this knowledge from social caretakers and peers. That knowledge is cultural, and music traditions play an important part in what music patterns are regarded positively or as pleasant. This is most likely how scales developed. They are embedded in the melodic structures and formal scale knowledge is not required required to make music within that scale. Few contemporary pop composers and musicians are formally trained. Many learn chords, which are shorthands, and combinations of chords, the characteristics of which are determined by western music traditions, which through blues, jazz, and rock have incorporated elements of other musical traditions. Except for serious musicians, most do not even have knowledge about keys, and can certainly not name the scales they use. Making music is thus possible without requiring a vast bank of knowledge that musicologists, as scientists, need to know and regard as essential.

Embedded in cultural knowledge, the essentials of music are about music soundwaves, music instruments (whichever way defined, and which for manufacturing requires technology), informal knowledge of scales (in the sense of which pitches are "allowed" to create a melody that is acceptable within a particular culture), and the "score" (in the sense of a composition, which is transferred audibly, and may not or may be written down if the culture has a symbolic written convention for music). The statement about which music is allowed does not refer to which music is normatively allowed, but which pitch combinations fit into the culturally acceptable scales—i.e. allowed by the scales. Breaking the scale is usually met with resistance by audiences.

Soundwaves are measured as frequencies. While musicians may not know the frequencies they produce, by its very nature the soundwaves they create can be measured as frequencies, even regardless of whether the musician knows the pitches or not within the cultural scale. If the design goal of a music ontology is an application, and as computers are better at handling explicit data, it is advisable to regard the frequency of soundwaves as the starting point. As humans, we are constrained by a physiological as well as psychological arrow of time. Music melody unfolds through time. Music is thus about the unfolding of a melody through time, expressed as soundwaves. Tuning is important, especially when fixed tuned instruments and variable tuned instruments are used together in orchestras. If tuning is not done properly, harmonic clashes result in unpleasant music.

Software applications should be able to handle the extensive existing stock of notational music scores. The pitches in these scores are not fixed to frequencies. To handle this, the software should allow the mapping of scores to Music Space, while pitch-frequency fixing can be selected just prior to performance, i.e. just before the software initiates the synthesizer to execute the score.

The core of music is as follows. Music is performed, following cultural norms. Performed music is expressed through soundwaves as frequencies that unfold through time. Cultural norms determine which pitch sets are "allowed," while the sets are defined in terms of ratios or intervals between individual pitches in a set. Cultural norms further guide patterns for compositions. Compositions may be formal, and often captured by some writing system or learned rote from mentors, or more *ad lib*, such as at jamming sessions. Instruments are made according to these cultural norms. Instruments are tuned to specific frequencies for performances, and the action of tuning thus fixes the pitches to definite frequencies. All other components are *about music*, not *music itself* (see Figure 1).

Figure 1. The core of music (performed music), its components, and how other disciplines relate to it

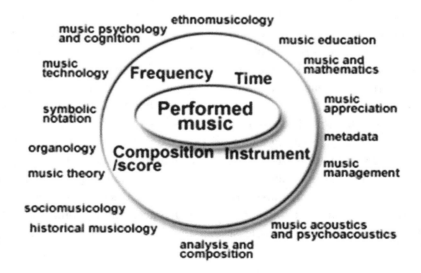

PITCH AND NOTES

For the purpose of this analysis, frequency and pitch are distinguished. Frequency is a discrete, measurable entity that can be determined with audio technologies. Before the advent of audio recording systems, writing systems could capture frequencies only relatively. As the actual frequencies might be unknown, the set of frequencies contained in a particular composition were described by expressing the relative relationships between the frequencies, and are called pitches. Without context, a single pitch in its written format is meaningless and only of theoretical interest. Even when performed a single decontextualized pitch is compositionally meaningless as songs by nature consist of repeated patterns, including variations on these patterns. The word "music" in its general, popular sense applies here, as music for mood, or experimental music may indeed consist of a single note, just as John Cage's "silence" consists not of notes, but the absence of music, and focused on the surrounding sounds. Drones of some cultures are also monotone, but given the vast stock of available music, these performances are exceptions rather than rules—even perhaps deliberate exceptions.

The relative relationship between pitches are indicated visually on the horizontal lines of CWMN but also on other visual systems. To map a particular pitch to a specific frequency, the tuning system as well as the scale must be known. In this context, scale refers to the relative frequencies between the individual notes assigned to a particular scale. It is evident that a particular pitch could be mapped to many different frequencies. Pitch is thus relative, while frequency is absolute.

In CWMN pitches are symbolized either with sticks and blobs, or with alphabet characters ranging from A...G, while flat and sharp signs indicate semitone variations. There is no natural relation between a pitch and an alphabet letter, and even less so between frequency and a letter.

It is interesting that given the potential music frequency spectrum, all human cultures only use a subset, and within the set, only some relationships between points on the continuum. This is most likely due to the physiological constraints of the human audio perception system, which includes the brain's capacity to filter out redundancies and highlight only a very small and limited set of possible incoming information. Neurologically, the focus is on what is regarded as pleasant. From this perspective, it would be redundant for any attempt at a music information architectural program to account for the entire music frequency as starting point. It is much more economical to start with what the human audio perception system is capable of distinguishing, and the subsets (as scales) already selected by cultures, as explained below.

The fact that ratios rather than isolated instances of pitches feature in all music, except for monotone drones, has the implication that for an economic description intervals should serve as starting point. Guiding this would be another fact: that for several thousand years the doubling of a frequency has been regarded as having special significance—i.e. the "octave." Ratios between pitches are typically declared within an "octave." So we can commence by using the "octave" as basis, then determining the ratios of "recognized" pitches, as defined by the different scales of different cultures.

CWMN is an amazing invention, despite its many shortcomings. CWMN is a very efficient (although not sufficient) symbolic music notation system, which serves the majority of music expressions in the world. It may not be sufficient for more experimental music, or for musical systems such as *gamelan*, but works for all popular music, much folk music, and lots more from all over the globe and history. Even before the invention of Cartesian coordinate system by Rene Descrates (1596-1650), music pitches were indicated on relative heights on staves (y-axis), and later the time signature on the x-axis. The basic design principle of CWMN (and I do not mean the graphic sticks and blobs but conceptually) could serve as the basis for designing a more powerful system. The notation system could easily be regarded as a frequency-time coordinate graph, keeping in mind that neither absolute frequency, nor absolute time is made explicit in CWMN. In the notation system, they are relative, and preciseness is implemented at execution or performance-based time, which depends on the whims of the performers, typically informed by years of training according to the interpretations of their masters.

A standard 12-tone octave is divided into 1200 cents, with 100 cent per semitone. Research into the smallest perceivable distinctions between pitches has been done since the 1800s, and variations of the early research is still being carried out (e.g. Houtsma & Smurzynksi, 1990; Tervaniemi, et al., 2005). The smallest perceivable distinction between adjacent pitches is known as *Just Noticeable Difference* (JND). Walker summarizes the perception of JND between tones as follows:

"Several studies in music perception of intervals as well as individual pitches, starting with Seashore, showed that highly trained musicians can detect differences as small as 10 cents. The limits of this perceptual ability were tested to produce what is known as the Just Noticeable Difference (JND), the smallest change in frequency which is detectable" (Walker, 2007, p. 252).

This means that trained musicians are able to distinguish 120 different pitches in a standard 12-tone octave—too many to label with the limited 26-character western alphabet. However, except for highly experimental music, such detailed distinctions is not practical. If the physical acoustics of music sounds is the focus of a general markup language for music, the question may arise on why using cents, which are relative. A cent measures the distance between musical intervals in a particular scale and tuning system. The measurement is done logarithmically from a base sound (or start of the scale in the octave). Cents are thus not absolute values, but relative and determined by the

particular scale. It is possible to design a markup language element for each step in frequency along the spectrum within the boundaries of human perception. It is possible to mark all the frequencies between, say 440Hz (A4) and 880Hz (A5). However, that would imply extreme redundancy. To describe the soundwaves of performance would be cumbersome and complex, as overtones and undertones not within the audible range may interfere with the audible sound by adding harmonics, and all of this will then need to be described. The range of frequency that can be heard is not consistent across different individuals, which implies that a statistical average "person" needs to be used, which would be an abstraction from physics. We thus continuously make abstractions and summarize the almost infinite possibilities of information that we wish to mark. Occam's razor applies here too!

Using the seven alphabet letters used by CWMN, recognized pitches in an "octave" could be indicated by A...G. Any other set of symbols could be used. Even the entire Latin alphabet could be used, but that would place quite a burden on the student of music having to learn the mapping of the alphabet to pitches. The absolute values of these symbols can only be assigned once a tuning system has been implemented. For an application for common use, in order to not introduce too much complexity for the average user, one of the major tuning systems (such as just, or well-tempered) could be used for factory settings, as is done presently by synthesizer manufacturers, while still allowing the mapping of pitches or written conventions to user-defined frequency settings. Within the "standard" 1200 cents per octave, pitches at 100 cent intervals are mapped to the letters A...G. Should smaller cent values be required, the proposed convention is to indicate the variation from the assigned pitch symbol with that symbol and a plus number value (or alternatively a minus number value attached to the previous symbol in the series). So a 45-cent positive variation to the pitch F will be expressed as F+45, and if the negative value needs to be expressed: G-55.

The CWMN symbol *A* is a !pitch! symbol. When in 1999 I designed the general Music Markup Language (MML) I had in mind for such symbols the meaning |pitch|, which was expressed in the MML language with <note>. This was a mistake, as commentators on MML (e.g. Haus & Longari, 2005) interpreted this to mean that MML is a notational markup language, perhaps because the examples given were of music scores. I take full responsibility for this non-deliberate confusion. The original reason why the CWMN letters were chosen was for their familiarity to non-technical readers. This was not made explicit enough, although hinted to on the MML website at http://www.musicmarkup.info/modules/notation/ with statements such as referring to the abstract nature of "note" in MML, and, for example, "... abstract MML 'note' can thus easily be translated into such a graphical representation as it contains all the necessary information for such a translation." The careful reader of MML would have noticed that the MML language consists of the core systems frequency and time, and that the notation system is an optional symbolic representation system. Thus, the notation system is not primary as commentators conclude, and the confusion should not have arisen.

MML's A...G maps onto CWMN's A...G, while the exact frequency (pitch) is determined by the tuning system (which is absent from CWMN). But MML's "notation" must be regarded as an expression of concepts—i.e. |notes|—not the symbols of CWMN—i.e. !notes!.

Ideally, each cent would be assigned a markup label. Pragmatically, this would be an over-kill. Apart from resulting in excessive markup code, it would be difficult for human readers to translate, hence not complying with the XML guideline to be human readable. The scale system would serve as an excellent shorthand selection of frequencies from the very large set of possible frequencies within the audible spectrum.

OCTAVE

The term "octave" is a bit of a misnomer, but well established in usage. The word is derived from the Latin word meaning "eighth," and on the modern piano if the white notes are counted, repeating cycles of the octave occur on every eighth note leading to the popular notion that an octave consists of 8 notes. There are of course more than 8 notes in our octave. Contemporary western music divides the octave into 12 pitches, Arabic music into 16 pitches, and Persian music into 24 pitches. Interval ratios between pitches are not universally consistent, and depend on the particular tuning system that is used. The octave could also consist of fewer than eight notes. The Javanese *sléndro gamelan* divides the octave into 5 pitches. To account for all the cultural variations, a better term for octave might be PitchSet, which will be used here. In the original MML NoteSet was used, but as explained, that lead to confusingly interpreting MML as a notation system, which it certainly was not.

Scales

Here a musical scale is regarded to consist of the pitches recognized to be members of some or other PitchSet (octave) system, while mode is a particular shorthand form, a nomenclature for a specific scale. What is regarded as pleasing music sound combinations is both cultural and neurological. Typically, to the human ear music consonance (pleasing sounds) differ depending on the context of the individual pitch, whether the pitch increases or decreases, and other factors. A particular pitch might have different preferred frequencies depending on whether the scale goes up or down. For example, in just intonation G# and A-flat have different frequencies.

From an applicaiton development point of view, developers could offer all the possible cultural scale systems as selectable options, while the technical details could be handled programmatically during the development phase.

For a quaint, but dated and politically incorrect view of cultures, and view on the intricacies of different cultural music systems, see Sachs (2008). One does not need to adhere to his eurocentric conclusions to appreciate his wealth of data. It is nevertheless a useful source for the different scales and modes used in the many different music styles on this planet.

TUNING SYSTEMS

The tuning system consists of a table of data, mapping pitches to frequencies. From an applicaiton point of view, users should be allowed to fine-tune frequencies, as well as to define the pitches. For example, given a well-tempered tuning table, a user should be allowed to insert a new pitch somewhere on the table, give that pitch a name, and map that pitch to a frequency.

For popular music, knowledge of tuning systems is not important, and cultures usually have widely accepted practices of how the relationships between pitches are "defined," or tuned on instruments. Before the advent of modern technologies, and an understanding of the physical acoustics of musical soundwaves and how harmonics are created, as well as what is culturally (perhaps biologically?) regarded as "in tune," the tuning of instruments was more an art (and subjective) than scientific, or rational. The modern western tuning system was only established as recently as around 1917, when it became possible to fix pitch ratios using tuning according to the findings of physics. This equal temperament tuning system divides the "octave" into more or less equal ratios. Of course, tuning without tuning forks or tuning devices might still be considered an art. However, the design goal of this chapter's content is aimed at computers, and for computers explicit tuning instructions would be very important.

For a computer application, conventional scales could serve as default settings, while allowing a user to create any possible set. This would be done by specifying the base note cycles of a PitchSet (e.g. 220, 440, 880, etc.), assign how many pitches are to be identified within the PitchSet, and then either assign specific frequencies to the pitches, or declare their relative intervals. The average user may not be interested in so many degrees of freedom, so manufacturers may fix default values following general standard practices of tuning.

TIME

Allen (1984) defines time with reference to action. He distinguishes between events that remain static over time which are captured by properties, and events that change over time, which are captured by occurrences. This distinction seems to follow Saussure's distinction between synchrony and diachrony. Computers operate in discrete steps, using static and discrete information. The only possible method to indicate change is to algorithmically change the parameters of one state, which will then be followed by this new state. Algorithms are creative constructs, and operate on information. The structures of information are also discrete. This means that the basics of computer processes depend on static structures, and that apparent change over time is an illusion caused by states following on one another. The discrete states can be mapped onto a timeline, while each instance on the timeline will have its own properties.

Raimond, Abdallah, Sandler, and Giasson (2007) distinguish between a universal timeline (a calendar) and an audio signal timeline (duration of the performance). The audio timeline refers to the specific audio event mapped onto a calendar datetime stamp. A three minute song executes somewhere on the universal timeline, such as 1 February 1990, 21:05. This audio timeline maps onto the x-axis of the abstract music space onto which music is mapped. This space can be linked to the universal timeline when known, but would nevertheless function adequately when unknown.

Common Western Music Notation is relative regarding time and frequency, as the absolute values are determined during performance. When absolute, time intervals may be mapped to some other other clock system. It references some or other widely accepted external time measurement convention. Even when the time referencing system is absolute, the time of the music event instance may be relative. An absolute datetime stamp may indicate when a song—i.e. a music event sequence—begins to play, but the actual tempo may be unknown until specified by the performer (which may be done when recording to MIDI or waveform). A device may be set to trigger a music song with relative tempo on a specific date and time (i.e. absolute). When the relative tempo is performed, it becomes absolute.

The tempo of systems, such as MIDI, are based on some or other clock—MTC, or SMPTE, which are absolute. Special algorithms need to be written to turn absolute computer time into relative time.

A timeline as reference point for music events is essential for the description of music architecture. There are of course many aspects of the whole discipline of music that do not require timelines—e.g. metadata, but for music itself, it is essential.

Several proposals have been made to address the timeline in markup languages. SMLD and HyTime were the first such attempts (Sloan, 1993). Haus and Longari (2002, 2005) proposed a spine as the reference line. Music as well as multi-media time can be represented on the x-axis in Music Space (Steyn, 2004). Time can be represented visually as an axis with intervals on which event instances can be plotted. Intervals may represent absolute or relative time.

Both pitch and tempo are relative, but both become absolute at the instance of performing that music. The relative nature of pitch and tempo are structural. Cultures developed systems of acceptable pitches, not in isolation of one another, but in sets of pitches. Music instruments were designed around these sets. These customs became ossified to such an extent that they are regarded as natural.

However, they are only cultural frameworks within which performed music occurs. Performance occurs in real absolute time, and music is expressed as soundwaves with definite frequencies. The tempo is never absolute, and can vary along the axis of absolute time. The same with pitches. Performers are not always able to map pitches to the ideal set of frequency intervals. From a computer application perspective, absolute time and frequency are the basics. Relative pitch and tempo are mapped onto this system, not the other way around.

MUSIC SPACE

Music Space (Steyn, 2004) was introduced as an abstract visual (and virtual) presentation space for multimedia events and objects. The main purpose of Music Space is to be able to map simultaneous music events onto a common timeline, but it is powerful enough to allow the mapping of music objects, and non-music events related to the performance. On this three-dimensional space, the x-axis represents time (intervals may be absolute or relative), the y-axis frequency or pitch, and the z-axis simultaneity, used for synchronizing events that start at the same time instances. The same coordinate space could also be used to specify locations, such as physical theater stages or virtual rooms. However, in such cases the axes will represent different properties—length, breadth, and height. Locations are visual phenomena. Hence, the coordinate system representing such spaces are semiotically once removed from the space it represents. Music space is at least twice removed, as music is audio, which needs to be expressed first, and then translated into visual representation—the translation of time-based music events onto a visual coordinate system. It seems best that for performance and production purposes a time-based space is fundamental, and that location spaces are instances mapped onto intervals within the time-based space, even if relational and not absolute. For example, props may change their position on a stage during a production. Those changes are time-based. Therefore, the snapshot of the visual location at time *A* will differ from the snapshot at time *B*. A time-based coordinate system, such as Music Space, is thus primary, and location spaces are mapped as instances (snapshots) to specific time slots in this space. The location coordinate system thus links to slots within the time coordinate system.

The fundamental representation of entities within time space is not always known. Events are actions executed by actors (human or non-human) at some or other time. There is thus always a time-dimension associated with events. Events have start points and end points. Even objects are event-based, as actors manage and manipulate objects. It is, however, not always necessary to stipulate the actors managing an object. For example, when a chair as prop needs to be put on stage, from a score point of view it is not necessary to stipulate the particular stage-hand who has to move the chair to its position, except of course for stage management, in which case the role of moving the chair needs to be assigned to a specific stage-hand or performer. A prop, as object, might thus just appear at a specific time slot within time space. Alternatively, the prop may be on stage from before the show started and remain fixed in the same spot for the entire performance. From the theatrical production perspective the prop is static, but given calendar time it is not, as there was a past calendar time when the prop was not in that position, and most likely a future calendar time when the prop will also not be in that spot. In a similar sense, symbolic music notation is not translated into events until performed. A score may be mapped onto a relative music space without any indication of its absolute time reference. Each note merely appears in the space as the user scrolls through the score—an intellectual exercise, because music is not performed. However, once the user assigns an absolute time reference to the score, as indicated by beats per minute, or by the conductor's indication of the

tempo, the location of a note can be predicted as it is then tied to an absolute time reference. This is what happens during any performance when a conductor sets the tempo, or changes the tempo during the performance.

From a software application point of view the time space and location space could visually display in separate synchronized windows. For the visual side of a production, the location space would dominate. From the sound side of a production, the time space would dominate. A musician may want to see how the music events unfold through the time progression of a movie; while a film director might want to see the video—which of course hangs on the time axis.

Serial Markup vs. Parallel Markup

Music Space itself does not need to be marked. It is a visual heuristic. Marking objects and events within this space is challenging—i.e. not the labeling part, but the structural design of the markup nodes. For a text document, markup nodal structure is straightforward. The markup structure could just follow the text structure as document text unfolds serially in time. In such cases, the markup structure would follow the x-axis of Music Space. Music, however, except for non-polyphonic music, always involves multiple events that happen simultaneously in parallel. This means multiple z-axis values have to be linked to the same intervals on the x-axis.

Given this complexity, the design question is this: should marking be event-series based (in the sense of all events for a single instrument), or should it be time-based (in the sense of marking all the different instrument events that occur in the same time-slot simultaneously).

Recall that markup is serial, and processors render the markup serially, not in parallel. This means, theoretically, that the timeline should be processed first, and that each series be processed in succession. In practice, this implies a huge memory burden, as the timeline for each instrument's events will need to be kept in memory, and then each successive series before synchronization can be processed. Alternatively, markup should be done in chunks, making explicit all the simultaneous events before moving onto the next interval. Such markup will be more difficult to follow by human readers. To explain this, here is a snippet describing three events for four instruments.

Serial Markup

```
<instrument id="1">
        <event eventid="1">...
        <event eventid="2">...
        <event eventid="3">...
</instrument>
<instrument id="2">
        <event eventid="1">...
        <event eventid="2">...
        <event eventid="3">...
</instrument>
<instrument id="3">
        <event eventid="1">...
        <event eventid="2">...
        <event eventid="3">...
</instrument>
<instrument id="4">
        <event eventid="1">...
        <event eventid="2">...
        <event eventid="3">...
</instrument>
(404 characters)
```

Parallel Markup

```
<instrument id="1">
        <event eventid="1">......
</instrument>
<instrument id="2">
        <event eventid="1">......
</instrument>
<instrument id="3">
        <event eventid="1">......
```

```
</instrument>
<instrument id="4">
        <event eventid="1">......
</instrument>
<instrument id="1">
        <event eventid="2">......
</instrument>
<instrument id="2">
        <event eventid="2">......
</instrument>
<instrument id="3">
        <event eventid="2">......
</instrument>
<instrument id="4">
        <event eventid="2">......
</instrument>
<instrument id="1">
        <event eventid="3">......
</instrument>
<instrument id="2">
        <event eventid="3">......
</instrument>
<instrument id="3">
        <event eventid="3">......
</instrument>
<instrument id="4">
        <event eventid="3">......
</instrument>
(696 characters)
```

It is evident from this example that in this format, parallel is not the most economical markup-wise, even though it may be less demanding on memory. When time is the basis of the markup structure, neither serial or parallel markup is efficient. Consider this event-based markup, which is for the same concepts as above:

```
<event eventid="1">
        <instrument id="1">...
        <instrument id="2">...
        <instrument id="3">...
        <instrument id="4">...
</event>
```

```
<event eventid="2">
        <instrument id="1">...
        <instrument id="2">...
        <instrument id="3">...
        <instrument id="4">...
</event>
<event eventid="3">
        <instrument id="1">...
        <instrument id="2">...
        <instrument id="3">...
        <instrument id="4">...
</event>
(357 characters)
```

Event-based markup for multiple simultaneous events is more economic than time-based markup. This demonstrates that for efficient design it is not only the information architecture defined by idealistic ontology that should guide the design of the markup, but also efficiency. From an information architectural perspective one might have wanted to begin with the instrument as parent node, as that would be based on our normal "intuitive" knowledge of performing music. For the efficiency of a specific artifact, the design should perhaps be guided by the System of Markup Expressions for the design of nodal relationships rather than only by the System of Abstract Theoretical Constructs.

CONCLUSION

If the design goal is to build a computer system for music, one first needs to determine what is meant by music, and secondly what the designed artifact will be used for. To determine the information architecture of the envisaged system, an ontological investigation needs to be launched. Ontology as used in Information Science is ambiguous, differs from the philosophical conception of the term, and originated within a positivist tradition. Various systems of description need to be considered during the ontological investigation:

theory (System of Explanation), concepts (System of Abstract Theoretical Constructs), language use (System of Human Language Description), and the written formats (System of Formal Symbolic Expression). Markup languages (System of Markup Expression) could be designed for any of these systems, including a markup language for the markup language itself! In the final analysis praxis rules, and not ontological idealism. The information architecture shows the structural relationships between concepts, but a markup language cannot blindly follow that structure, especially when memory efficiency is required.

An ontological investigation into what the basics of music are will result in different answers. In this chapter, the core of music is demarcated based on historically and culturally shared components. Music is about generating soundwaves by the use of some or other technological artifact—the instrument; but could also be restricted to the physiologically natural human voice. The process of generating music soundwaves does not utilize the entire available human audible spectrum of frequencies. Only a small portion is used, and in structural sets in which different pitches within the set are in strict interval relations with one another. The sets used are culturally defined pitches, which are confined to culturally defined scales. During performance, these pitches are expressed in absolute frequency values. Before performing, a pitch is mapped to a frequency through the use of a tuning system.

If the design goal is to build a computer system for music, the basic concepts that need to be accounted for are as follows. Music consists of a selection of base frequencies, which constitute a small subset of the available frequency spectrum. Base frequency refers to "pure" sine waves without any harmonics; thus an abstraction. Selected subsets of frequencies depend on culturally predefined sets in which relations between pitches are specified conventionally. Within repeating cycles (i.e. octaves) that define the boundaries of cycle sets, the number of pitches selected is culturally dependent, and through cultural history obtained fixed status, even to the extent of having names assigned to them (such as Dorian, sléndro, etc.). At performance time, the relative pitches and time are realized in absolute frequencies and time. This transition from pitch to base frequency is achieved through the conventions of the tuning system.

The above description is considered to be the basics of music, informed by an ontological investigation. All other ontologies are *about the music* object; not the *music object itself*. To describe the information architecture of this basic notion of music requires a description of the cultural set of pitches that are regarded to form a set, and which is informed by cultural scales. When this pitch-system (Figure 2) is expressed during music performance, it is based on some tuning. In pre-scientific eras the tuning might have been haphazardly done, while more recently a measurable consistent mapping convention is followed (in western music A4 at 440Hz or 442Hz).

Music unfolds through time. Even when a strict measure of tempo is not followed, or when time is variable, there is nevertheless a deployment through measurable time when performed. The beat may not be consistent, but the abstract tempo may be. It is possible for a musician with poor time-keeping ability to play inconsistently

compared to an absolute time. For emotional effect, music may slow down or speed up in relation to absolute time, while the tempo intervals may remain unchanged. However, as computers require absolute time, Music Space should start there, and map relative tempo to the absolute tempo. As absolute time is not always know, Music Space allows for the mapping of relative time on this space. However, before performance of such music can take place, a decision needs to be made as to how tempo translates into clock-time (see Figure 3).

The above constitutes the "essence" of music, as informed by acoustics. Once this core of music is expressed as information architecture, all other possible music ontologies can be mapped onto this system. Psychoacoustics interprets this music from a certain perspective; ethnomusicology from another perspective; symbolic notation systems are cultural conventions recording this music; music education teaches this; organology systematizes this; music theory is a theory about this; sociomusicology considers sociological aspects of this; and so forth. It seems that all other possible ontologies and information architectures revolve around this core. It is this core, which is what was expressed with the generic Music Markup Language when it was originally developed.

From an application point of view, a user might begin with setting up the system as follows. Music

Figure 2. The frequency/pitch system

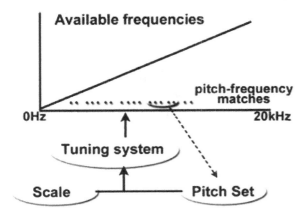

Figure 3. Frequency/pitch (y-axis) and time/tempo (x-axis)

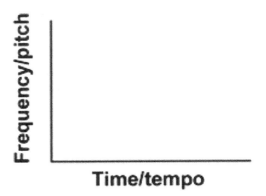

Space could be presented visually. On this space, the user selects whether time is absolute or relative. If relative, the intervals need to be specified. On this space, the user also indicates whether relative pitches or absolute frequencies are to be used. If frequency is selected, the frequencies of pitches need to be selected. Names are assigned to pitches, or a user could choose a default PitchSet, such as a scale within a well-tempered tuning system, in which case the pitches will populate automatically, yet allow the user to change individual frequency settings for each pitch. The selection of a particular PitchSet might be informed by established scales. For example, the user interface may allow the user to select between Dorian and Sléndro (which would offer only five pitches).

Onto such a basic set-up any kind of synthesis model could be deployed.

NOTE

Several sections in this chapter are based on a working paper for the MPEG4 group working on Symbolic Music Representation, which met in Paris in 2005.

REFERENCES

Allen, J. F. (1984). Towards a general theory of action and time. *Artificial Intelligence, 23*, 123–154. doi:10.1016/0004-3702(84)90008-0

Austin, J. L. (1975). *How to do things with words*. Cambridge, MA: Harvard University Press. doi:10.1093/acprof:oso/9780198245537.001.0001

Buitelaar, P., et al. (2006). *LingInfo: Design and applications of a model for the integration of linguistic information in ontologies*. Retrieved from http://www.dfki.de/~romanell/OntoLex2006.pdf

Chandrasekaran, B., Josephson, J. R., & Benjamins, V. R. (1999). What are ontologies, and why do we need them? *IEEE Intelligent Systems, 14*(1), 20–26. doi:10.1109/5254.747902

de Saussure, F. (1990). *Course in general linguitsics* (Harris, R., Trans.). London, UK: Duckworth.

Fong, S. (2002). On the ontological basis for logical metonomy: Telic roles and WORDNET. [Ontolex.]. *Proceedings of Ontolex, 2002*, 37–41.

Fonseca, F. (2007). The double role of ontologies in information science research. *Journal of the American Society for Information Science and Technology, 58*(6), 786–793. doi:10.1002/asi.20565

Gruber, T. R. (1992). *What is an ontology?* Retrieved from http://www-ksl.stanford.edu/kst/what-is-an-ontology.html

Harold, E. R. (2004). *Effective XML: 50 specific ways to improve your XML*. Boston, MA: Addison Wesley.

Haus, G., & Longari, M. (2002). Towards a symbolic/time-based music language based on XML. In Haus & Longari (Eds.), *MAX 2002: Musical Applications using XML: Proceedings First International Conference Laboratoria di Informatica Musicale*, (pp. 38-46). Milan, Italy: State University of Milan.

Haus, G., & Longari, M. (2005). A multi-layered, time-based music description approach based on XML. *Computer Music Journal, 29*, 70–85. doi:10.1162/comj.2005.29.1.70

Haus, G., & Longari, M. (2005). A multi-layered, time-based music description approach based on XML. *Computer Music Journal, 29*(1), 70–85. doi:10.1162/comj.2005.29.1.70

Houtsma, A. J. M., & Smurzynksi, J. (1990). Pitch identification and discrimination for complex tones with many harmonies. *The Journal of the Acoustical Society of America, 87*(1), 304–310. doi:10.1121/1.399297

Ingram, J. (2004). *A survey of the world's music notations with special emphasis on early, contemporary and non-European notations*. MusicNetwork.

James, J. (1993). *The music of the spheres: Music, science, and the natural order of the universe*. London, UK: Abacus. doi:10.1119/1.18443

Kania, A. (2007). The philosophy of music. *Stanford Encyclopedia of Philosophy*. Retrieved from http://plato.stanford.edu/entries/music/

Kuhn, T. S. (1962). *The structure of scientific revolutions*. Chicago, IL: University of Chicago Press.

Lenci, A. (2010). The life cycle of knowledge. In Huang, C., Calzolari, N., Gangemi, A., & Lenci, A. (Eds.), *Ontology and the Lexicon: A Natural Language Processing Perspective* (pp. 241–257). Cambridge, UK: Cambridge University Press. doi:10.1017/CBO9780511676536.015

Lucidovo, L. (2009). IEEE 1599: A multi-layer approach to music description. *Journal of Multimedia, 4*(1).

Music Ontology Specification. (2010). *Specification document*. Retrieved from http://www.musicontology.com/

Ng, K., & Nesi, P. (Eds.). (2007). *Interactive multimedia music technologies*. Hershey, PA: IGI Global. doi:10.4018/978-1-59904-150-6

Peeters, G., McAdams, S., & Herrera, P. (2000). Instrument sound description in the context of MPEG-7. In *Proceedings of ICMC*. ICMC.

Perry, R. (2002). The music encoding initiative (MEI). In Proceedings of the First International Conference MAX 2002: Musical Application Using XML. Milan, Italy: MAX.

Raimond, Y., Abdallah, S., Sandler, M., & Giasson, F. (2007). The music ontology. *Austrian Computer Society*. Retrieved from http://fgiasson.com/articles/ismir2007.pdf

Raimond, Y., & Giasson, F. (Eds.). (2010). *Music ontology specification*. Retrieved from http://musicontology.com/

Ridley, A. (2003). Against musical ontology. *The Journal of Philosophy, 100*(4), 203–220.

Ryle, G. (1965). *The concept of mind*. New York, NY: Barnes and Noble.

Sachs, C. (2008). *The rise of music in the ancient world: East and west*. New York, NY: Dover.

Sloan, D. (1993). Aspects of music representation in HyTime/SMDL. *Computer Music Journal, 17*(4). doi:10.2307/3680544

Steinberger, R., Hagman, J., & Scheer, S. (2000). *Using thesauri for automatic indexing and for the visualisation of multilingual document collections*. Paper presented at OntoLex 2000 – Workshop on Ontologies and Lexical Knowledge Bases. Sozopol, Bulgaria.

Steyn, J. (1999). *MML (music markup language)*. Retrieved from http://www.musicmarkup.info/

Steyn, J. (2002). Framework for a music markup language. In *Proceedings of the First International Conference MAX 2002: Musical Application Using XML*. Milan, Italy: MAX. Retrieved from http://www.musicmarkup.info/MAX/max2002paper.html

Steyn, J. (2004). Introducing music space. In *Proceedings of the 4ᵗʰ Open Workshop of MUSICNETWORK: Integration of Music in Multimedia Applications*. Barcelona, Spain: MUSICNETWORK. Retrieved from http://www.musicmarkup.info/papers/musicspace/musicspace.html

Steyn, J. (2007). Challenges of designing a markup language for music . In Ng, K., & Nesi, P. (Eds.), *Interactive Multimedia Music Technologies*. IGI Information Science. doi:10.4018/978-1-59904-150-6.ch006

Tervaniemi, M., Just, V., Koelsch, S., Widmann, A., & Schröger, E. (2005). Pitch discrimination accuracy in musicians vs nonmusicians: An event-related potential and behavioral study. *Experimental Brain Research, 161*, 1–10. doi:10.1007/s00221-004-2044-5

Vaggione, H. (2001). Some ontological remarks about music composition processes. *Computer Music Journal, 25*(1), 54–61. doi:10.1162/014892601300126115

Walker, R. (2007). *Music education: Cultural values, social change and innovation*. New York, NY: Charles C Thomas Pub Ltd.

Wand, Y., & Weber, R. (1990). An ontological model of an information system. *IEEE Transactions on Software Engineering, 16*(11). doi:10.1109/32.60316

Wand, Y., & Weber, R. (1993). On the ontological expressiveness of information systems analysis and design grammars. *Journal of Info Systems, 3*, 217–237. doi:10.1111/j.1365-2575.1993.tb00127.x

Whitehead, A. N. (1960). *Process and reality*. New York, NY: MacMillan.

Wittgenstein, L. (1953). *Philosophical investigations* (Anscombe, G. E. M., Trans.). New York, NY: Macmillan.

Wuyssusek, B. (2004). Ontology and ontologies in information systems analysis and design: A critique. In *Proceedings of the Tenth Americas Conference on Information Systems*, (pp. 4303-4308). New York, NY: Americas Conference.

Zuniga, G. L. (2001). Ontology: Its transformation from philosophy to information systems. In *Proceedings of the International Conference on Formal Ontology in Information Systems*, (pp. 187-197). ACM Press.

Chapter 2
The Physics of Music

Jyri Pakarinen
Aalto University, Finland

ABSTRACT

This chapter discusses the central physical phenomena involved in music. The aim is to provide an explanation of the related issues in an understandable level, without delving unnecessarily deep in the underlying mathematics. The chapter is divided in two main sections: musical sound sources and sound transmission to the observer. The first section starts from the definition of sound as wave motion, and then guides the reader through the vibration of strings, bars, membranes, plates, and air columns, that is, the oscillating sources that create the sound for most of the musical instruments. Resonating structures, such as instrument bodies are also reviewed, and the section ends with a discussion on the potential physical markup parameters for musical sound sources. The second section starts with an introduction to the basics of room acoustics, and then explains the acoustic effect that the human observer causes in the sound field. The end of the second section provides a discussion on which sound transmission parameters could be used in a general music markup language. Finally, a concluding section is presented.

INTRODUCTION AND BACKGROUND

This chapter intends to serve as an introduction for the different physical phenomena involved in music. It is aimed at an audience with a basic understanding on mathematics and physics, but without a formal education on acoustics. This chapter does not attempt to serve as a thorough tutorial or textbook on musical acoustics or physics of musical instruments. For these purposes, other excellent works can be found in the literature. The distinguished 'Science of Sound' (Rossing, 1990) provides a broad and easily understandable intro-

duction to acoustics and speech in general, and is being used as a primer on acoustics in several universities. Works by Reynolds (1981), Fahy (2001), and Blauert and Xiang (2008) provide perhaps a more thorough engineering approach to acoustics and vibrational physics of fluids and solids. The book *Physics of Musical Instruments* (Fletcher & Rossing, 1991) gives a rigorous explanation of various physical phenomena involved in musical instruments, and is mostly used as the basis for the section on musical sound sources below.

Aside from purely educational purposes, basic understanding of the physical phenomena that enable the creation of music is useful when deciding what musical features to markup in a general music

DOI: 10.4018/978-1-4666-2497-9.ch002

markup language. Using physical quantities, such as frequency, as markup parameters has some important advantages. Firstly, physical quantities are universal. Since higher-level musical concepts are derived from physical phenomena, a system using physical variables as its lowest-level representation would adapt well to changes higher up in the system hierarchy. For example, if the pitch is represented with a frequency in Hertz rather than the note name in the Common Western Notation (CWN), transporting the system between different notation systems becomes trivial.

Secondly, physical parameters can be used in controlling sound synthesizers. For physics-based sound synthesizers, the physical quantities can in many cases be directly used as control parameters. This enables more explicit control over the timbre of the synthetic instruments, since instead of feeding only the note name, velocity, and instrument name to a synthesizer, the user could for example explicitly state the length and material of a guitar string, as well as plucking location, and whether the string is plucked with a finger or plectrum, and so forth. Of course, some default parameter values or compound variables for such a system should be set, so that the user would not always have to define an extensive list of parameters, but he or she would have the freedom to do so, if in search for a specific musical timbre. For an extensive review of physics-based sound synthesis methods, see (Välimäki, et al., 2006). For abstract sound synthesis techniques (such as additive synthesis or frequency modulation), the physical parameters can be used, e.g. in defining the desired spectral form or amplitude envelope of the sound. This can be achieved by creating mapping rules from physical parameters for the control parameters of the particular abstract synthesis method. It must be noted that creating these mappings might not necessarily be as difficult task as it might seem at first, since many synthesis techniques already have some control parameters (such as pitch, amplitude, spectral density, etc.) that are indirectly related to physical properties of the source.

The objective of this chapter is to introduce the reader to the physical processes that enable us to create and hear music. Furthermore, the chapter should raise ideas on what features to markup in a general music markup language. The depth of coverage is defined by the potential markup parameters, so that the physics is discussed to the extent that is required for understanding these parameters.

What is Sound?

In everyday speech, the term "sound" represents a variety of concepts. For example, it can refer to the actual physical phenomena of moving air particles, a series of grooves on a vinyl disc, or the response of a human mind to the vibration of the eardrum and the corresponding neural firings inside the brain. This chapter considers sound as an air pressure disturbance that propagates as a function of time. In most cases[1], this pressure disturbance manifests itself as an oscillatory vibration of the air molecules. Sound is propagated in air as waves, similarly as the ripples propagate on the surface of a pond when a stone is thrown into the water. It is important to note that although sound waves (as well as other motion waves in a medium) transmit the vibrational movement created by the source, they do not transmit matter. In other words, the air molecules at the source do not travel far themselves, although the sound wave might travel long distances at a considerable speed.

The sound itself possesses some physical characteristics, which aid in analyzing how a human listener would perceive that particular sound. In addition, information on the operation of the sound source itself can be extracted from this analysis. One of the most important of these sonic characteristics is the sound spectrum. If the sound is recorded with a microphone, the spectrum gives the air pressure variation as a function of frequency, for a measured time interval. By moving this time window for continuous time, an explicit two-dimensional representation of the sound amplitude as a function of time and frequency is obtained. This time-varying spectrum can be illustrated as a spectrogram image for a given time and frequency range. For harmonic sounds, for example, important parameters such as the fundamental frequency, amplitudes of the individual harmonics, and the amplitude envelope, can be extracted from the spectrum. Also for non-harmonic sounds, the spectrum can reveal useful information, such as the distribution of energy among different frequencies.

Instead of focusing merely on the properties of the sound itself, it is better to consider the sound production mechanisms that are responsible for creating these sounds, in order to obtain a deeper understanding and a more thorough representation of the sonic phenomena. In the musical context, this means analyzing the vibrational mechanics of musical instruments and the acoustical processes related to sound transmission that provide tonal coloration for these sounds. Given the physical properties of a vibrating sound source, the properties of the sound (such as the spectrum) can be deduced, if required.

MUSICAL SOUND SOURCES

This section discusses the physics behind some of the most typical musical sound generation mechanisms, namely vibrating strings and bars, membranes and plates, and air columns. In addition, the effect of resonator structures, such as instrument bodies, is discussed. Finally, some physical parameters for a general music markup language are proposed.

Vibration of Strings and Bars

All vibrational movement results from the interaction of two or more opposing forces. In strings, the two most prominent forces are (1) the restoring force caused by the tension of the string, and (2) the inertial force caused by the moving mass

of the string. Force (1) opposes string displacement, so that it tends to return the string into its equilibrium position, while force (2) opposes the change of movement, so that it tries to make the string continue moving on a steady speed. These forces result from laws by Hooke and Newton, respectively, and are explicitly expressed by the wave equation for the ideal string:

$$\frac{\partial^2 y}{\partial t^2} - c^2 \frac{\partial^2 y}{\partial x^2} = \frac{f(x,t)}{\mu} \tag{1}$$

where y denotes the displacement of the string in one vibration plane, t is time, x is the longitudinal coordinate, $f(x,t)$ is an excitation force, and μ is the linear mass density of the string, i.e. the mass per unit length. The variable

$$c = \sqrt{T/\mu} \tag{2}$$

denotes the speed of the transversal wave on the string, and T is the tension of the string. As can be seen in Equation (2), increasing the tension or decreasing the mass of the string causes an increase in the wave propagation speed. This makes the string vibrate faster and thus raises the frequency of the vibration.

As its name implies, the ideal string is an imaginary concept – a perfectly flexible, lossless cord, fixed at its both ends. Although this model is a highly simplified image of a real string, important behavior of the string vibration can be revealed by studying the solution to the ideal string equation. One solution to Equation (1) was presented by Daniel Bernoulli (1700-1782):

$$y(x,t) = \sum_{n=1}^{\infty} \sin(\frac{n\pi x}{L}) \left[a_n \cos(\frac{n\pi ct}{L}) + b_n \sin(\frac{n\pi ct}{L}) \right] \tag{3}$$

where L is the length of the string, so that $0 \leq x \leq L$. As Equation (3) illustrates, the vibration of the ideal string is given as a sum of sinusoidal

Figure 1. (a) The first six modal shapes of an ideal vibrating string. Subfigure (b) illustrates the initial displacement and the individual modes for a string plucked in the middle. Note that due to the plucking location, the vibration consists only of odd modes. Subfigure (c) shows the case for a string plucked at 1/3rd of its length. Subfigure (d) depicts the modes that are missing in subfigure (c).

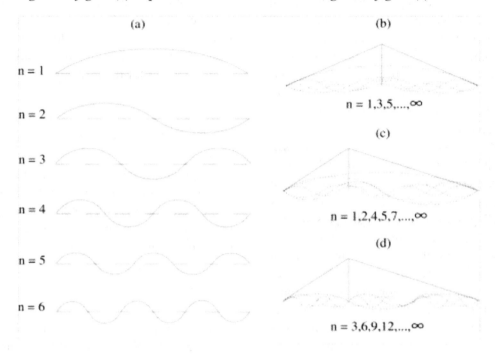

functions that depend on the spatial coordinate x and the temporal variable t. Furthermore, each of the sum indices $n = 1, 2, 3,...$ represents a unique vibrational form having a specific physical shape and vibration frequency. These forms are called vibrational modes. The lowest-frequency (i.e. the fundamental) mode corresponds to $n = 1$, the first harmonic (one octave higher than the fundamental) mode corresponds to $n = 2$, and so forth. The modal frequencies in an ideal string are perfectly harmonic, meaning that all the modal frequencies are an integer multiple of the lowest, or fundamental, frequency. In Equation (3), the symbols a_n and b_n are constants defining the modal amplitudes, that is, the level of each of the modes. In a plucked string, the modal amplitudes are mainly set by the excitation location, i.e. the place where the string is plucked. Figure 1 illustrates some of the first modal shapes on an ideal plucked string, fixed at both ends. As Figure 1 shows, the vibration of a plucked string consists of those modes that do not have a node at the plucking location. This is intuitive, since when a string is plucked at some point, it certainly will vibrate at that specific point, and thus cannot have a node there.

All real strings experience a loss of energy during their vibration. Since string terminations are never exactly rigid, vibrational energy is transmitted from the string to the instrument body. Frictional forces inside the string, at the terminations, and in the surrounding air also attenuate the movement of the string. The mechanical coupling between the string and the instrument body has a major impact on string vibration. This can be observed, for example, by comparing the sound radiating from a plucked electric guitar to the one radiating from a plucked acoustic guitar. Since the solid body of the electric guitar is considerably heavier than the thin top plate of the acoustic guitar, it is easier for the light vibrating string to move the latter. Thus, the motional energy of the acoustic guitar string is effectively transmitted into the top plate, making it to vibrate. The moving top plate, in turn, makes the vibration clearly audible by radiating it into the surrounding air as sound. On the other hand, the electric guitar string retains its vibrational energy longer, due to the poor coupling between the string and the instrument body. This results in a quiet sound with long sustain, since only a small amount of the string's energy is transmitted into the body. Of course, the vibration of the electric guitar string also eventually attenuates due to frictional forces and the direct sound radiation from the string. In practice, the energy transfer—as well as the friction—depends on frequency. Thus, different frequencies are attenuated at a different rate, typically so that high frequencies die out first.

Real strings also vibrate in different polarizations. In plucked strings, the most prominent polarizations are in the two directions transversal to the string itself. The vibration in the longitudinal direction, i.e. along the length of the string, has a smaller effect. In struck strings, such as in the piano, the coupling between the transversal and longitudinal polarizations causes some interesting phenomena, such as the generation of phantom harmonics (Conklin, 1999). In bowed strings, the torsional vibration of the strings also has a small role in the resulting sound (Bavu, et al., 2005).

Since the string terminations move differently in different directions, the decay rate is not the same for all polarizations. In plucked strings, this leads into a two-stage decay of the sound. Since one of the polarizations is more strongly coupled to the instrument body than the other, it makes a louder sound in the beginning, but then loses its motional energy faster. When the amplitude of the initially louder polarization has decreased below the amplitude of the other polarization, the overall decay rate of the vibration starts to follow the less steeply decreasing amplitude envelope of the latter polarization. In addition, the effective

length of the string varies between polarizations. This can be understood for example by considering an easily moving string termination to 'lengthen' the string, since it moves the rigid pivoting point of the motion further away from string's actual end. As a result, the modal frequencies of the two transversal polarizations can be slightly different, resulting in a slow amplitude modulation in the overall sound, the so-called beating effect.

An interesting effect in strings with bending stiffness (such as in the bass end of the piano) is the inharmonicity phenomenon. The bending stiffness of the string causes the transversal wave velocity to become a function of frequency, so that high frequencies travel faster on the string than low frequencies. This causes the modal frequencies to spread further apart, so that they no longer fall into exact integer ratios. The resulting sound is more 'bell-like' than with elastic strings. The modal frequencies f_n of a stiff string can be given as:

$$f_n = f_0 n \sqrt{1 + Bn^2} \qquad (4)$$

where f_0 is the fundamental frequency, n is the mode number, and B is an inharmonicity coefficient that can be derived from the physical properties of the string (Fletcher, Blackham, & Stratton, 1962). In physical terms, when the stiffness of a string is increased, it becomes bar-like, and the restoring force due to the internal stiffness overrides the force term of the externally applied tension. Thus, the need for fixed terminations becomes less significant. Stiff bars can vibrate with or without fixed terminations or end supports, although the presence or absence of them affects the resulting vibration spectrum. Among these termination types, the bar that is clamped at one end, but free to vibrate on the other end has the lowest vibration frequencies, while the freely vibrating bar has the highest vibration frequencies. The mode frequencies of a bar with simply supported (i.e. hinged) ends fall between these two cases. Musical bars are used in the glockenspiel and the marimba, for example.

The sound of a vibrating string also depends on the type of excitation. As illustrated in Figure 1, the excitation location affects the resulting sound spectrum. Perhaps not surprisingly, the properties of the object exciting the string also affect the string vibration. For plucked and struck strings, relatively soft and smooth objects (such as fingers) generally result in a sound where high frequencies are strongly attenuated. Harder or sharper objects (such as a nail or a plectrum) on the other hand usually produce a brighter sound.

For bowed strings, the excitation mechanism is nonlinear and the resulting vibration is more complicated. As noted by Helmholtz (1821-1894) (Fletcher & Rossing, 1991), the bowed string forms a triangular shape, consisting of two nearly straight lines, joined by an intersection angle. During the bowing action, the angle travels along an ellipsoidal path that crosses the string terminations. More specifically, the bow first attaches to the string and displaces it, forming the initial triangular shape. When the restoring force of the string under tension exceeds the frictional force connecting the string to the bow, the string slips and swings itself to the opposite direction. Finally, when the frictional force between the string and the bow exceeds the inertial force of the decelerating string, the bow re-attaches to the string, and the process repeats itself. Due to the continuous excitation by the bow, the resulting sound is strictly periodic, and remains largely unaltered during the bowing, provided that other control parameters, such as the length or tension of the string or bowing pressure are kept constant.

In addition to the bow-string interaction, there are also some other nonlinear phenomena that affect the tone of vibrating strings. These include the tension modulation nonlinearity (Legge & Fletcher, 1984), which causes the pitch of a heavily-plucked string experience a downward glide as the oscillation decays, the nonlinear felt compression in a piano hammer (see e.g. Hall, 1986) causing the piano timbre to vary with varying key velocity, and the nonlinear displacement constraint, manifesting itself, e.g. in the slap bass (Rank & Kubin, 1997). In general, the nonlinearities in musical instruments cause the timbre of the instrument to vary with the excitation amplitude.

Vibration of Membranes and Plates

When an ideal string is extended into two dimensions, an ideal membrane is obtained. This imaginary sheet shares many of the properties of its one-dimensional counterpart, such as losslessness and perfect elasticity. In order for sustained vibrations to occur, the membrane must be under tension. This is obtained by fixing the membrane edges to a frame of some sort. Thus, also in the case of the membrane, the two interacting forces are the inertial force caused by the moving mass and the restoring force caused by the external tension.

The modes of an ideal rectangular membrane with dimensions d_x and d_y can be seen as a combination of modes generated by two ideal strings of length d_x and d_y, respectively. More specifically, the modal frequencies of an ideal rectangular membrane can be given as (Fletcher & Rossing, 1991):

$$f_{mn} = \frac{1}{2}\sqrt{\frac{T}{\sigma}}\sqrt{\frac{m^2}{d_x^2} + \frac{n^2}{d_y^2}} \qquad (5)$$

where m and n denote the mode numbers for the two dimensions, T is tension, and σ is the mass density of the membrane (i.e. mass per unit area). As can be seen in Equation (5), the modal frequencies are no longer simply integer multiples of the fundamental frequency. As a result, the sound of a vibrating rectangular membrane does not have a single easily recognizable pitch. Also for circular membranes, the modal frequencies are inharmonic in general. In practice, the tension modulation phenomenon is often present in vibrating membranes. Similarly as for strings, it causes a downward glide of the modal frequencies during the decay of the vibration.

In musical instruments, vibrating membranes are typically found in percussive instruments, such as drums. Since membranes are approximately two-dimensional, they are more efficiently coupled to the surrounding air than strings, and thus radiate sound better. This is used in boosting the sound of a banjo, where the strings are coupled to a membrane via a wooden bridge. In drums, the sound volume of the vibrating membrane is in turn increased by coupling it to an air cavity inside the drum body. In practice, the coupling with air affects the membrane vibration similarly to an added mass, so that the modal frequencies are lowered from what presented, e.g. in Equation (5).

Similarly as introducing bending stiffness to a string resulted in a bar, adding internal bending stiffness to a vibrating membrane creates a vibrating plate. In a plate, the two interacting forces are again the inertial force of the mass and now the internal stiffness of the plate itself. Thus, there is no need for end supports in having a sustained vibration. Also just like in stiff strings, the modal frequencies of the plate are stretched upwards in frequency, although in this two-dimensional setting they were not harmonic even in the perfectly elastic case (see Equation 5). The vibration of musical plates is strongly affected by nonlinear phenomena. This means that the resulting sound spectrum depends in a complicated way on the magnitude of the excitation. More specifically, the nonlinear effects in vibrating plates cause the kinetic energy to move between different modes so that the spectrum of the resulting sound varies considerably in time. A typical example is a heavily struck tam-tam gong, where the vibration initially starts at low frequencies and then gradually extends to the upper frequency range, finally ending in a bright, 'shimmering' sound. Besides gongs, also other cymbals serve as examples of vibrating musical plates.

For wood plates, the vibration characteristics depend on the direction of the propagating wave, due to the inhomogeneous inner structure of wood. Although wood plates are usually not directly used as vibrating sound sources, they play an important part in music acoustics, since many musical instrument bodies are built using them.

Vibration of Air Columns

When an air mass confined inside a pipe experiences a pressure or volume disturbance, it starts to move back and forth, creating a vibrating air column. The two interacting forces in this case are the inertial force caused by the moving air mass, and the restoring force caused by the air compliance. If the diameter of the pipe is small compared to the wavelength of the vibrating air column, the vibration takes place only in the longitudinal direction of the pipe. This case is in fact quite similar to the vibrating string, although in strings, the vibration takes place mainly in the transversal direction. Furthermore, in musical strings, the end terminations are always more or less rigid, resulting in a phase-inverting termination. This is illustrated in Figure 2(a).

Figure 2. Wave reflection from (a) a fixed end in a string, (b) an open-ended pipe, and (c) a closed-ended pipe. The dotted lines indicate the shape of the fundamental frequency mode. In (c), one of the ends is open while the other is closed, creating a ¼ wave resonator.

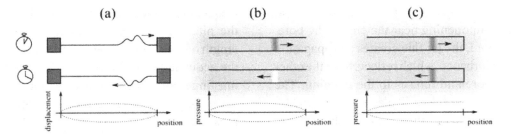

The pressure wave in a pipe, however, can experience both phase-preserving and phase-inverting reflections, as illustrated in Figure 2(b) and (c). Note that the maximum wavelength that a fixed-ended string (or an open-ended pipe) can sustain belongs to the wave having double the length of the string (or pipe). In other words, both the string and the open-ended pipe form a half-wave resonator structure. In a typical wind instrument, such as the clarinet or the saxophone, the player's end of the bore is seen as a closed termination by the wave inside the bore, while the other end opens to the surrounding air. This causes the wave to experience a phase-inverting reflection at the closed end, and a phase-preserving reflection at the open end, creating a ¼ wave resonator structure, as illustrated in Figure 2(c). Since there is a pressure maximum at the closed end of the pipe, all the even modes are missing in the spectrum, similarly as in the middle-plucked string in Figure 1(b).

At the open end of the pipe, the wave reflection point exceeds the pipe termination by a small distance. This elongation of the air column happens because a finite air mass outside the open end of the pipe gets coupled with the vibrating air inside the pipe. In addition, the amount of this additional elongation depends on the frequency of the vibration. For low-frequency modes, the elongation is relatively larger than for high-frequency modes, so that the modal frequencies do not fall at exact integer ratios but are spread further apart.

For making the air column inside the pipe oscillate in a sustained manner, a continuous excitation must be provided. In the case of wind instruments, it is the musician's lungs that provide this excitation. For flute-like instruments, the musician creates an air jet flue by blowing at the edge of an opening near the end of the bore. Inside the bore, the jet flue creates a propagating pressure disturbance, which reflects from the other end of the bore and returns to the opening. The returning pressure wave displaces the jet flue by either pulling it inside the bore or pushing it out,

depending on the type of bore termination. This creates another pressure wave inside the bore, and the process is repeated. This interplay between the excitation mechanism and the instrument bore results in a sustained oscillation. The excitation principle for other wind instruments is similar in nature, although instead of the jet flue, the excitation mechanism can be a single or double reed, or the lips of the musician.

Perhaps surprisingly, the abovementioned inharmonicity of the bore resonances does not lead to an inharmonicity in the sound of a wind instrument. This is because the excitation mechanism is continuous and nonlinear, resulting in mode locking between the excitation and the air column vibration. In other words, the excitation mechanism forces the air inside the pipe to vibrate periodically. Typically, the modal frequencies of the vibration are shifted slightly higher in frequency to provide a better fit with the inharmonic pipe resonance frequencies. In fact, for any sustained-tone instruments, the excitation mechanism must be nonlinear for the mode locking to occur. Mode locking between nonlinear excitation mechanisms and inharmonic resonators is more thoroughly discussed in Fletcher (1999).

Naturally, vibrational losses are also present in air columns (Fletcher & Rossing, 1991). Here, they are mainly due to the viscous drag between the airflow and the rigid pipe walls. Another source of losses comes from the thermal exchange between the air and the walls. Both viscous and thermal losses are more prominent for thin pipes, since the ratio between the tube circumference and the cross-section area is greater than for wide pipes. In addition, as with all mechanical energy dissipation mechanisms, the losses increase with frequency. Although in some wind instruments the pitch is directly controlled by altering the length of the pipe (such as in a trombone), usually the acoustic length of the tube is varied by adding fingerholes onto the instrument bore. When several consecutive fingerholes are left open, the pressure wave reflects as it would at the open end of the tube, thus creating an acoustic termination near the open fingerholes. In reality, the detailed effect of the fingerholes is more complex, and it is discussed more thoroughly, e.g. for woodwinds in Benade (1960).

The sound of a wind instrument is radiated not only at the open end of the pipe, but also through all other openings of the pipe, including the fingerholes. Since the vibration spectrum inside the pipe depends strongly on the location, the sounds emanating from different fingerholes (and from the open end) have different spectra. When combined with different radiation characteristics for each opening, the total sound spectrum can be a relatively complex function of direction. In many wind instruments, the open end of the pipe is flaring, creating a horn-like ending. The main reason for this is to enhance the sound radiation from the instrument by making the pressure wave exiting from the open end to experience a gradual, rather than an abrupt change when it enters the surrounding air[2]. A conical or flaring pipe profile also alters the tube resonance frequencies, as more thoroughly discussed in Fletcher and Rossing (1991).

Resonating Structures

The sound coupling from a vibrating air column to the surrounding air is strong because they both share the same medium. On vibrating plates, such as cymbals, the air coupling is relatively good due to the large contact area between the vibrating surface and air. On string instruments, however, the air coupling from the vibrating string itself is weak since the contact surface between the string and air is small. Therefore, the string is usually connected to a lightweight wooden plate, which increases the contact surface to the surrounding air. Furthermore, when many of these plates are connected together to form an enclosed structure, a resonating instrument body is formed. In addition to improving the sound radiation, the vibrating body—as well as the air mass inside the body

cavity—also considerably colors the sound and alters its spatial radiating pattern. It must be noted that the interaction between the sound generation mechanism (e.g. a vibrating string) and the resonating structure is two-directional, so that the properties of the instrument body also affect the vibration of the source. For wind instruments, however, the vibration of the bore does not affect the sound of the oscillating air column, since the resonances of the bore are typically located considerably higher in frequency than the air column resonances (Fletcher & Rossing, 1991).

In general, the tonal and radiational characteristics of an instrument body define the perceived quality of the instrument. Due to the complicated interactions between the string, instrument body, and the air inside and outside the body cavity, the dependency between the actual physical parameters and the quality of an instrument are still unknown, at least in the strict academic sense. This is exemplified by the fine violins made by Antonio Stradivari (1644-1737). Although the knowledge in physics has taken a giant leap after Stradivari's days, these string instruments are still—after roughly three hundred years from their creation—generally considered superior in comparison to modern ones.

Another important example of a resonating structure is the human vocal tract. This amazing resonator is able to continuously alter its shape, providing a time-varying coloration for the sound originating from the vocal chords. As a result, the rather crude, buzzing, sound from the vibrating vocal chords is transformed as intelligible speech or singing. The detailed operation of the vocal tract is extensively studied in the field of phonetics, and is not discussed further here.

Markup Parameters for Musical Sound Sources

For all tonal musical sounds, one of the most important parameters to markup is the fundamental frequency of the sound. For many instruments, it is crucial that the fundamental frequency is allowed to vary in time for the entire duration of the sonic event, to enable important phrasing techniques, such as vibrato. Therefore, the fundamental frequency should be given in a vector form by defining some key points in frequency and the corresponding time instants. For avoiding abrupt step-like frequency variations in the synthesized sound, the synthesis engine could use curve-fitting techniques for interpolating between the key points of the frequency vector. Another important parameter is the amplitude of the excitation (corresponding to note velocity in MIDI), which controls not only the sound volume, but also the timbre of the resulting sound, due to the inherent nonlinearities in many musical instruments. For continuously excited sound sources, such as bowed strings or wind instruments, also the excitation amplitude should be given as a vector. In addition to these perhaps obvious choices, there are many physical parameters that have an important effect on the resulting sound, although the relation is more complicated. Instead of marking up all the physical parameters in the equations related to the sound generation mechanisms, it is better to markup some central parameters that are intuitive for the user, and from which the other parameters may be evaluated by the synthesizer.

For string instruments, marking up the total string length together with the corresponding fundamental frequency of the open string defines the wave propagation velocity. In addition, marking up the gauge of the string defines the string volume, together with the string length. For evaluating the other basic physical parameters, there are two alternatives. The first option is to mark up the material of the string. Since this is not necessarily intuitive for an average user, the string material parameter could be for example selected from a predefined list of typical string materials on an Internet page, or the list could be embedded in the markup language documentation. From the string material and gauge parameters, the synthesis en-gine could deduce the mass density of the string. In addition, since the transversal wave velocity, linear mass density, and the applied tension are related by Equation (2), the tension of the string can be deduced by the system. Furthermore, once the string material and gauge are known, losses due to air damping and the internal dissipation mechanisms can be evaluated. The other alternative is to mark up the tension of the string, perhaps also from a list of typical string tension values for a set of different instruments. Using Equation (2), the system could then define the linear mass density of the string. From the linear mass density and the gauge parameters, the string material and the resulting loss parameters could automatically be calculated. It must be noted that the string length and the corresponding frequency are parameters for one string only and not for the entire instrument (unless it is a monochord, of course).

Alternatively to the low-level string markup parameters discussed above, some compound parameters combining the properties of the string and the resulting sound could be devised. For defining the overall decay parameters of a string, for example, an abstract measure for the overall decay rate, decay rate difference between polarizations, and the spectral tilt of the time-varying losses could be presented. For keeping things intuitive, these parameters could be presented on a normalized scale for which StringLosses=(0,0,0) would mean a long decay time, the same decay rate for both polarizations, and emphasized high-frequency content, while StringLosses=(1,1,1) would correspond to fast decay rate, large decay difference between polarizations (two-stage decay), and a quick decay of higher harmonics, resulting in a boomier, darker tone, respectively.

In the case of stiff strings or musical bars, the inharmonicity parameter B in Equation (4) could be an intuitive parameter to mark up. Some approximate range of musically useful inharmonicity parameters could be presented to the user. For perfectly harmonic strings $B = 0$, and it rises up to around $B \approx 0.005$ for a typical piano (Lattard, 1993). For the piano, a normalized measure for the hammer hardness could be used in fine-tuning the spectral details. Also for bowed strings, the bowing pressure could be used for the same purpose, perhaps even using a vector representation for enabling continuous bowing pressure variations. For the electric guitar, the amount of distortion could be defined, perhaps also on some normalized scale. It must be noted that even though usually considered merely as a sound effect, a distorting guitar amplifier is a crucial part of the electric guitar sound in some music genres[3]. In the synthesis phase, a guitar amplifier emulator plug-in could be used. For a review on different digital emulation methods (see Pakarinen & Yeh, 2009).

For musical membranes, an intuitive choice would be to markup the dimensions of the membrane, that is, the radius of a circular membrane or the length and width of a rectangular one. In addition, if the fundamental vibration frequency of the membrane were marked up, the synthesizer could deduce the tension-to-density ratio using Equation (5), or its circular version. Similarly as in the case of strings, if the membrane material were selected, the synthesizer could define some of the internal loss parameters, as well as the tension of the membrane. Since extracting the fundamental frequency for a vibrating plate might be challenging due to a high mode density, simply the material parameter (metal, glass, wood) together with the dimension measure (now including thickness), could be used. As discussed earlier, air loading alters the modal frequencies especially in the case of vibrating membranes and plates. It is, however, relatively straightforward to take this effect into account when the surface area of the musical object is known, since the properties of air can be considered to be constant for all instruments.

In wind instruments, a notion of whether the tube endings are open or closed is an important markup parameter, since it directly defines the presence or absence of even harmonics, as illustrated in Figure 2. Alternatively, given the bore length and the corresponding lowest fundamental frequency, the synthesizer could deduce the type of tube endings by itself[4]. The radius of the instrument bore is another intuitive and thus potential physical markup parameter, since it defines the loss parameters for both viscous and thermal losses. In addition, it would be important to mark up the excitation type (single reed, double reed, lip-reed, or jet flue), since it has a strong effect in the resulting sound spectrum. Furthermore, the profile of the bore (e.g. straight, conical, or flaring) could be used as a markup parameter for fine-tuning of the sound spectrum. Marking up the states of the fingerholes, i.e. which ones are open and which ones are closed, would enable more realistic synthesis (for example the use of multiphonics), but would on the other hand be quite tedious for the user. Thus, the fingerhole states could be left as an optional markup parameter only for special purposes.

For resonator structures such as instrument bodies, the detailed dependency between physical parameters and the resulting sound coloration is complex. However, some relations between approximate parameters and the tone color can be presented. For example, since large instrument bodies have more pronounced bass response than small instrument bodies, some physical size parameter could be used in controlling the spectral tilt of the tonal coloration by the body. For drums, in addition to the approximate volume of the body, also a notion if whether the drum is open or closed, i. e. if it has one or two membranes, could be used. At the synthesis stage, if the type of the instrument body were used as a markup parameter (for example using the parameter BodyType=AcousticGuitarJumbo for an acoustic guitar, or BodyType=FloorTomLarge for a drum), the effect of the instrument body could be implemented by filtering the sound of the source mechanism (e.g. string or a membrane) using a digital filter that resembles the acoustic effect of the body. For high-quality sound synthesis, the synthesis engine could even use pre-recorded impulse responses for the instrument body. The concept of the impulse response is discussed more thoroughly in the following section.

SOUND TRANSMISSION TO THE OBSERVER

In addition to the resonating instrument body, the sound transmission mechanism from the oscillating source to the eardrum of the listener plays an important role in coloring the tone of the instrument. In an anechoic environment, the coloration due to the surrounding space is virtually absent, apart from a very mild lowpass filtering effect due to the damping properties of the air. In practice, however, music is never played in perfectly anechoic environments. Even in the case of outdoor concerts, the sound from the performers reflects from the stage, audience, ground, and nearby buildings so that the sound arriving to the listener is a mixture of the direct sound and a myriad of densely located echoes. Inside buildings, this coloration effect is even stronger due to the larger number of reflecting surfaces. This section gives an introduction to some of the concepts that are used in characterizing the acoustical properties of rooms and the effect of the human listener. In addition, the last part of this section provides suggestions on which of these parameters could be used in a music markup language for improving the quality of synthesized or pre-recorded sound.

A Brief Introduction to Room Acoustics

The acoustical properties of a performance venue directly dictate what type of music can or cannot be played in that particular space. Historically, the architecture of music halls has been connected to the evolution of different music styles. Medieval chant music, for example, was best suited to an acoustic environment with long reverberation, such as large churches or cathedrals. Music in the Baroque era, however, consisted of more complex musical passages that required less reverberant environments, such as small palace rooms or theaters, to be perceived clearly. The performance space can be considered as an extension of an acoustic musical instrument, due to the strong tonal coloration and reverberation provided by the room. In fact, when musicians are asked to perform in an anechoic chamber (e.g. for instrument acoustic research purposes), they often find the sound of their instrument artificial, unpleasing, and "dead."

The acoustic coloration caused by the room can be understood with the concept of early reflections and late reverberation (Rossing, 1990). Consider a short impulsive sound generated by a start pistol on the stage of a small auditorium, as illustrated in Figure 3(a). If the wavelength of the sound under consideration is small compared to the dimensions of wall boundaries and the objects inside the room, the sound can be considered to propagate as rays, reflecting from the boundaries and objects. In Figure 3(a), a microphone for recording the resulting sound is located on the top row of the auditorium. As the sound rays propagate from the start pistol, they bounce back and forth inside the room, with some of the rays finally reaching the microphone. In the figure, only the first four sound rays (numbered 1 through 4) reaching the microphone are illustrated, for clarity. Figure 3(b) visualizes the output signal of the microphone, as a function of time.

Obviously, the sound ray reaching the microphone first is the ray traveling on the straight line from the sound source to the microphone. This impulse is referred to as the direct sound from the source, and it corresponds to the first impulse in the microphone output signal in Figure 3(b). Soon after the direct sound, a second sound ray, reflecting from the ceiling, arrives at the microphone. Some milliseconds later, the third and fourth sound rays, reflecting from the edge of the stage and the slanted ceiling above the stage, respectively, reach the microphone. After this, more and more sound rays, reflecting from the walls, ceiling, floor, seats,

Figure 3. Sound propagation from an impulse source to a microphone inside a room (a), and the corresponding impulse response signal (b), as recorded by the microphone

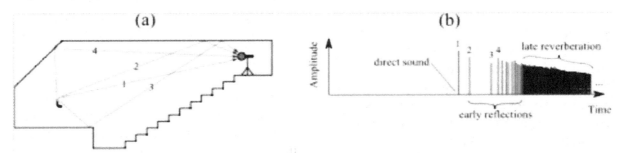

etc. hit the microphone with an increasing rate, until the individual impulses can no longer be distinguished from the microphone signal. Since each reflection from a surface—as well as the air itself—attenuates the sound rays, the impulses arriving later at the microphone are generally more damped than the ones arriving earlier. Thus, the amplitude envelope of the microphone signal in Figure 3(b) experiences an exponential decay.

The set of individual impulses after the direct sound are called early reflections (see Figure 3[b]), and they correspond to the sound rays experiencing at maximum only a couple of reflections before reaching the observation point. If the dimensions of the acoustic environment are large enough (in the range of tens of meters or more, such as in stadiums), some of the early reflections might be heard as individual echoes. With typical rooms, however, the early reflections arrive so rapidly that they rather tend to affect the perceived timbre of the sound source, instead of being perceived as separate sounds by a human listener. The remaining part of the impulse response signal in Figure 3(b) consists of the remaining sound rays arriving at the microphone after many reflections. This part of the impulse response is called the late reverberation (or the reverberation tail), and individual impulses can no longer be distinguished since they are so densely located. For a given sound source position and a single fixed observation point, the impulse response signal contains the entire 'acoustic fingerprint' of the room. More importantly, the acoustic effect[5] of any room can be artificially reproduced for any sound source by using the convolution function between the source signal and the impulse response of that room.

In reality, the reflection from a surface always scatters the sound wave more or less, so that the idealized mirror-like reflection depicted in Figure 3(a) does not hold. The amount of scattering depends on the frequency of the sound wave, as well as the reflective material. Also for low-frequency sounds, the wavelength can easily be comparable to the dimensions of the sound-reflecting objects. Then, the sound does not simply reflect from the surface, but experiences diffraction, so that the wave front changes its propagation direction by partially bending around the object. However, it must be noted that these phenomena do not weaken the accuracy of the impulse response technique discussed above, since if the impulse responses are measured using wideband excitation signals, the abovementioned phenomena will be present also in the impulse response recording.

An important parameter characterizing the amount of reverberation in a room is the reverberation time, given by Sabine's formula:

$$T_{60} \approx 0.163 \frac{V}{A_\alpha}, \tag{6}$$

where V is the volume (in cubic meters), and A_α is the equivalent absorption area (in square meters) of the room. The equivalent absorption area depends on all the sound reflecting materials inside the room, and can be understood as the area that would be required if all the sound absorbing surfaces in the room were to be replaced by single surface of an imaginary, perfectly sound absorbing material. The reverberation time T_{60} represents the amount of time it takes for an impulsive sound inside the room to attenuate 60 dB, that is, to one millionth of its initial amplitude. As can be seen in Equation (6), large rooms and small equivalent absorption areas yield long reverberation times. The desired reverberation time of a room depends on the purpose; for intelligible speech, a short reverberation time of about 0.8-1 seconds is required, whereas for concert halls a long reverberation time around 2 seconds is optimal (Barron, 2008).

It must be noted that real sound sources are not omnidirectional, that is, they do not radiate sound evenly to all directions. Moreover, the spatial radiation pattern of a sound source is frequency-dependent. This means that the room affects different sound sources and different sound signals differently. In addition, physical sound sources are not lumped, point-like elements, but the sound radiates from all spatially distributed points on a vibrating structure. In addition, in reality, the sound arrives to the observer from many directions. Thus, if a monophonic representation is used for the recorded sound signal, many important acoustic phenomena are neglected. The purpose for mentioning these points explicitly is not, however, to discourage the use of approximate techniques for modeling acoustic spaces, but to simply serve as a reminder that although the convolution of a monophonic sound by a room impulse response creates an impression that the sound is played in a real room, the real acoustic effect of the space is more complicated.

Loosely speaking, the average amount of reverberation is approximately the same for all points inside a room. The direct sound from the source, however, attenuates when the distance to the observation point is increased. At some distance from the source, the direct sound and the reverberant sound are equally loud. This is called the critical distance, and can be given as:

$$d_c = \sqrt{A_\alpha/V}. \tag{7}$$

Outside the critical distance, the observed sound is perceived highly reverberant, so that if the sound source is a human speaker, for example, the intelligibility of speech can be compromised.

The Effect of the Human Listener

As discussed earlier, any physical structure in the acoustic environment changes the sonic field by introducing absorption and reflections, among other things. For human listeners, especially the sound reflections from the shoulders, head, face, earlobes, etc. alter the sound pressure signal at the eardrum. In fact, the human brain uses these subtle sound colorations—along with the sound amplitude and arrival time difference at the two ears—as psychoacoustic cues in locating the direction of the incoming sound. In mathematical terms, the sound coloration effect of the human body can be represented as the Head-Related Transfer Function (HRTF). Given the desired direction of a sound source relative to the listener, the HRTF tells how the sound should be processed so that the listener would perceive it coming from the desired direction. Once obtained, the HRTFs can be used in virtually placing sound sources anywhere around the human listener, provided that the sounds are played through stereo headphones.

Since human anatomy is diverse, HRTFs are unique for each person. Individual HRTFs can be measured e.g. by placing small microphones to both ears of the person, playing sounds from different directions around him or her in an anechoic environment, and then analyzing the microphone outputs. In practical spatial sound applications, averaged HRTFs, obtained by analyzing the HRTFs for a large set of subjects, are often sufficient to create an approximately correct sensation of the direction of the incoming sound for most people. In practice, even with individually measured HRTFs, the front-back-confusion (typically meaning that the sounds positioned in front of the person are perceived to be coming from behind) can cause discrepancies between the intended and perceived sound directions.

If the HRTFs are measured using the setup mentioned above, they represent the sound transmission to the opening of the listener's ear canal. Naturally, the sound coloration does not end there, since e.g. the resonance of the ear canal and the mechanics of the ossicles (the small bones inside the middle ear) further alter the sound. However, since these properties—not to mention the various psychoacoustic mechanisms involved in hearing—are an inherent and unchangeable part of the listener, they are not useful in the context of the music markup language, and are thus not discussed further here.

Markup Parameters for Sound Transmission

Since the performance environment alters the sound of a musical instrument to a large extent, it is important to mark up some parameters of the acoustic space for realistic sound reproduction. Although adding the effect of the room into a synthesized sound source is probably the most obvious choice, it is not limited to this. In fact, the acoustical characteristics of a space can successfully be added to any recorded sound, provided that the recording is not too reverberant to begin with. For example, the signal from many electronic instruments, such as keyboards, can directly be used in conjunction with a room effects model.

The most basic physical room parameters worth marking up are the dimensions of the room. If the room is not rectangular, an additional shape parameter should be added, too. In addition, the average acoustic absorption of the room materials should be defined. This could be given on a normalized scale, where Absorption=0 would correspond to a room with highly sound reflecting, hard surfaces (such as in a typical bathroom), while Absorption=1 would correspond to a highly damped, soft surfaces (such as inside a wardrobe closet), for example. Once the room dimensions and the average absorption coefficient are known, it is straightforward for the system to calculate the room volume and the equivalent absorption area, and thus the reverberation time and the critical distance (see Equations [6] and [7], respectively). Using the reverberation time along with the absorption parameter, the reverberation inside the room under discussion can be approximated with any digital reverberation algorithm (for a tutorial on digital reverberation see Dattorro, 1997). In addition, knowing the critical distance parameter of the room enables the virtual adjustment of the physical distance between the sound source and the listener by tuning the amplitude balance between the direct sound and the reverberation effect.

For more accurate sonic imitation of the room, the impulse response of the room—or some of its frequency characteristics—could be used as a markup vector. As discussed above, this would allow a very accurate simulation of a particular room, but at the cost of considerably increasing the size of the markup file. Alternatively, a link to a pre-recorded impulse response file on a remote server could be used as a markup parameter. A set of impulse responses for certain concert halls and rooms are already freely downloadable in the Internet (see, e.g. http://irlibrary.org/). Another compact alternative for simulating the tonal coloration of a particular room is to include a coarse approximation of the frequency response characteristics, for example as small set of frequencies and their corresponding amplitudes, as a markup vector. In the sound reproduction stage, the system could select the frequency and amplitude resolution

Table 1. A collection of the proposed markup parameters for sound sources, resonating structures, and performance spaces

Interacting object	Parameter	Example code	Note
Any sound source	Excitation amplitude	Amplitude=0.7	Normalized scale
	Direction and distance from the listener	Direction&Dist=(15,-180,7)	For spatial sound reproduction
Tonal sound sources	Fundamental frequency	Frequency=(440;0,442;0.5)	Key points in time and frequency
Vibrating string	Length	StringLength=0.65	In meters
	Gauge	StringGauge=0.0011	In meters
	String material OR String tension	StringMaterial=Brass StringTension=83	Possibly selected from a predefined list
	Decay parameters	StringLosses=(0.2,0.6,0.1)	Normalized scale
	Inharmonicity	Inharmonicity_B=0.0001	From a list
	Excitation location	ExcitationLocation=0.2	W.r.t. string length
Plucked string	Plucking object	Plucker=finger	From a list
Struck string	Hammer hardness	HammerHardness=0.6	Normalized scale
Bowed string	Bowing pressure	BowingPressure=(0.1;0,1:2)	Key points
Electric guitar	Amount of distortion	Distortion=0.3	Normalized scale
Membranes	Dimensions	MembraneRadius=0.37	In meters
	Material	MembraneMaterial=leather	From a list
Plates	Dimensions	PlateDims=(0.35;0.0007)	Radius, thickness
	Material	PlateMaterial=steel	From a list
Wind instruments	Bore radius	BoreRadius=0.022	In meters
	Ending type OR Bore length	TubeEndings=closed-open BoreLength=0.55	Endings either open or closed, length in meters
	Excitation type	WindExcitation=LipReed	From a list
	Bore profile	BoreProfile=straight	From a list
	Fingerhole states	FingerHoles=(1,1,1,0,1,0,0)	If required
Resonator structures	Body type	BodyType=Contrabass	From a list
	Body size	BodySize=0.9	Normalized scale
Drums	Enclosure type	DrumEnclosureType=closed	Open or closed
Closed performance space	Dimensions	RoomDimensions=(10,7,2.5)	Possibly with a shape parameter
	Absorption	RoomAbsorption=0.2	Normalized scale
	Frequency response OR Impulse response	RoomFreqResp=(0;-10,2000;2) RoomImpRespURL=http://www…	Only for accurate simulation of a particular space

according to desired level of audio quality and the available computational resources.

For stereophonic loudspeaker reproduction, the left-right balance is an obvious markup parameter for defining the directions of the sound sources relative to the listener. For more advanced spatial sound reproduction systems, for example a multiple-loudspeaker setup or the HRTFs and headphones configuration, full three-dimensional coordinates for the directions of the sound sources could be used as markup parameters. In practice, this would most likely mean marking up the distance between the source and the listener, as well as the azimuth and elevation angles of the source directions.

CONCLUSION

This chapter reviewed the physics of different musical sound sources and the acoustics related to sound transmission between the instrument and the listener. The vibration of strings, bars, membranes, plates, and air columns were discussed, and their energy loss mechanisms due to dissipation and coupling were explained. For strings, also the effect of non-rigid terminations and different vibrational polarizations, as well the inharmonicity caused by stiffness, was studied. The motion of a bowed string was outlined, and some of the nonlinearities involved in vibrating strings were mentioned. For membranes and plates, the vibration modes were shown to be unevenly distributed in frequency, resulting in a highly inharmonic spectrum. In addition, the reason for connecting a resonating body to a vibrating string or membrane was explained. For musical pipes, different types of bore terminations was studied. The seeming inconsistency between the inharmonic bore resonances and the strictly harmonic wind instrument sound was resolved by explaining the concept of mode locking between the bore and the nonlinear excitation mechanism.

A short introduction to room acoustics was provided, and the concept of impulse response in characterizing the acoustic properties of a room was introduced. In addition, some of the most important room acoustic parameters, such as the reverberation time and critical distance, were discussed. The sound coloration effect of the listener's body was explained using the concept of head-related transfer functions. The operation of the human ear and psychoacoustic issues were not addressed, since they are practically irrelevant for music markup purposes.

As mentioned in the introduction, the main advantage of using physical quantities as markup parameters is that they allow the composer to more accurately control the timbral characteristics of the synthesized sound. For this reason, several physical parameters of the vibrating sound sources and acoustic spaces were suggested for use in a music markup language. These potential markup parameters are collected in Table 1. It must be noted that most of these parameters are specific to the type of the instrument. Furthermore, most of the parameters are optional, so that the user may explicitly define them if a certain musical timbre is required, but is not necessarily required to. In the latter case, the synthesizer would simply use default values for the given instrument. Even if physics-based synthesizers were not directly used in the sound rendering process, physical markup parameters provide a universal representation of musical instrument sounds, and are therefore a strong candidate for use in conjunction with any sound synthesis method.

REFERENCES

Barron, M. (2008). Raising the roof. *Nature*, *453*(12), 859–860. doi:10.1038/453859a

Bavu, E., Smith, J., & Wolfe, J. (2005). Torsional waves in a bowed string. *Acta Acustica united with Acustica, 91*, 241-246.

Benade, A. H. (1960). On the mathematical theory of woodwind finger holes. *The Journal of the Acoustical Society of America, 32*(12), 1591–1608. doi:10.1121/1.1907968

Blauert, J., & Xiang, N. (2009). *Acoustics for engineers: Troy lectures* (2nd ed.). Berlin, Germany: Springer-Verlag.

Conklin, H. A. (1999). Generation of partials due to nonlinear mixing in a stringed instrument. *The Journal of the Acoustical Society of America, 105*(1), 536–545. doi:10.1121/1.424589

Dattorro, J. (1997). Effect design, part 1: Reverberator and other filters. *Journal of the Audio Engineering Society. Audio Engineering Society, 45*(9), 660–684.

Fahy, F. (2001). *Foundations of engineering acoustics*. London, UK: Academic Press.

Fletcher, N. H. (1999). The nonlinear physics of musical instruments. *Reports on Progress in Physics, 62*, 723–761. doi:10.1088/0034-4885/62/5/202

Fletcher, N. H., Blackham, E. D., & Stratton, R. (1962). Quality of piano tones. *The Journal of the Acoustical Society of America, 34*(6), 749–761. doi:10.1121/1.1918192

Fletcher, N. H., & Rossing, T. D. (1991). *The physics of musical instruments*. New York, NY: Springer. doi:10.1007/978-1-4612-2980-3

Hall, D. E. (1986). Piano string excitation in the case of small hammer mass. *The Journal of the Acoustical Society of America, 79*(1), 141–147. doi:10.1121/1.393637

Lattard, J. (1993). Influence of inharmonicity on the tuning of a piano—Measurements and mathematical simulation. *The Journal of the Acoustical Society of America, 94*(1), 46–53. doi:10.1121/1.407059

Legge, K. A., & Fletcher, N. H. (1984). Nonlinear generation of missing modes on a vibrating string. *The Journal of the Acoustical Society of America, 76*(1), 5–12. doi:10.1121/1.391007

Pakarinen, J., & Yeh, D. T. (2009). A review of digital techniques for modeling vacuum-tube guitar amplifiers. *Computer Music Journal, 33*(2), 85–100. doi:10.1162/comj.2009.33.2.85

Rank, E., & Kubin, G. (1997). A waveguide model for slapbass synthesis. In *Proceedings of the IEEE International Conference on Acoustics, Speech, and Signal Processing*, (pp. 444-446). IEEE Press.

Reynolds, D. D. (1981). *Engineering principles of acoustics*. Boston, MA: Allyn and Bacon Inc.

Rossing, T. D. (1990). *The science of sound* (2nd ed.). Boston, MA: Addison-Wesley.

Välimäki, V., Pakarinen, J., Erkut, C., & Karjalainen, M. (2006). Discrete-time modelling of musical instruments. *Reports on Progress in Physics, 69*(1), 1–78. doi:10.1088/0034-4885/69/1/R01

ENDNOTES

[1]   As pointed out in Fahy (2001), the wave motion does not need to have an oscillatory nature. Consider, for example, a short, impulsive sound that propagates through a certain imaginary volume in air. When the acoustic disturbance has passed the volume, the air inside the volume simply returns to its undisturbed state, and does not continue to oscillate.

[2]   In engineering terms, the flaring end lowers the impedance mismatch between the pipe and the free-field, thus improving the sound energy transmission to the surrounding air. A more thorough discussion on the concept of acoustic impedance can be found in Fahy (2001).

3   In fact, some playing techniques, such as pinch harmonics or the controlled use of acoustic feedback are impossible without a distorting guitar amplifier.

4   Note that in this case, the system could not in theory choose between a pipe with both ends open and one with both ends closed, since the same bore length would produce the same fundamental frequency. However, this would probably not be a problem since the latter type is not usually used in a musical context.

5   Note that only monophonic signals and omnidirectional sources and microphones are considered here. For stereophonic signals, two impulse response signals would be required.

Chapter 3
Expressing Musical Features, Class Labels, Ontologies, and Metadata Using ACE XML 2.0

Cory McKay
Marianopolis College, Canada

Ichiro Fujinaga
McGill University, Canada

ABSTRACT

This chapter presents ACE XML, a set of file formats that are designed to meet the special representational needs of research in Music Information Retrieval (MIR) in general and automatic music classification in particular. The ACE XML formats are designed to represent a wide range of musical information clearly and simply using formally structured frameworks that are flexible and extensible.

This chapter includes a critical review of existing file formats that have been used in MIR research. This is followed by a set of design priorities that are proposed for use in developing new formats and improving existing ones. The details of the ACE XML specification are then described in this context. Finally, research priorities for the future are discussed, as well as possible uses for ACE XML outside the specific domain of MIR.

INTRODUCTION

Music Information Retrieval and Automatic Music Classification

Music Information Retrieval, or MIR (Downie, 2003), is a research domain that investigates theoretical and practical issues relating to the extraction of information of any kind from music

DOI: 10.4018/978-1-4666-2497-9.ch003

and to making this information accessible. MIR has a broad scope that includes symbolic musical data (musical scores, MIDI files, etc.), audio data (MP3 recordings, AIFF recordings, etc.) and cultural data (sales statistics, album art, etc.).

MIR researchers often make use of machine learning and data mining algorithms (Duda, Hart, & Stork, 2001; Witten & Frank, 2005) to extract meaningful information from music. This typically involves having computers automatically classify music in some way. For example, machine learning can be used to automatically classify music by title, genre, performer, composer, mood, geographical origin, etc. Other MIR tasks such as automatic pitch recognition, chord identification, key finding, melodic segmentation, tempo tracking, instrument identification, and structural segmentation also often make use of automatic classification technology.

Musical machine learning typically involves the following basic tasks:

- The collection of a musical dataset that can be used to "train" machine learning algorithms. This dataset is typically (although not always) annotated with labels, called "classes," that are considered to be reliably correct. Class labels are domain-specific, and can specify information such as song titles, genre names, etc. Such annotated datasets are called "ground truth." Each individual piece of data comprising the dataset (e.g., an audio recording, a musical score, an album art image, etc.) is called an "instance."

- Before training can actually be performed, the dataset must first have "features" extracted from it. Features are characteristic pieces of information of any kind that are believed to be potentially useful in discriminating between classes. Examples include low-level signal processing oriented features such as Spectral Flux, higher-level musical information such as the Range of Melodic Arcs, perceptually oriented information such as MFCCs, and cultural features such as Yearly Sales Volume. Sometimes "dimensionality reduction" algorithms are used to automatically determine which features, or which components of features, are the most likely to be useful for a given classification task.

- Training is then performed, whereby the machine learning algorithms use various methods to learn to associate particular

feature patterns to particular classes. The ground truth is typically partitioned into disjoint "training," "testing," and sometimes "publication" sets in order to help evaluate the reliability of learned models.

The effective implementation of musical machine learning requires well thought out representations of musical information, as this information must be provided to algorithms in effective ways, and it must also be possible to interpret the output of the algorithms in musically meaningful ways. Consequently, the particular file formats that are used in MIR can have an immense impact on the kinds of research that may be performed and on the quality of the results.

The overall efficiency of MIR research hinges on the ability of researchers to share data effectively with one another. Information such as ground-truth annotations, for example, can be very expensive to produce, and a great deal of repeated effort is avoided if researchers are able to share such information easily. Similarly, training and testing datasets themselves can be expensive to acquire, and since they cannot typically be distributed directly because of legal copyright limitations, the ability to share feature values can be very valuable. The ability to communicate metadata about features, instances, and classes can also be very useful.

Well-defined, flexible, and expressive standardized file formats are essential for distributing such information efficiently and effectively. The absence of such standardized formats poses a serious obstacle to the sharing of research information, with the result that each lab has a greater tendency to generate its own in-house data and file formats, which results in both wasteful repeated effort and, in general, lower quality data.

Introduction to ACE XML and jMIR

The ACE XML file formats are specifically designed to represent information that is relevant to MIR and automatic music classification. The representation of the following five fundamental types of information is the primary (but not exclusive) focus of ACE XML:

- Feature values extracted from instances
- Abstract information about features and their parameters
- Instance annotations
- Class ontologies
- Metadata related to instances, features, and classes

The design priorities behind ACE XML and the ways in which it stores this information are specified later in this chapter, as are the code libraries that support ACE XML parsing, writing, and processing.

The original Version 1.1 of ACE XML (McKay, et al., 2005) was developed as part of the jMIR automatic music classification project (McKay & Fujinaga, 2012). The significantly updated Version 2.0 of ACE XML, which is the focus of this chapter, was developed in response to changing needs of the MIR community and to the needs of the NEMA project, as described at the end of this chapter.

jMIR is a suite of software applications developed for use as general MIR research tools. Each of the jMIR applications can be used independently, and they can also be used as an integrated suite. jMIR includes the following primary components, in addition to ACE XML:

- **jAudio:** An audio feature extractor that includes implementations of 26 core features. jAudio also includes implementations of "metafeatures" and "aggregators" that can be used to automatically generate many more features from these core features (e.g., standard deviation, derivative, etc.).
- **jSymbolic:** A symbolic feature extractor for MIDI files. jSymbolic is packaged with 111 features, many of which are original.

- **jWebMiner:** A cultural feature extractor that extracts features from the Web-based on search engine co-occurrence page counts. Many user options are available to refine results, including search synonyms, filter strings, and site weightings.
- **ACE:** A meta-learning classification system that can automatically experiment with a variety of different dimensionality reduction and machine learning algorithms in order to evaluate which are best suited to particular problems.
- **jMusicMetaManager:** Software for managing and cataloguing large musical datasets, as well as detecting probable metadata errors in them.
- **Codaich, Bodhidharma MIDI and SAC:** MIR research datasets consisting of, respectively, MP3 files, MIDI files and matched sets of audio, MIDI, and cultural musical data.

Although most of the jMIR applications can process common file formats such as Weka ARFF and Apple iTunes XML, ACE XML 1.1 is the native format used to store and exchange data between them. All jMIR components are thus currently fully ACE XML 1.1 compatible. Efforts are currently underway to upgrade this to the much more flexible ACE XML 2.0. The jMIR components thus provide a ready to use and flexible set of software tools for producing and using ACE XML data.

Objectives of this Chapter

The main goal of this chapter is to introduce ACE XML 2.0 to the MIR community in particular and to researchers interested in computational musicology and music theory in general. It is hoped that ACE XML will be adopted as a standard format for communicating information between different research groups, and that the ACE XML processing libraries will be incorporated into a variety of software tools, as they already are in jMIR.

An additional objective of this chapter is the promotion of a critical discussion of existing file formats and associated design priorities. Whether or not ACE XML 2.0 is adopted as a standard, failure to meet needs such as those described in this chapter can have the consequence of limiting the quality of MIR research. For example, there is currently widespread agreement in the MIR community that the classification of music into only a single genre is a musically unrealistic constraint, yet almost all published work on automatic genre classification does just this, largely because the file formats that are currently popular are not able to properly represent multi-class membership.

BACKGROUND

Core File Format Technologies

There are several basic technologies that can be used as foundations for designing file formats. Each of these has its own strengths and weaknesses.

Binary files are computer files that use series of 1s and 0s to store any type of data. Information can be stored very efficiently in binary files, but they have significant disadvantages with respect to portability, readability, and longevity. Specialized software is needed to parse and write each binary file type, and stored data can be difficult to access if this software becomes obsolete or is otherwise unavailable.

Text files offer an alternative to binary files. Although text files are still at their core binary, they represent alphanumeric characters and reserved special characters according to widely accepted standards such as ASCII and Unicode, something that increases portability and assures some longevity, but also tends to reduce storage efficiency. Text files have the additional advantage of being human readable and writable. "Delimited" text files are files where data fields are separated by

designated characters such as tabs, and are often used to store machine readable data.

Markup languages offer another alternative. These text-based formats use more sophisticated annotations than delimited text files, with the result that they can usefully structure and constrain data. XML (Ray, 2003) is a popular and sophisticated markup language that provides users with the ability to specify custom "schemas" that create custom file formats. There are a variety of schema languages, one of the earliest and best known of which is the "Document Type Definition," or "DTD."

RDF (Powers, 2003) refers to a family of syntax specifications for representing relationships between different entities. These entities are typically distributed over the Internet, and are often addressed using URI references. Subject-predicate-object "triples" are the basic building blocks for specifying RDF ontologies. Each such triple indicates that the subject is related to the object with a relationship specified by the predicate. RDF is often implemented using XML, although there are alternative implementations as well.

OWL (Lacy, 2005) is another family of languages that can be used to represent ontologies. Some variants of OWL are partially compatible with RDF.

Existing MIR-Oriented File Formats

Although there are many formats for representing music, ranging from symbolic representations like MIDI, MusicXML (Good, 2006), or Humdrum (Huron, 1999) to audio representations like FLAC and MP3, such representations are poorly suited to representing the kinds of information that are needed for automatic music classification, namely feature values, instance labels and associated metadata. As a consequence, most MIR researchers have resorted either to using custom in-house file formats, which have serious disadvantages with respect to the sharing of research data, or to using formats designed for non-music specific use by the general data mining community.

Weka ARFF (Witten & Frank, 2005) is by far the most popular of these general purpose data mining formats among MIR researchers, probably because of the powerful and open source Weka machine learning library associated with it. ARFF is a text-based format that begins with a header listing feature and class names, as well as associated feature data types. This is followed by a comma-delimited list of feature values, where the features for each instance are contained on a single line, along with a class name, if appropriate. Many MIR feature extraction systems store extracted feature values in ARFF files, including the popular Marsyas (Tzanetakis & Cook, 2000).

RapidMiner (Mierswa, et al., 2006) is another general purpose machine learning framework. Unfortunately, from the perspective of MIR, the particular emphasis of RapidMiner XML files is on communicating experimental configurations rather than instance and class data itself.

Some of the more sophisticated audio file formats can be adapted to storing machine learning oriented information. SDIF (Schwarz & Wright, 2000) in particular has been used for storing audio features by the powerful CLAM (Amatrain, Arumi, & Ramirez, 2002) MIR software. Such files are less appropriate for dealing with cultural and symbolic data, however, and have a relatively limited expressivity with respect to pertinent metadata.

Mathworks MATLAB binaries are also used sometimes, since MATLAB is itself a powerful platform used by many MIR researchers. Unfortunately, MATLAB binaries suffer from the same portability and accessibility problems as all binary formats, particularly given the proprietary nature of MATLAB.

Music Ontology (Schwarz & Wright, 2000) is one of the few frameworks designed specifically with the needs of MIR in mind, and it has many powerful advantages. It is designed to represent musical ontologies of essentially any kind using RDF and, to a lesser extent, OWL. Music Ontol-

ogy is itself composed of several implemented ontologies. The Timeline and Audio Features ontologies are of particular interest to automatic music classification. Music Ontology is the main representational format used in the OMRAS2 project, and is supported by the Sonic Visualiser software (Cannam, et al., 2006).

CrestMuseXML (Kitahara, 2008) is another MIR oriented framework. It has yet to be fully published at the time of this writing, but it is very promising.

Problems with Existing File Formats

Weka ARFF and Music Ontology in particular are critically examined in this section, as they are the most popular and viable alternatives to ACE XML. These two frameworks are based on very different approaches and technologies, with the consequence that a consideration of their relative strengths and weaknesses can yield important insights that can be used in designing new formats and improving existing ones.

This critical analysis is in no way intended to denigrate either of these frameworks, as they are both exemplary in quality with respects to their own intended use cases. These domains only partially intersect the ACE XML's particular focus on automatic music classification, however, so it is to be expected that there will be some relative weaknesses.

ARFF files are intended for general data mining research, and as such certainly cannot be expected to meet the special needs of MIR. One serious such limitation of ARFF files is that there is no natural way to assign more than one class to a given instance without resorting to awkward and inappropriate workarounds. Although this is not a serious shortcoming for the majority of general pattern recognition applications, which only require classification into one and only one class, there are many MIR research areas where this limitation is problematic. For example, a performer classification system should be able to assign multiple performer labels. It should be possible, to extend this example, to label a symphony with the names of the conductor, the soloists, the orchestra as a whole, etc., or to label pieces on the *Kind of Blue* album with the names of Miles Davis, John Coltrane, Bill Evans, etc.

A second problem is that ARFF files store each instance only as a list of feature values and a class label, without any supplementary structuring or associated metadata. It is often appropriate in music to extract features over a potentially overlapping time series of windows, something that results in a set of ordered feature subsections for each piece. This is a fundamental requirement in applications such as recording segmentation or structural analysis, and is convenient in a wide variety of other MIR tasks. Furthermore, some features may be extracted for each window, some only for some windows and some only for each piece as a whole. ARFF files provide no way of internally associating features extracted from a window with the recording that the window comes from, nor do they provide any means of identifying recordings via metadata or of storing time stamps associated with each window.

A third problem is that ARFF files do not permit any logical grouping of associated features. ARFF files treat each feature as an independent entity with no relation to any other feature. In contrast to this, one often encounters multidimensional features in music, such as MFCCs, beat histograms and binary lists of instruments present. Maintaining a logical relationship between the values of such multidimensional features allows one to use classification algorithms that take advantage of their particular interrelatedness, particularly when using classifier ensembles (McKay, 2004).

A fourth problem is that there is no way to provide any metadata about features in ARFF files, other than in unstructured comments. This can be a problem, for example, when features are extracted from new instances added to a dataset that has already had features extracted from it. Such a scenario necessitates identical feature implementations and parameterizations to the ones previously used if the features values are to be combined. It is very helpful if information such as the roll-off point used to extract the Spectral Roll-Off feature, for example, can be stored and communicated in a standardized manner.

A fifth problem is that there is no way of specifying structuring of class labels in ARFF files. One often encounters hierarchical or other ontological class structures in music, such as in the cases of genre classes. ARFF files treat each class as distinct and independent. This means that there is no way to use classification algorithms that make use of structured ontologies, such as hierarchical tree classifiers, for example. This also means that there is no way to use weighted training strategies that penalize misclassifications into dissimilar classes more severely than misclassifications into similar classes.

It is apparent that many of the limitations of ARFF files are due to the format's lack of expressivity and generality. The limitations of RDF-based formats such as Music Ontology, in contrast, tend to be due to RDF's generality, simplicity, and abstract nature, qualities that are both its keys strengths and its key weaknesses. Although these characteristics allow RDF to be used to describe an almost limitless range of information in flexible ways, they can also introduce ambiguities and computational disadvantages. RDF offers greater flexibility and extensibility than a particular XML schema might, for example, but it does not offer the ability to quickly and easily define strict and sophisticated self-contained structures when it might be useful to do so, as can be done with XML schemas. As a result, XML is in general better suited to representing well-structured data than RDF, something that is typically advantageous in use cases involving machine learning.

The well-structured way in which data is represented in ACE XML carries corresponding benefits with respect specifically to machine learning relative to the RDF-based Music Ontology. Although Music Ontology's Audio Features ontology does focus on the music classification domain, this particular ontology is not as developed, flexible and convenient as ACE XML with respect to representing information such as feature values and instance labels. The Audio Features ontology is also designed specifically with audio features in mind, whereas ACE XML treats audio, symbolic, and cultural features equally and equivalently.

ACE XML files are also much more human readable than Music Ontology's RDF files, which are more oriented towards machine-only readability. ACE XML files are also simpler and more clearly structured, without the fundamental reliance on complex external dependencies inherent to RDF. This makes ACE XML easier for users to learn and understand. The majority of researchers in the MIR community and its associated disciplines are likely to be, in general, more familiar with XML than they are with RDF, with the consequence that they will likely be more willing to adopt an XML-based standard. This is particularly true for key areas of MIR research that are more oriented towards the humanities than to technical applications. A related advantage is that ACE XML only relies on simple XML parsing, and does not require the installation of packages for parsing additional standards such as OWL, for example, which can pose obstacles for some less technically oriented users. The simple structuring of ACE XML and its associated data structures also make it easier for MIR researchers to quickly learn to write code using them, something that is essential if a format is to be accepted as a standard.

Although the ease with which connections between distributed resources can be specified with RDF can certainly be a strong advantage in many contexts, the consequent reliance on the availability of these resources can also be a disadvantage when documents that are linked become inaccessible or inconsistent. This can be a particular problem in MIR given the limited longevity, legal vulnerability, and dynamic nature of many electronic musical resources, at least in the current climate. This reliance on distributed resources can also be a significant disadvantage in general if one does not have network access at a particular moment, for example, or if a remote resource is removed, renamed, or moved. If even one resource is eliminated it is possible that one will not only lose access to it, but potentially to all of the resources that it refers to as well. Self-contained XML files, on the other hand, do not carry this risk.

Furthermore, the ability to easily store information such as feature values and instance labels locally if desired can be an important advantage when dealing with many gigabytes of feature values. Limitations such as slow network connections and monthly bandwidth caps can pose serious obstacles when dealing with resources that are distributed on the Internet, but are less of a problem with self-contained files such as ACE XML that can be downloaded or uploaded when convenient, or only used locally if appropriate. RDF-based ontologies correspondingly tend to be better suited to relatively small amounts of textual data than to the very large feature sets that are associated with many MIR use cases, and to the even larger datasets that are likely to arise in the future as MIR research scales up to include larger quantities of music.

Having noted all of this, the *uri* triples that can be specified in ACE XML (see below) make it possible to link to external resources in a very general RDF-like way. The essential difference, however, is that none of the essential expressivity of ACE XML is contingent on these links. This brings many of the advantages of RDF to ACE XML without the associated disadvantages. One important exception, however, is that ACE XML is not currently compatible with powerful query technologies such as SPAQL that can be used with RDF data.

In general, it can be said that Music Ontology is likely a better choice than ACE XML for representing weakly structured musical data unrelated to automatic music classification and for linking to data that is already distributed on-line. ACE XML, in turn, is likely preferable in the specific domain of automatic music classification, particularly with respect to feature extraction and instance labeling. Music Ontology can certainly be used for such purposes as well, however. In the long-term, it is possible that RDF-based approaches and the Semantic Web in general will be able to truly capitalize on the power of their generality. This promise of RDF and the Semantic Web has yet to be achieved, however, despite efforts dating back over a decade. In the meantime, more strongly structured approaches such as ACE XML have significant practical advantages for the use cases associated with most MIR classification research, both academic and commercial.

PROPOSED DESIGN PRIORITIES FOR MUSIC CLASSIFICATION FILE FORMATS

The following list outlines a set of priorities that are proposed for consideration in the design of representational frameworks intended to be used in automatic classification research. This list was derived from a critical analysis of the shortcomings of existing file formats that have been used in such research, as well as from general experience arrived at while performing music classification research:

- File formats should be as simple and easy to understand as possible. This makes it easier for users to learn the formats, adopt them, and implement software that uses them. It also decreases the probability of unforeseen conflicts and inconsistencies.
- File formats should be as flexible and expressive as possible, within the constraints of avoiding unnecessary complexity and redundancy.
- The data stored in the files should be conveniently machine readable. If a file format is difficult to write parsers for or is parsed

into inconvenient data structures then it will be difficult to convince users to adopt it as a standard.

- The data stored in the files should ideally be human readable. This is useful when debugging, and it also allows humans to write files manually when the design of specialized annotation software would be inappropriate or unnecessarily time consuming.
- The data should be stored as efficiently as possible, in order to avoid excessively large files, within the constraint of not compromising other design priorities such as flexibility and readability.
- Some widely accepted and well-known existing standard technology, such as XML, should be used. This increases the likelihood that new file formats will be themselves adopted as standards because they will be based on a proven technology, because users are likely to be already be at least somewhat familiar with the technology and because parsing libraries will already be available. It also helps to promote longevity.
- File formats should rely on as few external technologies as possible. Each technology that is used increases the probability that any given programming language used for application development will not include parsing libraries for that technology, that a parsing library will not function under a given operating system or that a component of the system will soon become obsolete.
- The fundamental types of information that need to be represented are: feature values extracted from instances, class label annotations of instances, abstract descriptions of features and their parameters, and ontological structuring of candidate class labels.
- It should be possible to express features extracted from audio, symbolic, and cul-

tural sources of information, and to treat these features equivalently so that they can easily be combined.

- Users should be free to associate arbitrary metadata fields with instances, classes, and features.
- It should be a simple matter to combine information of the same type, such as in the case of features extracted during different feature extraction sessions.
- It should be easy to reuse files for different purposes, such as in a case where the same audio feature values are used for both genre classification and artist identification.
- It is useful to emphasize a clear separation between the feature extraction and classification tasks in order to promote portability. This contrasts with traditional formats such as Weka ARFF, which combine feature values with class labels. A separation between these two types of data is important because individual researchers may have reasons for using particular feature extractors or particular classification systems. It should therefore be easy to use any feature extractor to communicate features of any type to any classification software. This portability makes it possible to process features generated by different feature extractors with the same classification software, or to use a given set of extracted features with multiple classification applications.
- It should be a simple matter to package files expressing related types of information (e.g., feature values extracted from particular instances and abstract information about the features themselves) together when appropriate, but also to separate them out when convenient. This helps to ensure data accessibility and integrity, as well as flexibility.

- It should be possible to reference external sources of information, but in such a way that doing so does not introduce dependencies on external resources that may no longer be available in the future or that might changes unexpectedly.
- It should be possible to assign an arbitrary number of class labels to each instance and sub-instance.
- It should be possible to express relative weights for these class labels.
- It should be possible to group the dimensions of multi-dimensional features and to logically associate related features and their values with one another.
- It should be possible to associate unique metadata with instances so that they can be identified, both internally and externally.
- It should be possible to specify relationships between specific instances, in both ordered and hierarchical ways. In the case of the former, this could be a time series of analysis windows, for example. In the case of the latter, it could be a hierarchical ranking of, from bottom to top, features extracted from individual analysis windows of a recording, features extracted from recordings as a whole, features extracted from many recordings associated with a particular performer, etc. In any case, it should be at least be possible to express both feature values and class labels for both overall instances and ordered subsections of them.
- For ordered instance data, it should be possible for section labels to overlap with one another.
- For ordered instance data, it should be possible for analysis windows to have variable sizes, rather than requiring them all to be the same size.
- It should be possible for feature values to be present for some instances and/or sub-

instances, but not others. For example, some features may be extracted for all analysis windows, some only for some windows, and some only for each recording as a whole.

- Related to this, it should be possible to abstractly specify the appropriateness of different features for different contexts. For example, some features might only be appropriate to extract for a whole recording, not its analysis windows, or some features might only be possible to extract once one or more windows have already been calculated (e.g., spectral flux).
- It should be possible to specify custom feature extraction parameters.
- It should be possible to specify relationships between different class labels, both hierarchical and otherwise. This is important for the specification of class ontologies that can be taken advantage of by machine learning strategies.
- It should be possible to relatively weight the associations between class labels.

THE ACE XML 2.0 SOLUTION

Overview of the ACE XML 2.0 Formats and Justification of Design Choices

The ACE XML file formats are designed with the goal of fulfilling the design priorities proposed above to the greatest extent possible. Although ACE XML is designed to meet specific needs of automatic music classification, it can also certainly be effectively adopted to other musical research domains or even non-musical applications as well.

Summarized as briefly as possible, the overarching design priorities behind ACE XML are the maximization of expressivity, flexibility and extensibility while at the same time maintaining as much simplicity and accessibility as possible.

These two sets of often opposed design priorities are addressed by making many of the ACE XML elements and attributes optional so that they can be included or omitted as needed. This makes it possible to use simple and concise files when this is all that is necessary, and to only necessitate the use of those particular additional options that are needed when more expressivity is required.

As implied by their name, ACE XML files are all XML-based. XML was chosen because it is not only a standardized format for which parsers are widely available, but is also extremely flexible while at the same time able to clearly specify data structuring that can be as rigid as needed. XML is verbose, with the consequence that it is less space efficient than formats such as ARFF, but this verbosity has the compensating advantages of increasing human readability and of allowing greater flexibility and extensibility.

There are five types of ACE XML files that perform the following core purposes:

- **Feature Value:** These files express feature values extracted from specific instances.
- **Feature Description:** These files express abstract information about features themselves (but not extracted feature values).
- **Instance Label:** These files associate class labels with specific instances and their subsections. They can be used to express either ground truth labels or predicted labels output by a classification system.
- **Class Ontology:** These files express relationships between classes. They can be used to simply catalogue candidate class labels, or for more sophisticated purposes such as expressing weighted ontological relationships between classes.
- **Project:** These files indicate associations between related groups of ACE XML files and other resources.

This is only a brief outline of the expressivity offered by each of the file types, however, as is evident from the individual descriptions of each of them in the sections below. Of particular note, all of the ACE XML file types offer functionality for specifying a variety of useful metadata.

Each of these XML file types may be used independently, or they may be associated with one another and integrated in software using unique identifiers. It is not in any way necessary to provide each of the ACE XML file types for any application if this is not appropriate or needed. For example, if a classifier is already trained and is to be used to classify unknown patterns, then there is no need for an Instance Label file, although one may be produced during processing to express predicted classes.

The ACE XML code base, discussed briefly below, automatically constructs implied data for missing file types in a way that is hidden from the user. For example, if only a Feature Value file and an Instance Label file are specified, the software can automatically construct a flat class ontology based on the labels present in the Instance Label file, and can also automatically generate feature descriptions based on the characteristics of the features present in the Feature Value file, such as the dimensionality of each feature.

The decision to use multiple different file types rather than the more typical single file type is unorthodox, and requires some justification. As discussed above, it is useful to incorporate a separation between feature values and instance labels. This is important for data reusability, such as in a case where one might extract features once from a large number of recordings, and then reuse the single resulting Feature Value file for multiple purposes, such as classification by performer, composer, genre and mood. If there were only one ACE XML file type, then feature values would need to be repeated for each of these applications. With the ACE XML approach, however, the Feature Value file can remain unchanged and be reused with a different Instance Label file for each classification task. Similarly, one can imagine a case where the same model classifications contained

in one Instance Label file are used for separate sets of features extracted from symbolic, cultural, and audio data contained in three different Feature Value files.

Feature descriptions and class ontologies are each distributed in separate files as well in order to emphasize their independence from particular instances. For example, a Feature Description file could be published on its own to catalogue the features that can be extracted by a particular feature extraction application in general, or to express specific extraction parameters that were found to be effective for a particular research domain. Similarly, class ontologies could be published in a way that is independent of particular instances and features, or even of a particular dataset as a whole.

Such file type separations emphasize the abstract nature of many of the types of data that are useful in music classification, and allow the files to be distributed and used either independently or together, as appropriate, rather than artificially forcing connections where they may not always be appropriate. The use of separate file formats also has advantages with respect to data longevity and convenience when updating data. If new features become available after a Feature Value file has been generated, for example, it would only be necessary to update the Feature Value and Feature Description files since the data stored in the other two file types could be reused unmodified. Similarly, if a class ontology changed over time, it would not be necessary to update Feature Value or Feature Description files.

Overall, and most importantly, the separation of different types of data into different file types makes it possible to distribute and use one type of file for arbitrary purposes without needing to impose particular choices with respect to the types of data described by the other file types. The separation into multiple files types also makes it easier to conceptualize and represent sophisticated arrangements of information with a divide and conquer approach.

It was decided to use XML DTDs rather than some other XML schema to define the ACE XML file types. Although other schemas can in general be more expressive than DTDs, DTDs are nonetheless sufficiently expressive for the purposes of ACE XML. They also have the advantages of being simpler and easier to understand, thereby making the ACE XML formats more attractive to new users. This is a particular advantage considering the variety of alternative schemas that are available. The average member of the MIR community is less likely to be familiar with any particular one of these alternative schema languages, particularly in the cases of those specialized schemas that provide enough increased expressivity to have advantages over simple DTDs. Furthermore, DTDs tend to be easier to learn for those users who might not know any XML at all. The ACE XML DTDs are specified in each ACE XML file along with the file's data, which means that each ACE XML file is packaged with an explanation of its data structuring.

Incorporating ACE XML 2.0 into Existing and New Software

A key factor in the effectiveness of any effort to encourage music researchers to adopt new standardized file formats is the ease with which they can parse and write to them in their own existing and new software. The ample data structures and processing functionality offered by the Weka code base have certainly contributed to its broad adoption, for example.

Specialized code libraries have thus been implemented to support the ACE XML file formats. These include functionality for parsing, writing and merging ACE XML files as well as performing various utility functions such as batch annotating files into an Instance Label file, generating Instance Label files based on simple tab delimited text files or accessing data from iTunes XML files. These libraries also include data structures for storing ACE XML data that

can be accessed by external code via simple and well-documented APIs. This data can be used and manipulated directly using these libraries, or it can be exported to individual developers' own data structures.

These code libraries are open source and are distributed for free with a GNU GPL. They are implemented in Java in order to ensure portability, and do not rely on any technologies beyond Java that require any kind of special installations. The resulting portability is important in helping to encourage adoption by less technically oriented users.

Functionality has also been implemented to automatically convert data stored in ACE XML data structures into Weka data structures, and vice versa, in order to take advantage of the convenient and well-established functionality built into Weka. This also makes it possible to use Weka data structures as intermediaries for conversion to yet other formats. jMIR also includes utilities for directly translating back and forth between Weka ARFF and ACE XML files, although data that fundamentally cannot be represented in ARFF files is lost when doing so.

An ACE XML GUI editor is also implemented as part of the ACE software. This makes it possible to conveniently view, edit, and save ACE XML files. Of course, ACE XML files can also be edited using simple text editors or specialized software like Altova XML Spy. The jMIR applications also include functionality for writing and, when appropriate, reading ACE XML files.

Linking ACE XML 2.0 Files to External Resources

As described in the sections below, each of the ACE XML file formats allow unlimited numbers of optional *uri* clauses to be added in a wide variety of contexts. Each *uri* element has an optional *predicate* attribute in order to make it possible to specify RDF-like triples, such that the file context where the *uri* element is found indicates the subject, the contents of the *uri* element specifies the object, and the *predicate* attribute specifies the relationship between the two. So, for example, in the case of an Instance Label ACE XML file providing information about genre labels, the following *uri* statement could be placed in a *class* clause associated with Afro-Cuban jazz in order to provide a link to useful background information:

```
<uri predicate="http://en.wikipedia.
org/wiki/Music_genre">
http://www.allmusic.com/cg/amg.
dll?p=amg&sql=77:2601</uri>
```

Such *uri* elements provide a powerful and flexible way of linking ACE XML files to external resources. This can be used simply to provide links to references, or it can be used to provide hooks to formally integrate ACE XML files into frameworks like RDF ontologies *uri* elements are by no means obligatory in ACE XML files, however, and it is perfectly acceptable to omit them if desired. They are not in fact used in any core ACE XML or jMIR functionality, so ACE XML files can still be used in an entirely self-contained way even if no *uri* tags are present. In other words, the *uri* tags are provided only to facilitate integration with external resources or into external frameworks, but they in no way introduce dependencies that limit the usability of ACE XML files if these resources become unavailable, as can be the case with RDF ontologies, and they do not compromise the backwards compatibility of future updates to ACE XML

In the special case of related ACE XML files, each of the ACE XML file formats offers the option of using a *related_resources* clause. Such a clause can be used to reference one or more related ACE XML Feature Value, Feature Description, Instance Label, Class Ontology or Project files, respectively referenced via *feature_value_file, feature_description_file, instance_label_file, class_ontology_file* or *project_file* elements. Although related ACE XML files can also be

grouped using an ACE XML Project file, the *related_resources* element provides the option of forming more general connections with a scope broader than just a particular project. *uri* tags may also optionally be used inside a *related_resources* clauses to reference as many external resources as desired that are relevant to the document as a whole.

THE ACE XML 2.0 FILE FORMATS

ACE XML 2.0 Feature Value Files

Feature Value files are used to express feature values that have been extracted for instances as a whole, for subsection regions of instances or at quantized coordinates in an instance. This can be useful, for example, when dealing with windowed audio feature extractions or with symbolic feature extractions where features are extracted separately for different sections of a score. The Feature Value DTD is shown in Figure 1.

The fundamental units of Feature Value files are *instance* clauses. A number of different kinds of metadata may be expressed for an instance by including the following elements within its *instance* clause:

- *instance_id:* The contents of this obligatory element specify a unique identifier for an instance. This may be a network URI, a file path, a publication number, a title, a hash code, or any other type of identifying string that is convenient, as long as it is uniquely used with reference to the given instance. *instance_id* tags are also used to link extracted feature values with corresponding class labels stored in ACE XML Instance Label files.
- *uri:* Described in the section above.
- *extractor:* This optional element may be used to specify the name of the feature extraction software that was used to extract

Figure 1. The XML DTD for the ACE XML 2.0 feature value format

```
<!ELEMENT ace_xml_feature_value_file_2_0 (comments?, related_resources?,
                                          instance+)>
<!ELEMENT comments (#PCDATA)>
<!ELEMENT related_resources (feature_value_file*,
                             feature_description_file*,
                             instance_label_file*,
                             class_ontology_file*,
                             project_file*,
                             uri*)>
<!ELEMENT feature_value_file (#PCDATA)>
<!ELEMENT feature_description_file (#PCDATA)>
<!ELEMENT instance_label_file (#PCDATA)>
<!ELEMENT class_ontology_file (#PCDATA)>
<!ELEMENT project_file (#PCDATA)>
<!ELEMENT uri (#PCDATA)>
<!ATTLIST uri predicate CDATA #IMPLIED>
<!ELEMENT instance (instance_id,
               uri*,
               extractor*,
               coord_units?,
               s*,
               precise_coord*,
               f*)>
<!ELEMENT instance_id (#PCDATA)>
<!ELEMENT extractor (#PCDATA)>
<!ATTLIST extractor fname CDATA #REQUIRED>
<!ELEMENT coord_units (#PCDATA)>
<!ELEMENT s (uri*,
        f+)>
<!ATTLIST s b CDATA #REQUIRED
          e CDATA #REQUIRED>
<!ELEMENT precise_coord (uri*,
                    f+)>
<!ATTLIST precise_coord coord CDATA #REQUIRED>
<!ELEMENT f (fid,
        uri*,
        (v+ | vd+ | vs+ | vj))>
<!ATTLIST f type (int | double | float | complex | string) #IMPLIED>
<!ELEMENT fid (#PCDATA)>
<!ELEMENT v (#PCDATA)>
<!ELEMENT vd (#PCDATA)>
<!ATTLIST vd d0 CDATA #REQUIRED d1 CDATA #IMPLIED d2 CDATA #IMPLIED
          d3 CDATA #IMPLIED d4 CDATA #IMPLIED d5 CDATA #IMPLIED
          d6 CDATA #IMPLIED d7 CDATA #IMPLIED d8 CDATA #IMPLIED
          d9 CDATA #IMPLIED>
<!ELEMENT vs (d+,
         v)>
<!ELEMENT d (#PCDATA)>
<!ELEMENT vj (#PCDATA)>
```

features. A separate *extractor* clause is needed for each feature. The contents of an *extractor* clause indicate the name of the feature extractor, and the obligatory *fname* attribute indicates the name of the feature

that is to be associated with this extractor. This arrangement accommodates scenarios where different feature extractors are used to extract the same feature for different instances, as well as scenarios where different features are extracted by different feature extractors for the same instance.

- *coord_units:* This optional element may be used to specify units for the coordinate values associated with the *b, e,* and *coord* attributes described below.

Actual feature values and instance subdivisions are specified after this metadata in *instance* clauses. In the case of subsections, the feature values are wrapped in an *s* clause that includes obligatory *b* and *e* attributes to specify the beginning and end coordinates of the section, respectively. There may be multiple subsections within an instance that may or may not overlap, that may or may not be of equal size and that may or may not comprehensively cover the overall instance. This makes it possible to have, for example, overlapping analysis windows of arbitrary and potentially varying sizes. There is nothing about the *b* and *e* attributes that specifically associates them with time, although they often are in practice. They could just as easily be used to specify a range of pixels in an image of album art, for example.

In the case of a subsection that corresponds to a quantized point (e.g., a single audio sample or a single pixel), with only a single corresponding coordinate, a *precise_coord* clause is used instead of an *s* clause, with a single *coord* attribute specifying the point within the instance that is referred to. Both *s* and *precise_coord* clauses may make use of optional *uri* tags to refer to external resources.

Each instance or subsection may contain an arbitrary and potentially differing number of features in an arbitrary and potentially differing order. This makes it possible to omit features from some instances or subsections if appropriate or if they are unavailable.

The value(s) of a feature are specified within an *f* clause. A separate *f* clause is used for each feature. The *f* element may be specified within an *instance* clause at the root level or within a subsection *s* clause or a *precise_coord* clause. The following information may be specified within each *f* clause:

- *fid:* The contents of this obligatory element specify a unique identifier for a feature. This identifier may be any string, as long as it is only used in reference to the feature in question. *f_id* tags may be used to link Feature Value files to ACE XML Feature Description files in order to access more information about individual features if desired.
- *type:* This optional attribute may be used to specify the data type that should be used to store the feature value. The options are integers, doubles, floats, complex numbers, and text strings. Although this typing is not strictly necessary for jMIR, it is sometimes necessary for other software. *type* is assumed to be double by the jMIR ACE XML parser if it is not specified in an *f* clause, but this not an intrinsic assumption of the Feature Value format. Feature types may also be specified in an associated Feature Description file, in which case the they can be omitted from the Feature Value file for the sake of brevity.
- *v, vd, vs,* or *vj:* Feature values themselves are enclosed in any one of these elements. These are each described below.

Before proceeding to explain the differences between these four feature value tags, it is useful to first provide several examples. Figure 2 demonstrates a case where only features extracted for an instance overall are encoded, Figure 3 adds features extracted over subsections of the instance, and Figure 4 adds a variety of metadata. These examples illustrate how ACE XML files can be kept relatively sparse and simple if appropriate, but can also be very expressive if needed.

One essential requirement for a file format designed to express feature values is the ability to represent feature arrays of arbitrary dimensionalities, not just single value features or feature vectors. In addition, some features may have a dimensionality that varies from extraction to extraction, so it should be possible to accommo-

Figure 2. An excerpt from an artificial ACE XMLE 2.0 feature value file indicating feature values extracted for a single instance that, in this case, is an MP3 file. This example specifies two single-value features extracted from the recording as a whole. The identifier for the instance is a file path in this case, but it could just as well be a URI, a fingerprint string or any other unique key.

```
<instance>
    <instance_id>C:\Audio\song_57.mp3</instance_id>

    <f>
       <fid>Duration</fid>
       <v>257</v>
    </f>
    <f>
       <fid>Bit Rate</fid>
       <v>160</v>
    </f>
</instance>
```

Figure 3. An excerpt from an artificial ACE XMLE 2.0 feature value file indicating feature values extracted for a single instance. This example expands on Figure 2 by adding features extracted over two overlapping analysis windows. Two features are extracted for each window.

```
<instance>
    <instance_id>C:\Audio\song_57.mp3</instance_id>

    <s b="0" e="150">
       <f>
          <fid>Spectral Centroid</fid>
          <v>1016.8</v>
       </f>
       <f>
          <fid>RMS</fid>
          <v>0.1559</v>
       </f>
    </s>
    <s b="125" e="257">
       <f>
          <fid>Spectral Centroid</fid>
          <v>980.5</v>
       </f>
       <f>
          <fid>RMS</fid>
          <v>0.1229</v>
       </f>
    </s>

    <f>
       <fid>Duration</fid>
       <v>257</v>
    </f>
    <f>
       <fid>Bit Rate</fid>
       <v>160</v>
    </f>
</instance>
```

Figure 4. An excerpt from an artificial ACE XML 2.0 feature value file indicating feature values extracted for a single instance. This figure builds upon Figure 3 by adding several kinds of metadata, including a link to an imagined RDF ontology associated with the instance, the name of the feature extraction software used to extract each feature, the units used to denote subsection coordinates and the data type of each feature.

```
<instance>
    <instance_id>C:\Audio\song_57.mp3</instance_id>
    <uri predicate="http://www.mpeg.org/">
        http://audio.datastte.org/files/song_57.rdf</uri>
    <extractor fname="jAudio">Spectral Centroid</extractor>
    <extractor fname="jAudio">RMS</extractor>
    <extractor fname="jAudio">Duration</extractor>
    <extractor fname="Audacity">Encoding</extractor>
    <coord_units>ms</coord_units>

    <s b="0" e="150">
        <f type="double">
            <fid>Spectral Centroid</fid>
            <v>1016.8</v>
        </f>
        <f type="double">
            <fid>RMS</fid>
            <v>0.1559</v>
        </f>
    </s>
    <s b="125" e="257">
        <f type="double">
            <fid>Spectral Centroid</fid>
            <v>980.5</v>
        </f>
        <f type="double">
            <fid>RMS</fid>
            <v>0.1229</v>
        </f>
    </s>

    <f type="int">
        <fid>Duration</fid>
        <v>257</v>
    </f>
    <f type="int">
        <fid>Bit Rate</fid>
        <v>160</v>
    </f>
</instance>
```

date this. Another essential consideration is efficiency of representation, since files can quickly become very large if there are many features extracted over many subsections of many instances, particularly when features have high dimensionalities. It should also be possible to specify sparse arrays, or arrays that are missing some elements. Finally, one would ideally like feature values to be relatively human readable for debugging purposes, although this is not the most important consideration.

As mentioned above, there are four different elements that may be used to represent feature values in Feature Value files. Each of these have different strengths and weaknesses with respect to the above considerations, and are each suitable for different kinds of features. An efficient file writer may use different encodings in the same file in order to minimize file size, so each *f* clause may use any one of the four feature encoding tags, independently of what is used in any other *f* clauses. Each of the four encoding formats works as follows:

- *v:* This simple approach permits only single-value features or non-sparse feature vectors. A separate *v* element is used for each value of a feature vector, with the index of the value implied by the order in which the *v* clauses appear.

- *vj:* Arrays with any number of dimensions may be expressed using JSON array notation. JSON is a well-established and relatively human readable text-based data interchange format for representing simple data structures. JSON arrays are expressed using simple square bracket notation, which are in turn enclosed in *vj* elements in ACE XML 2.0. So, for example, a feature vector of size three consisting of the numbers one, two and three would be represented as *<vj>[1,2,3]</vj>*. JSON arrays can be nested in order to represent arrays of arbitrary dimensionality. A table with two identical rows, for example, each containing the values one, two and three would be represented as *<vj>[[1,2,3],[1,2,3]]<vj>*. A similar approach could have been achieved by using nested XML elements, but the JSON representation is standardized and more compact. There are also open source JSON libraries available in many languages that can parse JSON arrays quickly, which offloads some of the work from that would otherwise need to be performed by the ACE XML parser. A disadvantage of the JSON approach, however, is that JSON is not ideally suited to rep-

resenting sparse arrays. In addition, JSON can be less human readable than some of the alternative approaches.

- *vd:* This approach involves explicitly notating the coordinates of entries in feature arrays using ten attributes numbered *d0* to *d9*. If there is only one coordinate (i.e., a feature vector), then only the d0 attribute would be used, if there is a three-dimensional array then the d0, d1 and d2 attributes would be used, and so on. This approach is less space efficient than JSON, but can represent sparse arrays very well and is relatively human readable. There is a limitation to only ten dimensions, but each of these dimensions may be of any size, and very few features used in MIR need arrays with more than ten dimensions. Although it would be ideal to have such an approach for N dimensions, it is not possible to specify an arbitrary number of attributes in an XML DTD schema. To give an example, the *JSON* feature vector *[1,2,3]* would be represented as:

```
<vd d0="0">1</vd><vd d0="1">2</vd><vd d0="2">3</vd>
```

```
<vd d0="0" d1="0">1</vd><vd d0="0" d1="1">2</vd><vd d0="0" d1="2">3</vd>
<vd d0="1" d1="0">4</vd><vd d0="1" d1="1">5</vd><vd d0="1" d1="2">6</vd>
```

- *vs:* This final option may be used to represent arrays of any dimensionality, including sparse arrays, and is the only option with this degree of generality. Its disadvantage is that it is less concise than JSON and potentially less human readable than the other options. Each *vs* clause contains one *d* element for each dimension, and this *d* element is used to specify the coordinate value in its corresponding dimension. The dimension corresponding to a *d* element is implied by the order in which the *d* elements appear. Each *vs* clause also contains a single *v* clause to specify the feature value for the array at the corresponding coordinate. To give an example, the *JSON* feature array *[[1,2,3],[4,5,6]]* would be represented as:

```
<vs><d>0</d><d>0</d><v>1</v></vs>
<vs><d>0</d><d>1</d><v>2</v></vs>
<vs><d>0</d><d>2</d><v>3</v></vs>
<vs><d>1</d><d>0</d><v>4</v></vs>
<vs><d>1</d><d>1</d><v>5</v></vs>
<vs><d>1</d><d>2</d><v>6</v></vs>
```

Figure 5 demonstrates the use each of the four encoding formats.

Figure 5. An excerpt from an ACE XML 2.0 feature value file indicating artificial feature values for a single instance. This figure demonstrates how features of different dimensionalities can be expressed using each of the v, vd, vs, and vj tags.

```
<instance>
    <instance_id>Artificial Example</instance_id>
    <f>
        <fid>Single Value</fid>
        <v>1</v>
    </f>
    <f>
        <fid>1-D Vector</fid>
        <v>1</v>
        <v>2</v>
        <v>3</v>
    </f>
    <f>
        <fid>Another 1-D Vector</fid>
        <vd d0="0">1</vd>
        <vd d0="1">2</vd>
    </f>
    <f>
        <fid>2-D Table</fid>
        <vd d0="0" d1="0">1</vd>
        <vd d0="0" d1="1">2</vd>
        <vd d0="0" d1="2">3</vd>
        <vd d0="1" d1="0">11</vd>
        <vd d0="1" d1="1">22</vd>
        <vd d0="1" d1="2">33</vd>
    </f>
    <f>
        <fid>The Same 2-D Table</fid>
        <vs><d>0</d><d>0</d><v>1</v></vs>
        <vs><d>0</d><d>1</d><v>2</v></vs>
        <vs><d>0</d><d>2</d><v>3</v></vs>
        <vs><d>1</d><d>0</d><v>11</v></vs>
        <vs><d>1</d><d>1</d><v>22</v></vs>
        <vs><d>1</d><d>2</d><v>33</v></vs>
    </f>
    <f>
        <fid>3-D Array</fid>
        <vj>[[[[1],[2],[3],[4]],
            [[11],[22],[33],[44]],
            [[111],[222],[333],[444]]],
           [[[4],[5],[6],[7]],
            [[44],[55],[66],[77]],
            [[444],[555],[666],[777]]]]
        </vj>
    </f>
</instance>
```

It should be noted that all of these figures only indicate data for a single instance each. In practice, Feature Value files typically include data for multiple instances, with the consequence that they contain multiple instance clauses.

As noted above, it is possible to link feature values for instances stored in Feature Value files to class labels and other metadata associated with the same instances that is stored in ACE XML Instance Label files. Similarly, features extracted in Feature Value files can be linked to feature parameters and other general feature metadata stored in ACE XML Feature Description files. This can be done using matching *instance_id* and *fid* tags, respectively. Although this can certainly be helpful, Feature Value files can also stand on their own, as the ACE XML software libraries can automatically implicitly deduce information such as the dimensionality of features without Feature Definition files if needed. It can often be more efficient to store information such as feature data types in Feature Definition files, however.

ACE XML 2.0 Feature Description Files

Feature Description files are used to express abstract information about features in a way that is independent of particular feature extractions. Feature Description files do not specify actual feature values or other information related to specific instances, as this information is instead specified ACE XML Feature Value files. The Feature Description DTD is shown in Figure 6.

Feature Description files can be used to accompany associated Feature Value files in order to specify feature constraints, such as data types or dimensionalities, in a way that is more efficient than encoding this information in the Feature Value files directly. Additional useful metadata about features, such as extraction parameters, can be matched to extracted feature values by using both of these file types.

There are also many possible applications for self-contained Feature Description files. Examples include a catalogues of features that can be extracted by a particular feature extraction application, or a list of features and associated parameters that have been found to be useful for a particular research application, such as instrument classification or pitch classification.

Information on each feature is expressed in a separate *feature* clause. Each such clause can include the following information about the feature:

- *fid:* The contents of this obligatory element specify a unique identifier for the feature. This may be a simple feature name, a URI, or any other type of unique identifying string. *fid* tags are used to link feature information with corresponding extracted feature values stored in ACE XML Feature Value files.
- *description:* This optional element may be used to provide qualitative information about the feature.
- *related_feature:* This optional element can be used to specify other features that are related in some way to the feature under consideration. This could be used, for example, to note that one feature is an alternative implementation of another. Each *related_feature* clause contains an *fid* sub-clause identifying the related feature, an optional *relation_id* element that can be used to specify the nature of the relationship, optional *uri* tags to link to external resources and an optional *explanation* element to provide a qualitative description of the relationship between the features.
- *uri*
- *scope:* The parameters of this obligatory element indicate whether the feature can be extracted for an instance as a whole, for subsections of an instance or at quantized points in an instance.

Figure 6. The XML DTD for the ACE XML 2.0 feature description format

```
<!ELEMENT ace_xml_feature_description_file_2_0 (comments?,
                                                related_resources?,
                                                global_parameter*,
                                                feature+)>
<!ELEMENT comments (#PCDATA)>
<!ELEMENT related_resources (feature_value_file*,
                             feature_description_file*,
                             instance_label_file*,
                             class_ontology_file*,
                             project_file*,
                             uri*)>
<!ELEMENT feature_value_file (#PCDATA)>
<!ELEMENT feature_description_file (#PCDATA)>
<!ELEMENT instance_label_file (#PCDATA)>
<!ELEMENT class_ontology_file (#PCDATA)>
<!ELEMENT project_file (#PCDATA)>
<!ELEMENT uri (#PCDATA)>
<!ATTLIST uri predicate CDATA #IMPLIED>
<!ELEMENT feature (fid,
                   description?,
                   related_feature*,
                   uri*,
                   scope,
                   dimensionality?,
                   data_type?,
                   parameter*)>
<!ELEMENT fid (#PCDATA)>
<!ELEMENT description (#PCDATA)>
<!ELEMENT related_feature (fid,
                           relation_id?,
                           uri*,
                           explanation?)>
<!ELEMENT relation_id (#PCDATA)>
<!ELEMENT explanation (#PCDATA)>
<!ELEMENT scope (#PCDATA)>
<!ATTLIST scope overall (true|false) #REQUIRED
                sub_section (true|false) #REQUIRED
                precise_coord (true|false) #REQUIRED>
<!ELEMENT dimensionality (uri*,
                          size*)>
<!ATTLIST dimensionality orthogonal_dimensions CDATA #REQUIRED>
<!ELEMENT size (#PCDATA)>
<!ELEMENT data_type (#PCDATA)>
<!ATTLIST data_type type (int | double | float | complex | string) #REQUIRED>
<!ELEMENT global_parameter (parameter_id,
                            uri*,
                            description?,
                            value?)>
<!ELEMENT parameter (parameter_id,
                     uri*,
                     description?,
                     value?)>
<!ELEMENT parameter_id (#PCDATA)>
<!ELEMENT value (#PCDATA)>
```

- *dimensionality:* The *orthogonal_dimensions* attribute of this optional element can be used to constrain the number of orthogonal dimensions that values for this feature have (e.g., 1 for a feature vector, 2 for a table structure, etc.). The dimensionality clause can contain a separate *size* element for each such dimension that specifies the size of each of each corresponding dimension (e.g., the length of a feature vector, the number of rows and the number of columns in a table structure, etc.). *uri* clauses may also be used to link to external information. The dimensionality element should be omitted for features that vary in dimensionality, in which case the ACE XML parsing software will automatically dynamically vary the dimensionality of stored features as appropriate.
- *data_type:* The *type* parameter of this optional element makes it possible to specify whether the values of the feature are integers, doubles, floats, complex numbers, or strings. This information may also be specified directly in ACE XML Feature Value files, but Feature Description files take precedence in the case of contradictions, and represent the information more efficiently. Although data typing is not necessary for the jMIR components, it is sometimes necessary for other applications.
- *parameter:* Specific parameters may be associated with a feature, such as the roll-off point for the Spectral Roll-off feature, for example. Such parameters can significantly impact extracted feature values, so it is important that they be specified so that future feature extractions will be consistent. A separate *parameter* clause may be specified for each such parameter of a feature, and each such clause contains a *parameter_id* element specifying a unique identifier for the feature parameter, optional *uri* links for the parameter, an optional

qualitative *description* of the parameter and the numerical (or other) *value* of the parameter.

It is also possible to specify global parameters for all features in a Feature Description file using the *global_parameter* element. This is useful for specifying overall pre-processing of files before features are extracted, for example, such as down sampling or amplitude normalization. The mechanics of *global_parameter* clauses are the same as for the *parameter* clauses.

Figure 7 provides an example of how information for a single feature can be described in a Feature Description file. In practice, Feature Description files typically contain multiple *feature* clauses, not just one.

ACE XML 2.0 Instance Label Files

Instance Label files are used to specify class labels and miscellaneous metadata about instances and subsections of instances. These files are typically used to express ground truth class labels or predicted labels, but there are certainly other possible uses as well. The Instance Label DTD is shown in Figure 8.

Just as is with ACE XML Feature Value files, *instance* clauses are the fundamental units of Instance Label files. Each *instance* clause can include the following information about a particular instance as a whole:

- *instance_id:* The contents of this obligatory element specify a unique identifier for the instance. This may be a network URI, a file path, a publication number, a title, a hash code, or any other type of identifying string that is convenient, as long as it is uniquely used with reference to this instance. *instance_id* tags are used to link the information stored in Instance Label files to corresponding extracted feature values stored in ACE XML Feature Value files.

Figure 7. An excerpt from a sample ACE XMLE 2.0 feature description file indicating information about a single beat histogram feature. It is noted that this feature is related to another feature called tempo peak that can be calculated from the beat histogram feature. A URL is also provided that indicates background information on beat histograms. In terms of more technical information, it is noted that this feature is configured to only be extracted for musical files as a whole, that it consists of a single vector of size 161, that feature values are stored as doubles and that the bin values are normalized.

```
<feature>
    <fid>Beat Histogram</fid>
    <description>Tempo histogram calculated using autocorrelation</description>
    <related_feature>
        <fid>Tempo Peak</fid>
        <relation_id>derivative feature</relation_id>
    </related_feature>
    <uri predicate="reference">http://www.music-ir.org/evaluation/mirex-
                             results/articles/tempo/tzanetakis.pdf</uri>
    <scope overall="true" sub_section="false" precise_coord="false"></scope>
    <dimensionality orthogonal_dimensions="1">
        <size>161</size>
    </dimensionality>
    <data_type type="double"></data_type>
    <parameter>
        <parameter_id>normalized</parameter_id>
        <value>true</value>
    </parameter>
</feature>
```

- *role:* This optional attribute of the *instance_id* element can be used to specify whether the instance's class label is ground truth intended for classifier training, ground truth intended for classifier testing and evaluation, or a label output by a classification system.

- *misc_info:* This optional element can be used to specify miscellaneous metadata about an instance. The metadata field is identified using the *info_id* element, and the metadata itself is put in an *info* clause. *uri* elements may also be used to link to external resources.

- *related_instance:* This optional element may be used to specify a relationship of any kind between the instance and any other instance, referred to via its *instance_id*. For example, it might be noted that one musical recording is a cover of another musical recording. The *relation_id* element can be used to identify the specific kind of rela-

tionship, and the *explanation* element can be used to provide a qualitative description of the relationship. *uri* links may also be specified.

- *uri*

- *coord_units:* This optional element may be used to specify units for the coordinate values associated with the *begin, end* and *coord* attributes described below.

Each *instance* clause can also contain one of more *class* clauses specifying information about the class labels associated with the instance. Multiple classes can be specified by including multiple *class* clauses, or *class* clauses can be omitted entirely if no class labels are available. The following information may be specified within each *class* clause:

- *class_id:* This element is used to specify a unique identifier for the class. This element can be used to link to class data stored in

Figure 8. The XML DTD for the ACE XML 2.0 instance label format

```
<!ELEMENT ace_xml_instance_label_file_2_0 (comments?,
                                           related_resources?,
                                           instance+)>
<!ELEMENT comments (#PCDATA)>
<!ELEMENT related_resources (feature_value_file*,
                             feature_description_file *,
                             instance_label_file*,
                             class_ontology_file*,
                             project_file*,
                             uri*)>
<!ELEMENT feature_value_file (#PCDATA)>
<!ELEMENT feature_description_file (#PCDATA)>
<!ELEMENT instance_label_file (#PCDATA)>
<!ELEMENT class_ontology_file (#PCDATA)>
<!ELEMENT project_file (#PCDATA)>
<!ELEMENT uri (#PCDATA)>
<!ATTLIST uri predicate CDATA #IMPLIED>
<!ELEMENT instance (instance_id,
                    misc_info*,
                    related_instance*,
                    uri*,
                    coord_units?,
                    section*,
                    precise_coord*,
                    class*)>
<!ATTLIST instance role (training | testing | predicted) #IMPLIED>
<!ELEMENT instance_id (#PCDATA)>
<!ELEMENT related_instance (instance_id,
                            relation_id?,
                            uri*,
                            explanation?)>
<!ELEMENT relation_id (#PCDATA)>
<!ELEMENT explanation (#PCDATA)>
<!ELEMENT misc_info (info_id,
                     uri*,
                     info)>
<!ELEMENT info_id (#PCDATA)>
<!ELEMENT info (#PCDATA)>
<!ELEMENT coord_units (#PCDATA)>
<!ELEMENT section (uri*,
                   class+)>
<!ATTLIST section begin CDATA #REQUIRED
                  end CDATA #REQUIRED>
<!ELEMENT precise_coord (uri*,
                         class+)>
<!ATTLIST precise_coord coord CDATA #REQUIRED>
<!ELEMENT class (class_id,
                 uri*)>
<!ATTLIST class weight CDATA "1">
<!ATTLIST class source_comment CDATA #IMPLIED>
<!ELEMENT class_id (#PCDATA)>
```

ACE XML Class Ontology files that contain matching *class_ids*.
- *uri*
- *weight:* This attribute permits weighted class membership. So, for example, a given musical recording might be labeled with the Blues genre with a weight of 2 as well as with the Jazz genre with a weight of 1. Depending on context, this could mean either that the recording is a member of both

the Blues and Jazz genres, but the influence of the former is twice that of the latter, or it could mean that a classifier is unsure whether the piece is Blues or Jazz, but believes that the former label is twice as likely as the latter. If the weight attribute is not specified for a class, then it is assigned a value of 1 by default. All weight values are proportional, so the absolute value of a weight has no meaning other than its value relative to the weights of other class labels.

- *source_comment:* This optional attribute specifies the source of the class label, such as an expert human annotator's name or the name of a piece of classification software.

Each *instance* clause can also specify information about subsections of the instance, denoted with a *section* element, as well as information about quantized points within the instance, denoted with the *precise_coord* element. Both of these elements can include *class* sub-clauses that operate exactly as *class* clauses for overall instances, as well as *uri* elements. The scope of each subsection is denoted using *begin* and *end* attributes, and the coordinates of quantized points are denoted with the *coord* attribute.

Subsections can be potentially overlapping and can be of potentially varying sizes. This arrangement permits two partially overlapping regions, where each region is labeled with a different class name, and the overlapping portion is associated with both labels. Such an occasion might occur, for example, in the ground truth for a music/applause discriminator where the applause in a live performance begins before the music ends. Such a situation could be equivalently expressed as either two sections with one label each overlapping in time or as three non-overlapping consecutive sections where the outer sections have one label each and the central section has two labels.

As noted above, it is possible to link instances to ACE XML Feature Value files in order to associate class labels with feature values, or to ACE XML

Class Ontology files, in order to access information on the connections between different class labels. The former is fundamental to machine learning, and the latter enables certain powerful structured classification algorithms. Instance Label files can also be used entirely independently as well, such as, for example, as the save format used by annotation software.

Figure 9 provides an example of how information for a single instance can be described in an Instance Label file. In practice, an Instance Label file will typically contains multiple *instance* clauses, not just one.

ACE XML 2.0 Class Ontology Files

Class Ontology files can be used to specify the candidate class labels for a particular classification domain and to specify weighted ontological relationships between classes. They do not, however, specify the labels of any actual instances, as this is the domain of Instance Label files, although they can be linked to Instance Label files. The Class Ontology DTD is shown in Figure 10.

The ability to specify ontological class structuring has several important benefits. From a musicological perspective, it provides a simple machine readable way of specifying a variety of musical relationships. From a machine learning perspective, it has the dual advantages of enabling the use of potentially very powerful hierarchical classification methodologies that take advantage of this structuring (e.g., McKay, 2004) as well as the use of learning schemes utilizing weighted penalization, such that misclassifications during training into related classes are penalized less severely than misclassifications into unrelated classes.

Information on each class is expressed in a separate *class* clause. Each such clause can include the following information:

- *class_id:* This obligatory element is used to specify a unique identifier for the class.

Figure 9. An excerpt from an artificial ACE XML 2.0 instance label file indicating class labels for a MIDI file. As indicated by the role attribute, the labels are automatic classifier outputs. As indicated by the misc_info metadata, the subsections are classified by form and the overall instance is classified by composer. It can be seen that the piece has for the most part been structurally classified according to sonata form, although from the period of 505,787 ms to 515,938 the classifier is unsure whether it is a sonata recapitulation or an allegro in a symphony. The classifier is also unsure whether the piece is by Haydn or Mozart, but it believes that it is three times as likely to be by Haydn. In the context of a ground truth role, of course, such ambiguity would not be present.

```
<instance role="predicted">
    <instance_id>C:\Symbolic\piece_42.midi</instance_id>
    <misc_info>
        <info_id>Classification format</info_id>
        <info>
            Overall instances are classified by composer and
            sections are classified by form.
        </info>
    </misc_info>
    <coord_units>ms</coord_units>

    <section begin="0" end="85673">
        <class>
            <class_id>Sonata Exposition</class_id>
        </class>
    </section>
    <section begin="85674" end="278894">
        <class>
            <class_id>Sonata Development</class_id>
        </class>
    </section>
    <section begin="278895" end="525419">
        <class>
            <class_id>Sonata Recapitulation</class_id>
        </class>
    </section>
    <section begin="505787" end="515938">
        <class>
            <class_id>Symphonic Allegro</class_id>
        </class>
    </section>

    <class weight="3">
        <class_id>Haydn</class_id>
    </class>
    <class weight="1">
        <class_id>Mozart</class_id>
    </class>
</instance>
```

This element can be used to link to instances stored in ACE XML Instance Label files that are labeled with classes with matching *class_ids*.

- *uri*
- *misc_info:* This optional element may be used to specify miscellaneous metadata

about a class. The metadata field name is specified with the *info_id* element, and the metadata itself is put in an *info* clause. Links to external resources may also be made with *uri* tags.

- *related_class:* This optional element is used to specify general ontological re-

Figure 10. The XML DTD for the ACE XML 2.0 class ontology format

```
<!ELEMENT ace_xml_class_ontology_file_2_0 (comments?,
                                    related_resources?,
                                    class+)>
<!ATTLIST ace_xml_class_ontology_file_2_0 weights_relative (true|false)
                                                    #REQUIRED>
<!ELEMENT comments (#PCDATA)>
<!ELEMENT related_resources (feature_value_file*,
                             feature_description_file *,
                             instance_label_file*,
                             class_ontology_file*,
                             project_file*,
                             uri*)>
<!ELEMENT feature_value_file (#PCDATA)>
<!ELEMENT feature_description_file (#PCDATA)>
<!ELEMENT instance_label_file (#PCDATA)>
<!ELEMENT class_ontology_file (#PCDATA)>
<!ELEMENT project_file (#PCDATA)>
<!ELEMENT uri (#PCDATA)>
<!ATTLIST uri predicate CDATA #IMPLIED>
<!ELEMENT class (class_id,
                 misc_info*,
                 uri*,
                 related_class*,
                 sub_class*)>
<!ELEMENT class_id (#PCDATA)>
<!ELEMENT misc_info (info_id,
                     uri*,
                     info)>
<!ELEMENT info_id (#PCDATA)>
<!ELEMENT info (#PCDATA)>
<!ELEMENT related_class (class_id,
                         relation_id?,
                         uri*,
                         explanation?)>
<!ATTLIST related_class weight CDATA "1">
<!ELEMENT relation_id (#PCDATA)>
<!ELEMENT explanation (#PCDATA)>
<!ELEMENT sub_class (class_id,
                     relation_id?,
                     uri*,
                     explanation?)>
<!ATTLIST sub_class weight CDATA "1">
```

lationships between other classes. This relationship is unidirectional by default. Bidirectional relationships can be formed by declaring the reverse relationship in the other class' *related_class* clause.

• *sub_class:* This optional element makes it possible to specify explicitly hierarchical relationships between classes, as an alternative to the more general *related_class* approach. Classes referred to in *sub_class* clauses are hierarchically subordinate to the class from in which the *sub_class* clause is found. Tree-like structures can be built by having subordinate classes include other classes in their own *sub_class* clauses. There is no need to indicate parent classes in any way, as this relationship is implicit. *related_class* and *sub_class* clauses may each contain the following information:

- *class_id:* The identifier of the related class.
- *weight:* This attribute indicates the strength of the relationship between the classes. If the weight attribute is not specified for a class, it is assigned a value of 1 by default. Weights can be either absolute or relative, as defined by the global *weights_relative* attribute, which must be either *true* or *false*.

- *relation_id:* An optional attribute identifying the kind of relationship between the classes.
- *explanation:* An optional qualitative explanation of the inter-class relationship.
- *uri*

Figure 11 demonstrates how both hierarchical and general ontological class relationships can be

Figure 11. An excerpt from an artificial ACE XML 2.0 class ontology file indicating class labels consisting of names of blues musicians and bands. Two kinds of relationships between classes are specified, namely musicians influenced by other musicians and musicians who were members of groups. In this example, there is no relationship from Robert Johnson to the other musicians because he was not influenced by them. Both of the other musicians are influenced by Johnson, however. Clapton is more influenced by Johnson than by Muddy Waters, and Muddy Waters is slightly influenced by Clapton, as indicated by the weight values. There is also a hierarchical relationship specified between Cream and Clapton, since Clapton was a member of Cream.

```
<class>
    <class_id>Robert Johnson</class_id>
</class>

<class>
    <class_id>Muddy Waters</class_id>
    <related_class weight="10">
        <class_id>Robert Johnson</class_id>
        <relation_id>Influenced By</relation_id>
    </related_class>
    <related_class weight="1">
        <class_id>Eric Clapton</class_id>
        <relation_id>Influenced By</relation_id>
    </related_class>
</class>

<class>
    <class_id>Eric Clapton</class_id>
    <related_class weight="30">
        <class_id>Robert Johnson</class_id>
        <relation_id>Influenced By</relation_id>
    </related_class>
    <related_class weight="10">
        <class_id>Muddy Waters</class_id>
        <relation_id>Influenced By</relation_id>
    </related_class>
</class>

<class>
    <class_id>Cream</class_id>
    <sub_class>
        <class_id>Eric Clapton</class_id>
        <relation_id>Had As Member</relation_id>
    </sub_class>
</class>
```

specified, how both unidirectional and bidirectional links can be declared, and how relationship weights can be used.

ACE XML 2.0 Project Files and ZIP Files

The advantages of having four different core ACE XML formats have been made clear above. However, users in practice will often want to use multiple ACE XML files together. This can be done using *related_resources* clauses in each component file, but it would be clearer and more convenient to have an external way of specifying all of the files that are associated with any one project or application, particularly if this can be done in a way that does not compromise the reusability of the component files for entirely different projects.

The ACE XML Project file format makes this possible. This format allows users of an application such as one of the jMIR components to simply specify a single Project file, and then rely on the application to itself automatically open all of the files referred to by the Project file and update them if appropriate.

ACE XML Project files include an element corresponding to each of the four core ACE XML formats. These can be used to specify zero, one or many files of each type. The ACE XML parsing software automatically performs a data structure merge if multiple files of the same type are specified. Class Ontology files are the exception to this, since only one such file can be specified at a time because merging different ontologies can lead to significant inconsistencies if not supervised carefully. It is also possible to specify a path to a trained classification model and to a Weka ARFF file, as well as to multiple external resources via *uri* tags if desired. The Project file XML DTD is shown in Figure 12.

Although ACE XML Project files do make the combined use of multiple ACE XML files together more convenient, they are an imperfect solution on their own. Users must still maintain the individual files, and must be careful not to delete, rename, or move them without making appropriate changes in the Project file.

The ACE XML ZIP file format is a solution to these problems. This solution involves packaging related sets of ACE XML (or other) files together into a single ZIP file. This has advantages with respect to reduced maintenance and increased convenience, while retaining the advantages of having separate files. Each component file stored in an ACE XML ZIP file remains self-contained

Figure 12. The XML DTD for the ACE XML 2.0 project file format

```
<!ELEMENT ace_xml_project_file_2_0 (comments?,
                                    feature_value_id,
                                    instance_label_id,
                                    class_ontology_id,
                                    feature_description_id,
                                    weka_arff_id?,
                                    trained_model_id?,
                                    uri?)>
<!ELEMENT comments (#PCDATA)>
<!ELEMENT feature_value_id (path*)>
<!ELEMENT instance_label_id (path*)>
<!ELEMENT class_ontology_id (#PCDATA)>
<!ELEMENT feature_description_id (path*)>
<!ELEMENT weka_arff_id (#PCDATA)>
<!ELEMENT trained_model_id (#PCDATA)>
<!ELEMENT uri (path*)>
<!ATTLIST uri predicate CDATA #IMPLIED>
<!ELEMENT path (#PCDATA)>
```

and can be easily extracted from the ZIP file and used on its own or with other projects if desired.

Another significant advantage is that ZIP files are compressed formats, which means that they can dramatically reduce space and bandwidth requirements. This is significant, as ACE XML files can be quite large, particularly in cases where many windowed features are extracted from large collections of data.

jMIR's ACE libraries include a number of open-source utilities designed to facilitate the use of ACE ZIP files. Each ACE XML ZIP file is associated with an ACE XML Project file that serves as a key for accessing the files stored in the ZIP file, as well as their context. This Project file is either specified by the user upon creation of the ZIP file, in which case the associated ACE XML files are automatically added to the ZIP file when it is created, or auto-generated by the ACE XML utilities if ACE XML files are instead specified individually.

FUTURE RESEARCH DIRECTIONS

The NEMA Project

The NEMA (Networked Environment for Music Analysis) project is a multinational and multidisciplinary effort to create a general music information processing infrastructure. NEMA is funded by the Andrew W. Mellon Foundation, and involves research groups from McGill University, University of Illinois at Urbana-Champaign (UIUC), University of Southampton, University of Waikato and Goldsmiths and Queen Mary at University of London.

ACE XML 2.0 has been adopted as one of the primary technologies used in the NEMA project. Correspondingly, many of the updates from ACE XML 1.1 have resulted from the needs and excellent suggestions of various NEMA members. Particular efforts have been made to facilitate the integration of ACE XML with Music Ontology,

which is also being used by NEMA, something that enables ACE XML to be integrated into networks of musical data with a scope much greater than automatic music classification.

Future updates to ACE XML will be implemented in response to the needs of the NEMA project. Efforts will also be made to promote the use of ACE XML as a standard submission format for the yearly MIREX MIR contest run by UIUC.

Increasing the Accessibility of ACE XML

An important emphasis of future research will be on efforts to encourage and facilitate general adoption of ACE XML by the MIR community. The porting of the ACE XML processing libraries to widely used languages such as Mathworks MATLAB, C++, and Python will help to achieve this. Although the existing Java libraries can already be accessed by such languages via external calls, it is desirable to make this process even easier.

The implementation of ACE XML plug-ins for commonly used musical feature extraction and machine learning software is also planned. This has already been done with Weka and jMIR.

Another important priority is the implementation of translation and integration tools that will make it possible to access information stored in alternative file formats. This work has already begun with ARFF translation utilities and the incorporation of *uri* tags for linking to Music Ontology data, and will continue with respect to other formats.

Uses of ACE XML beyond MIR

The ACE XML file formats are designed to meet the specific needs of MIR research in automatic music classification. There is nothing about them that limits them to this specific domain, however, and they can easily be used for more general data mining applications, including ones unrelated to music.

The ACE XML formats can also be adopted for many musical applications and research domains, not just automatic music classification. Examples include general musical representation, computational musicology, computational music theory, physical audio analysis and psychological models and data. The potential of even ACE XML Class Ontology files alone with respect to outlining musical ontologies of many kinds in a standardized yet simple form is significant with respect to many of these fields.

The conception of what ACE XML features, classes and instances are can be interpreted in a very broad sense. The ability to specify feature and class information for instances as a whole, for subsections of instances and for quantized instance coordinates, as well as the ability to easily represent different types of information in parallel, make it possible to flexibly express very broad kinds of musical information. The ACE XML formats are also appropriate for dealing with essentially any type of music, including Popular, Classical and Traditional musics.

Future research will therefore include efforts to design illustrative examples of how ACE XML can be used to usefully express information outside the scope of automatic music classification. Providing examples of how ACE XML could be used to first describe symbolic scores and then encode concurrent harmonic, melodic and rhythmic theoretical analyses might be a good starting point, for example. Such an example could then be built upon by placing each such piece in the context of multiple parallel musicological ontological frameworks specifying related pieces, composers and musical movements, for example.

CONCLUSION

This chapter has emphasized the need for effective file formats for use in MIR and automatic music classification research, and has proposed a set of design guidelines for such formats. ACE XML 2.0 was presented as an implementation of these guidelines, and was described in detail. It is hoped that these guidelines in general and ACE XML in particular will help to facilitate communication and data sharing between research groups involved in the computational study of music, and correspondingly reduce wasted duplicate efforts and increase the quality of results.

REFERENCES

Amatrain, X., Arumi, P., & Ramirez, M. (2002). CLAM: Yet another library for audio and music processing? In *Proceedings of the ACM Conference on Object Oriented Programming, Systems, and Applications,* (pp. 22–23). ACM Press.

Cannam, C., Landone, C., Sandler, M., & Bello, J. P. (2006). The sonic visualiser: A visualization platform for semantic descriptors from musical signals. In *Proceedings of the International Conference on Music Information Retrieval,* (pp. 324–327). ACM.

Downie, S. (2003). Music information retrieval . In Cronin, B. (Ed.), *Annual Review of Information Science and Technology* (*Vol. 37*, pp. 295–340). Medford, NJ: Information Today.

Duda, R. O., Hart, P. E., & Stork, D. G. (2001). *Pattern classification.* New York, NY: John Wiley & Sons Inc.

Good, M. (2006). MusicXML in commercial applications. In Hewlett, W. B., & Selfridge-Field, E. (Eds.), *Music Analysis East and West* (pp. 9–20). Cambridge, MA: MIT Press.

Huron, D. (1999). *Music research using humdrum: A user's guide.* Stanford, CA: Center for Computer Assisted Research in the Humanities.

Kitahara, T. (2008). *A unified and extensible framework for developing music information processing systems.* Unpublished Manuscript.

Lacy, L. W. (2005). *OWL: Representing information using the web ontology language*. Victoria, Canada: Trafford Publishing.

McKay, C. (2004). *Automatic genre classification of MIDI recordings*. (M.A. Thesis). McGill University. Montreal, Canada.

McKay, C., Fiebrink, R., McEnnis, D., Li, B., & Fujinaga, I. (2005). ACE: A framework for optimizing music classification. In *Proceedings of the International Conference on Music Information Retrieval*, (pp. 42–49). ACM.

McKay, C., & Fujinaga, I. (2012). jMIR: Tools for automatic music classification. In *Proceedings of the International Computer Music Conference*. ACM.

Mierswa, I., Wurst, M., Klinkenberg, R., Scholzn, M., & Euler, T. (2006). YALE: Rapid prototyping for complex data mining tasks. In *Proceedings of the ACM SIGKDD International Conference on Knowledge Discovery and Data Mining*, (pp. 935–940). ACM Press.

Powers, S. (2003). *Practical RDF*. Sebastopol, CA: O'Reilly Media.

Raimond, Y., Adbdallah, S., Sandler, M., & Giasson, F. (2007). The music ontology. In *Proceedings of the International Conference on Music Information Retrieval*, (pp. 417–422). ACM.

Ray, E. T. (2003). *Learning XML*. Sebastopol, CA: O'Reilly Media.

Schwarz, D., & Wright, M. (2000). Extensions and applications of the SDIF sound description interchange format. In *Proceedings of the International Computer Music Conference*, (pp. 481–484). ACM.

Tzanetakis, G., & Cook, P. (2000). Marsyas: A framework for audio analysis. *Organized Sound*, *4*(3), 169–175. doi:10.1017/S1355771800003071

Witten, I. H., & Frank, E. (2005). *Data mining: Practical machine learning tools and techniques*. New York, NY: Morgan Kaufman.

Chapter 4
Towards an Encoding of Musical Interaction

Antoine Allombert
University of Bordeaux, France

Myriam Desainte-Catherine
University of Bordeaux, France

ABSTRACT

While representing musical processes or musical scores through Markup Languages is now well established, the authors assume that there is still the need for a format to encode musical material with which a musician can interact. The lack of such a format is especially crucial for contemporary music that involves computing processes. They propose such a formal representation for composing musical scores in which some temporal properties can be interactively modified during their execution. This allows the creation of scores that can be interpreted by a performer in the same way a musician can interpret a score of instrumental music. The formal representation comes with an XML format for encoding the scores and also interfacing the representation with other types of Markup Language musical description.

INTRODUCTION

As contemporary music involves more and more signal processing during the compositional process and more and more interaction during the performance, the notions of interpretation and consequently of scores are in complete mutation. The musical material of such interactive musical pieces is often represented by samples, signal processing programs as well as temporal information often represented as cue-lists. Obviously, such

material cannot be qualified as a score for several reasons. Firstly, a score is written by a composer for the musician to interpret. The score contains musical information as well as instructions for the musician. Secondly, a score is based on an abstract notation that does not describe the resulting music in detail. The only information presented to the musician is: instrument, pitches, volumes, dates and durations of the notes. A score never describes, as a signal processing program, how the sound is produced by the instrument. As a consequence, the notions of score and interpretation need to be formalized in this new context.

DOI: 10.4018/978-1-4666-2497-9.ch004

Let us imagine for a moment what a score for contemporary electro-acoustic music consists of. For instrumental scores, it should contain a description of the instrument. Because computer music instrument are often part of the creation of a musical piece, such a description cannot be limited to a label but it should provide information about sets of samples, sound synthesis, and processing functions. It should also contain a temporal organization of musical events. Some of those events are musician gestures controlling sound synthesis or triggering samples, and others are synthesized sound automatically played by the computer. Moreover, such scores should display the musician gestures in a readable way according to a convenient symbolic notation and following a left to right temporal ordering.

The question that is raised concerns the nature of the link that should bind this kind of score and the usual musical material, which lies in the core of the computer during performance. By contrast with a paper score, a numeric score has the property to be an executable document. Moreover, by contrast with a paper score, which is physically separated from the instrument, a numeric score lies in the computer as well as the musical material composing the piece. As a consequence, this document should ideally be used on the one hand by the musician to execute the gestures that are provided by the score, and on the other hand by the computer to acquire the gestures information according to the temporal organization of the score and execute the corresponding signal processing programs during performance.

To complete this introduction, let us imagine how interpretation of contemporary music should be defined and formalized. Taking interpretation of instrumental pieces as an example, a performer would be able to control dates and durations of the musical events as well as sound and musical parameters in some limits given by the composer. As a consequence, the execution of a score, instead of being read in a deterministic way, should provide the musician with all the interpretation choices

specified by the composer. Thus, a musical piece can be seen as a set of interpretations defined by a composer and among which the musician makes his choice.

To reach this objective, we introduce the notion of Interactive Scores. Objectives are written by the composer and they can also be performed and executed by the musicians. These interactive scores are based on a temporal formalism allowing the performers to control the dates and the durations of the musical events as in a traditional score, according to the freedom that the composer has given to them. We aim at creating a system, including an environment of assisted composition that allows the composers to create interactive scores, and an execution machine used by the performers in order to interpret the scores. We have already developed part of such a system that we called Iscore (Allombert, et al., 2007).

The Iscore system needs a backup format to encode the scores that are created with it. We address this issue with a transcription of the formalism into an XML format. More than a simple backup copy system, the Iscore-XML format can be applied to the more general representation of pieces of music allowing interaction. This is the point of view that we take here.

First, we present the abstract formalism of interactive scores. Then we explain why a specific format to encode them is needed, while one can find similarities with existing formats for multimedia documents. Finally, we show some applications of this format that we have developed, and imagine some perspectives of research and use.

BACKGROUND

As stated, our model of interactive scores was introduced to answer the question of the interpretation in electro-acoustic music context. Indeed, this question remains widely open (Dahan, et al., 2008) since the pieces of this type of music are supportive, and the possibilities to interact with them during execution are very limited. To develop these possibilities, we base our approach upon a formalization of interpretation in the context of instrumental music, developed by Jean Haury (2012). He identifies four ways for an instrumentalist to interpret a piece of music:

- **Dynamic Variations:** i.e. continuous variations of the volume
- **Accentuation:** Which consists in locally modifying the volume of some notes
- **Articulation:** i.e. the way the musician will bind successive notes
- **Agogic Modifications:** Which are the temporal delays or anticipations on the beginning and end of notes compare to what is written on the score

Haury shows that in addition to these liberties given to the musician, the composer defines a frame to enclose them, to guide the performer during the execution and to prevent him from misrepresenting the meaning of the score. In the case of instrumental music, these limits are expressed with some guidelines put on the score. Each one of the interpretations can be enclosed by the composer with explicit indications. For example, the dynamic variations will be guided by information of volume such as *piano*, *forte*, etc. The musician will also find some linking symbols that gather groups of notes that must be played in the same phrase, in order to design the articulation of the score. Regarding the agogic variations, the composer can give an informative value for the tempo, which in fact allows for a range of possible values around this nominal value, and he indicates the possible variations during the execution: continuous variations by modifying the global tempo (*accelerando*) and local variations on a single note (*fermata*).

In summary, this formalization of interpretation in instrumental music shows that the system of classical notation gives to the musician the liberty to move away from the exact reproduction of the score, but also includes specific indications to limit the distance between the performance and the reference of the score. As a consequence, a score does not represent a unique execution, but a (possibly wide) set of executions, or more precisely, a restricted space of executions, delimited by the indications of the composer. Under this approach, an interpretation can be considered as a particular exploration of this space.

In the design for the system *Iscore*, we only considered the agogic variations and restrict the interaction to discrete controls. In the context of instrumental music, this type of interaction corresponds to modifying the date of the beginning or the end of some notes. The composer can explicitly define which notes he allows to be modified. He can include a group of notes in a tempo modification which implies changes to the beginnings and ends of these notes (delay in case a of slow down, anticipation in case of an acceleration), or he can add a *fermata*, which allows the musician to delay or to anticipate the end of a single note or *pause*. In this last case, the temporal variation of the end of the pause can be considered as a variation of the beginning of the note that follows the pause. To qualify the beginnings and ends of note, which can be modified during the execution, Haury introduces the notion of *interaction points*. An interaction point represents the possibility for the musician to trigger a note beginning or end, at a different time from what is written on the score. A period of tempo change corresponds to a set of interaction points, while a fermata corresponds to a single one. As we can see, like the other ways of interpretation, the agogic variations are closely defined by the composer. However, a large part of the frame limiting these variations is implicit and relies on a set of *temporal relations* between the *time intervals* of the score.

Time Intervals

To explain the notion of time interval, we have to define the notion of events.

Definition: *An event within a score is either the beginning or the end of a note within that score.*

A time interval is associated to any couple of events. Naturally, a note or a pause corresponds to the time-interval between its beginning and its end, but it is possible to define an interval between two events taken in the score. In addition, it is possible to evaluate the time interval by introducing *date* functions over the events of the score. These date functions are expressed by using the beginning of the score as the time origin. There are two date functions:

- The logical date function (*lo-date*) expressed in beats.
- The real date function (*re-date*) expressed in seconds.

During the execution, there will be a mapping between the logical time (expressed in beats) and the real time (expressed in seconds). Without any interaction from the performer, this mapping is totally determined by the value of the tempo, which sets the value of a beat expressed in seconds.

The value of the time interval defined between an event e1 and an event e2 is then the difference between their dates. As there are two date functions, there are two possible values for a time interval.

Definition: *For e1 and e2, two events of the score, the time interval defined between them, its two values are defined as following:*

$$lo\text{-}val(I) = lo\text{-}date(e2) - lo\text{-}date(e1)$$

$$re\text{-}val(I) = re\text{-}date(e2) - re\text{-}date(e1)$$

Without any interaction, we can see that there is a proportional relation between the two values of an interval:

Propriety: Let r(t) be the ratio between logical-time and real-time defined by a given tempo t, and I a temporal interval of the score:

$$re\text{-}date(I) = r(t).lo\text{-}date(I)$$

As we can see, the interpretation limits fixed by the composer on the tempo of a score, lead to a limitation of the possible values of time intervals of the score. Of course, the interaction of the performer leads to change the mapping between the logical time and the real time. But in the case of a tempo change, since the possible values of the tempo are given, the possible values of the time intervals remain under the control of the composer. A *fermata* is a quite particular case since it corresponds to a local change of the value to an interval, out of the influence of the tempo. In general, the expression by the composer of limits upon the agogic modifications leads to limitations on the values of time intervals of the score.

Temporal Relations

Another important part of the frame, which constrains the agogic variations, is mostly implicit and consists in temporal relations between the events of a score. The presence of such relations can be understood by noticing that events, which define a time interval, can be involved in other time intervals of the score. For example, when describing the effect of a fermata, we showed that a variation of the end of a pause *p* can be considered as a variation of the beginning of the note *n* which follows *p*. This means that the interval corresponding to *n* (*I(n)*) is bound to a time interval corresponding to *p (I(p))*. This link can be interpreted by the fact that the end of *I(p)* coincides with the beginning of *I(n)*. One can see that these links between the time intervals define an partial order between the events of the score.

In fact, this partial order between the events depends on the articulation of the score by the performer. For a given articulation strategy of the score, a set of relations between the time intervals can be deduced. As example, we now present an example taken from an instrumental piece, and deduce from it some temporal relations between its events.

Figure 1. A bar extracted from the Rhapsody in Blue by George Gershwin. There are several directives by the composer: a range of values for the tempo and also a trill indication. In addition, there are two fermatas.

A Case Study

In Figure 1, we present one bar taken from the *Rhapsody in Blue* by George Gershwin. In this example, we find different instructions from the composer to the performer. First, one can notice the term "*molto moderato*" which indicates a medium tempo. An acceptable range tempo may range from 80 bpm to 100 bpm. This range, limits the possible values for the tempo. In addition, we can find two fermatas that allow the musician to choose the value of *re-date* for the end of the notes which are controlled by a fermata. One is on the first note of the first triplet of the melody - it allows the musician to delay the end of this note. Introducing a variation on the *re-date* of this note will lead to change the *re-date* of the end of the bar. Since there is a second voice whose end has to be synchronized with the end of the first voice, one can find another fermata on the whole notes of the bass chord. Thanks to this fermata, the musician can change the *re-date* of the end of these notes to follow the voice of the melody.

One can empirically demonstrate why a delay on the first note of the triplet will automatically delay the end of the bar. We can also formally express the reason for such a phenomenon by exhibiting the implicit temporal relations between the events of the score. To show these relations, we present in Figures 2, 3, and 4 three possible mappings of the logical time of the score into the real time referential. In each of these pictures, we present the notes of the bar as a time segment between the real date of its beginning and the real date of its end. In addition, we represent on a time line, the real dates of the events as a sorted list. We use in the three s, the following notations:

- The real date of the beginning of a note *n* (*re-date(start(n))*) is denoted by *ds(n)*.
- The real date of the end of a note *n* (*re-date(end(n))*) is denoted by *de(n)*.

Figure 2 depicts a non-interpreted mapping between the logical time and the real one. The real dates of the events are proportionally computed from the logical ones by a conversion with a given ratio, which is supposed to be in the range of values imposed by the composer. This mapping can be seen as a direct representation of the logical dates with the tempo used as a scale between the two time frames.

As a consequence, the events which share the same logical date (i.e. they appear on the same beat) also share the same real date. This mapping is an ideal one and is widely non-realistic. It may even be said that it is esthetically irrelevant.

The mapping presented in Figure 3 is closer to what could be produced by a musician. We suppose here that the performer plays the first part of

Figure 2. A mapping between the logical time and the real time for the bar of Rhapsody in Blue. In this example, there is no interpretation. The mapping is a proportional computation from the logical dates to the real ones.

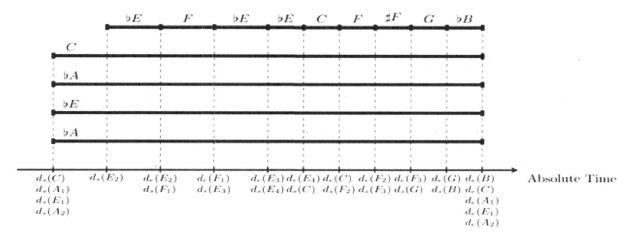

Figure 3. A mapping between the logical time and the real time for the bar of Rhapsody in Blue. In this example, the first part of the bar is interpreted "staccato." This means that the notes of the first part are temporally detached. The second part is played "legato," this means that if a note B follows a note A, then A and B overlap in the real time.

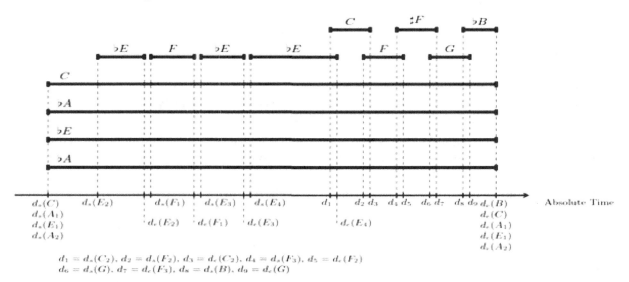

the bar "*staccato*." This means that he separates the notes of the melody and then introduces an interval of silence between the end of a note and the beginning of the one which follows it.

We also suppose that the second part of the bar is played "*legato*." In this type of interpretation, the notes are bounded and we can notice a short period of overlapping between a note and the

Figure 4. A mapping between logical time and the real time for the bar of Rhapsody in Blue. In this example, the choices of interpretation are the same in the example of Figure 3, but the musician changes the tempo and sets a faster tempo for the first part, and a slower tempo for the second part.

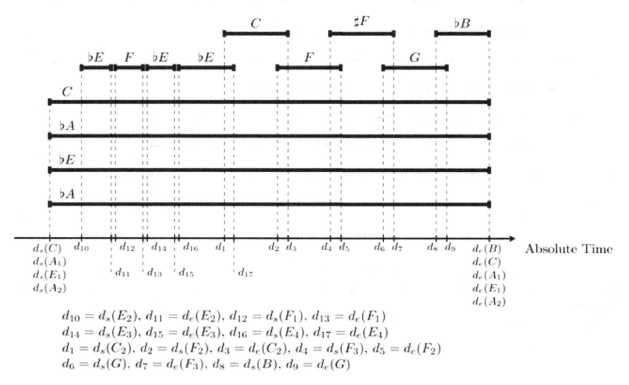

note, which follows it. In addition, the musician takes benefits of the fermata on the first note of the triplet. He makes this note lasting more than what one could expect in regard of the tempo.

We can notice that in this second example, some relations between the dates of notes found on the first example are no more respected. In the case of a note B that follows a note A, we have the relation:

$$lo\text{-}date(end(A)) = lo\text{-}date(start(B))$$

but in the mapping of Figure 3:

$$re\text{-}date(end(A)) \neq re\text{-}date(start(B))$$

However, we can notice some temporal relations between the events of the score, which are permanently respected.

First, we can identify what we call the *coherence* constraints. This type of constraint denotes the fact that the date of the beginning of a note must appear before the date of the end of the note.

Propriety: *Let n be a note,*

$$re\text{-}date(start(n)) \leq re\text{-}date(end(n))$$

Secondly, when a note B follows a note A we can deduce a relation between the real dates of the beginnings of these two notes.

Propriety: *Let A and B be two notes,*

$$(lo\text{-}date(end(A)) = lo\text{-}date(start(B)) \Rightarrow (re\text{-}date(start(A)) \leq re\text{-}date(start(B)))$$

The relations between the real dates of the ends of the notes depends on the choice of interpretation made by the musician. This propriety led

Jean Haury to conclude that the interpretation of a score deals only with the ends of the notes.

Other relations can be found in most cases, such as the one, which denotes the fact that two notes which are written to start on the same beat, always begin at the same real date.

Propriety: *Let A and B be two notes,*

(lo-date(start(A)) = lo-date(start(B)) ⇒ (re-date(start(A)) = re-date(start(B)))

One can find an exception to this property in the specific case of the "melody lead." This is a particular type of interpretation used by pianists. In such cases, the musician does not synchronize his two hands at some moment but introduces a short delay (30ms) between the melody and the chords (Palmer, 1996).

However, we do not want to list all the relations that could exist between the events of a score, but rather to focus on the bindings between the events that they introduce. These relations are limited to the notes we presented. Indeed, by considering the relations, which we presented, and some transitivity rules, one can deduce some temporal relations between events, which are "far from each other" in the score. This is why we can talk about a framework defined by all these relations.

After presenting some relations between the dates, we want to focus on some constraints on the time intervals. We present on Figure 4 another mapping for the Rhapsody in Blue bar, in which we suppose the musician chooses the same interpretation styles than the ones in Figure 3: "*staccato*" in the first part and "*legato*" in the second one. However, we also suppose that he plays these two parts with different tempi. Precisely, he plays the first part faster than in the previous example, and the second part slower. Let us denote by *r1* and *r2* this two tempi. Since the composer indicates a range of possible values for the tempo, r1 and r2 with respect to this limitation:

$$80 \le r1 \le 100$$

$$80 \le r2 \le 100$$

We explained before that, "without an interpretation by the musician," for an interval *I* and a ration *r* associated to a given tempo, we introduce the equation:

$$re\text{-}val(I)=r.lo\text{-}val(I)$$

In the example of Figure 4, we can find intervals with no modification due to interpretation between the start of two following notes. For example, the first two notes of the melody *(bE* and *F)*. With *I = start(F) – start(bE),* we have:

$$lo\text{-}val(I)=1$$

since there is one beat between these two events. And then:

$$1/100 \le re\text{-}val(I) \le 1/80$$

This illustrates the fact that the instructions of a composer impose constraints on the values of the time intervals.

The important thing to notice in this background presentation is the way in which a composer can specify how a performer can interactively interpret the information of the score, in the context of instrumental music, and at the same time, how the composer can limit the liberties of the performer. Secondly, by describing a score in terms of events, time intervals and binds between them, allow us to deduce some constraints from the composer's indications. The word constraint must be understood here in the sense of computer science: a relation between the value of some variables that must be satisfied. Here the variables are the real dates of the events and the real values of the interval. With this point of view, we can formalize why the delay on the first of the triplet will delay the end of the bar. When a modification of the value of a variable leads to invalidate a constraint (i.e. the relation between the variables is no more respected), new values are found for the variables, in order to satisfy the relation. Since the end of a note must occur before the end of the bar, delaying the end of the first note of the triplet implies to delay the end bar to keep the relation satisfied. This approach using events, dates, and constraints is the one we adopt for our formalism of interactive scores.

FORMALISM OF INTERACTIVE SCORES

The formalism that we built is a generalization of the Haury's model of interpretation. Since we are interested in the representation of electro-acoustic music, the notions of pitch or rhythm are not relevant. However, we base our vision of interpretation upon the definition by the composer

of a temporal framework by defining temporal constraints between the events of the score.

In the context of electro-acoustic music, the question of the representation of the scores is crucial; the theoretical representation (structures involved in the logical representation) as well as the graphical representation. For both representations, we base our formalism upon the environments of computer assisted composition *Boxes* (Beurivé, 2000) and the OpenMusic Maquettes (Assayag, et al., 1999). Both allow the creation of pieces seen as temporal organizations of "out-of-time" elements. As the pieces are not necessarily tonal or rhythmic, the musical elements which constitute the scores are represented as boxes placed over an horizontal time-line, while the vertical axis has no specific meaning. Figure 5 presents a score in the *Boxes* environment.

In addition, there is the possibility to hierarchically organize the scores by including some elements into others. A box that contains other ones represents a sub-part of the score with its own

Figure 5. A screen shot of the computation environment boxes

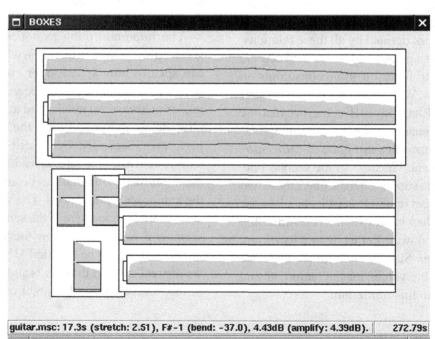

Figure 6. The Allen relations

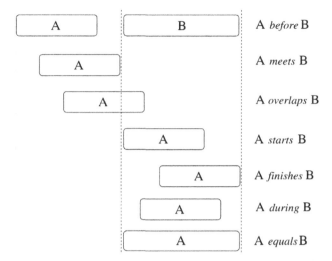

temporal reference whose time-origin coincides with the beginning of the box.

We base the system of interactive scores on the same time model. The elements of the scores that we call *temporal objects* denote the executions of processes, which bear the musical content of the scores. Thiese processes are supposed to be "out-of-time" elements that are put in "time" through the objects of the scores. As we did with the instrumental music, we denote by "events" the beginnings and the ends of the temporal objects. We add to this model a set of temporal relations, which are defined between the events of the score. Since the scores do not necessarily represent rhythmic music, they do not contain as much implicit temporal relations as the instrumental scores. In fact, the only type of implicit relations in the interactive scores is the "coherence" relations, which impose that the end of an object must occur after its beginning. The other temporal relations must be explicitly defined by the composer, and they are seen as a compositional organization of the time. We add to the time model, a set of temporal relations that can be used by the composer.

We choose Allen relations as such a set of relations (Allen, 1983). These relations have

been introduced by J. F. Allen in 1983 to describe the temporal relative organization of two events with non-zero duration. As a linguist, he used them to analyze the temporal information given in a conversation, and deduce implicit relations between events, thanks to transitivity rules. Allen relations are presented on Figure 6.

Since their introduction, these relations have been used in several fields of computer science, especially in artificial intelligence and the specific topic of temporal information maintenance. However, they also spread through other fields. We aim at using them as imperative constraints between the objects of the scores. By introducing a temporal relation between two objects, the composer tells the system that he wants this temporal constraint to be always maintained. The system has the charge to maintain it during the edition of the score, when the composer modifies the score. The system must also maintain it during the performance, since the relation constitutes a limit of the interpretation liberties. By introducing some Allen relations in the score, the composer will define the temporal framework for the interpretation

Figure 7 presents an example of such a score. It is constituted by a main structure (*S1*) which

Figure 7. An example of an interactive score

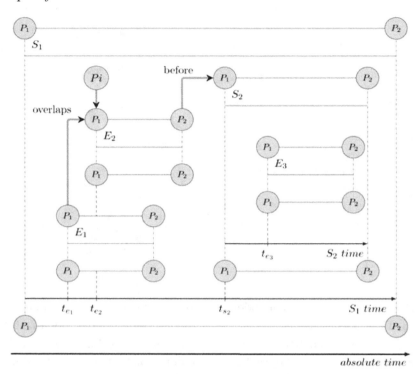

contains 3 objects: two simple objects representing the execution of processes (*E1* and *E2*) and a structure (*S2*) which contains a simple object (*E3*). Each structure defines its own time-line and the dates of beginning and end of the objects are defined relatively to the beginning of the structure which owns them. Finally, the composer defines an *overlap* and a *before* Allen relation.

Interaction Points

In addition, we propose that the composer adds some interaction points, which allows the performer to dynamically trigger some events of the score during the performance. When an interaction point is defined, the written score represents one proposition of execution among an infinity of others. The written score has the same status as in the case of instrumental music. It represents logical values for the dates of the events of the score. When a musician plays the score, he makes

a mapping between this logical time and the real one. The interaction points allow the musician to introduce some modifications into this mapping. Naturally, the temporal relations defined in the score limit the possibilities of modification and the system must keep the relations satisfied during the execution. This means that the system will recompute values for the real dates of the events when the value of one of them is modified by the musician. Formally, during the execution of a score, the system executes a constraints satisfaction algorithm. The variables are the real dates of the events while the constraints are inequalities between them, imposed by the Allen relations. Before the beginning of the performance, each variable is assigned a value that corresponds to a direct mapping from the logical time to the real time, such as the one presented on Figure 2. These values are not definitive ones, and will be accepted during the performance if no modifications are performed by the musician. In the example of

Figure 7, the beginning of the object *E2* is set dynamic with an interaction point *Pi*.

While the score is executed, more and more variables are definitively assigned. For the *static* events (not controlled by an interaction point), if no modification made by musician has an impact on them, they are assigned with their predefined values.

For the *dynamic* events (those controlled by an interaction point), they are assigned with the real date when the musician triggers the interaction point. This date has a great chance to be different from the predefined value.

Suppose now that the value assigned to a dynamic event through an interaction point, breaks some constraints, which involve the modified date. Since the date of the dynamic event cannot be modified, the system must compute new values for the other dates to maintain the constraints. Of

course, the system cannot compute new values for the dates that have already been definitively assigned. This would be like trying to change the past. Then the system only modifies the future, i.e. the dates, which have not been definitively assigned. One can notice that modifying the value of some dates to maintain a constraint could lead to break other constraints. That is why the system globally resolves the constraints problem. A modification introduced by an interaction point can then be propagated far in the future from the dynamic event.

Figure 8 presents a mapping for the score of Figure 7 where the interaction points have been delayed. As a consequence, other dates have been changed to respect the Allen relations defined by the composer and the coherence relations.

Figure 8. A mapping between the logical time into the real time for the score of Figure 7. In this mapping, the interaction point has been delayed.

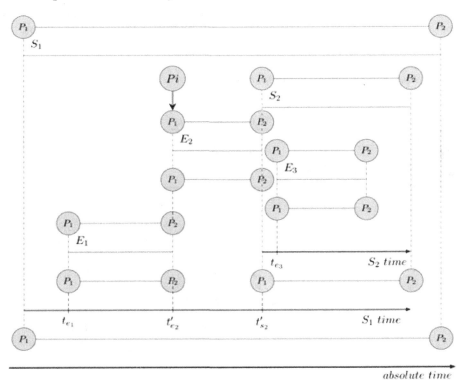

Implementation

We developed several implementations for the *Is-core* system. The most complete one takes place in the *Maquettes* environment of *OpenMusic*. Since the time model of our formalism is the same as the one used in the *Maquettes*, we introduced in this composition environment the possibility to define Allen relations between the objects and to set some events dynamic. The main limitation of this implementation is that the hierarchy is limited to one level. There is a root structure and all the objects are children of this root.

The temporal relations must be satisfied all the time, even during the edition phase of the score. We use a constraints satisfaction library called *Gecode* (Schulte, et al., 2005) to maintain the constraints during the edition.

In Figure 9, we present a screenshot of this environment while the user is defining an Allen relation between two objects.

For its execution, we use a model based on Petri nets (Diaz, 2008) to prevent the system from heavy real-time computation.

Since we are not interested in the operations performed by the processes involved in the scores, we use external applications to produce the sound material of the pieces. The processes defined in these applications are supposed to accept duration modifications. The execution of the processes is controlled by messages sent by the system during the execution of a score. We only control the beginning and the end of a process, then each object is associated with two messages: one sent when the object starts and one when it ends. We use the OSC (Open Sound Control—http://www.opensoundcontrol.org) protocol for the communication between *Iscore* and the other applications. When an interaction point is defined, during the execution the point is controlled by the reception of an OSC message.

We present the architecture of the system in Figure 10. Here, we suppose that the composer uses the application Max-MSP to synthesize the sounds of the piece. *Iscore* triggers the events of the score but has no action during the execution of the processes. However, it possible to control some parameters of the processes directly in the application which executes them.

Figure 9. A screen shot of the Maquettes in OpenMusic

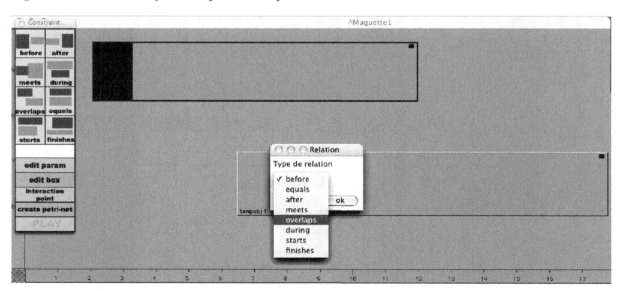

Figure 10. The diagram of an example of using Iscore with Max MSP

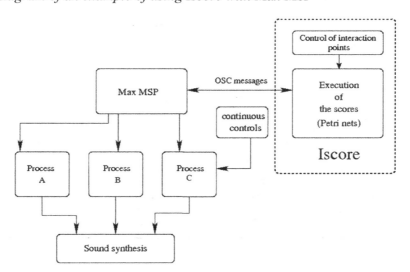

For this implementation, we need a file format to save the works of the composers. We decided to create an XML format because of the existence of several implementations that will use this format, so we created a DTD for our application. However, one could ask why we did not use an existing XML format.

EXISTING FORMATS

The scores we manipulate in our formalism and encode in our format are constituted by musical elements organized in time, bound with temporal relations defined between them, with some events set as dynamic. By some aspects, an interactive score is then comparable to a multimedia document. This approach questions the necessity of a specific format for encoding the scores. Indeed, different formats have arisen with the development of applications manipulating this type of documents. After the appearing of proprietary formats from particular applications (QuickTime, 1991), some tried to standardize this type of format. The most important ones are certainly Hytime (1992) and SMIL (2008) which are both SGML formats as is Iscore-XML. They show some possibilities to specify temporal constraints between their elements, and also a way to specify interactive behaviors. Erfle (1993) shows how it is possible to use the relative dates system of Hytime, and its HyOp and HyFunk to specify some Allen relations between the elements of the document, or to define some temporal constraints based on arithmetic expressions and then, to force a time interval to have a constant value. Erfle presents some cases of simple interaction, as well as an interesting study on the possibility of some current formats, regarding the interaction. Wirag *et al.* (1995) use the same HyTime format to create documents which accept more elaborate interaction, such as jumps between different parts of the document, or choices between different executions of the document. These articles constitute important efforts to formalize the way a creator can "write" the time of a multimedia document, and the ways a user can interact with it during the execution of the document. Nevertheless, even if this approach seems to show many similarities between general multimedia documents and our specification of interactive scores, they present such a specificity in their description and the way a musician can interact with them, that they need a specific format to encode them.

Figure 11. An example of an interactive score created with OpenMusic

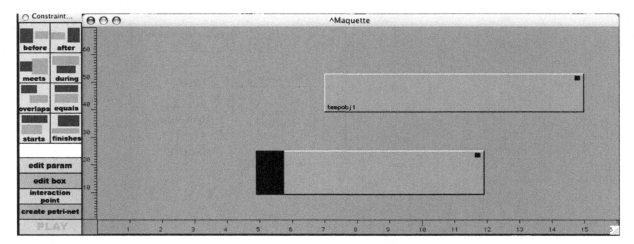

XML FORMAT

In our approach, the first version of an XML application is designed for saving the interactive scores created with *Iscore*. The DTD of the format is then a direct adaptation of the formalism and is linked to the architecture of the system implemented in *OpenMusic*. As a consequence, the processes are encoded as two OSC messages, the start message and the end message.

We now present an example of a file of an encoded score. The file corresponds to the score presented in Figure 11.

In this example, two objects are linked with an *overlaps* relation. The upper one is called *tempbj1* while the lower one is called *tempobj*. The beginning of the object called *tempobj* is set dynamically with an interaction point.

The file associated with this score is shown in Algorithm 1.

The element <score> represents the root of the score. Information about the piece and the composer are given in a header. The element <applications> encodes information about the external applications used by the score, those to which the system sends OSC messages. In our example, only one application has been defined as: *Pure Data*. The file contains information about the network address of the applications, which permit-

ted to communicate with it. Following this there is the list of the temporal objects of the score. For each of them, we encode a name and information for the graphical representation. Temporal information is also given, the date of the beginning is given in the time reference of the parent structure of the box - this information is encoded into the markup <start-date>, while the duration of the box is given with the element <duration>. The application which executes the process associated to a box is encoded with a key defined in the markup of the application. Knowing the application which executes the process allows the system to send the OSC messages which controls the process. These OSC messages are of course encoded in the elements <start-message> and <end-message>. If the beginning or the end of an object is set to be dynamic, the associated interaction point is encoded in the markup of the box. In our example, the beginning of the object "tempobj" is set dynamic. Since in the system implemented in OpenMusic the interaction points are triggered through the reception of OSC messages, the message associated with an interaction point is declared with the element <control-message>. The Allen relations defined between the objects are encoded after the objects. Finally, the listening port of the system is encoded in the element <receiving-port>.

Algorithm 1. File associated with the score

```
<!DOCTYPE iscore SYSTEM "iscore.dtd">
<score>
 <title>
  Girl
 </title>
 <composer>
  Hooray Henrys
 </composer>
 <date>
  Today
 </date>
<applications>
  <application id="app1">
   <name>
    Pure Data
   </name>
   <ip>
    127.0.0.1
   </ip>
   <port>
    3000
   </port>
  </application>
 </applications>
<boxes>
  <box id="bx1" name="tempobj1"
              id-application="app1"
              start-date="7000"
              duration="8000"
              posy="53"
              height="14">
   <start-message>
    /note-1/start
   </start-message>
   <end-message>
    /note-1/stop
   </end-message>
   <interaction-points>
   </interaction-points>
  </box>
  <box id="bx2" name="tempobj"
              id-application="app1"
```

Algorithm 1. Continued

```
              start-date="5000"
              duration="7000"
              posy="77"
              height="13">
   <start-message>
    /note-1/start
   </start-message>
   <end-message>
    /note-2/stop
   </end-message>
   <interaction-points>
    <interaction-point event="0">
     <control-message>
      /control
     </control-message>
    </interaction-point>
   </interaction-points>
  </box>

 <allen-relations>
  <allen-relation type="overlaps">
   <motherbox>
    bx2
   </motherbox>
   <childbox>
    bx1
   </childbox>
  </allen-relation>
 </allen-relations>

<osc-receiving-port>
  1999
 </osc-receiving-port>
</score>
```

95

This version remains simple and is designed to encode basic scores. This simplicity of the scores might lead one to think that the documents which we encode are generic multimedia documents. But since the formalism is based on a model of musical interpretation and aims to represent musical pieces, the evolutions of the formalism and the format will specify them for musical documents. Nevertheless, we are involved in a research project for adapting our formalism (called *Virage)* for the theater. Stage managers in live theatre use more and more computer tools to control numerical content (video, sounds, light shows, etc.). They need to organize events in time and interactively control the execution of the processes to follow. The solution we propose for music can be adapted to the way of writing and executing the multimedia scenarios involved in theater shows. However, we have insisted on the fact that our formalism is specific to musical interaction for the interpretation of written pieces.

APPLICATIONS

The main application for the system *Iscore* is naturally the composition and the interpretation of electro-acoustic pieces. Some experiments were done with composers.

Beyond this direct application, several other ones can be imagine. One important application is a playback system that could follow a musician. The system has the charge to play an accompaniment which could be synchronized with the playing of the musician through interaction points. For this application, the score executed by the system would be transcriptions of some instrumental scores. A transcription of a score by hand would be very tedious. It consists in creating a temporal object for each note and adding temporal relations between them deduced from the rhythm of the score. We are trying to develop a system of automatic transcription. This functionality is based upon the XML format of the interactive

scores. The facilities for developing conversion systems between different XML formats make it possible. Here we try to make a conversion from MusicXML files into Iscore-XML files. Such a conversion must perform the operations explained above. The main difficulty for this conversion is to deduce to temporal relations from the classical description. We started to develop such a module and found some encouraging test results.

Another application is in the pedagogical field. This would allow people who do not have enough skills to nevertheless play a piece and to experiment with the possibilities of interpretation of the piece. For such an application, an interactive score could be adapted to the skill of the musician by modulating the number of interaction points. The more skillful the player is, the more interaction there could be. This is suitable for novice musicians or even non-musicians. This application could also offer the possibility for physically handicapped people who cannot manipulate classical instruments to be able to interact with compositions. For such an application, an automatic conversion from a format such as MusicXML would be important.

PERSPECTIVES

We have several plans to develop and extend the system and its applications. First we are developing the formalism of interactive score to introduce more complex strategies of adaptation to a modification from an interaction point. Some of these strategies are inspired by instrumental music (tempo change, rubato) while others are novel approaches. We also want to introduce the possibility to define loops on objects and pieces with multiple ways of execution.

Concerning the format, we are of the opinion that making the system evolve with the formalism could lead to a general format to encode musical pieces. In fact, the computer representation of pieces of electro-acoustic music or even contemporary music is more complicated than pieces of instrumental music. A more developed formalism could be the base of a general way to represent musical pieces. This type of representation becomes crucial since people do not know how to preserve the starting points of interactive electronic music snippets. This problem mainly results from the fast obsolescence of machines and software. A general format such as the one we propose could be the basis for representing the pieces in ways not linked to particular hardware or a software.

To reach such a goal, different steps have to be achieved. The power of musical expression of the formalism must be increased in the manner suggested. We also have to find a way to represent the processes, which are involved in the pieces. We plan to use some existing formalisms and formats for this part. In fact, some work is required on representing and encoding musical or sound processes. Faust (Gaudrain, et al., 2003), which is a programming language that allows the description of algorithms involved in sound processing is a possibility; or MML (Music Markup Language www.musicmarkup.info), which is an XML format that encodes processes for synthesizing sounds or applying effects on them.

Another development for the format concerns the graphical representation of the scores. Some composers have developed specific nomenclatures to write their scores. In addition, a graphical representation by boxes does not give information about the nature of the processes involved in a piece. We would like to develop the possibility of graphical representation of the scores to allow the composers to give specific representations of the objects. One solution consists in creating some graphical style sheets using SVG (www. w3c.org/Graphics/SVG/). Applying such a style sheet with an XML file describing a score would produce a graphical representation of it. Exporting the graphical representation of the scores in SVG would allow users to print them or to broadcast them on the Web.

As far as broadcasting on the Web is concerned, we plan to develop a module to transform a file in the Iscore-XML format into a format for multimedia documents (SMIL for example). This transformation would remove all things that cannot be encoded in the multimedia format. Then we could provide some demos of the pieces that could be played with the players associated to the exporting format.

CONCLUSION

We presented a formalism of interactive scores for writing and interpreting interactive electro-acoustic pieces of music. With this formalism, a composer can describe the temporal organization of the processes involved in the production of the sound of his piece. He can also add some interaction points, which allow a musician to dynamically change the date of an event of the score. This formalism designed for contemporary music is inspired by an analysis of the interpretation of musical pieces. From this formalism, we developed a composition environment called *Iscore* in which a composer can create pieces and let musicians interpret it. We created a XML format to encode the scores written with this tool. This format must be specific because the documents encoded are musical pieces and not generic multimedia documents.

From a simple functional point of view, for saving the scores, the format will become an interface with other type of formats, such as for importing scores from MusiclXML files or exporting to graphical files or multimedia documents files. Finally, we defined processing on our format to apply transformations on a file and generate a new version of the score.

Using an XML format was helpful in two ways: it made easy the design of the format from the theoretical formalism and easy to develop the interface with other XML formats.

REFERENCES

Allen, J. F. (1983). Maintaining knowledge about temporal interval. *Communications of the ACM, 26*(11), 832–843. doi:10.1145/182.358434

Allombert, A., Assayag, G., & Desainte-Catherine, M. (2007). A system of interactive scores based on petri nets. In *Proceedings of the 4th Sound and Music Computing Conference*. Lefkada, Greece: ACM.

Assayag, G., Rueda, C., Laurson, M., Agon, C., & Delerue, O. (1999). Computer assisted composition at IRCAM: From PatchWork to OpenMusic. *Computer Music Journal*. Retrieved from http://recherche.ircam.fr/equipes/repmus/RMPapers/CMJ98/

Beurivé, A. (2000). Un logiciel de composition musicale combinant un modèle spectral, des structures hiérarchiques et des contraintes. In *Proceedings of the 5th Journées d'Informatique Musicale (JIM 2000)*. Bordeaux, France: JIM.

Dahan, K., & Laliberté, M. (2008). Réflexions autour de la notion d'interprétation de la musique électroacoustique. In *Proceedings of the 13th Journées d'Informatique Musicale (JIM 2008)*. Albi, France: JIM.

Diaz, M. (2008). *Petri nets: Fundamental models, verification and applications*. Oxford, UK: Wiley-Blackwell.

Erfle, R. (1993). Specification of temporal constraints in multimedia documents using HyTime. *Electronic Publishing, 6*(4), 397–411.

Gaudrain, E., & Orlarey, Y. (2003). *A Faust manual*. GRAME.

Haury, J. (2012). *La grammaire de l'exécution musicale au clavier et le mouvement des touches*. Unpublished.

HyTime. (1992). *HyTime: Information technology - Hypermedia/time-based structuring language (HyTime). ISO/IEC DIS 10744, 8*. HyTime.

Palmer, C. (1996). On the assignment of structure in music performance. *Music Perception, 14*, 23–56. doi:10.2307/40285708

QuickTime. (1991). *QuickTime developer's guide*. QuickTime.

Schulte, C., & Tack, G. (2005). Views and iterators for generic constraint implementations. In *Proceedings of the Fifth International Colloquium on Implementation of Constraint and Logic Programming Systems, CICLOPS 2005*. CICLOPS.

SMIL. (2008). *SMIL 3.0 W3C recommendation*. Retrieved from http://www.w3c.org

Wirag, S., Rothermel, K., & Wahl, T. (1995). Modelling interaction with HyTime. In *Proceedings of the GI/ITG Kommunikation in Verteilten Systemen*, (pp. 188-202). GI/ITG.

Chapter 5
Chronicle:
XML–Representation of Symbolic Music and Other Complex Time Structures

Wijnand Schepens
University College Ghent, Belgium

Marc Leman
Ghent University, Belgium

ABSTRACT

Chronicle is a new universal system for representing time-related data. Although the system was developed for the representation of symbolic music, it is readily applicable to other types of data with complex time structure, such as audio, multimedia, poetry, choreography, task scheduling, and so on.

Different levels of complexity are supported. The lowest level deals with a stream of events ordered in time. Subsequent higher levels add the possibility to organize the data in groups and subgroups forming a hierarchical structure, local timing, automatic layout of sequential or parallel sections, association of data with other elements, working with multiple timescales, time mappings, and more.

The system is primarily concerned with the treatment of time and structure. The domain developer is free to choose the event data types; timescales and organizational constraints most suited for the application.

The Chronicle system defines an XML-based encoding based on a set of level-specific DTDs, but it also offers software support in the form of classes, interfaces, libraries for reading and writing XML, tools for level reduction, etc.

It is hoped that developers of new XML-encodings in different domains can use Chronicle as a powerful base layer. The software can also be useful for researchers who need an easy and flexible way to store XML-data.

DOI: 10.4018/978-1-4666-2497-9.ch005

INTRODUCTION

The design of an encoding format for music is far from trivial. Apart from the actual symbolic content (such as notes, lyrics, chords, etc.), the designer has to solve typical problems that have to do with time, structure, groups, repetition. Wiggins (2009) and Steyn (2002) propose a number of essential features that a qualitative encoding should exhibit, such as readability, conciseness, expressive power, openness to extension and so on. However, so far, few or no encoding formats are available that can stand these criteria.

The present chapter introduces a new approach to the encoding of symbolic music and other complex time structures, by means of the Chronicle system. The core idea behind the Chronicle system is based on the notion of "an event," which is a thing that happens at a certain moment in time, refers to a certain amount of data, and is structured in relation to other events. The supported types of event data can be freely chosen. For instance, one can decide to use events for the encoding of note onsets, note offsets, bar lines, chords, clefs, key signatures, slur starts, slur stops, section names, metadata like song-title or composer, and so on. The Chronicle system offers powerful and versatile support for grouping events and for dealing with timescales and timescale mappings, and a unique mechanism for non-intrusive association of information. The Chronicle system offers solutions to some important issues related to the representation of time and structure, without having to specify content-specific aspects of what is represented.

The Chronicle system consists of several components. The most "visible" part is an XML-based file format or, to be more precise, a set of four XML-schemas, each one representing a different "level." Next to this external representation, Chronicle will also provide internal representations in the form of object models in a number of programming languages. The third component comprises software libraries and tools for the manipulation of Chronicle data, for reading and writing XML, for converting between levels, etc. The idea behind Chronicle is thus based on a general representational format for events that occur in time. Given the fact that music can be conceived as events over time, it is straightforward to apply the Chronicle system to the musical domain.

It is our hope that format developers may use Chronicle as the skeleton for new encodings. Instead of starting from scratch, they can benefit from the general organizational mechanisms and software support provided, allowing them to concentrate on domain-specific issues. It should be noted that Chronicle can be used not only for different types of music (non-western, contemporary, ancient, pop, …) but for all kinds of systems involving time and structure like poetry, dance, planning and scheduling, etc. Although the primary focus is on symbolic music, Chronicle is also appropriate for tagging and labeling events in audio or multimedia, musical gestures recorded by motion capture systems, or to represent intermediate data that is used e.g. in music algorithms (e.g. chroma-vectors in information retrieval, key-fields in pitch spelling, etc.).

The present chapter gives an introduction to the Chronicle system. The first part situates the Chronicle system in a multitude of already existing encoding schemes for music. The second part gives an introduction to the Chronicle system. The third part contains the discussion and the conclusion.

BACKGROUND

Since the late 1980s and early 1990s, many proposals have been made for music representations (Wiggins, et al., 1993; Selfridge-Field, 1997; Ng & Nesi, 2007). Haus and Longari (2005) provide an overview of several attempts that address the problem of representing music at a general level, including the relationship to XML standards. According to these authors, the main motivation for the development of a general representational structure comes from the multitude of formats in audio (such as wav, ogg, aiff), controls (such as MIDI or Csound), notational (NIFF, Sibelius, Finale), and compositional representations of music (PD, Max), and the need to structure these different formats in view of cataloging and archiving. SMDL (Sloan, 1993) is considered as a conceptually meaningful attempt, with historical importance, because it contains an intrinsic description for space-time relationships between, for example, notes on a staff and the timing of notes in an audio file. The SMI-encoding proposed by Haus and Longari (2005) has recently been developed into the IEEE 1599 standard Lucidovo (2009). We will come back to this in the discussion. Other important attempts include MEI (Perry, 2002), MML (Steyn, 2002), MusicXML (Good, 2001), WEDELMUSIC (Bellini & Nesi, 2001), and many others. For an overview see e.g. Cover (2006).

The variety of encodings reflects the variety of types of musical information. First of all, most formats either encode audio information (e.g. WAV, mp3) or symbolic information. Within the realm of symbolic formats, one can distinguish between representations of score or sheet music (e.g. MusicXML, LilyPond) and representations of performance instructions (e.g. MIDI, OSC). Furthermore, encodings may target different musical styles or cultures: classical music, contemporary music, pop music, jazz, opera, Chinese folksongs, Gregorian chant, and so on. There are score formats for different kinds of sheet music like Common Western Music Notation (CWMN), historical notations like Gregorian notation, all kinds of graphical scores for contemporary music, guitar tablature, drum scores, chord sheets, lead sheets, non-western notations etc. Some encodings focus on particular instruments, voice, percussion, orchestra, electronic equipment, etc., often with instrument-specific indications such as lyrics, pedal, fingering, sound bank, etc.

Many software applications use their own file format, which usually reflects the internal object structure. These formats are not intended for sharing with other software and are often proprietary and binary (e.g. Finale, Sibelius). Other formats were designed with the explicit intention of being shared between different software applications, and/or being readable and writable by humans. Needless to say that there are several similarities between all these encodings. The approaches so far have learned that the most important common factors for music encoding are time and structure, and that a very careful design is needed that relates time and structure to abstract representations that can be linked with a multitude of data types. As Steyn (2004) points out, one of the most challenging aspects of symbolic music representation is to develop a system that can handle time-based and time-less (or unmeasured) music.

This problem was addressed by HyTime (Goldfarb, 1991), the Hypermedia/Time-based Structuring Language. HyTime is an SGML application that forms the basis of SDML (Sloan, 1993). Although both HyTime and SDML are international standards published by the ISO/IEC, and have been very influential, they are not used anymore. One of the main reasons for this failure is without any doubt their complexity. In contrast, Chronicle is designed to be simple and easy to use.

Related time-based approached can be found in the domain of multimedia. Encodings like SMIL (Bulterman, et al., 2008), ZYX (Boll, Klas, & Westermann, 1999), and MHEG-5 (Hofmann, 1996) are used for the scheduling and synchronization of presentations (movies, images, sound). Recently, the time-specific part of SMIL has been extracted in Timesheets 1.0: "an XML timing language that makes SMIL 3.0 element and attribute timing control available to a wide range of other XML languages" (Vuorimaa, Bulterman, & Cesar, 2008). Very simple timing schemes are used for movie subtitles and karaoke. Compared to multimedia, symbolic music is more complex. As Steyn (2007) points out "the challenge for a music XML is that multiple layers of events need to be synchronized as micro-objects, not only the generic high-level multimedia objects." Our Chronicle system bears resemblances with these multimedia systems, such as sequential and parallel groups, but offers more advanced time references and timescale mappings, which makes it more appropriate for the encoding of symbolic music.

We use the word "time" in a loose manner. One can distinguish between musical time and real (clock) time, between absolute and relative time, etc. A time-coordinate can even be interpreted as a space-coordinate: on a music score, if we make abstraction of staff group breaks, time is mapped onto the graphical x-axis. This idea is essential in Music Space (Steyn, 2004, 2007), where the x-axis is used to denote time/space, the y-axis to denote pitch/frequency, and the z-axis to denote musical parts or voices. Similarly, in HyTime the time-coordinate is generalized to a coordinate in a Finite Coordinate Space (FCS). Compared to Steyn's Music Space, Chronicle is not concerned with pitch (the y-coordinate). However, it does support the representation of time/space and even the explicit mapping from time to space! In addition, structural mechanisms like groups can be used to specify parts or voices.

A distinction can be made between point-based and interval-based timing systems (Boll, Klas, & Westermann, 1999). In a point-based system, every element has a specific start (and stop) time. In an interval-based system, every element has a specific duration, and in a sequence of elements, the (start) time of each element is calculated from the start time and duration of its predecessor. Most symbolic music encodings use such an interval scheme for notes in a melody. Although an interval-based approach is handy for melodies (monophony), it runs into trouble when faced with overlapping notes (polyphony). A limited form of polyphony can be supported by introducing 'chords' consisting of notes of equal length. For full polyphony, some encodings refrain to inelegant solutions such as jumping back in time (cf. MusicXML) or inserting invisible elements.

A point-based scheme (specifying note start times) is more suitable for polyphony. On the other hand, an interval-based scheme (specifying note durations) is more handy in the case of simple melodies. The Chronicle system tries to reconcile both views by working with events at the lowest level while supporting note-like elements and sequences via grouping-mechanisms at a higher level. At the lowest level, Chronicle uses *events*. Unlike notes, events have zero duration. They just "happen" at a definite time. A note is represented by (at least) two events: the start (onset) event and the stop (offset) event. In between those two, other events can happen, such as the start of a different note, which is the key to polyphony. Extra note-related events can be used; for example to specify ADSR (attack-decay-sustain-release) envelopes. In Chronicle, one can either encode the individual note events separately, or join them in a (note-like) group.

Many symbolic music encodings, especially those that are focused on CWMN, use *measures* for basic structuring. Typically, a song is modeled as a sequence of measures, and each measure as a sequence of notes. In that conception, a "measure" serves multiple functions: it indicates down beats (metric structure), sets boundaries for local accidental changes, is used for layout (discouraging line splits). Musicians use measure numbers as a means of indexing, allowing fast lookup.

However, it may be desirable or necessary *not* to encode measures. Chord sheets for pop music, for instance, specify only chord symbols and lyrics. In audio files and a large portion of MIDI-files metric information is not available. Some types of music do not use measures at all (e.g. Gregorian chant, non-Western music, some contemporary music). In polymetric music, different measure structures are superimposed. Therefore, a simple sequence of measures is not always adequate, and it is not a good idea to base an encoding scheme on a concept that is so heavily influenced by a historical Western music style.

As in the case of notes versus events, Chronicle tries to offer the best of both worlds, namely by enabling but not enforcing measure structure. Moreover, Chronicle offers different ways to specify metric structure. The same mechanisms that allow the encoding of measures can be used for larger organizational units, like phrases, movements, song-parts (e.g. chorus, verse), etc. Related to this issue is the eternal discussion whether musical information should be organized horizontally (part by part) or vertically (measure by measure or frame by frame). Here too, Chronicle leaves the choice to the user and offers tools to transform between these viewpoints.

Following the majority of music encodings, Chronicle is based on discrete or quantized time, which implies the representation of time moments by means of timestamps and durations in terms of integer numbers. However, Chronicle supports multiple timescales and mapping between timescales, as will be explained. It should be noted that Chronicle is not directly concerned with "musical time" or "note values" (whole note, half note, etc.) which is considered to be a notational issue. A note value can always be expressed in terms of some basic time unit (tick or pulse).

A further aspect concerns Chronicle's open format, using XML. In the last ten years, there has been a tendency towards open formats instead of proprietary formats, and towards text-based formats instead of binary formats, for a number of reasons. Text-based formats have the advantage of being readable, writable, and corrigible by humans. The fact that text-based encodings use more space has become less of an issue. Within the class of text-based formats, there has been a boom of XML-based formats. Markup-based formats in general have the advantage of being readable, in principle writable (albeit often verbose) and for a large part self-documenting. XML-based formats in particular can benefit from a wealth of available tools and software libraries.

THE CHRONICLE SYSTEM

The Chronicle system is organized in different levels with increasing complexity. In level 0, the most basic level, the only building blocks are simple events. Level 1 adds the possibility to collect events in groups, subgroups etc., forming a hierarchy. Within groups, elements have a local time, which can be either explicitly stated or determined by a layout-scheme. Level 2 introduces special events and groups that have non-local times, and can be used to associate elements with other elements, to refer to specific timescales and even to provide mappings between timescales.

The organization in levels is reflected directly in the XML-representation. Every level has a corresponding DTD (or schema), which is a superset of the lower level DTDs. This means that a level-x file is also a valid level-y file, for all y > x. Because Chronicle does not "care" about the actual content, the DTD is quite simple, with only a couple of possible elements and attributes.

The paragraphs that follow are organized in a bottom-up fashion. They describe the Chronicle system starting from level 0 and introducing new concepts along the way, which are illustrated in example XML Boxes.

Level 0: Event Stream

Level-0 Chronicle data consists of a list of events, ordered in time. An event is taken to "happen" at a certain instant in time, and it has no duration. At this level, we choose to represent event timestamps by *integer* numbers, specified via the attribute time. These timestamps are to be interpreted as *absolute* values (not as relative "delta" times) in a certain *timescale*, as will be explained further on. Time increases monotonically: an event time must be equal to or greater than that of its predecessors.

Apart from a timestamp, an event can also carry data. The Chronicle system deals primarily with

Box 1. Example with musical information similar to MIDI

```
<?xml version="1.0" encoding="UTF-8" ?>
<!DOCTYPE chronicle SYSTEM "chronicle.dtd">
<chronicle version="2.0" level="0">
        <event time="0">  <midi:note_on  key="60" channel="0" /> </event>
        <event time="0">  <midi:note_on  key="67" channel="0" /> </event>
        <event time="192"> <midi:note_off key="67" channel="0" /> </event>
        <event time="192"> <midi:note_on  key="65" channel="0" /> </event>
        <event time="384"> <midi:note_off key="65" channel="0" /> </event>
        <event time="384"> <midi:note_on  key="64" channel="0" /> </event>
        <event time="768"> <midi:note_off key="64" channel="0" /> </event>
        <event time="768"> <midi:note_off key="60" channel="0" /> </event>
</chronicle>
```

the timing-information, not the actual content. The user is free to choose the type of event data, as will be illustrated throughout the text. As an example, consider Box 1, which encodes musical information similar to MIDI.

All data is included in the root-element chronicle. The attributes version and level indicate the version-number of the software and the level of the encoded data. Events are encoded in XML-elements called event and event-timestamps via attribute time. In this case, the event-data are inner elements, either note_on or note_off, from a namespace with prefix midi. The key-numbers specify keys on a MIDI-keyboard (60 is C4 or "middle C," 61 is C#4, etc.). The time-values indicate *ticks* in a certain (unspecified) tempo. The types of event-data elements make up the *domain* of the application, which is free to choose.

In contrast with Box 1, it is possible to explicitly specify the domain and/or the timescale used. This is illustrated in the Box 2, which encodes a chord sheet (lyrics and chord symbols).

The domain-attribute points to a URI (uniform resource identifier), which uniquely identifies the domain used. As usual in XML, this does not need to be a real URL. The timescale-attribute is a label that can be used by processing software. In this case, the timestamps indicate "frames" or "rendezvous points," e.g. the lyric "me" and the chord "Fmaj7" start at the same time. The relation

Box 2. Chord sheet

```
<chronicle version="2.0" level="0" timescale="frames"
        domain="http://wikifonia.org/chronicle/domains/chordsheet" >
        <event time="0" type="lyric"> Hello </event>
        <event time="0" type="chord"> Am    </event>
        <event time="1" type="chord"> G6    </event>
        <event time="2" type="lyric"> is it </event>
        <event time="3" type="lyric"> me    </event>
        <event time="3" type="chord"> Fmaj7 </event>
</chronicle>
```

between the frames-timescale and real timing (e.g. in milliseconds) is not specified here—timestamps are merely used to impose ordering—but this can be done (see further).

Optionally, one can specify the type of event-data by an attribute type. Here the event data are simply text strings, but the type-attribute distinguishes between chords and lyrics. The type-indications are not interpreted by the Chronicle system but serve as labels that can be used by human users or domain-specific software.

Level 0 data is ideally suited for *event processing* software, such as MIDI-players, score-viewers, format converts and so on, where events are parsed and handled sequentially. A software tool can choose between real-time processing (inserting time delays between events as indicated by the event timestamps, and if needed handling the events asynchronously) and batch processing (handling the events synchronously, one after the other, ignoring the time information).

The Chronicle-system offers software-support for reading and parsing Chronicle XML-files into objects (in this case of class Event). The parsing of event-data is handled by domain-specific parser-classes, which must be provided by the domain designer. These internal objects can then be used by domain-specific software, e.g. for playing the notes. Vice versa, Chronicle can convert internal object to XML with the aid of domain-specific event-data writer-classes.

Level 1: Groups, Hierarchical Structure, and Local Timing

Level 1 introduces the concept of groups. A group can contain events and/or subgroups, which in turn can contain other events and/or subgroups and so on, thus creating a hierarchy or tree structure. The tree leaves are events. The root of this tree is a special group called the root-group. Every element (event or group) except the root-group has a parent-group.

Optionally, one can give a group a *name* (unique within its parent group) and/or a *type*. Groups are useful for organizing the data. The choice of group structure is entirely free.

In Box 3 the note_on and note_off events are collected in note-groups, which in turn are elements of a larger group. The outer group has been given the name "notes," while the individual note-groups are unnamed.

It is important to note that groups do not have a timestamp and that event timestamps *do not* have to be ordered in level 1! The note_off-event of the first note, for instance, has time 768, which is larger than the onset times of the following notes. Like in level 0 timestamps indicate absolute times in a certain timescale.

In general, different kinds of groupings are possible and one is free to choose the most appropriate one. Box 4 illustrates how lyrics and chords from Box 2 can be put into different "horizontal" groups.

Level Reduction

The Chronicle software provides tools to *reduce* level 1 data to level 0. In this reduction process, groups are *serialized* or flattened into a list of events, and events are *ordered* in time. For example, Box 3 can be reduced to Box 1, and 4 to 2. It should be clear that different level-1 data structures can reduce to the same level-0 data. During this reduction the events are renumbered in natural order: id=0, 1, 2, etc.

Processing software can either target level-1 data or level 0-data. In the latter case, a user may choose to encode his data in level-1, using any grouping structure he deems most appropriate, use a tool to reduce the data to level-0, and feed this data to the level-0 processor. Thus, a level-0 processor is more general in scope.

Note that level-0 data is also valid level-1 data! Technically one could say that the level-0 DTD is a subset of the level-1 DTD. This means that

Box 3. note_on and note_off events collected in note-groups

```xml
<group name="notes">
        <group type="note">
                <event time="0">   <midi:note_on   key="60" channel="0" /> </
event>
                <event time="768"> <midi:note_off key="60" channel="0" /> </
event>
        </group>
        <group type="note">
                <event time="0">   <midi:note_on   key="67" channel="0" /> </
event>
                <event time="192"> <midi:note_off key="67" channel="0" /> </
event>
        </group>
        <group type="note">
                <event time="192"> <midi:note_on   key="65" channel="0" /> </
event>
                <event time="384"> <midi:note_off key="65" channel="0" /> </
event>
        </group>
        <group type="note">
                <event time="384"> <midi:note_on   key="64" channel="0" /> </
event>
                <event time="768"> <midi:note_off key="64" channel="0" /> </
event>
        </group>
</group>
```

Box 4. Horizontal groups

```xml
<group name="lyrics">
        <event time="0" type="lyric"> Hello </event>
        <event time="2" type="lyric"> is it </event>
        <event time="3" type="lyric"> me    </event>
</group>
<group name="chords">
        <event time="0" type="chord"> Am    </event>
        <event time="1" type="chord"> G6     </event>
        <event time="3" type="chord"> Fmaj7 </event>
</group>
```

Box 5. Event-time is 100+4*10 = 140

```
<group time="100" scale="4">
   <event time="10" />
</group>
```

level-1 software, which can handle groups and events, can also handle the trivial case of only events. In that case, reduction is a null-operation.

Furthermore, Chronicle is designed for *embeddability*. This means that any Chronicle element (event or group) can be copied to a different group, even in a different file. It is also possible to insert the content of a complete Chronicle file as an element in another file. This can be done by textual copy-paste, or using the tag include.

Level 2: Timescales

Level 2 introduces the multiple timescales, mappings between timescales, and automatic layout.

In general, a timestamp is an integer number, which is to be interpreted relative to a certain timescale. Mathematically, one could write this as a tuple *(value, timescale)*. It is possible to express the same timestamp in a different timescale if a mapping from the original timescale to the new timescale is defined. For example, *(2000,ms)* can be mapped to *(2, s)* if the mapping from *ms* (milliseconds) to *s* (seconds) is known.

Chronicle provides two general mechanisms for timescale mapping. The first is translation and scaling of local time values. The second is substitution of time references.

Local Timing

In the two former examples, only the events carry a timestamp. In level 2, however, it is also possible to specify time for a group. This time is interpreted as the starting time of the group, with respect to its parent. Time values of the group elements are interpreted as being relative to the group starting time, that is they have to be added to the group starting time. A group can also define a scale-factor by which the element times must be multiplied (default is one). Scaling is carried out before shifting.

In Box 5 the event-time is $100+4*10 = 140$. It is important to note that, from the point of view of the element (in this case the event), the group itself plays the role of a timescale, called the *internal* timescale. At the same time the group time and scale factor define a *transformation* or *mapping* from the group's internal timescale to its *external* timescale (the timescale of its parent group), composed of a scaling followed by a translation (shift).

If an element does not explicitly set a time value, then a default value of zero is used (unless the a group layout is specified, see further).

This powerful feature makes it easy to work with sections starting at different times. An elegant use of group timing is illustrated in Box 6, an alternative for Box 4 using "vertical" groups.

Box 7 is a more elaborate example. The section named "chorus1" starts at time=4000. The element times within this group are shifted accordingly, yielding values of 4000, 4000, 4192, and 4384 respectively. Within these note-groups the note_off elements are shifted even more, giving 4768, 4192, 4384 and 5768. This box also illustrates the possibility of mixing "horizontal" groups with "vertical groups": both the notes- and the chords-group start at the same time (4000).

An important consequence of the technique of local timing within groups is the possibility

Box 6. Group timing

```
<group type="frame" time="0">
        <event type="lyric"> Hello </event>
        <event type="chord"> Am     </event>
</group>
<group type="frame" time="1">
        <event type="chord"> G6      </event>
</group>
<group type="frame" time="2">
        <event time="2" type="lyric"> is it </event>
</group>
<group type="frame" time="3">
        <event type="lyric"> me     </event>
        <event type="chord"> Fmaj7 </event>
</group>
```

to embed an existing group (including subgroups) into a larger group, or to move or copy groups to a different place or even include complete files, without losing the internal timing in the group.

In addition, it is clear that if a group in the tree has zero (or unspecified) time, then the element times are not shifted. If all groups in a tree have time equal to zero and scale equal to one, then all timestamps can be interpreted as *absolute* times relative to the *global* timescale, which is exactly what is expected in level 1! It is therefore equivalent to say that level-1 data only uses absolute times, or to say that level-1 groups must have default starting time (zero) and scale factor (one).

Parallel and Sequential Layout

An additional feature of level 2 is the possibility to let the system calculate times according to a layout scheme. First of all we introduce the notion of *duration*. By default the duration of a group is equal to the largest time of its elements (including sub-elements!), according to the internal group timescale. For example, the duration of the notes-group in Box 7 is 768. The duration can also be set manually to override the

default. If one agrees events to have a duration equal to zero, it is clear that every element has a definite duration.

Element groups often occur in a *sequential* organization. This means that an element starts when its predecessor has stopped. Technically the start-time of the $(i+1)$-th element is equal to the stop-time of the i-th element, for every i. If the duration of all elements and the start time of the first element are known, then the start times of all elements and the duration of the group can be calculated. A sequential layout scheme is illustrated in Box 8.

The duration of the third group is calculated to be 25. After the layout process, the group reduces to Box 9.

A similar case is *parallel* layout. Here all element start-times are set to zero and the total duration of the group is equal to the largest of the element durations. If the layout in Box 8 would have been "parallel," it would have resulted in Box 10.

The same result is achieved by omitting the internal timestamps—in other words, parallel layout is the default. Note that element times determined by a group layout are still relative

Box 7. More elaborate example

```
<group name="song">
        <group name="verse1">
                . . .
        </group>
        <group name="chorus1" time="4000" >
                <group name="notes">
                  <group time="0">
                     <event>            <midi:note_on  key="60" /> </event>
                     <event time="768"> <midi:note_off key="60" /> </event>
              </group>
                  <group time="0">
                     <event>            <midi:note_on  key="67" /> </event>
                     <event time="192"> <midi:note_off key="67" /> </event>
                  </group>
                  <group time="192">
                     <event>            <midi:note_on  key="65" /> </event>
                     <event time="192"> <midi:note_off key="65" /> </event>
                  </group>
                  <group time="384">
                     <event>            <midi:note_on  key="64" /> </event>
                     <event time="384"> <midi:note_off key="64" /> </event>
                  </group>
                </group>
                <group name="chords">
                     <event time="0"> <chord>C</chord>     </event>
                     <event time="384"> <chord>C7</chord>    </event>
                </group>
        </group>
        <group name="verse1" time="6400">
                . . .
        </group>
        ...
</group>
```

to the internal group timescale. Groups with and without layout schemes can be nested freely. The layout process is carried out bottom-up. This is necessary because the layout of a group depends on the duration of its elements—if these elements are in turn groups then their duration depends on their internal layout and so on. Box 11 shows a combination of layout schemes.

Identification

We have discussed the transformation of times in a group from the internal to the external timescale. Next, we will describe a second mechanism for timescales transformation based on mappings between element id's and timestamps. To do this we must first elaborate on the identification of elements.

Box 8. Sequential layout scheme

```
<group layout="sequential">
        <group duration="10"> ... </group>
        <group duration="30"> ... </group>
        <group>
                <event time="0">...</event>
                <event time="25">...</event>
        </group>
        <group duration="20"> ... </group>
```

Box 9. Group reduction

```
<group duration="85">
        <group time="0"  duration="10"> ... </group>
        <group time="10" duration="30"> ... </group>
        <group time="40" duration="25"> ... </group>
        <group time="65" duration="20"> ... </group>
</group>
```

Box 10. Parallel Box 8

```
<group duration="30">
        <group time="0" duration="10"> ... </group>
        <group time="0" duration="30"> ... </group>
        <group time="0" duration="25"> ... </group>
        <group time="0" duration="20"> ... </group>
</group>
```

Within a group each element (either event or subgroup) has a unique *local ID*, represented by an integer number. By default elements are numbered 0, 1, 2, …, but it is possible to set a local ID explicitly, with the important constraint that it has to be strictly larger than the ID of its predecessor.

It follows that every element in the full hierarchy can be uniquely identified by specifying its local ID, the local ID of its parent group, etc., up to the root group. Such a *global ID* can be notated conveniently as a *path expression* by concatenating the local ID's separated by slashes, starting from the root, similar to a file path or URL. By convention, the root-group is notated as "/". In Box 10

for example, the song-group has global ID "/0," the verse1-group "/0/1," the chords-group "/0/1/1" and the D7-chord "0/1/1/2." If available, one can also use element-names instead of numbers. Thus the global ID of the D7-chord can also be written as "/song/verse1/chords/2." This is convenient for human users, but is should be kept in mind that this is only "syntactical sugar" for the more fundamental number-based format.

Time References

Element times are normally integer numbers (*local* or *relative* time) which are added to the group

Box 11. Combination of layout schemes

```
<group name="song" layout="sequential">
        <group name="intro"> ... </group>
        <group name="verse1" layout="parallel">
                <group name="voice" layout="sequential" >
                    <group duration="2"> <event> <note pitch="d5" /> </event> </
group>
                    <group duration="4"> <event> <note pitch="c5" /> </event> </
group>
                    <group duration="2"> <event> <note pitch="bb4" /> </event>
</group>
                    <group duration="8"> <event> <note pitch="eb5" /> </event>
</group>
                        ...
                </group>
                <group name="chords" layout="sequential" >
                    <group duration="8"> <event> <chord>Gm</chord> </event> </
group>
                    <group duration="4"> <event> <chord>Cm7</chord> </event></
group>
                    <group duration="4"> <event> <chord>D7</chord> </event></
group>
                        ...
                </group>
        </group>
        <group name="chorus"> ... </group>
        <group name="verse2"> ... </group>
        <group name="chorus"> ... </group>
        <group name="outro"> ... </group>
</group>
```

time. However, if a time-value is not a number but a path expression, then a different mechanism takes place: the time value is *substituted* by the time-value of the element indicated by the path expression. This is illustrated in Box 12.

The staccato-accent time refers to /song/notes/1, which is interpreted as the second note in the notes-group (e4) which has time 2 (relative to some unspecified scale). The resulting accents-group after substitution is shown in Box 13.

Alternative Path Expressions

Up to here, we have only used *absolute* paths like /song/notes/1. Similar to file paths, it is also possible to use *relative* paths, using .. to denote "parent group." For example, the time-reference of the staccato-accent in group L can also be written as ../../notes/1. Although this notation is more complex it has the important benefit that it doesn't depend on the location of the song-group

Box 12. Substitution

```
<group name="song">
        <group name="notes">
                <event time="0">  <note pitch="d4" /> <event>
                <event time="2">  <note pitch="e4" /> <event>
                <event time="10"> <note pitch="f#4" /> <event>
                <event time="12"> <note pitch="a4" /> <event>
                ...
        </group>
        <group name="accents">
                <event time="/song/notes/1"> <accent type="staccato" /> </
event>
                <event time="/song/notes/3"> <accent type="strong" /> </event>
        </group>
</group>
```

Box 13. Accents-group after substitution

```
<group name="accents">
        <event time="2">  <accent type="staccato" /> </event>
        <event time="12"> <accent type="strong" /> </event>
</group>
```

in the tree. This means that the song-group can be moved or copied or embedded at will. In general it is advisable to avoid absolute references.

A path notation like ../../notes/1 still requires the relative location of the notes-group with regard to the accents-group to be fixed. To soften this restriction we introduce a third syntax: @ notes refers to the first element called "notes" encountered upward in the tree. This is similar to referring to a variable in a programming language with nested scopes: look up the variable in the enclosing scope; if not found look it up

in the parent scope etc. In the example we could write @notes/1. In practice the @-notation turns out to be the most convenient, and sufficient for most purposes.

It is interesting to mix the behavior of local time shifting with time references. For example, the accents group above can also be written as in Box 14.

In this group, the local times are added to the last part of the time reference path (in this case 0+1=1 and 0+3=3). Note that it is essential not to write @notes instead of @notes/0. Recall that the

Box 14. Accents group

```
<group name="accents" time="@notes/0" >
        <event time="1"> <accent type="staccato" /> </event>
        <event time="3"> <accent type="strong" /> </event>
</group>
```

use of names in addresses is merely syntactical sugar. That means that @notes resolves to /song/notes which is the same as /song/0, whereas @notes/0 is equal to /song/notes/0. Applying the shift-behavior to /song/0 would result in accents referring to /song/1 and /song/3, the second and fourth group in the song-group, which is not what was meant.

Association

Time references can be used to associate data with non-local elements. In Box 12 accents are associated with notes. Note that the time reference is specified in the time-attribute. Although this may be counterintuitive at first, it is an essential feature of Chronicle. In a sense, every note is an instant in time from the point of view of the accents. What happens when a time reference path does not point to an existing element will be explained shortly.

An attentive reader may wonder why the accents are in a separate group—could they not be specified in the notes-group, either as extra events or as extra note-data? The answer is that this is possible, of course, but it requires changing the note-data. Association is a *non-interruptive* technique that achieves the same result. One of the great things about this is that it can be used to associate information with *external* data (data outside the chronicle-file), and even with non-

Chronicle data, such as audio or multimedia data. The only requirement is that the elements in the external file have a unique timestamp (or in general a unique ID), such as frame number or sample index.

A second objection might be that one can directly state the "resolved" timestamps as in Box 13, instead of referring to notes as in Box 12. Why the detour? The point is that the associated accents will automatically have the correct time *if the note times are changed.*

Association is very useful for referring to groups or ranges of elements, to indicate slurs, tuplets, pedal-section, ottava-section, motifs, rhythmic or melodic cells, measures, volta's, chords, etc. Box 15 is an example showing the association of a slur and a chord with notes from different groups.

Timescales

In Box 12 accents were associated with notes via time references. Another way of viewing this is that the notes group acts as a timescale to which accent times refer. Suppose the note-times are measured in "ticks," and we now that every tick takes 10 milliseconds. Box 16 shows how this can be encoded using two groups.

The second note (e4) for instance has local time 2, which is resolved by the notes-group to

Box 15. Association of a slur and a chord with notes from different groups

```
<group type="slur" time="@soprano/notes/8">
        <event                type="slur_start" />
        <event time="4" type="slur_stop" />
</group>
<group type="chord">
        <event type="chordsymbol">Em7</event>
        <event time="@soprano/notes/14" />
        <event time="@alto/notes/12" />
        <event time="@tenor/notes/10" />
        <event time="@bass/notes/8" />
</group>
```

Box 16. Note-times measured in "ticks"

```
<group name="ticks" time="@realtime/ms/0">
        <event time="0"/>
        <event time="10"/>
        <event time="20"/>
         <event time="30"/>
        ...
</group>
<group name="notes" time="@ticks/0">
        <event time="0">  <note pitch="d4" /> <event>
        <event time="2">  <note pitch="e4" /> <event>
        <event time="10"> <note pitch="f#4" /> <event>
        <event time="12"> <note pitch="a4" /> <event>
        ...
</group>
```

@ticks/0+2 = @ticks/2. This is interpreted as an association with the third ticks-element (whose implicit local ID is 2), resolving to @realtime/ms/20. The ticks-group in effect defines a *timescale mapping* from @ticks to @realtime/ms, using ID and time of its element as key-value pairs.

In practice, defining a time mapping for every possible time-value can result in an extremely list of mapping elements. In order to alleviate this complication, Chronicle makes it possible to specify a limited list of mapping elements and use linear interpolation for references falling in between elements. Note that this is the reason why local ID's can be specified explicitly. Box 17 illustrates this.

Box 17. Limited list of mapping elements

```
<group name="ticks" time="@realtime/
ms">
        <event id="0"  time="0"/>
        <event id="10" time="100" />
        <event id="20" time="250" />
</group>
```

Substituting this mapping in Box 16, the resulting note times are shown in Box 18.

Note that it is possible to refer to an element whose time is itself a reference. In that case, substitutions are chained. For example, if we combine Box 14 and 16, the staccato-accent time @notes/1 resolves to @ticks/2 which in turn resolves to @realtime/ms/20. It is also possible to mix time references with local timing and with automatic layout.

To conclude: the mechanism of time references used for association can also serve for mappings between timescales. We see that @xxx can be interpreted as a timescale-label.

Level Reduction

The Chronicle system provides tools to *resolve a group* by shifting the local times, laying out, and substituting time references of all elements and sub-elements. Care must be taken to assure the correct order of this resolution process. If after this resolution all elements and sub-elements of a group refer to (the internal timescale of) the group itself, then that group is called "free." Groups containing only elements with local time are

Box 18. Substitute mapping of Box 16

```
<group name="notes" >
        <event time="@realtime/ms/0">    <note pitch="d4" /> <event>
        <event time="@realtime/ms/20">   <note pitch="e4" /> <event>
        <event time="@realtime/ms/100"> <note pitch="f#4" /> <event>
        <event time="@realtime/ms/130"> <note pitch="a4" /> <event>
        ...
</group>
```

automatically free. Groups containing elements with time references are free if those references can be resolved *internally*, that is if they do not refer to elements outside the group. For example in Box 12 the notes-group is free, but the accents-group is not. However, the song-group is free because the accent times can be resolved within the song-group.

Any free group can be reduced from level 2 to level 1 by setting the times of element groups equal to zero (see Local Timing above). In Box 16 the ticks-group refers to an external timescale @realtime/ms. If this group is part of the root-group (the chronicle element), then the root group can only be free if it explicitly defines a global timescale as in Box 2.

The net result of resolving the root-group containing Box 16 and 17 is presented in Box 18. This is level-1 data because there are no more time-references or layout and no groups have non-zero time. Such a reduction from level-2 to level-1 is only possible if all (sub-)elements somehow refer to a single "global" timescale. As before, the resulting level-1 data can be further reduced to level 0.

DISCUSSION

The Chronicle system is an encoding system that is useful when it is linked with data types of a specific domain. For that purpose, the domain

Box 19. Net result of resolving the root-group containing Box 16 and 17

```
<chronicle level="2" timescale="realtime/ms">
        <group name="ticks">
                <event id="0"  time="0"/>
                <event id="10" time="100" />
                <event id="20" time="250" />
        </group>
        <group name="notes">
                <event time="0">    <note pitch="d4" /> <event>
                <event time="20">   <note pitch="e4" /> <event>
                <event time="100"> <note pitch="f#4" /> <event>
                <event time="130"> <note pitch="a4" /> <event>
                ...
        </group>
</chronicle>
```

and the types of event data (e.g. notes, pitches, lyrics, chords) need to be identified and linked with the encoding of events. Optionally a global timescale can be specified. This is sufficient for level-0 applications, which deal with events only. It is also possible to make use of higher-level features and add constraints. For example, a specific group-structure (e.g. song containing parts containing measures) can be defined, restrictions can be imposed on the use of time reference, and so on. As explained, a user can always choose to use a higher-level encoding for convenience, and use tools for level reduction. On the other hand, the software should accept lower-level encodings, as long as domain-specific constraints are not violated. The same holds for embedding or including data in Chronicle files.

Remember that apart from an XML-representation, the Chronicle system is also concerned with "internal" representation (classes, objects), tools for reading, writing, manipulating. Software developers can use the Chronicle classes as a foundation for new applications. Alternatively, they can opt to use Chronicle merely as an XML parser and writer, by providing a mapping between Chronicle elements and non-Chronicle data.

Compared with most symbolic music formats such as MEI (Perry, 2002), MML (Steyn, 2002), MusicXML (Good, 2001), WEDELMUSIC (Bellini & Nesi, 2001), we believe that Chronicle offers more powerful mechanisms for handling time.

Following SMDL (Sloan, 1993), many encodings try to separate graphical score information from performance information, often by introducing a middle layer called "logical" layer. In SMI (Haus & Longari, 2005) the essential content of the logical layer is the so-called "spine" or "backbone" which contains unique "essential" musical elements (such as notes) with a time-coordinate and a spatial (x-) coordinate. These coordinates define a mapping between the graphical and the performal domains. In Chronicle, such a spine can easily be implemented as a mapping between the t-timescale and the x-timescale. Moreover, Chronicle offers a hierarchical structuring of these events. Chronicle can be seen as a general representational schema for 'musical events,' which includes the possibility of having hierarchical events that occur in time, on top of which inferential aspects can be added.

Chronicle also exhibits some of the key features of a music representational system listed by Wiggins (2009). The construction of multiply hierarchical structures and referential annotations is supported via the mechanism of time references. The same mechanism also allows a domain developer to define different musical surfaces. Domain labeling of syntactic elements is possible because the developer has the freedom to choose the representation of domain-specific data. Moreover, every element is identified uniquely using a global ID, which allows the expression of distinguished co-reference relations.

The Chronicle system is still in progress. At the time of writing this chapter, we are developing a reference implementation in Java. There are also plans for an extra level (level 3), which will add support for reducing unnecessary repetition and space overhead via parameterized templates, transposition and smart lists, default and override elements etc. Chronicle is completely open source. Documentation, DTDs, tools, and source code can be found at (1).

As a test example, we are working on an XML-based MIDI-wrapper. In the near future we are planning to use Chronicle for storage and editing of chord sheets (in collaboration with wikifonia.org), of harmonic and rhythmical data produced audio analysis algorithms (in collaboration with the Speech Laboratory at Ghent University), and of data involving the synchronization and analysis of score, audio, video and body-related data (in collaboration with the Institute of Psychoacoustics and Electronic Music—IPEM—at Ghent University). We hope that other researchers and developers will follow.

CONCLUSION

In this chapter, we have situated the Chronicle system within the broad context of music encoding. The Chronicle system was then presented in the form of a tutorial. The focus was on the Chronicle levels and on the process of level reduction. Level 0 data consists of events with absolute time in a single timescale. Level 1 allows to structure the data in groups. Level 2 offers a set of mechanisms for timescale management, such as local group timing, group layout, and time references. These can be used for non-intrusive association or tagging of data, but also for mapping between timescales.

New encodings are still being developed every day, as proprietary formats for new software, as open formats targeting a new combination of musical information aspects, or simply to improve intrinsic qualities such as expressiveness, readability, conciseness, extensibility. We believe that the Chronicle system offers solutions to some important issues related to the representation of time and structure, without having to specify content-specific aspects of what is represented.

REFERENCES

Bellini, P., & Nesi, P. (2001). WEDELMUSIC format: An XML music notation format for emerging applications. In *Proceedings of the First International Conference on Web Delivering of Music*. Florence, Italy: ACM.

Boll, S., Klas, U., & Westermann, W. (1999). *A comparison of multimedia document models concerning advanced requirements. Technical Report – Ulmer Informatik-Berichte No 99-01*. Ulm, Germany: University of Ulm.

Bulterman, D., Jansen, J., Cesar, P., Mullender, S., Hyche, E., & DeMeglio, M. … Michel, T. (Eds.). (2008). *Synchronized multimedia integration language (SMIL 3.0)*. Retrieved July 6, 2009, from http://www.w3.org/TR/2008/REC-SMIL3-20081201/

Cover, R. (Ed.). (2006). *XML and music*. Retrieved July 6, 2009 from http://xml.coverpages.org/xmlMusic.html

Goldfarb, C. (1991). Standards: HyTime: A standard for structured hypermedia interchange. *IEEE Computer Magazine, 24*(8).

Good, M. (2001). MusicXML: An internet-friendly format for sheet music. In *Proceedings of XML 2001*. Orlando, FL: XML.

Haus, G., & Longari, M. (2005). A multi-layered, time-based music description approach based on XML. *Computer Music Journal, 29*, 70–85. doi:10.1162/comj.2005.29.1.70

Hofmann, P. (1996). *MHEG-5 and MHEG-6: Multimedia standards for minimal resource systems. Technical Report*. Berlin, Germany: Technische Universitat.

Lucidovo, L. (2009). IEEE 1599: A multi-layer approach to music description. *Journal of Multimedia, 4*(1).

Ng, K., & Nesi, P. (Eds.). (2007). *Interactive multimedia music technologies*. Hershey, PA: IGI Global. doi:10.4018/978-1-59904-150-6

Perry, R. (2002). The music encoding initiative (MEI). In *Proceedings of the First International Conference MAX 2002: Musical Application Using XML*. Milan, Italy: MAX.

Selfridge-Field, E. (Ed.). (1997). *Beyond MIDI: The handbook of musical codes*. Cambridge, MA: MIT Press.

Sloan, D. (1993). Aspects of music representation in HyTime SMDL. *Computer Music Journal, 17*, 51–59. doi:10.2307/3680544

Steyn, J. (2002). Framework for a music markup language. In *Proceedings of the First International Conference MAX 2002: Musical Application Using XML*. Milan, Italy: MAX.

Steyn, J. (2004). Introducing music space. In *Proceedings of the 4th Open Workshop of MUSIC-NETWORK: Integration of Music in Multimedia Applications*. Barcelona, Spain: MUSICNET-WORK.

Steyn, J. (2007). Challenges of designing a markup language for music . In Ng, K., & Nesi, P. (Eds.), *Interactive Multimedia Music Technologies*. Hershey, PA: IGI Global. doi:10.4018/978-1-59904-150-6.ch006

Vuorimaa, P., Bulterman, D., & Cesar, P. (Eds.). (2008). *SMIL timesheets 1.0 - W3C working draft*. Retrieved July 6, 2009, from http://www.w3.org/TR/2008/WD-timesheets-20080110/

Wiggins, G. (2009). Computer-representation of music in the research environment. In Crawford & Gibson (Eds.), *Modern Methods for Musicology: Prospects, Proposals and Realities*. Oxford, UK: Ashgate.

Wiggins, G., Miranda, E., Smaill, A., & Harris, M. (1993). A framework for the evaluation of music representation systems. *Computer Music Journal, 17*, 31–42. doi:10.2307/3680941

ENDNOTES

[1]   http://code.google.com/p/chronicle-xml/

Chapter 6
Representing Music as Work in Progress

Gerard Roma
Universitat Pompeu Fabra, Spain

Perfecto Herrera
Universitat Pompeu Fabra, Spain

ABSTRACT

In this chapter, the authors discuss an approach to music representation that supports collaborative composition given current practices based on digital audio. A music work is represented as a directed graph that encodes sequences and layers of sound samples. The authors discuss graph grammars as a general framework for this representation. From a grammar perspective, they analyze the use of XML for storing production rules, music structures, and references to audio files. The authors describe an example implementation of this approach.

INTRODUCTION

The widespread adoption of Internet access has raised great expectations with respect to music creation. On one hand, networks extend the possibilities for collaborative composition using computer-based tools by allowing intermediate objects to be shared. On the other, these tools can be accessed by a larger audience, and designed to be used by people with little or no musical training.

The recent focus on media sharing by Internet users is reinforcing such expectations. The habit of sharing multimedia objects has facilitated an explosion in the culture of creative repurposement and recombination. Specifically in the case of sound recordings, there is a long tradition in sharing files for creative reutilization. Content in sites such as freesound.org, soundsnap.com, or sampleswap.org is typically downloaded to be reused in music and multimedia products. This trend in the use of sound samples can be seen as an expression of an audio culture (Cox & Warner, 2004), influenced by a number of aesthetic traditions that have exploited the specific constraints of sound recordings, such as Musique Concrète, Plunderphonics, soundscape composition and acoustic ecology, or Hip Hop. The wide use of digital technologies has thus allowed using digital

DOI: 10.4018/978-1-4666-2497-9.ch006

audio as matter for musical discourse, in a way that can no longer be represented using traditional music notation. Since understanding sound files is now part of the standard computer literacy, this kind of discourse can now be used as a means for expression by many computer users without the need of formal music training. As computers keep invading different areas of music production, sound files have become prevalent as a way to represent musical events. Samplers and sample-based synthesizers are among the most commonly used tools, offering simplicity and realism over other types of synthesis. On the other hand, most music is at some point edited in some sort of audio sequencer or multi-track editor as an organized ensemble of sound files.

Some tools have appeared that attempt to relate the use of audio sequencers with the explosion of social networking and social media. Companies such as SoundCloud (http://www.soundcloud.com) are offering Web hosting of audio tracks, and sites such as Indaba Music (http://www.indaba-music.com) are already offering online tools for basic audio mixing and sequencing. The makers of one of the most popular programs for audio sequencing, Ableton Live (http://www.ableton.com), currently offer a collaboration feature based on progressive uploading and downloading of audio clips.

While these movements toward the use of network servers for storing audio are promoting greater degrees of collaboration, current tools and their interfaces are still focused on single user operation, in many cases under the influence of classic western music notation. Currently, popular programs do little to represent deep music structure, especially for practices based on digital audio manipulation. Moreover, most music is stored in proprietary formats and cannot be moved from one program to another.

The difficulties of understanding music, and especially musical structure, when using sound recordings were largely explained in Schaeffer's Traité des Objets Musicaux (Schaeffer, 1966).

Given the impossibility to describe the practices that magnetic tapes made possible from the established music theory, Schaeffer frequently borrowed concepts from the linguistic theories of Saussure and Jackobson (an analysis of the relationships between music and language in the Traité can be found in Chion [1983]). In the 1970s, pioneers of computer music like Curtis Roads and Otto Laske proposed the adaptation of formal grammars to the practice of composing music with sound objects. While the use of grammars has been established in fields such as computational musicology, the early use of grammars for sample-base music composition provides a ground for current needs with respect to collaborative recombination of shared media.

The separation of musical structure from audio signals allows the use of hosting services and shared databases for the audio, while musical structure can be represented and exchanged using text markup formats such as XML (Figure 1). In composition activities, music structure can be typically stored in lightweight documents that may change frequently, and transmitted through established text communication channels such as email. Each music document may make reference to a number of bigger sized audio files. Transmission and local caching of these files can be dealt independently between each participant and the remote location through standard Web technologies and services, which avoids the need of potentially complex specialized p2p tools for the synchronization of audio collections among different participants.

In collaborative composition, though, the exchange of music documents does not need to be reduced to a single document representing a complete work: much of this activity works through sharing and reusing lower level building blocks. Formal grammars provide a framework for the representation of different structural levels in music composition. Formal languages already allow high levels of cooperation in computer music. For example, Music-N style languages and

Figure 1. Separation of structure and content allows for faster collaboration on successive versions of music document

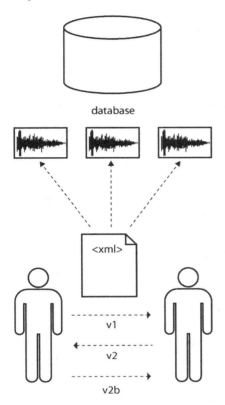

environments are very often driven by lively communities that continuously exchange code and knowledge. We propose similar approach to support collaboration in sample-based music composition.

MUSIC REPRESENTATION WITH FORMAL GRAMMARS

Formal Grammars

Formal grammars were introduced by Noam Chomsky in the 1950s as a means for formal analysis of natural language (Chomsky, 1956). The view of grammars as mathematical devices has since then remained at the foundation of Computer Science. From the point of view of linguistics, it was an important revolution that introduced a generative perspective: grammars served as language theories that could explain and predict linguistic phenomena by generating them from a formally defined set of laws.

In the 1970s and 1980s, the idea of modeling music with grammars became very popular. Formal grammars can be used to generate expressions of a language, and they can also be used to parse existing expressions, and give an interpretation of how they were generated. Thus, grammars were used, on one hand, for automatic or computer-aided music composition, and on the other for musicological analysis. Both directions can be thought as complementary: in some cases, grammars are learned from existing musical works and then used to generate new ones.

For the case of collaborative music composition, grammars provide a suitable framework for sharing, reusing, and assembling parts of music compositions. In this sense, a grammar can support the metaphor of a common language, as a means for the computational representation and manipulation of musical fragments. From the point of view of analysis, grammars can be used for computational modeling of the style of different participants or groups in collaborative applications. From the perspective of generation, they can serve to facilitate creativity by producing new combinations of sounds, or to assist the search of suitable sounds for a given musical context.

A formal grammar is usually defined as a 4-tuple (V, Σ, S, P), where:

- Σ is a terminal alphabet, a set of symbols that are used to form sentences in the language. In common music notation, terminals could be notes, durations or chords, while in sample-based music they can be sound objects.
- V is an alphabet of non-terminal symbols or variables. Variables represent strings of terminal or non-terminal symbols in inter-

mediate stages of the generation. In a music composition process, variables can be used, for example, to represent groups of terminals that are often used together.

- S is the start symbol, a special variable that is used to begin the generation process.
- P is a set of production rules that allow a given string to be replaced by another string. For example, they can specify how a part of a musical piece can be replaced by its subparts.

In summary, a formal grammar can be explained as a set of rules that rewrite a string of symbols with another one. For example, the rule $A \rightarrow AB$ defines that a string composed of the symbol "A" can be replaced (rewritten) by the string "AB." This rule can be used to generate the string "AB" in presence of string "A." Thus, the rule could be applied again to "AB" to produce "AAB," and so on. In addition, it can give one possible explanation of how the string "AB" (or "AAB" for that matter) was produced in a given language. This is the idea behind the generative linguistics methodology: a set of rules that is able to generate all observable sentences of a language constitutes a theory of that language that is able to predict (i.e. generate) unobserved sentences and provide a possible explanation of how the observed ones were produced.

Intuitively, grammars can be understood as a formal way to specify structural groupings of a language. For example we can state that all sentences in a natural language are composed of a "noun'" sub-sentence and a "verb" sub-sentence, and then define a rule that describes this decomposition using abstract symbols (say $S \rightarrow NV$). Thus, they can be used to specify the structure of a musical piece. For example we could define a structure that is always composed by a sequence of themes "ABBA."

Chomsky defined a hierarchy for formal languages and their associated grammars that has become standard in linguistics and computer science. The most general class, type 0, is the class of recursively enumerable languages. Grammars that parse or generate such languages are not subject to restrictions in the production rules. Type 1 is the class of context-sensitive languages. Production rules for grammars that generate these languages can only replace a string with another string of equal or greater length. Still, context-sensitive rules such as aAb -> aBb are allowed. Type 2 is the class of context-free languages. Grammars that produce these languages are subject to a second restriction, which forbids context-sensitive productions. The left side of productions must consist only of a non-terminal variable. In addition, the right side of productions cannot consist exclusively of the empty word. Intuitively, context-sensitive rules seem to have many applications in music. However, the most general types of grammars are also the most complex ones, and in practice, they are difficult to parse efficiently. Thus, it is common to use context-free grammars, sometimes augmented with transformation rules or control mechanisms. Context-free grammars are also widely used to describe and design programming languages. Finally, type 3 defines regular languages, the most limited class of formal languages. In addition to the above restrictions, the right side string of a production in a regular grammar can only consist of a terminal symbol and a non-terminal variable. Chomsky described this model as an equivalent to Markovian processes and dismissed them for the analysis of natural language mainly because of their inability to describe nested structures. The stochastic nature of Markovian processes does not affect this fundamental limitation. The same reason applies to their use for music analysis or generation. Despite this limitation, Markov chains have been very popular as a simple mechanism for algorithmic music composition (Ames, 1989). It can be argued, though, that the use of Markov chains does not justify by itself the grammar paradigm: Markov chains are represented simply using transition matrices.

Grammars in Music Composition

The application of grammars to collaborative composition can rely on a long tradition in the use of grammars for computer music. A brief review of some of the approaches can be helpful to understand their potential.

One of the first documented efforts to use formal grammars in music composition is due to Curtis Roads. In Composing Grammars (Roads, 1978) he described a system for music composition based on context-free grammars augmented with control procedures. The system provided the composer with a workflow for experimenting with structural and semantic aspects of composition. First, the composer would specify a grammar using a specialized language (Tree) and an associated compiler (Gram). The program would generate a compiler for the specified grammar. The composer would then work on valid derivations according to the grammar to create the syntactic surface. A second language (CoTree) and its corresponding compiler (GnGram) would aid in the generation of the score. A final task, the lexical mapping, consisted in pairing the terminals of the grammar with sound objects previously created by the composer. Such amount of relatively low-level tasks reflects the kind of interaction that computers supported at that time. Still, the emphasis on the lexical mapping and the use of sound objects makes this pioneering work interesting in the context of social media.

In Grammars as representations for music (Roads, 1979), Roads presented a synthesis of formal grammar theory and surveyed the use of grammars for music analysis. Perhaps more importantly, he summarized the powers and limitations of the grammar approach. Considering iconic (i.e. based on analogies) and symbolic (based on convention) representations, it is quite obvious that, as symbolic representations, grammars rely on a discretization of the sound material. This limitation is however less restrictive for compositional purposes than for analysis.

An example of discrete treatment of sound is the Schaefferian concept of sound object (Schaeffer, 1960). A second limitation is the compromise in complexity. As we mentioned, the most complex types of grammars are often too complex to parse, while simple grammars can be too trivial and less effective than other models. A third limitation is that grammars are purely structural and hence they do not deal with the semantic and social implications of music. Despite these limitations, the scope of grammars for modeling different kinds of music is huge. In computer music, where most applications rely on some sort of storage, grammars can be used to represent structure in a very broad sense.

Holtzman's Generative Grammar Definition Language (GGDL) was developed as a tool for investigation of structural aspects of music using a computer (Holtzman, 1980). The language could be used both by composers and musicologists. GGDL allowed to specify type 0 (i.e. free) grammars and provided support for phrase structure rules and transformational rules. Phrase structure rules are standard formal grammar string rewriting rules. Since many rules can be applied at a given point, the system provided a mechanism for defining functions to control this choice. For example, "blocked" generation allows random choice of rules but restricts the use of a rule until all the possible selections have been made. Meta-productions are a special type of rewrite rule that allow the generation of rewrite rules at initialization time, before actual variables are initialized. Transformation rules modify the strings generated by phrase structure rules in different ways, such as transposing them or inverting them. Finally, GGDL provided a means for mapping abstract symbols to actual sounds synthesized with the possibilities offered by computers of the time. Holtzman provided a complete example of the generation of a piece. As a given grammar can generate a large number of pieces, the composer is encouraged to experiment with the program until an acceptable result is obtained. This resort to manual experimentation can be seen as an effect of the lack of restrictions that the language imposes to grammars. The author also explained how Schonberg's Trio could have been generated by the example grammar. Still, the system doesn't provide any automatic support for such musicological analysis.

Kippen and Bel's development of the BOL processor system (Kippen & Bel, 1988) has been extensively documented along different phases. The system was originally conceived for linguistic analysis of North-Indian tabla music, a highly formalized system that uses an oral notation system of mnemonic symbols called Bols. Tabla music is usually improvised, typically involving permutations of a reference pattern. Expert musicians can assess whether a given permutation is correct or not. On this basis, the authors tailored several formal grammars that reflected correct variations. The particularities of tabla music led to the introduction of different context-sensitive rules, such as negative contexts (a string is replaced except if found in a given context) in order to reflect the description of the rules by musicians. The main components of the systems are the inference engine, which generates sentences from the grammar, and the membership test that determines whether a given sentence belongs to the grammar. A graphical interface allowed users to perform both analysis and synthesis. In order to parse strings introduced in the graphical editor without the full formal structure specification, a system of templates was introduced. A second iteration of the Bol processor, named BP2 targeted grammar-based music composition from a more general perspective, allowing composers to specify their grammars to generate sound object compositions. Because of this focus on composition, BP2 omitted the parser mechanism and allowed a more free approach to grammar specification, subordinating the issue of correctness to aesthetic considerations.

Finally, one of the most well known uses of grammars for music composition is David

Cope's Experiments in Music Intelligence (EMI) (Cope, 2001). Over the years, Cope has refined a database-driven system that imitates the compositional style of classic composers. The works of the target composers are segmented and described in a database, and each fragment is assigned to a category according to a system called SPEAC: Statement, Preparation, Extension, Antecedent, and Consequent. Such categories attempt to define a basic formalization of the dynamics of tension and relaxation in western tonal music. Thus, the system defines a set of rules that make a sequence of patterns of different categories correct. For example, an Antecedent fragment can only be followed by an Extension or a Consequent fragment. The music generation engine is based on an Augmented Transition Network (Woods, 1970), which allows for faster parsing and generation of context-sensitive rules.

One issue of music grammars that is not covered by linguistics or formal languages literature is parallelism (Roads, 1982). Both Roads and Holtzman made use of parallel rules, where two parallel tokens are meant to start at the same time. However, parallel rules introduce some ambiguity. For example if we have a musical sequence "AB" and a parallel rewriting rule "A → D/E" (meaning that D and E start at the same time), it is not clear, upon replacement of A, if B will follow after D or after E. Graph grammars provide a general framework that allow us to deal explicitly with sequential and parallel structures.

Graph Grammars

Graph grammars were introduced by Pfaltz and Rosenfeld in the late 1960s (Pfatz & Rosenfeld, 1969) as an extension of traditional grammars to languages of directed graphs. A directed graph is defined as a tuple (N,E) where N is a set of nodes and E a set of edges that connect nodes in a certain direction. Clearly, strings are a class of directed graphs where symbols are nodes and edges define the sequence of symbols. In this sense, edges of a string define a total order relation. If cycles are forbidden in a directed graph (where cycles are defined as loops involving more than one node), the set of edges defines a partial order relation on the nodes, which allows the generalization of string grammars to acyclic directed graphs.

A graph grammar can be defined in similar terms to string grammars. However, graph-rewriting productions are more complex than string rewriting productions as they have to define how to connect the result of the production to the enclosing graph. Thus, productions are defined as triples (α, β, E) where α is the (sub)graph to be replaced and β is the replacement, while E defines the embedding of β in the host graph. Graph grammars can be categorized in the same way as string grammars. For example, node replacement grammars (Engelfriet & Rozenberg, 1997) are context-free graph grammars where the left hand of each production is restricted to a single node.

Development of graph grammars has continued over the years both at a theoretical and at a practical level fostered by applications in very diverse fields such as image recognition or graphical languages for engineering (Ehrig, Engels, Rozenberg, & Kreowski, 1999). The extension of strings to graphs seems naturally suited for music representation by allowing parallelism. However, explicit mention of graph grammars for music is rare in the literature. Some works (Cook & Holder, 2000; Madsen, 2003) have showed their use for mining classical music scores represented as graphs with multiple possible connections between consecutive notes. Since these connections are not specified in the score, this approach bears a high level of complexity that is not needed in the context of music composition. In the tradition of composing grammars, music surface may be represented by a rooted tree, where the direction of links indicates temporal sequences (note that this is different from parse tree that could represent a musical piece as a vertical hierarchy). A rooted tree can be defined as a directed acyclic graph with a root node where there is a unique

path from the root node to any node. Intuitively, this structure forbids two things. On one hand, no cycles can exist in the graph. This means that edges define a partial order relation, which allows them to represent time sequences. Also as shown by Pfatz and Rosenfeld (1969), acyclic graphs have the property of being contractible, which allows the definition of grammar expansion rules. One problem with acyclic graphs is that it's quite common in music to use cyclic structures. Since loops (i.e., edges from one node to itself) are still possible with respect to the partial order relation, musical cycles can be understood as a finite number of repetitions of a single node, to which a graph has been contracted (Figure 2). A second restriction of this representation is that a given node can only be the target of one edge. Two edges arriving at the same target would imply the scheduling of the same node (and all the following structure) at two different moments in time, which has the effect of creating multiple auditory tracks from the same graph specification, and breaking the intuition of the temporal sequence of the representation.

The rest of this chapter presents and discusses XML representation of music as a network of sound samples using graph grammars. This implies the representation of music at three distinct levels: grammar rules, musical surface, and lexical map-

Figure 2. A cycle can be avoided by contracting and repeating the graph

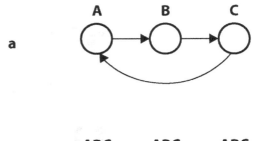

ping. Grammar rules represent patterns that can be extracted from musical compositions. If a normative approach is pursued, compositions must validate against these rules. In the field of computer music composition, we have seen that grammars have been used by composers to define the rules that govern their pieces. The process of composition then consists in the application and refinement of the rules. Other examples of normative forms are conventional pop songs or sonatas. Representation of music grammars can be used by music editing programs both to parse and validate compositions created by users. Rules can also be understood as frequent patterns that are mined from several musical pieces and used to model the style of a user, group, or community, and generate new pieces that follow these patterns. At the surface level, it is useful to represent music structure in an analog way to what is presented to the listener. This is the most common

kind of document that is used to store and exchange music. The grammar approach provides the appropriate framework for the representation and computational manipulation of different fragments of the surface representation. Finally, we need to represent the mapping of the symbols in the surface representation to actual sounds and their physical location. This mapping can be defined as a direct link to sound resources, or it can be specified as an abstract description of a sound segment (see Figure 3).

GRAMMAR RULES

We have described how grammars can be used both to parse or analyze the structure of musical compositions and to generate new compositions. This implies that a grammar can be used as a compositional aid to analyze and model the style

Figure 3. Representation of a drum pattern as a graph

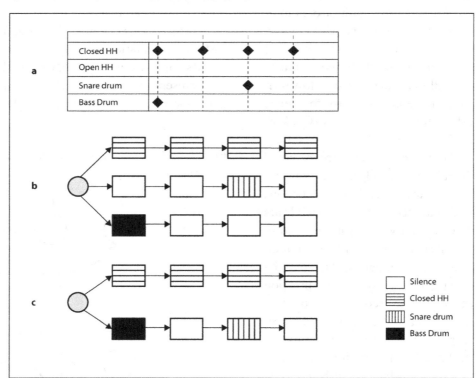

of different users or groups, and suggest potential interesting combinations of sounds. A grammar can also be seen as an agreement between remote collaborators working in different parts of a musical work. A central issue is how can we encode grammars in XML documents so that they can be shared among different programs and still remain human-readable.

The most well known representation of (context free) grammars is the Backus-Naur Form (BNF). Essentially, it defines a grammar as a set of production rules, each one composed of a non-terminal symbol (the left hand side of the production) and a set of alternative possible replacement strings, composed of both terminal and non-terminal strings. Several variations of this form exist and are widely used in the definition of programming languages and protocols. An example of XML representation of grammars that is equivalent to a BNF variant can be found in the speech recognition grammar specification (http://www.w3.org/TR/speech-grammar), which provides the option of ABNF and XML representations. Rule definitions have an attribute that uniquely identifies the rule within a document. Thus, the Universal Resource Identifier (URI) of a rule is absolutely defined by the URI of the document and the identifier attribute of the rule. A rule definition contains rule expansions, which may be tokens, rule references, or sets of any of both (sequences, alternatives and repeats). This limits the scope of these grammars to context-free grammars, where each rule represents a variable in the grammar and can be expanded to sequences or alternatives of variables and terminals. Tokens are terminal symbols (in the case of speech recognition grammars, tokens are usually text). Rule references are simply references to URIs of other rules. Sequences are defined by the order of XML elements, while alternatives are defined by a specific tag. Repeats are marked by an attribute in the repeated element.

This example illustrates some straightforward aspects of the design of XML representations of grammars, such as the nesting of rules and the use of references. For music representation, it is common to try to preserve context sensitivity, depending on the level of automation that is needed. Context-sensitive grammars are usually quite complex for computational manipulation, but as we have reviewed, some composers chose to manually deal with such grammars in the 80s. Context sensitivity implies that both the left hand and the right hand of a production rule can be represented as a compositions of tokens and references to other rules. On the other hand, musical grammars will need to accommodate parallelism, so these compositions can be represented as graphs. The representation of graphs is discussed in the next section. However, graph grammars introduce the issue of embedding, which must be taken into account for the representation of rules.

A graph grammar-rewriting rule defines that a given subgraph (embedded in a host graph) can be replaced by another subgraph. The problem is: how will this new subgraph connect to the host graph? In string grammars, embedding is trivial. A string can be seen as a simple graph where each token is a node connected to the following token with a directed edge. A string replacement rule obviously implies connecting the first token of the new string to the token that preceded the replaced string, and the last token to the token that followed the replaced string. In graph grammars, the replaced subgraph can have an arbitrary number of connections to the host graph depending on the problem. Again, this can be simplified in the case of context-free grammars. Several strategies, such as Node Label Controlled (NLC) embedding have been defined for node replacement grammars (Engelfriet & Rozenberg, 1990). In NLC grammars, embedding rules are defined globally for all rules as relations among nodes with some specific labels. It has been shown that this kind of grammars is less general for the purpose of graph rewriting than other grammars where embedding rules are defined locally. However, this mechanism can be used as a simple approach to define musical grammars. For example, one may concede that any music fragment has a starting point and an ending point. A node replacement grammar can then be defined so that when a node is replaced by a graph, the starting point inherits incoming edges of the replaced node, and the ending point inherits its outgoing edges. The ending node does not need be the one that ends last. Continuing with the example of a drum loop, the last cymbal sound in a drum pattern can be less important than the last bass drum or snare sound to define the end of the pattern. This strategy does not allow maintaining parallel connections among "tracks" in a single expansion. Still, it can be argued that the need of such parallel connections implies the need of separate rules. On the other hand, synchronous start of several sounds (parallelism) will require the addition of a virtual initial node with no sound. An example implementation of this idea is described later.

MUSIC SURFACE

The concept of surface structure was introduced in the context of linguistics by Chomsky to emphasize the power of grammars to describe the "deep structure" of a language. From the point of view of a generative grammar, the observable structure of sentences is able to convey meaning because it has been generated by the rules of a grammar. Jackendoff and Lehrdal (1981) popularized the identification of the score representation of music in the western tradition with the "musical surface." While the score representation is limited with respect to other musical cultures, the use of structured documents to represent musical surface can be used to share musical ideas of a wide range of styles and cultures. The point of the grammar approach is that the surface representation should reflect sequences and parallelism as relationships among musical events, and not merely represent their position in a time line. In this sense, the general use of timed events for storing and reproducing

music implies that the actual musical structure is not taken into account by programs, which hinders their use for collaborative composition.

Many XML representations of music surface have been proposed for traditional western notation. Since they are subdivided in parts and measures, music scores can be represented naturally in XML as hierarchies. This is the case for example of MusicXML and MDL (Good, 2001). Still, there is a wide variety of musical practices that cannot be represented with western notation. A representation of music as an ensemble of audio segments can be used for some of them. This approach was enabled by the MPEG-7 standard (Manjunath, Salembier, & Sikora, 2002) with the definition of the Segment Descriptor Scheme (DS), a description scheme for multimedia objects that allows defining them as compositions of segments. The MPEG-7 Segment DS allows the definition of hierarchies and arbitrary relationships between media segments such as audio. Still, the standard is more oriented to the description of existing content (e.g. for indexing and navigation) than to the creation of the new content. On the other hand, the standard addresses all kinds of multimedia content, including video, images, and 3D. This generality adds a lot of overhead by introducing many complexity layers that are not needed for music composition.

As described earlier, a relatively general approach to music surface representation is to use a graph where nodes represent sound objects that can be linked to audio files. By restricting this graph to a rooted tree, we can then easily cut and collapse fragments of a music document into grammar variables, or meaningful units that can be shared and reused. From a conceptual standpoint, the main issue with this approach is that silence is no longer considered an empty space, but a part of the composition. This contrasts with the "ruler-style" representation of time that has become general in music sequencers, although not with the representation of silence in traditional music notation. In this sense, the use of graph notation assumes that the samples associated to terminal tokens of the grammar already have an appropriate length with respect to the rhythm of the piece. The lexical map should allow to specify start and end points if the represented object is a fragment of the referenced sound file.

We can now simply focus on the representation of music fragments as graphs. A graph is usually described as a set of nodes and a set of edges. A general approach to representing graphs in XML is GraphML (http://graphml.graphdrawing.org). GraphML documents basically contain lists of node and edge elements. Node elements have a mandatory identifier attribute, and edges refer to node identifiers in their source and target attributes. A node identifier is necessarily unique only within a graph document, and is used to represent the structure of the graph. Thus, it cannot be used to represent any other information. Additional data can be defined for nodes and edges but is kept separate from the structure. GraphML aims to gather some consensus as a general way to exchange graph data. In this sense, using GraphML for music applications could enable the use of general purpose graph drawing programs and libraries for music editing. However, GraphML is not targeted at the definition of grammars. On the other hand, music applications can benefit from a more specific format that defines music-oriented restrictions directly in the XML schema definition. For the case of music surface representation, nodes represent terminal tokens that at some point are associated to sounds. While in GraphML nodes can be absolutely identified by the document URI and the node identifier, it may be convenient that node elements can directly point to their lexical mapping (in the case of the musical surface) or to a rule definition (when graphs are used in the grammar specification). With respect to edges, additional information may typically not be necessary, but some uses can be described. For example for the representation of algorithmic compositions, edges can be labeled with probability values.

LEXICAL MAP

The interest in formal grammars for music composition was mainly influenced by their success with natural language. In linguistics, formal grammars have made possible an understanding of the importance of structure in the transmission of information with independence of the meaning of words. In natural languages, the meaning of words has generally nothing to do with their written or phonetic representation but is conventionally defined. Musical objects, such as notes, generally do not refer to real objects or concepts, but they are articulated into higher level structures like in other languages. This parallelism in the use and articulation of discrete symbol systems has been related to a more general principle of self-diversifying systems (Merker, 2006).

The concept of a lexical map between terminal tokens of a grammar and actual sound objects was investigated by Roads (1979). Roads defined three general forms of lexical mapping. The first form is arbitrary mapping. The other two forms require a lexicon of sound objects that is grouped according to some acoustic features. This grouping is understood as relevant to a grammatical function, so that the mapping is not arbitrary. In our drum loop example, this could be illustrated by a classification of percussion instrument sounds. Roads distinguished between injective (each terminal maps to one sound from the ordered lexicon) and polymorphic (one-to-many, many-to-one) mappings. Polymorphic mappings were regarded as a complex situation equivalent to context-sensitive rules.

Current audio description technologies based on feature extraction and machine-learning techniques (see e.g. Kim, Moreau, & Sikora, 2006) allow us to establish functional groupings. This means that grammars that use discrete descriptors as their terminal alphabet can be used for analysis and generation of music based on audio segments. Generally speaking, a lexical map will describe how the alphabet of terminals used in the production rules is assigned an actual sound object. In this sense, we will consider any alphabet to be a partition of a collection of sound objects, so that all elements of the database are mapped to some symbol of the alphabet. If the partition is hard (i.e., each sound belongs to only one group), the mapping is equivalent to "one-to-many" ("injective" mapping being a particular case when there is one sound per group). Soft partitions, such as fuzzy or overlapping partitions will pose additional problems. For example mining patterns in musical graphs where each node can have more than one label will result in a combinatorial explosion. A perhaps preferable approach is to consider different perceptual facets (e.g. pitch, timbre, loudness ...) where hard partitions can be used to obtain a discrete symbol system, and use different grammars for each facet.

One question with regard to a partition of a database is how many symbols are desirable. While the answer to this question will depend on the application, it may be desirable to consider symbol hierarchies. One example of hierarchy could be the general classification of musical instruments into families and subfamilies. This approach allows the extraction of patterns with different levels of detail. If patterns have to be found in a small amount of audio graphs, it may be easier to work at a higher level in the hierarchy. This generality can be called the "lexical level" of an alphabet. Many hierarchical clustering algorithms allow the construction of such hierarchies (Jain & Dubes, 1988). Supervised approaches based on hierarchies of classifiers are also common in audio data mining (Zhang & Kuo, 1999).

THE *GRAPHEME* REPRESENTATION

As part of our ongoing research in collaborative composition systems, we have implemented a music representation based on the ideas exposed in this chapter. The system evolved from the graph representation used in freesound radio (http://ra-dio.freesound.org), an online radio station based on sounds from freesound.org where a genetic algorithm generates recombinations of sounds from the compositions created by users (Roma, 2008; Roma, Herrera, & Serra, 2008). The composition program in freesound radio and the associated graph representation were developed with the perspective that the sound file sharing community could benefit from greater possibilites for collaborative composition based on the sounds from the database. While the graph representation had a general good reception, it lacked the modularity of the grammar approach. The current framework based on graph grammars makes it possible for users to share intermediate representations, and to exploit the generative aspect of grammars as a compositional aid.

Our current prototype consists of a music creation program based on sounds from the freesound database. This database currently holds more than 100,000 sounds. The interface allows a user to search for sounds in the database, with the help of a partition performed by a clustering algorithm. Selected sounds are added to a palette, from which they can be dragged to a composition canvas. The composition interface allows the piece to be specified as a set of relationships between objects, rather than placing them in a predefined temporal grid. It is possible, though, to arbitrarily add silence nodes, as well as to edit start and end points of audio clips. However, an important restriction with respect to the previous version is that cycles are not allowed, which, as discussed, makes subgraphs contractible. The user is presented an initial and final special nodes that facilitate the embedding of any graph as a node of another graph. Since cycles involving several nodes are not possible, the only way to create a loop is to effectively contract a subgraph. This, along with the space limitation of the canvas, forces the user to continuously define the groupings that are meaningful in the composition, and hence the compositional process is split in several structural levels. We refer to these graphs as sample patches.

Each of the patches is stored in an XML file that describes the structure of the composition, as well as an automatically rendered audio file and a bitmap file for representing the node in higher-level compositions. A simple example is listed in below. All of the groupings made during the composition process are stored and optionally shared with other users, which facilitates collaborative building of higher-level structures. The XML document is divided between a "mappings" section and a "graph" section. The mappings section contains the lowest level lexical mappings, which refer

Box 1.

```
<xml>
    <audiograph name="4keys" author="simple machines">
        <maps>
            <map
                id = "9185__melack__claus_2#66267_141725"
                url = " http://www.freesound.org/download/9185/9185_melack_
claus_2.wav"
                start="66267"
                end="141725"
                    type="audio"
                icon = " http://media.freesound.org/data/9/images/9185__
melack__claus_2.png"/>
        </maps>
        <graph start="0" end="1">
            <nodes>
                <node id="0" x="-9" y="250"/>
                <node id="1" x="970" y="250"/>
                <node id="2" x="180" y="252"
                        map="9185__melack__claus_2#66267_141725"/>
                <node id="3" x="401" y="268"
                        map="9185__melack__claus_2#66267_141725"/>
                <node id="4" x="604" y="277"
                        map="9185__melack__claus_2#66267_141725"/>
                <node id="4" x="795" y="269"
                        map="9185__melack__claus_2#66267_141725"/>
            </nodes>
            <edges>
                <edge source="2" target="3"/>
                <edge source="3" target="4"/>
                <edge source="4" target="5"/>
                <edge source="5" target="1"/>
                <edge source="0" target="2"/>
            </edges>
        </audiograph>
</xml>
Sample markup.
```

to actual sound files (terminals) or other graphs (variables). In the first case, the mapping may include segment boundaries. The graph section consists of a sequence of nodes and a sequence of edges. Each node refers to one of the mappings, and many nodes can refer to the same mapping. Nodes with no mapping are virtual nodes used to mark the beginning and end of the patch and are used for embedding of patches in other patches.

A sample patch can be seen as a grammar rule that expands a node into a graph. Hence, the surface of a complete piece is obtained by recursively expanding all of the referenced subgraph using the embedding rules based on virtual start and end nodes. This expansion is based on the embedding rules: these consists simply in wiring the incoming edge of the replaced node to the nodes in the replacement patch that are connected to its start node, and the outgoing edges to the node in the replacement patch that is connected to its end node (Figure 4). This means that all of the authors involved in the piece can be tracked.

Figure 4. Example of the embedding process: the host patch (a) contains two nested patches as nodes. The first one is replaced by the replacement patch (b) using the start and end nodes (c).

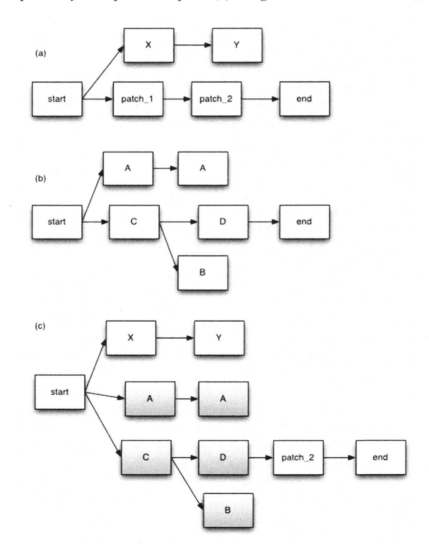

Higher-level lexical mappings are generated in the same format using information stored in a generic database used by the application. These mappings depend on partitions of the database computed by a clustering algorithm. Thus, for the same graph, we can derive multiple expansion rules at different levels of lexical generality, which allows us to detect common patterns among users. Initial experiments with this system were described in Roma and Herrera (2010). The current version of the prototype can be accessed at http://radio.freesound.org.

CONCLUSION AND FUTURE DEVELOPMENTS

Current practices in computer-aided music composition often imply the manipulation and organization of sound objects represented as digital audio files. Most current representations are based on a single document, where the evolution of the composition is stored in successive revisions. In order to facilitate collaborative creation of music based on audio samples, we propose a general framework that involves distinct representations of intermediate products that reflect the work in progress.

We have shown that graph grammars provide a theoretical ground for the development of such framework. Grammars provide mechanisms for analysis and generation of music that can be used in networked applications with simple interfaces. As an extension of string grammars, graph grammars allow the manipulation of both sequential and parallel structures. Representation of audio graph grammars can be encoded in XML.

We have presented an example implementation of this approach. Still, many possibilities remain to be explored. The described language has originated from a specific application but aims to be generalizable. We plan to evaluate it in several applications related with popular practices such as rhythm programming or soundscape composition. Specific applications can benefit from the definition of appropriate sound object ontologies. Finally, probabilistic grammars (where each expansion rule is assigned a certain probability) can be used when many example compositions are available.

REFERENCES

Ames, C. (1989). The Markov process as a compositional model: A survey and tutorial. *Leonardo Music Journal*, *22*(2). doi:10.2307/1575226

Casey, M. (2005). Acoustic lexemes for organizing internet audio. *Contemporary Music Review*, *24*(6). doi:10.1080/07494460500296169

Chion, M. (1983). *Guide des objets sonores*. Paris, France: Buchet/Chastel.

Chomsky, N. (1957). *Syntactic structures*. The Hague, The Netherlands: Mouton.

Cook, D., & Holder, L. B. (2000). Graph data mining. *IEEE Intelligent Systems*, *15*(2). doi:10.1109/5254.850825

Cox, C., & Warner, D. (Eds.). (2004). *Audio culture: Readings in modern music*. New York, NY: Continuum.

Engelfriet, J., & Rozenberg, G. (1990). Graph grammars based on node rewriting: An introduction to nlc graph grammars . In *Graph-Grammars and Their Application to Computer Science* (pp. 12–23). Bremen, Germany: Springer-Verlag. doi:10.1007/BFb0017374

Engelfriet, J., & Rozenberg, G. (1997). Node replacement graph grammars . In Rozenberg, G. (Ed.), *Handbook of Graph Grammars and Computing by Graph Transformation* (pp. 1–94). Singapore, Singapore: World Scientific Publishing Co. doi:10.1142/9789812384720_0001

Good. (2001). MusicXML for notation and analysis. In W. B. Helwet & E. Selfridge-Field (Eds.), The Virtual Score. Cambridge, MA: MIT Press.

Jackendoff, R., & Lehrdal, F. (1981). Generative music theory and its relationship to psychology. *Journal of Music Therapy, 25*(1).

Jain, A. K., & Dubes, R. C. (1988). *Algorithms for clustering data*. Upper Saddle River, NJ: Prentice Hall.

Kim, H., Moreau, N., & Sikora, T. (2006). *MPEG-7 audio and beyond: audio content indexing and retrieval*. Hoboken, NJ: Wiley and Sons.

Lerdahl, F., & Jackendoff, R. (1983). *A generative theory of tonal music*. Cambridge, MA: MIT Press.

Madsen, S. T. (2003). Automatic discovery of parallelism and hierarchy in music. (Master Thesis). University of Arhus. Arhus, Denmark.

Manjunath, B. S., Salembier, P., & Sikora, T. (2002). *Introduction to MPEG-7*. New York, NY: Wiley and Sons.

Merker, B. (2006). Layered constraints on the multiple creativities of music . In Deliège, I., & Wiggins, G. (Eds.), *Musical Creativity: Multidisciplinary Research in Theory and Practice*. New York, NY: Psychology Press.

Pfaltz, J., & Rosenfeld, A. (1967). *Web grammars*. Paper presented at the Joint International Conference on Artificial Intelligence. Washington, DC.

Roads, C. (1978). Composing grammars. In *Proceedings of the 1977 International Computer Music Conference*. San Francisco, CA: ACM.

Roads, C. (1979). Grammars as a representation for music. *Computer Music Journal, 3*(1). doi:10.2307/3679756

Roads, C. (1982). An overview of music representations. In Baroni, M., & Callegari, L. (Eds.), *Musical Grammars and Computer Analysis*. Firenze, Italy: Leo S. Olschi.

Roma, G. (2008). Freesound radio: Supporting collective organization of sounds. (Master Thesis). Universitat Pompeu Fabra. Barcelona, Spain.

Roma, G., & Herrera, P. (2010). Graph grammar representation for collaborative sample-based music creation. In *Proceedings of the 5th Audio Mostly Conference*. Audio Mostly.

Roma, G., Herrera, P., & Serra, X. (2009). *Freesound radio: Supporting music creation by exploration of a sound database*. Paper presented at the Computational Creativity Support Workshop (CHI 2009). Boston, MA.

Rozenberg, G. (Ed.). (1997). Handbook of graph grammars and computing by graph transformation. Singapore, Sinapore: World Scientific Publishing Co.

Schaeffer, P. (1966). *Traité des objets musicaux*. Paris, France: Seuil.

Woods, W. A. (1970). Transition network grammars for natural language analysis. *Communications of the ACM, 13*(10). doi:10.1145/355598.362773

Zhang, T., & Kuo, C.-C. J. (1999). Hierarchical classification of audio data for archiving and retrieving. Paper presented at the IEEE International Conference on Acoustics, Speech, and Signal Processing. Phoenix, AZ.

Chapter 7
Structuring Music–Related Movements

Alexander Refsum Jensenius
University of Oslo, Norway

ABSTRACT

The chapter starts by discussing the importance of body movement in both music performance and perception, and argues that for future research in the field it is important to develop solutions for being able to stream and store music-related movement data alongside other types of musical information. This is followed by a suggestion for a multilayered approach to structuring movement data, where each of the layers represents a separate and consistent subset of information. Finally, examples of two prototype implementations are presented: a setup for storing GDIF-data into SDIF-files, and an example of how GDIF-based OSC streams can allow for more flexible and meaningful mapping from controller to sound engine.

INTRODUCTION

Looking at the last century of music research, particularly what has been done within musicological departments, we find an overwhelming focus on analyses of symbolic music notation, particularly in the form of scores. The focus on scores as the centre that much of western music theory is circulating around is obviously because their symbolic nature allows for an easily quantifiable representation that can be used for many different types of analyses. This is probably also one of the reasons why much of computer based

music analysis have focused on scores as the basic material, which again has led to an interest in developing various types of markup languages for representing the scores.

While scores can undoubtedly reveal many interesting aspects of the powers of music, we should we should not forget that they are mainly a representation of the composer's intention of musical structures to be performed. This also means that although many parameters can be derived from the score, others can only be found when listening to the musical sound. The advent of faster computers have made it possible to carry out analysis on the musical sound itself, and a large community of researchers have developed various

DOI: 10.4018/978-1-4666-2497-9.ch007

methods and tools for extracting features ranging from low (signal), middle (perceptual) and high (cognitive/emotional) levels. This has again led to standardisation needs for such audio based descriptors, e.g. the Sound Description Interchange Format (SDIF) and MPEG-7 descriptors.

The last couple of decades have seen yet another shift in attention among music researchers, mainly that of studying music not only as notes in a score or the physical and perceptual properties of musical sound, but rather to investigate body movement involved in both music performance and perception. While there are few that dispute the importance of body movement in performance and perception of music, comparably little attention has been given to movement when music has been analysed and discussed. While thinking about music as "organised notes," or "organised sound" seems mainstream, it is still radical to suggest that music could be thought of as "organised movement." Recent research goes even further in arguing that not only is body movement crucial for the performance of music, but that we also think about music through mental imagery of sensations originating in the body (see e.g. Godøy, 2004). This is the background for our interest in studying music-related movements in both performers and perceivers, and some theoretical discussions, observation studies and experiments on this can be found in e.g. Godøy and Leman (2009).

This chapter is concerned with how we can create representations of music-related body movement, covering topics such as synchronisation of multidimensional data streams, classification of movements, and issues related to streaming and storing of such data.

BACKGROUND

A major obstacle to music-related movement research is the lack of appropriate formats and standards. Working with hardware and software tools that cannot efficiently interchange information is a limitation not only for the single researcher, but it also effectively blocks collaboration between researchers and institutions. Rather than analysing data, this makes researchers spend a lot of time and effort just getting their data transferred from one system to another. Developing formats that can be used in music-related movement research therefore seems of great importance, and is something that can also benefit other fields, e.g. music technology and human-computer interaction.

Data streaming and storage has been a major challenge in our research group for a long time. Only storing data from a single sensor interface, and synchronise these data with simultaneously recorded audio and video files is not a trivial task. In the beginning, we stored raw sensor data in text files, with references to the corresponding audio and video files. However, since we did not store any information about the setup, scaling and filtering used, etc., these data files quickly became useless as we continued to change our experimental setups. In later studies, we were more careful about taking notes, and including these with the data sets, but we still ended up with lots of problems relating to synchronisation between the data files and the audio and video files.

After talking to other researchers in the field, and starting formal collaboration with some other groups, we realised that nobody seemed to have a general solution to store their experimental data coherently and consistently. This was the reason I started sketching out a suggestion for the Gesture Description Interchange Format (GDIF), of which a first proposal was presented at the Conference on New Interfaces for Musical Expression (NIME) in 2006 (Jensenius, et al., 2006). Over the last years several prototype setups have been developed to test out GDIF ideas in practice: using hand movements to control sound spatialisation in realtime (Marshall, et al., 2006), analysing violin performance (Maestre, et al., 2007), and using multilayered GDIF streams in a networked setup (Jensenius, 2007). GDIF was also discussed in a workshop of the EU COST Action 287 ConGAS4 in Oslo in December 2006, and was discussed in a panel session on music-related movement formats at the International Computer Music Conference (ICMC) in Copenhagen in August 2007 (Jensenius, et al., 2007).

A number of formats exist that are related to, and cover parts of, our needs to stream and store music-related movement data. Some of these formats are directly linked to the motion capture systems they are accompanying, such as the AOA format used with the optical tracker systems from Adaptive Optics, the BRD format used with the Flock of Birds electromagnetic trackers, and C3D used with the Vicon infrared motion capture systems. Of these three, C3D seems to have emerged as the de facto standard format for many motion capture applications. There are also several formats that have been developed for using motion capture data in animation tools and software, such as the BVA and BVH formats from Biovision, the ASF and AMC formats from game developer Acclaim (Lander, 1998), and the CSM format used by Autodesk 3ds Max.

Some of these motion capture formats are used in our community of researchers on music-related movement, but often these formats create more problems than they solve. One problem is that they are proprietary and often closely connected to a specific hardware system and/or software solution, which makes them inflexible and impractical for our needs. Another problem is that they often focus on full-body motion descriptors, based on a fully articulated skeleton. This may not always be convenient in setups where we are only interested in a specific part of the body, or if unspecified objects (e.g. an instrument) is also being recorded. Yet another problem is that most of these standards are intended to store only raw data and/or basic movement descriptors, which leaves little room to store analytical results and annotations, as well as various types of music-related data (audio, video, MIDI, OSC, notation, etc.).

Another type of format that could be interesting for our needs is the large number of XML-based formats used in motion capture and animation, for example the Motion Capture Markup Language (MCML—Chung & Lee, 2004), Avatar Markup Language (AML—Kshirsagar, et al., 2002), Sign Language Markup Language (Elliott, et al., 2000), Multimodal Presentation Markup Language (MPML—Prendinger, et al., 2004), Affective Presentation Markup language (APML—De Carolis, et al., 2004), Multimodal Utterance Representation Markup Language (MURML—Kranstedt, et al., 2002), Virtual Human Markup Language (VHML—Beard & Reid, 2002), etc. Again, none of these languages are directly useful for our needs, but there are certainly interesting parts that could be used and which should be evaluated more closely.

The MPEG series of formats and standards are also relevant. Developed by the Motion Picture Expert Group (MPEG), these standards have gained a strong commercial position and wide distribution, and allow for audio and video compression (MPEG-1, MPEG-2, and MPEG-4—Hartmann, et al., 2002), as well as for storing metadata and annotations (MPEG-7—Martinez, et al., 2002; Manjunath, et al., 2002). While these standards could potentially solve many of our storage problems, including synchronisation with audio and video, MPEG-7 lack a number of features that are vital for our needs.

When it comes to streaming and storing low-level movement data, the Gesture Motion Signal (GMS) format is particularly interesting. GMS is a binary format based on the Interchange File Format (IFF) standard (Morrison, 1985), and was developed by the ACROE group in Grenoble and partners in the EU Enactive Network of Excellence. GMS provides a solution for structuring, storing, and streaming basic movement data (Evrard, et al., 2006; Luciani, et al., 2006), but unfortunately such files do not make it possible to include mid- and higher level features. This, on the other hand, has been the focus in the development of the Performance Markup Language (PML—McGilvray, 2007), and the Music and Gesture File

(MGF—Pullinger, et al., 2008) formats developed at the University of Glasgow. PML is an extension to the Music Encoding Initiative (MEI—Roland, 2002), and the main idea is to facilitate the analysis and representation of performance in the context of the musical score. PML allows the description of performance events and analytical structures with reference to the score and external sources such as audio files. The current version uses MusicXML as a basis for score representation, though PML can be used with any XML based score representation.

Finally, we should not forget the Sound Description Interchange Format (SDIF), the inspiration for GDIF. SDIF was developed jointly by CNMAT at University of California, Berkeley, IRCAM in Paris and the Music Technology Group at Pompeu Fabra University in the late 1990s, as a solution to standardise the way audio analysis is stored (Wright, et al., 1998). Although SDIF may not be the most well known format, it is supported and used in several audio programs and programming environments (Schwarz & Wright, 2000). Most importantly, the SDIF specification and software implementations have tackled a number of challenges relating to the synchronisation of multiple streams of high-speed data, and, by necessity, it ensures synchronisation between audio and other types of data. That is also the reason why GDIF development has focused on being an add-on to SDIF. That said, GDIF development is mainly focusing on laying the ground for creating structured representations of music-related movement at various levels, and an XML-based implementation is certainly something that is feasible (and also partially implemented, see Maestre, et al., 2007).

NEEDS

We have a number of different needs when creating solutions to stream and store music-related movement data, some of which will be presented in this section. First, we need a structured and coherent approach to handling a large number of different types of raw movement data and associated analytical results, including:

- **Raw Data:** Unprocessed data from sensing devices, for example motion capture systems, game controllers, MIDI devices, and custom built controllers.
- **Pre-Processed Data:** Filtered, scaled and normalised data that are the basis for further analysis.
- **Analytical Results:** The data resulting from both quantitative and qualitative analysis of the above mentioned data.

The idea is that all these data may be streamed and stored next to each other, as illustrated in Figure 1. A GDIF file may therefore contain a number of different time-synchronised streams so that it is possible to retrieve all the data from any point in time. It should also be possible to add new data streams resulting from various types of analyses, something that will allow different researchers to work on the same material.

Different Types of Raw Data

Let us start by looking at some of the different types of raw data typically being used in music-related movement research, all having different features and properties:

- **Motion Capture Systems:** Such systems usually output data at high speeds (up to 4000 Hz) for a number of multidimensional markers, anything from 2 to 50, sometimes even more. Each of the markers can be tracked with 3 or 6 degrees of freedom; position in XYZ coordinates and sometimes also orientation (azimuth, elevation, roll). Many commercial motion capture systems use their own proprietary software and formats to retrieve and store the data, although several seem to be able to export data in the C3D format.

Figure 1. A sketch of the different types of raw data and analytical results that could be streamed and stored in GDIF

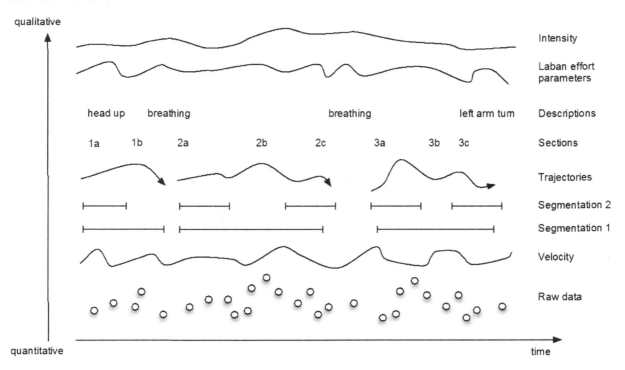

- **MIDI Devices:** Most commercial music controllers and instruments output MIDI. Since the MIDI standard is an event-based protocol, there is no information about the movements associated with the control messages. As such, MIDI is not particularly suited for streaming or storing continuous movement related data, but due to its widespread use, we need to find solutions to include data from such devices. This should not be too problematic since the MIDI specification is clear, and the messages are well defined. MIDI streams are typically output at fairly low sampling rates (up to a 100 Hz), and low bit-rates (7-bit).

- **Generic Controllers:** Game controllers, graphical tablets, and other commercial devices often use well-known protocols (e.g. Human Interface Device—HID) and use more or less well-defined ranges and resolutions. As is the case for MIDI devic-es, such general input devices mainly focus on control aspects, and not the body movements associated with these control messages, although the continuous control of a joystick may provide valuable information about the movement of the hand that is used to control the device.

- **Custom-Made Controllers and Instruments:** Such devices are more problematic to make general specifications for, since they often only exist as a single prototype. That said, custom-made controllers are often built with standard sensors, and use sensor interfaces based on a well-known protocols for data transfer (e.g. MIDI or Open Sound Control—OSC), which may be used as a starting point for a general specification.

Most of these devices have some sort of native format and messaging structure that should be preserved in later markup for backwards compatibility. This is also important in experiments, where it may be necessary to check the raw data in case there are problems or uncertainties with the formatting or analysis resulting from the markup in a new format.

Time and Synchronisation

One of the major challenges when it comes to finding a solution to structuring music-related movement, is that of *time coding* and *synchronisation*. Only structuring the raw data as mentioned above, poses a number of challenges when it comes to different sampling rates, number of streams, etc., and this is complicated further by the necessity to maintain time coding within streams, and synchronisation between streams of data.

First, time coding data that come from commercial motion capture systems that claim to operate with a "fixed" sampling rate should be an easy task. However, we have experienced that many of these systems are not as accurate as they claim to be, and there may be a substantial drift over time. This is particularly evident when recording data from high-speed systems that demand a lot of computer memory, disk access, and CPU processing. To keep up with the idea of being able to get back to the original raw data, our solution is to store both the time code from the device itself, along with a global time code for our own research setup.

Another challenge related to time coding inside streams is that several devices (for example MIDI) operate with delta time, based on specifying events relative to the preceding and/or succeeding events. The messages from such devices are typically sent at an uneven rate, transmitting only when they are active. Several challenges arise when synchronising data streams from devices using relative time coding with data sets using a fixed sample rate, and it is necessary to find a solution to handling such a time coding consistently. Here an important question is whether all streams should be time coded and sampled with

the same time code. This would allow for easier synchronisation, but it would probably also lead to redundant information being stored. For example, if data from a MIDI device is to be synchronised with data from a high speed motion capture system, the MIDI data would have to be recorded at a much faster rate than they are output from the MIDI device. Again, our solution is to allow each stream to operate with its own time coding, and create a system to secure synchronisation between the streams.

A third challenge is related to synchronising the various data streams with simultaneously recorded audio and video. Fortunately, there are several industry standards for both audio and video time coding and synchronisation, one of the most commonly used being the SMPTE time code. Using a video time code as the basis for time coding data in GDIF may not be the best option, though, since several of these time codes are based on a combination of time and video frames. In addition, the question of time code is related to the media formats and codecs being used. A research format that is intended to live for a while should not rely on specific audio and video formats/codecs (e.g. QuickTime, Windows Media Audio/Video, etc.), so we need to find a more generic solution to synchronise such media with the movement data.

Finally, we also have to tackle challenges related to synchronising data and media that are not based on a specific time code. Music is largely based on relative timing, often defined by a musical score, and different performances of the same piece often vary considerably in duration and timing. It is therefore important to develop solutions to synchronise the absolute or delta time codes of movement data, with the relative time codes of musical scores. This will probably have to be based on solutions to "time warp" data sets, or set musical "keyframes" that define synchronisation points.

REQUIREMENTS

When it comes to the format itself, there are several criteria that are important to make it versatile and useful in music-related movement research. The format should be:

- **Open:** The specification and the implementations should be free and open (as in open source) so that everyone can use them and expand them as they see fit.
- **Human-friendly:** It should be possible to easily understand what the data means by looking at the data stream or file, or there should be converters readily available if storing in a binary format.
- **Multiplatform:** Cross-platform and cross-software support is essential to ensure compatibility with systems past, present, and future.
- **Compatible:** It is important to ensure that the format will work with other relevant formats and standards. As far as possible, it should also be based on other well-known standards to allow for easy adaptation.
- **Simple:** The basic set of descriptors should be as small and simple as possible so that it is easy to get started using the format.
- **Extendable:** The format should allow for a great deal of flexibility when extending it to cover new areas that were not thought of in the original specification.
- **Efficient:** Since the main focus here is that of offline research, the above mentioned elements are the most important, and many of these contradict efficiency. That said, efficiency will also be a goal as long as it does not come in conflict with the other aims.

These requirements have been the basis for our choice of solutions and implementations that will be described in the following sections.

SOLUTION: A MULTILAYERED APPROACH

While many data formats often focus only on storage, we believe it is important to create a solution that allows for both streaming and storage. This allows for using the format not only for experimental setups, but also as a tool for realtime control in installation or performance. In fact, even though streaming and storage may seem as two widely different domains, they are often closely connected when working with music, since both sound and movement unfold in time. Streaming data from a controller and mapping these data to features in a music engine, involves many of the same types of processing and analyses as recording data to a file. In addition, since we see GDIF development as much about conceptualisation as it is about computer formats, both streaming and storage should be included in the process.

Streaming and Storage

GDIF is currently being developed in multiple directions: an implementation for realtime control of sound synthesis, and two different storage solutions, which is sketched out in Figure 2. The idea is that features from the recorded sound and sensor data will be converted to OSC streams and passed on using network communication (typically UDP/IP or TCP/IP). These OSC streams can then be mapped directly for use in a realtime model, or they can be passed on for storage.

For storing data from the OSC streams we are currently using the IRCAM's FTM library for the graphical programming environment Max/MSP/Jitter (Schnell, et al., 2005) to record files using the SDIF specification. This allows for synchronisation with audio, audio analysis and MIDI, and makes it possible to use the analytical tools available to SDIF to analyse GDIF data. For a more structured approach, and to be compatible with other software solutions, we have also developed

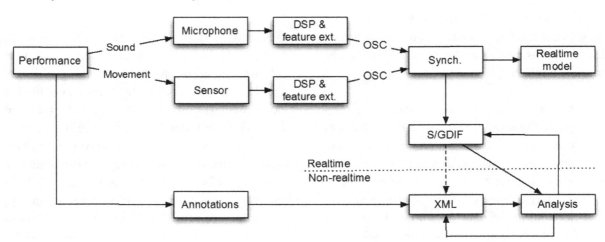

solutions for storing GDIF data in XML files. An example of this, in the context of analysing the movements in violin performance is discussed in Maestre et al. (2007).

The streaming/storage solution suggested in Figure 2 is but one of many ways to stream and store the data. In fact, we believe that the biggest challenge in future research is to work on the descriptors and specification of the content to be stored. For this reason, we have been focusing on understanding how different types of data are related, and how we can create solutions to structure them. An important starting point here is to differentiate between the different levels of data. Both practically and conceptually, it helps if we manage to separate between raw data coming from sensors, pre-processed data and the data resulting from various types of qualitative or quantitative analyses. A sketch showing one approach to this and a suggested namespace to use in OSC is shown in Figure 3. In this example, raw and pre-processed data of both sound and movement are separated into different streams called raw and cooked. Then a descriptive layer is suggested for handling analysed data that are directly referring to features in the sound and movement that can be described using techniques such as Laban Movement Analysis (LMA) (Laban, 1980), or

features from Schaeffer's typomorphological structures (Schaeffer, 1966; Godøy, 2006). The structure and properties of the different layers will be discussed in the following sections. The organisation of sound features will be left out in this discussion, and have just been included in the sketch to show that mid- and high-level features usually have to be considered from a multimodal perspective.

Acquisition Layers

The acquisition layers in Figure 3 refer to pre-analysed data: raw data coming from the device (raw) and pre-processed data (cooked). In the following discussion OSC-style namespaces are used as examples since this provides for a more compact notation, but the structures may also easily be formatted using XML tags. An important thing to remember is that all layers suggested here are optional and may be skipped if there is no need for them. The idea of having multiple layers is not to create large sets of redundant messaging, but rather suggest a structure for the way different types and levels of data could be communicated.

The raw layer is used to pass on raw data coming from the device. Here the idea is that the namespace should be constructed so that it reflects

Figure 3. Sketch of the multilayered approach suggested for the GDIF OSC namespace

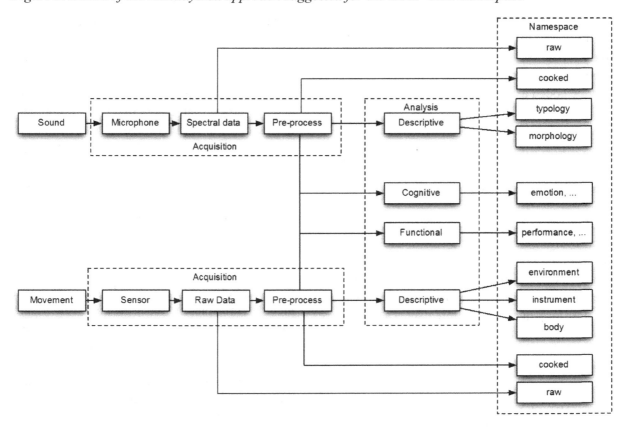

the way the data was received from the device. Game controllers, MIDI devices and other types of commercial controllers all have more or less well defined messages that can easily be turned into raw messages. For example, the namespace for a simple controller could be:

```
/raw/name/<controller number> <value>
```

Similarly, data from a MIDI keyboard could be coded as:

```
/raw/keyboard/<note> <velocity> <channel>
```

It is more difficult when it comes to data from custom-built controllers, in which the values often depend on the sensor interface being used. Here it might be relevant to code the strings from either the device, the sensor interface or the sensor:

```
/raw
        /device/<sensor number> <value>
        /sensor-interface/<sensor number> <value>
        /sensor/<sensor name> <value>
```

This could result in messages like:

```
/raw
        /cheapstick/2 32
        /teabox/4 255
        /sensor/accelerometer 24 54 40
```

Such messages may not be particularly useful without some extra information about the device, but, as will be described later, the idea is to allow metadata to be available in the system to provide information about what the data mean.

The structure of the cooked layer is similar to the raw layer, except that the data may have been filtered (for example using a low-pass filter to remove noise in the signal), and/or scaled to a useful range. For example, data from a joystick may be coded as:

```
/cooked/joystick/<controller number>
<0. - 1.>
```

Descriptive Layers

The descriptive layers are used for structuring data resulting from the analysis of the raw and cooked data layers. A first step here is often to clearly define which analytical perspective is used when describing data, and in the following, we will look at this from three separate layers: device, body, and environment.

Device Layer

The device layer represents data analysed with respect to the sensor, instrument, or controller used, totally independent of the performer and the performer's movements. The idea is that the device layer should be fairly generic, in the sense that devices with similar properties should be coded in the same way. This could be accomplished by creating a "device library," a collection of standardised namespaces for devices that share similar properties. For example, even though most commercial joysticks have a varying number of buttons and look differently, they still behave more or less similarly. Thus, it is possible to create generic device specifications for various popular devices, for examples joysticks, gamepads, mice, graphical tablets, etc. These specifications can then be used as the basis for all devices that have a similar (but not necessarily identical) functionality. This will allow for more flexibility and the possibility to interchange devices without having to worry about whether the raw data they output are identical.

One question in the device layer is how the values should be grouped. For example, the raw data from a joystick is usually transmitted as separate strings containing a control number and the associated value. But sometimes several such control numbers may be linked and dependent on each other, such as the two control numbers used to describe the tilt (x,y) of a joystick, and the rotation of the stick. Should all these messages be passed together in one message, or be split into multiple messages? Wright et al. (2001) argued for the former, and suggested that data from a joystick could be represented as:

```
/joystick/b xtilt ytilt rotation ...
```

when button "b" is pressed. Here they even included information about the buttons in a long string containing a number of different messages. This is a computationally efficient way of passing the data, but the problem is that the end user will not necessarily know what the different values mean. A more verbose and human-friendly, although less computationally efficient, way of structuring the message could be:

```
/device
    /joystick/tilt <x, y>
    /joystick/rotation <-1. - 1.>
```

An even more structured approach would be to pass on all messages as separate strings:

```
/device
    /joystick/button/b <1/0>
    /joystick/tilt/x <-1. - 1.>
    /joystick/tilt/y <-1. - 1.>
    /joystick/rotation <-1. - 1.>
```

This makes for more readable messages, and makes it very easy to parse the messages, but it will increase the traffic and computational load in the system, since the number of communicated bits is much higher than for the combined messages.

Ranges and Units

Notice that the range used in the above example is -1.–1. This is because a joystick will typically have a centre position around which it can be tilted and rotated in either direction. Using a -1.–1. range will secure that the centre position is at (0, 0), which seems more intuitive than having a centre position at (0.5, 0.5). Notice also that the above example is hierarchically organised around the functional aspect (tilt) of the device, rather than the dimensional (x,y). In some cases, however, it may be better to do it the other way around, for example:

```
/device
        /joystick/x/tilt <-1. - 1.>
        /joystick/y/tilt <-1. - 1.>
```

Such structural differences should be allowed, as long as they are clearly documented and implemented. However, we should be careful about allowing for too many different solutions, since one of the main goals of GDIF is to create a specification that will standardise the way messages are communicated.

An important issue in handling music-related movement data is the way units are used and defined. As far as possible it should be advised to use meaningful units, if they are known. However, when this is not possible, it is probably better to use a generic normalised range like 0.–1. or -1.–1 than sticking with some arbitrary range defined by the bit rate. For example, in the case of a joystick it may be better to convert the 8-bit (0-255) range returned from the HID protocol to a degrees when describing the rotation of a joystick:

```
/device/joystick/rotation <0 - 360>
```

The next question is how the unit should be described. Should it be part of the message:

```
/device/joystick/rotation <0 - 360>
degrees
```

```
/device/joystick/rotation/unit de-
grees
/device/joystick/rotation <0 - 360>
```

Again, this may depend on the usage. In a system where the units are fixed and well defined, the latter solution could be useful. However, other times it may well be that it could be useful to switch between Cartesian and polar coordinates, something which would make the former example a better choice.

Body Layer

The body layer describes the body and the body's movement in relation to the device, controller or instrument, as seen "through the eyes" of the performer. While the device layer describes activity in terms of the different elements of the device (e.g. joystick and buttons), the body layer focuses on movement of parts of the body (e.g. hands and fingers). Such body movement may sometimes be directly inferred from the raw sensor data (e.g. using a joystick), while other times they will have to be more loosely described. An example namespace of the movements associated with a joystick could be:

```
/body
    /hand/right/finger/2/press <1/0>
    /hand/right/location/horizontal
<-1. - 1.>
```

Notice that the namespace only refers to the body, and no information is available about the device. This opens for a more intuitive mapping process, and may allow for devices with similar movement properties to be exchanged unobtrusively.

There are a number of issues that will need to be addressed when developing the specification of the body layer. First, what type of coordinate system(s) should be used to describe the body? What type of naming convention(s) should be used? Should values be defined absolute or relative to a specific point in the body? If so, where should the reference point be? For a prototype setup of control of spatialisation with hand movements (as described in Marshall et al., 2006), we used a mirrored body model as shown in Figure 4. Here a positive movement space was defined for each hand in the forward, upward, outward quadrant of the body, which is typically where most of the movement takes place. The result was positive values when subjects moved their arms outwards, to the front, and upwards, something which simplified the mapping process in the setup.

One reason why the mirrored body model turned out to be so easy to work with is probably because it reflects the way we think and talk about our body. For example, we often think about an arm movement as "outwards," and not "left" or "right." Thus, creating such perceptually relevant namespaces may allow for a more intuitive mapping process. That said, further development of the body layer should probably also look at various types of biomechanical models used in motion capture systems, and see how they can fit into such a perceptual and descriptive paradigm.

Environment Layer

The *environment* layer is intended to code information about the relationship between various bodies and devices in a space. For example, in the prototype spatialisation setup described above, the orientation of the person was used to control the location of sound in the space. Further development of this layer can be done in collaboration with the Spatialisation Description Interchange Format (SpatDIF) developed at McGill University (Peters, 2008).

Functional Layers

The *functional* layers will be independent of both the technical and body-related descriptors presented above, and focus on describing the functional aspects of the movement. This can be based on the taxonomy of music-related movements presented as: *sound-producing, sound-facilitating, sound-accompanying* and *communicative* (Jensenius, et al., 2009). It can also be based on traditional music performance vocabulary, such as describing the dynamics of the performance (e.g. *ppp – fff*) or the playing style (e.g. *staccato* or *legato*). There is still a lot of conceptual work to be done before these layers can be specified, and it could be interesting to investigate how the structure from the *Performance Markup Language* (PML) could be used to create suitable namespaces.

Figure 4. Sketch of the mirrored and human-focused body model used in a prototype setup to control sound spatialisation with hand movements (Marshall, et al., 2006). Notice that the body is split in two, and two positive quadrants are defined on either side.

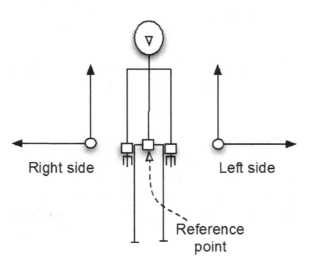

Cognitive Layers

The *cognitive* layers are intended to store data relating to higher-level features, for example abstract representations, metaphors, and emotional states. In many ways, this level is the most interesting when it comes to understanding and representing our experience of music, but it is also one of the most challenging to formalise and create a consistent structure of. For example, a metaphor like "intensity" may be used to describe music verbally, but it is not a trivial task to develop taxonomy for such a descriptor, and relate it to the low-level features of musical sound and movement. There is a growing body of research on these topics that could form the basis for creating relevant descriptors, for example by Bresin and Friberg (2000) and Camurri et al. (2003). They have been working on systems to analyse and model "expressive gestures" based on emotion parameters such as anger, fear, grief, and joy. So further development need to be done in close collaboration with researchers working on these topics.

PROTOTYPE IMPLEMENTATIONS

Over the last years we have developed a number of prototype setups using GDIF, and we shall here look at two of these, one for the recording of music-related movements in lab experiments,

and another for a simple mapping example. These examples should also help to illustrate some of the benefits, but also challenges, that we are facing in future development of formats for handling music-related body movement.

A Multilayered Setup for Motion Capture Studies

We are currently working on explorations of coarticulation and goal-points in music performance (Godøy, et al., 2008), and have created a laboratory setup using a multilayered GDIF-based recording system (Jensenius, et al., 2008). This modular setup, developed using components and modules in the Jamoma open source project for Max/MSP/Jitter (Place & Lossius, 2006), allows for quickly setting up observation studies with various combinations of motion capture equipment, video cameras and audio devices.

Table 1 shows an overview of some of the input devices we typically work within our setups, the number of values recorded, and the sampling and bit rates used. All of these are very different in nature, yet we still need to be able to record everything in a synchronized and structured manner.

Data from each of the devices (except for audio and video) are being converted to OSC streams at the first possible stage, and passed over the network to the master computer writing one combined SDIF file. As sketched in Figure 5, the

Table 1. List of data used in our setup, columns from left: input device, sampling rate in Hz, number of channels, resolution in bits, approximate bitrate in kbps

Input	# values	SR (Hz)	Bit
Optitrack IR motion capture	3-150	100	12
Phidgets accelerometers	3-30	60	32
Polhemus electromagnetic tracker	12	60	32
Biosensors	1-10	100	7
Video	1-3	86	8
Audio	2-8	44100	16
MIDI	3-20	100-1000	7

Figure 5. Sketch of GDIF data written to a SDIF file. The various streams consist of different types of frames and matrices, each of which have different resolution and sampling rates.

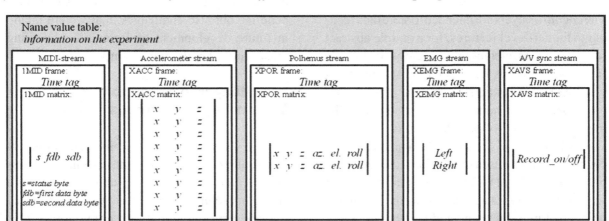

SDIF file contains separate *streams* recorded along a common timeline, where each stream consists of time-tagged *frames* within which the actual data are stored as *matrices* (Wright, et al., 1998). The frames and matrices are type-specific, meaning that different frame types consist of a different number of matrices, and different matrix types consist of a different number of rows and columns. This allows for handling data at various resolutions and speeds while still being synchronised.

The data are referred to with a set of custom defined frame and matrix types. For storing position and orientation data, we have defined three different matrix types:

```
1MTD XPOS { X, Y, Z }
 1FTD XPOS { XPOS position; }
1MTD XORI { azimuth, elevation, roll
}
 1FTD XORI { XORI orientation; }
1MTD XPOR { X, Y, Z, azimuth, eleva-
tion, roll}
 1FTD XPOR { XPOR position_and_orien-
tation; }
```

In the future, it may also be desirable to open for position descriptions using polar coordinates, but for the moment, we are using Cartesian coor-

dinates for the descriptions of points in space. We have also found the need for storing both velocity and acceleration data, and have defined two matrix types for this:

```
1MTD XVEL { X, Y, Z }
1FTD XVEL { XVEL velocity; }
1MTD XACC { X, Y, Z }
1FTD XACC { XACC acceleration; }
```

Since audio and video files are recorded on a separate computer, we use a synchronisation stream containing a binary on/off message recorded into a stream called XAVS:

```
1MTD XAVS { record_on }
 1FTD XAVS { XAVS audio_video_sync;
}
```

The end result is a structured SDIF/GDIF file where all data is tightly synchronized, and where the A/V sync stream also makes it possible to play back the data together with the recorded audio and video files. With custom built modules for Max/MSP and a toolbox for Matlab, it is possible to both record and playback data and media in Max/MSP and carry out non-realtime analyses in Matlab (Figure 6).

Figure 6. Example of SDIF/GDIF module in Max/MSP playing back recorded accelerometer data synchronised with video (left). Matlab script for reading SDIF/GDIF files and plotting the data.

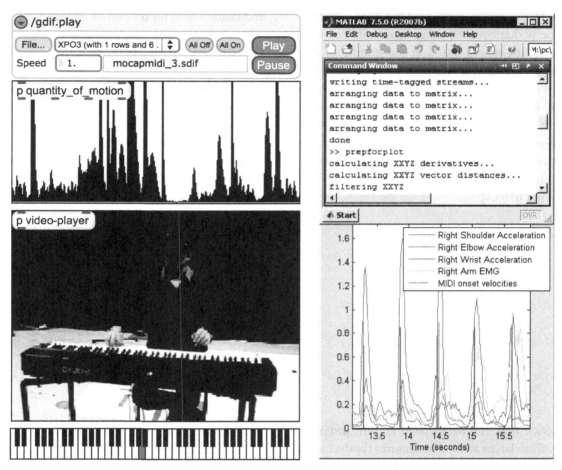

Mouse Mapping

Mapping between controller inputs to sound engine parameters is one of the most important aspects when creating new electronic instruments. While this may be hard-coded in either hardware or software, taking a more structured approach could greatly help in improving the time spent when creating mappings, but also the perceptual quality of the mappings being made. This section will briefly present an example of how a GDIF-based OSC namespace can help in setting up mappings from a computer mouse to a sound engine.

Rather than using the raw data coming from a computer mouse for setting up a mapping, we can define a set of descriptive layers that are more perceptually relevant from a user's point of view. As mentioned above, the device layer is focused around the functionality and elements of the device. The device layer for a mouse can be implemented with the following namespace:

```
/gdif/device
/mouse/button/1/press <1/0>
/mouse/location/horizontal <-1. - 1.>
/mouse/location/vertical <-1. - 1.>
```

Except for the different naming, this layer could be seen as fairly similar to how a raw and cooked layer could look like. One important difference is that here the range is normalised to a range -1.–1., where 0,0 is in the middle of the screen. This could be seen as more useful than for example having screen pixel values originating at the top left corner, which is the values being sent from the operating system.

The body descriptive layer, which describes the values from the perspective of the performer using the device, could be implemented with the following namespace:

```
/gdif/body
/hand/right/finger/2/press <1/0>
/hand/right/location/horizontal <-1.
- 1.>
/hand/right/location/vertical <-1. -
1.>
/hand/right/motion/quantity <-1. -
1.>
/hand/right/motion/direction <0. -
360.>
```

Notice how the namespace is built progressively from larger to smaller features (body, hand, finger), and that the specifications of the hand (right) and finger (2) are parts of the namespace. Here numbers are used to indicate the fingers, but we should work towards a better and more uniform terminology of the various parts of the body. As the mapping example in the next section will show, this allows for wildcards when parsing the values. This body layer will necessarily have to be subjective and context-dependent, so here the hand and finger that I use with the mouse have been chosen. Regarding the device layer, I also find it practical to use a -1.–1. range with the home position in the middle (0,0) of the movement space. In addition to the location, the body layer also displays the direction and quantity of motion, since it is often more interesting to use such movement data for control purposes. This is yet another way of making the returned values less dependent on the specific device being used, and rather focus on properties of the movement.

Header Information

All of the above mentioned data types and streams refer to dynamic data. However, it could also be useful to have access to "static" information that can be stored as header information at the beginning of a file, or be queried for in realtime. First, general information about the location and the setup should be defined, for example:

```
/general
/date 2009.01.01
/time 12:44:00 CET
/location "FourMs lab, University of
Oslo"
/author "Alexander Refsum Jensenius"
/experiment "Mouse-Joystick"
/session 1
/devices "Trust GM-4200 and Saitek
ST290"
/description           "Testing if us-
ers prefer a mouse over a
joystick in the control of a VST soft
synth running in Max."
```

It may also be necessary to include more specific information about the devices listed in the general information. They could be defined based on the generic device type they represent, such as:

```
/device
/type mouse
/name GM-4200
/manufacturer Trust
/id S12116847
/dof 3
/buttons 5
/description "A right handed computer
mouse"
```

The idea is that all relevant information should be available at any time. In realtime situations, this may allow for networked setups in which a new user could browse the network for available devices, find their properties, and set them up for control. These data could also be written in the headers of the stored files, so that it is possible to identify what the data mean, how they were recorded, and which devices they were recorded from.

Flexible and Meaningful Mapping

One of the main ideas behind the realtime implementation of GDIF is to allow for the quicker and easier creation of mappings between controllers and sound engines. The mapping system suggested by Malloch et al. (2007) is a good example of how such a structured approach could simplify the mapping process. Here the idea is to use a mapping patch that will automatically list all the available devices and their namespaces, and allow for mapping between controllers and sound engines by dragging lines between the various parameters.

The possibility to create flexible mappings is important, but even more important is to work towards solutions for creating meaningful mappings. This is something, which was explored in ESCHER, a modular system where the descriptions of the movements carried out with a controller are separate from the parameters of the synthesis engine, and where mappings are created with an intermediate abstract parameter level between the movement and the sound parameter levels (Wanderley, et al., 1998). These ideas have later been developed into models focusing on using several perceptual mapping layers: one layer for movements, one for sound, and one between movement and sound (Hunt & Wanderley, 2002; Arfib, et al., 2002). This makes it possible to create mappings between actions and sounds based on perceptually relevant features, rather than technical parameters.

Creating mappings based on meaningful parameters would be closer to how composers and performers usually think about movement and sound, for example in relation to the body: "I want a forward movement of my right hand to control the brightness of the sound" or "I want to control granularity in the sound with this gentle finger tapping." Rather than forcing everyone into the constraints of the technical system, we should try to create setups that make it possible for mappings to be created at such a meaningful level. If the idea is to have a forward movement in the right hand to control the brightness of the sound, it might not be important whether that movement is done with a bow, a joystick or a custom built controller, since the quality of the movement will be the same. If the mappings were created at this level, it would also be possible to retain the mappings even though either the controller or the sound system (or both) were changed.

A very simple example of such a meaningful mapping process is shown in the Max/MSP patch shown in Figure 7. This example patch retrieves data from two devices, a computer mouse and a joystick, and codes the data into body layer GDIF streams. The point of the patch is to show that it is possible to use either device to control a sound synthesis model, and to switch between them without having to create any new mappings between the control values and the parameters in the sound synthesis model. This is because the mappings are created at a body level, and only refer to the movement of the hand used in the interaction. Here both the mouse and joystick are controlled by the right hand, and they both allow for horizontal and vertical movement of the hand. It is therefore possible to use these body movement features to control the sound model. This is but a simple example, but similar meaningful mappings can also be developed between multi-dimensional controllers and sound engines.

CONCLUSION

The chapter has presented some general thoughts on challenges related to structuring music-related

Figure 7. An example of mapping movements from either mouse or joystick to a simple sound synthesis using a GDIF namespace. Since the values from both devices are coded using the same body-related descriptors, it is possible to switch between the devices without having to create new mappings. Note that a star (*) is used as a wildcard for choosing either left or right hand movements.

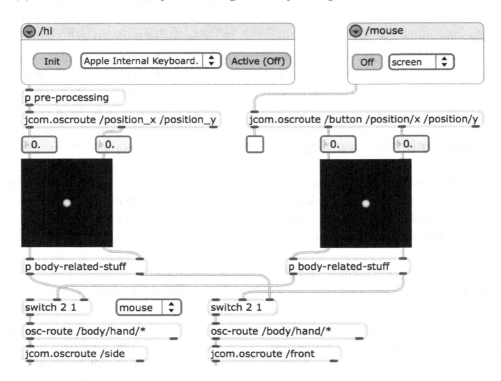

movement data, and also shown examples of how some of these thoughts have been tested in various prototype GDIF setups using both SDIF-files for storage and OSC streams for realtime control. GDIF development started out as an attempt to create a practical solution to store data from our observation studies, but we soon realised that the real challenge is not on the technical side but rather to create taxonomies of the different types and layers of movements that we are studying. This development will, obviously, have to mature with the continuous efforts of a number of research groups currently engaged in exploring music-related body movement.

Developing formats and tools can therefore be seen as an attempt to define a vocabulary for music-related movement in general. Fortunately, considering the many researchers that are currently involved in the field makes it possible that we may eventually succeed in creating a common format to stream and store music-related movement data.

ACKNOWLEDGMENT

Thanks to Rolf Inge Godøy and Marcelo M. Wanderley for supervising the PhD dissertation on which this chapter is based. Thanks to the GDIF community for further development of the thoughts presented in the chapter, and to Kristian Nymoen for the illustrations in Figures 5 and 6.

REFERENCES

Arfib, D., Couturier, J.-M., Kessours, L., & Verfaille, V. (2002). Strategies of mapping between gesture data and synthesis model parameters using perceptual spaces. *Organised Sound, 7*(2), 135–152. doi:10.1017/S1355771802002054

Beard, S., & Reid, D. (2002). MetaFace and VHML: A first implementation of the virtual human markup language. In *Proceedings of the AAMAS Workshop on Embodied Conversational Agents-Let's Specify and Evaluate Them. AAMAS.*

Bresin, R., & Friberg, A. (2000). Emotional coloring of computer-controlled music performances. *Computer Music Journal, 24*(4), 44–63. doi:10.1162/014892600559515

Camurri, A., Lagerlof, I., & Volpe, G. (2003). Recognizing emotion from dance movement: Comparison of spectator recognition and automated techniques. *International Journal of Human-Computer Studies, 59*(1-2), 213–225. doi:10.1016/S1071-5819(03)00050-8

Chung, H., & Lee, Y. (2004). MCML: Motion capture markup language for integration of heterogeneous motion capture data. *Computer Standards & Interfaces, 26*(2), 113–130. doi:10.1016/S0920-5489(03)00071-0

De Carolis, B., Pelachaud, C., Poggi, I., & Steedman, M. (2004). APML: A mark-up language for believable behavior generation . In Prendinger, H., & Ishizuka, M. (Eds.), *Life-Like Characters: Tools, Affective Functions and Applications* (pp. 65–85). Berlin, Germany: Springer-Verlag.

Elliott, R., Glauert, J. R. W., Kennaway, J. R., & Marshall, I. (2000). The development of language processing support for the visicast project. In *Proceedings of the Fourth International ACM Conference on Assistive Technologies*, (pp. 101–108). New York, NY: ACM Press.

Evrard, M., Couroussé, D., Castagné, N., Cadoz, C., Florens, J.-L., & Luciani, A. (2006). *The GMS file format: Specifications of the version 0.1 of the format*. Technical report. Grenoble, France: INPG, ACROE/ICA.

Godøy, R. I. (2004). Gestural imagery in the service of musical imagery. *Lecture Notes in Artificial Intelligence, 2915*, 55–62.

Godøy, R. I. (2006). Gestural-sonorous objects: Embodied extensions of schaeffer's conceptual apparatus. *Organised Sound, 11*(2), 149–157. doi:10.1017/S1355771806001439

Godøy, R. I., Jensenius, A. R., & Nymoen, K. (2008). *Production and perception of goal-points and coarticulations in music*. Paper presented at the ASA-EAA Conference. Paris, France.

Godøy, R. I., & Leman, M. (2009). *Musical gestures - Sound, movement, and meaning*. New York, NY: Routledge.

Hartmann, B., Mancini, M., & Pelachaud, C. (2002). Formational parameters and adaptive prototype instantiation for MPEG-4 compliant gesture synthesis. [Computer Animation.]. *Proceedings of Computer Animation, 2002*, 111–119.

Hunt, A., & Wanderley, M. M. (2002). Mapping performer parameters to synthesis engines. *Organised Sound, 7*(2), 97–108. doi:10.1017/S1355771802002030

Jazzmutant. (2006). *Extension and enchancement of the OSC protocol*. Paper presented at the OSC-meeting at NIME 2006, IRCAM. Paris, France.

Jensenius, A. R., Camurri, A., Castagne, N., Maestre, E., Malloch, J., & McGilvray, D. … Wright, M. (2007). Panel: The need of formats for streaming and storing music-related movement and gesture data. In *Proceedings of the 2007 International Computer Music Conference*, (pp. 13–16). Copenhagen, Denmark: International Music Conference.

Jensenius, A. R., Kvifte, T., & Godøy, R. I. (2006). Towards a gesture description interchange format. In N. Schnell, F. Bevilacqua, M. Lyons, & A. Tanaka (Eds.), In *Proceedings of the 2006 International Conference on New Interfaces for Musical Expression*, (pp. 176–179). Paris, France: IRCAM – Centre Pompidou.

Jensenius, A. R., Nymoen, K., & Godøy, R. I. (2008). A multilayered GDIF-based setup for studying co-articulation in the movements of musicians. In *Proceedings of the 2008 International Computer Music Conference*, (pp. 743–746). Belfast, Ireland: ACM.

Kranstedt, A., Kopp, S., & Wachsmuth, I. (2002). MURML: A multimodal utterance representation markup language for conversational agents. In *Proceedings of the AAMAS Workshop on Embodied Conversational Agents – Let's Specify and Evaluate Them*. AAMAS.

Kshirsagar, S., Magnenat-Thalmann, N., Guye-Vuillome, A., Thalmann, D., Kamyab, K., & Mamdani, E. (2002). Avatar markup language. In *Proceedings of the Workshop on Virtual Environments 2002*, (pp. 169–177). Aire-la-Ville, Switzerland: Eurographics Association.

Laban, R. V. (1980). *Mastery of movement* (4th ed.). Plymouth, MA: MacDonald & Evans Ltd.

Lander, J. (1998, January). Working with motion capture file formats. *Game Developer*, 30–37.

Luciani, A., Evrard, M., Castagné, N., Couroussé, D., Florens, J.-L., & Cadoz, C. (2006a). A basic gesture and motion format for virtual reality multisensory applications. In *Proceedings of the 1st International Conference on Computer Graphics Theory and Applications*. Setubal, Portugal: ACM.

Luciani, A., Evrard, M., Courousse, D., Castagne, N., Summers, I., Brady, A., … Pirro, D. (2006b). *Report on gesture format: State of the art*. Partners' propositions. Deliverable 1 D.RD3.3.1, IST-2004-002114-ENACTIVE Network of Excellence.

Maestre, E., Janer, J., Blaauw, M., Pérez, A., & Guaus, E. (2007). Acquisition of violin instrumental gestures using a commercial EMF tracking device. In *Proceedings of the 2007 International Computer Music Conference*. Copenhagen, Denmark: ICMA.

Malloch, J., Sinclair, S., & Wanderley, M. M. (2007). From controller to sound: Tools for collaborative development of digital musical instruments. In *Proceedings of the 2007 International Computer Music Conference*. Copenhagen, Denmark: ICMA.

Manjunath, B., Salembier, P., & Sikora, T. (2002). *Introduction to MPEG-7: Multimedia content description interface*. New York, NY: John Wiley and Sons.

Marshall, M. T., Peters, N., Jensenius, A. R., Boissinot, J., Wanderley, M. M., & Braasch, J. (2006). On the development of a system for gesture control of spatialization. In *Proceedings of the International Computer Music Conference*, (pp. 360–366). New Orleans, LA: ICMA.

Martinez, J., Koenen, R., & Pereira, F. (2002). MPEG-7: The generic multimedia content description standard, part. *IEEE MultiMedia*, *9*(2), 78–87. doi:10.1109/93.998074

McGilvray, D. (2007). *On the analysis of musical performance by computer*. (PhD Thesis). University of Glasgow. Glasgow, UK.

Peters, N. (2008). Proposing spatdif - The spatial sound description interchange format. In *Proceedings of the 2008 International Computer Music Conference*. Belfast, Ireland: ACM.

Place, T., & Lossius, T. (2006). Jamoma: A modular standard for structuring patches in max. In *Proceedings of the 2006 International Computer Music Conference*, (pp. 143–146). New Orleans, LA: ICMA.

Prendinger, H., Descamps, S., & Ishizuka, M. (2004). MPML: A markup language for controlling the behavior of life-like characters. *Journal of Visual Languages and Computing*, *15*(2), 183–203. doi:10.1016/j.jvlc.2004.01.001

Pullinger, S., McGilvray, D., & Bailey, N. (2008). Music and gesture file: Performance visualisation, analysis, storage and exchange. In *Proceedings of the 2008 International Computer Music Conference*. Belfast, Ireland: ACM.

Roland, P. (2002). The music encoding initiative (MEI). In *Proceedings of the First International Conference on Musical Applications Using XML*, (pp. 55–59). ACM.

Schaeffer, P. (1966). *Traité des objets musicaux*. Paris, France: Editions du Seuil.

Schnell, N., Borghesi, R., Schwarz, D., Bevilacqua, F., & Muller, R. (2005). FTM – Complex data structures for Max. In *Proceedings of the 2005 International Computer Music Conference*, (pp. 9–12). Barcelona, Spain: ICMA.

Schwarz, D., & Wright, M. (2000). Extensions and applications of the SDIF sound description interchange format. In *Proceedings of the 2000 International Computer Music Conference*, (pp. 481–484). Berlin, Germany: ICMA.

Sinclair, S., & Wanderley, M. M. (2007). Defining a control standard for easily integrating haptic virtual environments with existing audio/visual systems. In *Proceedings of the 2007 Conference on New Interfaces for Musical Expression*. New York, NY: NIME.

Wanderley, M. M., Schnell, N., & Rovan, J. B. (1998). Escher-modeling and performing composed instruments in real-time. In *Proceedings of the 1998 IEEE International Conference on Systems, Man, and Cybernetics*, (vol. 2, pp. 1080–1084). San Diego, CA: IEEE Press.

Wright, M., Chaudhary, A., Freed, A., Wessel, D., Rodet, X., & Virolle, D. … Serra, X. (1998). New applications of the sound description interchange format. In *Proceedings of the 1998 International Computer Music Conference*, (pp. 276–279). Ann Arbor, MI: ICMA.

Wright, M., Freed, A., Lee, A., Madden, T., & Momeni, A. (2001). Managing complexity with explicit mapping of gestures to sound control with OSC. In *Proceedings of the 2001 International Computer Music Conference*, (pp. 314–317). La Habana, Cuba: ICMA.

Chapter 8
Expressiveness in Music Performance:
Analysis, Models, Mapping, Encoding

Sergio Canazza
University of Padova, Italy

Antonio Rodà
University of Padova, Italy

Giovanni De Poli
University of Padova, Italy

Alvise Vidolin
University of Padova, Italy

ABSTRACT

During the last decade, in the fields of both systematic musicology and cultural musicology, a lot of research effort (using methods borrowed from music informatics, psychology, and neurosciences) has been spent to connect two worlds that seemed to be very distant or even antithetic: machines and emotions. Mainly in the Sound and Music Computing framework of human-computer interaction an increasing interest grew in finding ways to allow machines communicating expressive, emotional content using a nonverbal channel. Such interest has been justified with the objective of an enhanced interaction between humans and machines exploiting communication channels that are typical of human-human communication and that can therefore be easier and less frustrating for users, and in particular for non-technically skilled users (e.g. musicians, teacher, students, common people). While on the one hand research on emotional communication found its way into more traditional fields of computer science such as Artificial Intelligence, on the other hand novel fields are focusing on such issues. The examples are studies on Affective Computing in the United States, KANSEI Information Processing in Japan, and Expressive Information Processing in Europe. This chapter presents the state of the art in the research field of a computational approach to the study of music performance. In addition, analysis methods and synthesis models of expressive content in music performance, carried out by the authors, are presented. Finally, an encoding system aiming to encode the music performance expressiveness will be detailed, using an XML-based approach.

DOI: 10.4018/978-1-4666-2497-9.ch008

INTRODUCTION

The meaning of musical experience and how it can be described is extensively debated issue. According to Hanslick (1854), music consists of forms related to each other, but without a precised meaning; the content of music are moving sonic forms and any other meaning is a subjective interpretation of some music cues which are culturally significant. Nevertheless, many evidences support the idea that music can communicate information intended by a producer (composers or performers) to a listener, by means of a (more or less) shared code (Campbell & Heller, 1981). The results of studies on emotional response to music (see, e.g., Juslin & Sloboda, 2001) showed that subjects can describe their listening experience by means of emotional categories and the statistically significant similarities in the subjects' answers imply that this experience is shared at least in a given cultural contest. The power of music to induce in listeners different affective states or moods is a well known characteristic, but music experience is not evidently limited to emotions. Music experience is a complex issue, that can be analyzed from different point of views. A piece of music can interest a musicologist, because of its historical and stylistic relations with the cultural environment in which it has been composed. At the same time, another listener can be attracted by the same piece of music, because of the emotions or the sensations induced by that music or that performer. Even for the same person, the experience can vary depending on the musical aspects on which he is focused. Another issue is how music experience can be described: linguistic descriptions can capture only partial aspects of the musical experience and non-linguistic metaphors are used to represent other features that cannot be conveyed verbally.

The aim of the present chapter is to summarize empirical findings from Sound and Music Computing research field that are relevant to the analysis and representation of musical experience. Attention is paid to the aspects related to the way a performer can convey *expressive intentions* by means of music.

The pages that follow have been organized as follows. In the next section, the authors provide broad definitions and discussions of the understanding and modelling of music performance carried out in the last years. In the section *Models of music performance,* the methodology employed to obtain insight into the phenomena of the expressiveness in music performance will be described. Some examples of the experimental methods that yield them will be detailed in the section *Analysis of music performances.* Finally, in the section *Encoding: The representation of music performance features*, an encoding system aiming to encode the music performance expressiveness will be detailed, using an XML-based approach.

Since 2005, the term Web 2.0 has gradually become a hot topic on the Internet. Users' participation is the core of Web 2.0: open, shared, communication and growing-up together, as its primary characteristics, has been an inspiration to everyone. In this scenario, the authors firmly believe that the future of the audio interaction in a Web 2.0 scenario will be the use of expressive content: an interaction should allow a gradual transition (morphing) between different expressive intentions. Starting from a technologically oriented point of view, a computational model of human expression by means of music will be proposed in the section *Future trends*. This model is incorporated in a Web 2.0 framework that allows expressive processing, collaborative creativity and sharing of music content. Such a model is useful for multimedia/multimodal interaction systems (rhythms games and a new social interaction music-based platform, such as *freesound* or *soundpedia*), that could be integrated in the browser engines of the music community services.

BACKGROUND

Humans usually interact with music in complex and various ways. Depending on the context, music can assume different functions: e.g. the result of a creation process, a score to interpret, structured sound to listen, or an object to study from an historical and cultural perspective. For these reasons, it is difficult to design effective systems for technological-mediated access to music, able to cover all the requirements of the human-music interaction. Concerning software platform for the access to music content, a still open issue is which music-related information needs to be codified and how this information can be appropriately structured. In the last years, several works addressed this issue, focusing from time to time on specific applicative context.

Some proposals deal with the representation of audio signal (e.g., Gazon & Andriarin, 2001), with the symbolic representation of music (for a review of the main proposals, see Haus & Longari, 2002), with the definition of an XML-based framework (Haus & Longari, 2002; Bellini & Nesi, 2001) for the structured representation of different aspects of music contents such as musical sheet (or an equivalent symbolic representation), audio recordings, video recordings, etc.

Other proposals, instead, are focused on metadata. A piece of music can be associated with a large set of information. On the basis of the application context and/or the user's interest some information is more relevant than other.

Most of the projects deal with editorial information. These projects propose systems to generate and manage editorial information on popular music, such as titles, authors, performers, and track listings. Some examples of these editorial systems are CDDB (Gracenote, 2009); MusicBrainz (Swartz, 2002), a large database of music metadata, which contains over 300,000 records, collected by means of users' contributes; AMG (Allmusic, 2009); Muze (MuzeMusic 2.0, 2009), which include information on artists and

songs, created by experts. MoodLogic (Kalbach, 2002) is able to associate metadata to songs automatically thanks to two basic techniques: (1) an audio fingerprinting technology able to recognize music titles on personal hard disks, and (2) a database collecting user ratings on songs, which is incremented automatically, and in a collaborative fashion. MoodLogic relies entirely on metadata obtained from user ratings and does not perform any acoustic analysis of songs. However, collaborative music rating does not exhaust the description potential of music.

Beside editorial information, some systems also began to take into account acoustic information. An interesting example is the CUIDADO Project (Pachet, et al., 2006). The project covers the areas of editorial metadata, acoustic metadata, and other aspects concerning the metadata exploitation, the management and sharing of metadata among users. This system distinguishes between consensual information, or facts about music titles and artists, and content description of titles, albums, or artists. Whereas the first category does not raise any particular problem, as this information is universal by nature—at least for popular music there is generally a large agreement on artist and songs name, albums and tracks listing, group members, date of recording for a given title and so on; the second category is more problematic. Content description includes information such as artist style, artist instruments, song mood, song review, song or artist genre and more generally attributes aiming at describing the intrinsic nature of the musical item at stake (artist or song). These descriptions are useful to the extent that they can be used for musical queries in large catalogues, but it is hard or impossible to have a consensus about them. The approach of CUIDADO is based on the analysis of acoustic features: these can be objective data on which to base the organization of the metadata. In particular, the system is able to automatically extract: the time series of percussive sounds in music signals of popular music; the perceptual energy, i.e., whether a song is thrilling and exciting (e.g., swing, jumpin' jive, rock'n'roll), or relaxing and calm (e.g., *New Age* music); the global timbral quality; a descriptor that takes into account whether a given tune contains singing voice or only instrumental sounds.

All these projects are mainly addressed to popular music. Their aim is to make it easier to manage a large-scale music database. Their target users are music listeners, seeking for tools to effectively browse their *mp3* collections or to quickly retrieve songs of interest in the online music stores databases. The interaction with music content is limited to the choice of the musical object, but after the choice has been made the user is mostly a passive listener. In particular, almost all the aspects related to music performance are not considered.

The present authors believe that the formalization of aspects related to music performance may extend the possibility of technology-mediated interaction with music contents. Information about music performance, structured as metadata, could further the development of new application such us automatic expressive performance or active listening, and offer a contribution to improve systems in the context of content-based retrieval, entertainment, and music education.

Several problems hinder the definition of data structures to represent music performance cues. First of all, music performance cues are heavily related to cultural aspects, so it is difficult to find an objective way to describe them. There is generally no consensus on whether a music performance is a good or a bad performance, and which words can describe that.

Moreover, expressiveness in music is an ill-defined concept, and there is not a common opinion on what music express. The communication of expressive content by music can be studied at three different levels, considering: (1) the composer's message, (2) the expressive intentions of the performer, and (3) the listener's perceptual experience. Studies for (1) are histori-

cally more developed (Repp, 1992, 1995, 1998, 1999; Gabrielson & Lindstrom, 2001; Bigand, 2005). Generally, they analyze the elements of the musical structure and the musical phrasing that are critical for a correct interpretation of composer's message. This chapter considers the broader term *expressive intention* (Gabrielsson, 1997), including emotions, affects as well as other sensorial and descriptive adjectives or actions. Furthermore, this term evidences the explicit intent of the performer in communicating expression.

Most studies on the performance expressiveness aim at understanding the systematic presence of deviations from the musical notation as a communication means between musician and listener (see, at least: Todd & McAngus, 1995; Palmer, 1997). Deviations introduced by technical constraints (such as fingering) or by imperfect performer skill, are not normally considered part of expression communication and thus are often filtered out as noise. The analysis of these systematic deviations has led to the formulation of several models aiming to describe *where*, *how* and *why* the score notation is rendered, sometimes unconsciously. It should be noticed that, although deviations are only the external surface of something deeper and often not directly accessible, they are quite easily measurable, and thus widely used to develop computational models in scientific research and generative models for musical applications.

FROM ABSTRACT TO CONCRETE: THE EXPRESSIVE INFORMATION PROCESSING

The Mapping: Expressive Spaces

Understanding of musical (and/or dance) performance can be carried out through different layers/steps following a bottom-up approach (Camurri, et al., 2005):

- **Layer 1:** Physical Signals: audio sampled data.
- **Layer 2:** Low-level features and statistical parameters: Measures for a collection of audio cues are calculated. The extracted values can be processed by means of statistical methods. Examples of these low-level features are the onset and inter-onset timing, the maximum of the sound level envelope.
- **Layer 3:** Mid-level features and maps: "In this layer, the purpose is to represent expression in gestures by modeling the low-level features in such a way that they give an account of expressiveness in terms of events, shapes, patterns or as trajectories in spaces or maps" (Camurri, et al., 2005). A performance is divided in "musical gestures." Each of them is characterized by the measures of the different cues extracted in the previous step.
- **Layer 4:** Concepts and structures: for example, emotional content and KANSEI (e.g., basic emotions, information on arousal [Hashimoto, 1997]). This high-level information is built from low-level and mid-level features, using various analysis techniques (statistical, time series, etc.).

Following this scheme, we can (1) identify low-level cues in a complex sequence and (2) associate them with qualities deemed important for expressive communication (layers 3).

One aim of understanding could be to assign category labels that identify expressive intentions in music performance. However, such labels are very poor descriptions. In addition, humans use a daunting number of labels to describe their intentions. For example, in research on emotion, Plutchik (1994) who takes a relatively conservative view of what emotion is, found hundreds of descriptors. It is difficult to imagine artificial systems beginning to match the level of discrimination that those lists imply. For this reason, a dimensional

approach in describing expressive intentions is advisable. In this framework, understanding at layer 3 may involve representation as maps or low-dimensional spaces. In literature, different approaches are described to represent such spaces. Plutchik (1980) has offered a formulation of *emotion wheel* as referring to positions in an *activation-evaluation* space (Russel, 1980). It is a representation that is both simple and capable of capturing a wide range of significant issues in emotion. It rests on a simplified treatment of two key themes: (1) Valence, "the clearest common element of emotional states is that the person is materially influenced by feelings that are valenced, i.e., they are centrally concerned with positive or negative evaluations of people or things or events" (Cowie, et al., 2001); (2) Activation level, "the strength of the person's disposition to take some action rather than none" (Cowie, et al., 2001). The axes of activation-evaluation space reflect those themes. The vertical axis shows activation level and the horizontal axis evaluation.

Juslin (2001) presented a study on emotional expression in music performance. He uses the five *basic-emotions* (happiness, sadness, anger, fear, love/tenderness) that have been studied most extensively. His two-dimensional space (valence vs. activity) combines categorical (e.g. "happiness") and dimensional (activity level) approaches to emotional expression. The placement of musical performances is partly based on the results of Whissell (1989). Since the first study this space was used successfully in a computational model for emotion understanding (e.g. Picard, 1997; Cowie, 2001).

Bigand et al. (2005) proposed a novel methodology to measure the subjects' response to musical stimuli without using linguistic descriptions: participants were encouraged to entirely focus on their own emotional experience of the musical excerpts and to group those that conveyed similar subjective emotions. Multidimensional scaling methods were then used to analyze the psychological dimensions underlying the listeners' judgment. It resulted that listeners organized musical stimuli along two dimensions that authors associated to the emotional properties of valence and arousal. According to the hierarchical cluster analysis, listeners grouped the musical stimuli in four groups, characterized by different levels of valence and arousal: a cluster with High Arousal and High Valence (HAHV); a cluster with High Arousal and Low Valence (HALV); a cluster with Low Arousal and High Valence (LAHV); a cluster with Low Arousal and Low Valence (LALV).

Most research results on low-dimensional spaces deals with emotions; the general issue of expressive intentions is less investigated, because they are weakly defined. Canazza et al. (2003) explores a different approach to dimensional understanding on a small, but significant, subset of expressive intentions in a sensory domain. Some performances, played according to different expressive intentions, are evaluated in listening experiments. The understanding step consists in deriving a low dimensional structure by multivariate analysis of response data (Juslin, 2000, 2001).

Models of Music Performance

In order to develop the structure of the model and to find its parameters, researchers rely on different strategies. The analysis-by-measurement and analysis-by-synthesis are the most prevalent, although some methods deriving from artificial intelligence are currently being developed (machine learning and case based reasoning).

Analysis by Measurements

The first strategy, analysis-by-measurement, is based on the analysis of the deviations that characterise human performances. It aims at recognizing regularities in the deviation patterns and to describe them through a mathematical model, relating score to expressive values: see Gabrielsson (1999) for an overview of the main results.

First and foremost, an accurate selection of good and/or typical performances is required. Often better results are obtained with rather small sets of performances. The performer is usually asked to play according to his own taste, although sometimes he/she may be asked to play according to specific instructions, e.g. to convey a particular emotion, for experimental purposes.

Every single musical note has many physical properties (e.g. duration, intensity, frequency, envelope, note vibrato) that are subjected to variations. The instrument used for the experiment and the technical possibility available, as well as the working hypothesis related to the aims of the study, helps to determine which parameters to consider in the analysis. The reliability and consistency of the data obtained with the physical measurements must then be verified, classifying the performance in different categories, with different characteristics that keep in consideration the collected data. A statistical analysis of the data is carried out and a mathematical interpretation model of the data is developed. Sometimes multidimensional analysis is applied to performance profiles in order to extract independent patterns. The hypothesis that deviations deriving from different patterns or hierarchical levels can be separated and then added is often implicitly assumed. This helps the modeling phase, although it may be an oversimplification.

Different methodologies of approximation of human performances were developed consist of the generation of a parametric model, of which the parameters at best approximate a set of given performances are estimated (Bresin, 1998; Friberg, 2004): fuzzy logic approach, neural network techniques, and the linear vector space theory, using a multiple regression analysis algorithm. Alternatively, some researchers carried out controlled experiments collecting and studying performances based on the idea that measurements may reveal some underlying mechanisms if one parameter of the performance is manipulated (e.g. the instruction to play at a different tempo—Repp, 1994).

Analysis by Synthesis

The analysis-by-synthesis strategy focuses on the perception of the performance, and continues the process started with the analysis-by-measurement. Considering the results previously obtained, many performances of the same piece are gathered in order to have different sets of physical variables (duration, intensity, etc.) that systematically vary. At this point, it is necessary to express a judgment on the synthesized versions, paying particular attention to the most relevant experimental variables and referring to useful evaluation scales. It is crucial to trust the listeners' judgments, therefore the use of control methods is necessary (possibly sorting the listeners into classes).

Some relations between the performances with manipulated physical variations and the selected variables can be observed by asking questions such as: are the listeners sensitive to the manipulations? If so, in which way? Are there general effects or interactions among different variables? Which are the most important variables? Can someone be eliminated?

The process described so far should be repeated in an interactive manner until the results converge, that is until the relations of the selected variables of the performance converge to the experimental variables.

The above scheme can be modified and extended, though the main idea remains unchanged: systematic variations must be introduced in the synthetic versions of the performances in order to verify the hypothesis produced by the analysis of the real performances. With respect to such variations, it is worth remarking that only one factor at a time should be modified. The resulting performance will sound rather different from a real

one, where physical variables can change. Further experiments and long series of working sessions are required to gather significant data about the effects caused by a variable on the others. This strategy derives models, which can be described with a collection of rules, using an analysis-by-synthesis method. The most important is the KTH rule system (Friberg, 1991), which quantitatively describes the deviations to be applied to a musical score in order to make a mechanical performance—resulting from a literal playing of the score—sound more musical, i.e. more appealing to the human ear. Each deviation that a human performer is likely to insert is predicted (and explained with musical or psychoacoustic principles) by a rule. In the beginning, rules are defined from indications provided by professional musicians, using engineering paradigms. Some listeners evaluate the performances produced by the application of those rules, allowing further tuning and development of the rules. Rules can be grouped according to the purposes that they apparently have in music communication. Differentiation rules appear to facilitate the categorization of the pitch and the duration, while grouping rules appear to facilitate the grouping of notes, both at micro and macro level. As an example of such rules, let us consider the Duration Contrast rule: it shortens and decreases the amplitude of notes with a duration between 30 and 600 ms, according to their duration with respect to a suitable function. The value computed by this rule is then weighted by a quantity parameter k. Another very interesting rule system was developed by Ramirez and co-workers (Ramirez, et al., 2005, 2008). This is based on an evolutionary approach to inducing a generative model of expressive music performance for jazz saxophone. Starting with a collection of audio recordings of real jazz saxophone performances, Ramirez extracted a symbolic representation of the musician's expressive performance and then applied an evolutionary algorithm to the symbolic representation in order to obtain computational models for different aspects of expressive performance. Finally, they used these models to automatically synthesize performances with the timing and energy expressiveness that characterizes the music generated by a professional saxophonist.

Machine Learning

In the traditional way of developing models, the researcher usually makes some hypothesis on the aspects of the performance she/he wants to model, and then she/he tries to establish the empirical validity of the model by testing it on real data or on synthetic performances. A different approach, pursued by Widmer (1996), attempts to extract new and potentially interesting regularities and performance principles from many performance examples by using machine learning and data mining algorithms. The aim of these methods is to search for and discover complex dependencies on very large data sets, without any preliminary hypothesis. The advantage is the possibility of discovering new (and possibly interesting) knowledge, avoiding any musical expectation or assumption. Moreover, these algorithms normally allow an intelligible description of the discoveries, which are mainly accepted according to their degree of generality, accuracy, and simplicity. It is worth noticing that results are more understandable by the use of rules for categorical decisions (e.g. play faster or slower) rather than for computing an exact value.

Case-Based Reasoning

An alternative approach, much closer to the observation-imitation-experimentation process observed in humans, consists in the direct use of the implicit knowledge carried by the samples of human performances. Out of the assumption that similar problems have similar solutions, the Case-Based Reasoning (CBR) approach (Arcos, 2001) attempts to solve new problems by using

the same (or adapted) solutions which responded well to previously solved problems. Two basic mechanisms are used: (1) retrieval of solved problems (called cases) using suitable criteria and (2) adaptation of solutions used in previous cases to the actual problem.

The CBR paradigm comprises a variety of methods that may be described with a common subtask decomposition: the retrieved task, the reused task, the revised task, and the retained task. There are different CBR methods according to their specific ways of carrying out the tasks. The first one, the retrieved task, aims at recovering a set of previously solved problems that show some similarities with the present one. This task, in turn, is divided in three subtasks: (1) identify, (2) search, and (3) select tasks.

1. The identify subtask determines the set of relevant aspects of the current problem, using domain knowledge.
2. The search subtask uses the relevant aspects obtained from the previous task as similarity criteria to retrieve a set of precedent cases.
3. The select subtask ranks the sets of the precedent results, using domain knowledge.

The ordered set of precedent solved cases recovered by the retrieve task is the starting point for the construction of a solution for the current problem, which is the goal of the reuse task. The ranking over cases is interpreted as a preference criterion. A common policy is to consider only the maximal precedent determined by the select subtask.

If the generated solution is incorrect, then the system is given a chance to learn. The revisioned task detects the errors of the current solution and modifies the solution using repair techniques: the results are obtained by applying the solution to the real world (or by asking a teacher). This phase, though, is not always present in all CBR methods. Finally, the retained task incorporates the new solved problem into the system in order to help the resolution of future problems. This task consists of selecting which information to retain and how to integrate it in the memory structure.

CBR performs better, where many examples of solved problems are available and a large part of the knowledge involved in the solution of problems is tacit, difficult to verbalize and generalize. Moreover, new solutions to problems can be checked by the user and memorized, making the system learn from experience. Yet, a large amount of well-distributed previously solved problems is not easy to collect, and unfortunately, to a great extent the success of the CBR approach depends on that.

Expression Recognition Models

The methods presented in the previous sections aim to explain how expression is conveyed by the performer and how it is related to the musical structure. However, the accumulation of the research results recently opened the way to new models that aim to extract and recognize expression from a performance. In particular, a style classifier for interactive performance systems was proposed by Dannenberg (1995) employing a machine learning approach. The features he used to classify are simple parameters that can be extracted from trumpet performances played by one performer and recorded as MIDI data. The classified styles consist of a range of performance intentions: frantic, lyrical, pointillist, syncopated, high, low, quote and blues.

Juslin et al. (2002) developed a system that tries to predict what emotion the performer is trying to convey in his or her performance by combining a low-level cue extraction algorithm with a listener model. One or more types of listener panels can be stored as models, and are then used to simulate judgments of new performances based on the results from previous listening experiments. The following parameters are computed for each tone entered as audio data: interonset duration, relative articulation, peak sound level, attack velocity, and spectral ratio. The spectral ratio is simply defined as the difference in sound level below and above 1000 Hz. The acoustic cues are obtained by computing running averages and standard deviations of the parameters. An estimation of the strength of each intended emotion (happy, angry, sad) is obtained from a regression equation taking the standardized cue values as input variables.

Mion (2003) employed Bayesian Networks for the recognition of expressive content in musical improvisations. The features that can be extracted from MIDI piano improvisations are: note number, intensity, articulation, inter-onset duration, features pattern. The expressive intentions described by sensorial adjectives that can be recognized are: slanted, heavy, hopping, vacuous, bold, hollow, fluid, tender.

Analysis of Music Performances

Over the last decade, several analyses of musical performances have been carried out by the Sound and Music Computing Group of the Padova University. The analyses concern various musical pieces using different instruments, performers, and repertoires: performances of pieces for clarinet (Canazza, et al., 1997c), piano (Battel & Fimbianti, 1997; Canazza, et al., 2002), or violin (De Poli, et al., 1998) belonging to a classique-baroque repertoire; jazz piece played by saxophone (Canazza, et al., 1997a); popular melodies played by violin, flute, or guitar (Mion & De Poli, 2008); improvisation played by piano (Bonini, et al., 2006). As examples of the analysis by measurement method, we will illustrate and discuss analyses of piano and violin performances. The piano performances can be recorded as MIDI-like information, allowing the analysis of longer music piece. Moreover, piano performances are more suitable for studying timing information and aspects related to polyphony. The violin, on the contrary, is an instrument that offers the performer many expressive resources, i.e. a continuous control of sound amplitude and timbre, a rich set of articulation nuances, portamento, vibrato, etc. The analysis on the violin performances allow us to deal with many aspects of the music expressiveness. At the same time, a detailed analysis of the acoustic signal requires not fully automatic signal processing techniques that suggest to apply the analysis only on short musical piece.

The most important results in conveying expressive intentions will be presented in the next Subsections, comparing them with other studies.

Methodological Issues

In order to measure a music performance it is necessary to define a set of quantitative parameters able to describe the characteristics of that performance, what differentiate it from other performances and what makes it similar to other ones. This step is complicated by several factors. The audio recordings are not directly interpretable, i.e. the audio signal needs to be processed in order to extract parameters that are comparable with those of other performances. Moreover, the audio recordings contain a lot of measurable nuances: the amplitude envelopes and the spectrum change continuously; the notes are almost never played *a tempo*. Not all these nuances, however, are relevant from a perceptual point of view.

The basic assumption is that as the melodies remain the same in different expressions, whatever effects appear in listener's judgments or in acoustic measures should mainly be the result of the performer's expressive intention. To have performers playing the same piece of music with different kinds of expression might seem *unnatural* from a musical point of view. However, this design is necessary to secure the internal validity of the experiments: if different intentions are expressed by different melodies, it would be impossible to know whether the obtained effects on listener judgments or performance measures are due to the melody, the performance, or some complex interaction between the two.

In verbal and non-verbal communication two channels have to be distinguished: one transmits explicit messages, which is represented by the text or the musical score; the other transmits implicit messages about the expressive intentions of speaker or performer. Both research and technology have invested enormous efforts in understanding the first, explicit channel, but the second is not as well understood. Understanding the expressive intentions is one of the key tasks associated with the second, implicit channel.

MIDI Performances

The majority of performance studies analyze the note duration by measuring the Inter-Onset Interval (IOI) between the beginning of two successive tones, and the duration (DR) between the beginning and the end of a tone. These parameters are particularly easy to measure when recordings are in MIDI format where the information of note-on and note-off are available. Notice that in MIDI, note-off indicates the beginning of the decay and not the effective end of the note.

In Canazza et al. (2002) a professional pianist was asked to perform some musical excerpts, inspired by two sets of adjectives (expressive intentions). The choice of the adjectives was based both on studies concerning the basic emotions and on the skills of the authors that tested various sets of adjectives in previous experiments. Knowledge of the close analogy between the musical experience and the emotional one, as well as aiming at increasing the expressive nuances analyzed, suggested to us to choose the following affective adjectives (see Juslin, 2001; Gabrielsson, 1995; Plutchik, 1994): Anger, Disgust, Fear, Happiness, and Sadness. A neutral performance, described by the locution *No expression*, was also added and used as a standard measure of comparison in the analysis of the various interpretations. The basic hypothesis of our model is that the *No expression* version is approximately influenced only by the musical structure of the score.

The choice of the musical excerpts was suggested by the following requirements: (1) the score should present no technical difficulties, so that the performer could address his attention exclusively on the expressive content of the interpretation; (2) the score have to be sufficiently varied in its inner dynamism, as well as in the rhythmic configuration and in the musical texture; (3) the score have to be as neutral as possible, i.e. it had not to be deeply characterized from an expressive point of view, so that its mechanical performance didn't sound particular dramatic or glad. On account of these requirements, the following two excerpts was chosen: the Mozart's *Canzonetta* in G major, whose performance has concerned only the melody on the right hand, with the repetition (following the pianist's indication) of the first *ritornello*; and the Beethoven's *Sonatina in Sol* in G major, bars 1-24, without any repetition.

The *Canzonetta* by Mozart is separated in two periods of 16+16 bars: the first one is composed by the first 8 bars and by the *ritornello* replication.

The Key velocity arranges the performances in two clusters (see Figure 1). The first one groups fear, sadness and happiness, the second one disgust, no expression and anger. In general, it can be noticed that the values increase at the beginning of the sub-phrases in the second period. In the score, there are the annotations mf (mezzoforte) in the firsts two sub-phrases (events 37-44 and 45-53) and *f* (forte) in the third one (events 63-71). In addition, the last sub-phrase starts with a *mezzoforte*, but this trend is obscured by the characteristic final *diminuendo*. Disgust has a particular behaviour. The values of the beginning notes for each sub-phrases in first period must be noticed (events 1-4, 10-13, 19-22, and 28-31). In particular, its behaviour in events 10-13 must compared with the mean values (see Figure 1): disgust has an opposite trend. As a consequence, in this performance the musical accents are out of phase: a note with a strong accent becomes weak and vice versa. The listeners impression is a "no-musical" sensation.

Figure 1. Comparison among the different profiles of key velocity in Canzonetta

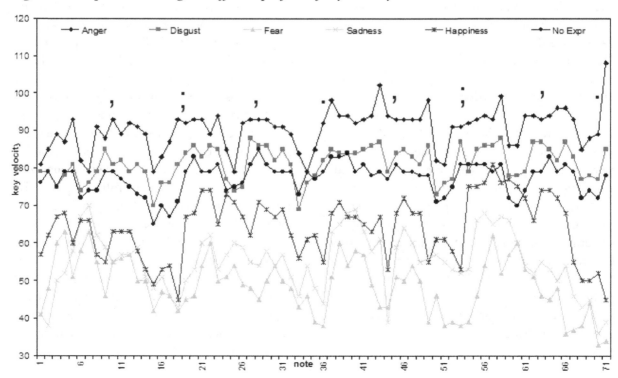

Figure 2. Average profile of key velocity in Canzonetta

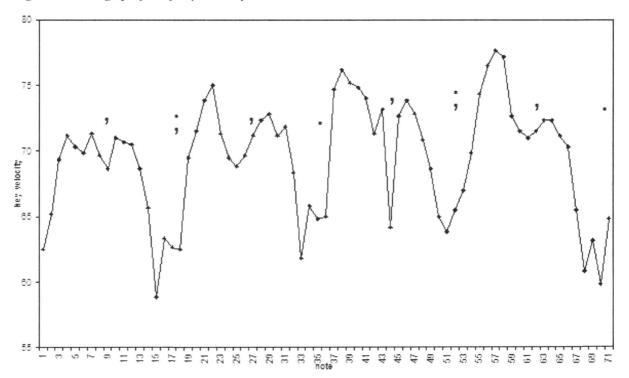

The average profile of key velocity in Mozart's *Canzonetta* is presented in Figure 2. The crescendo in the events 1-4, 19-22 and 54-57 are manifest. The events 14-18, 32-36, 54-57, and 67-71 have a characteristic "W" trend: it is evident in the finals notes. An effect of cadenza is so obtained, emphasizing the final part of the performance.

Figure 3 shows the regression curves applied to Local Tempo for anger, fear, happiness and no expression calculated following the partition suggested by the least square regression carried on the whole phrase. No expression is displayed as comparison. For these performances, the musician emphasized the accelerando/ritardando, which underlines the phrasing, putting in evidence an approximation parabola with a high degree of curvature coefficient. On the contrary, no expression does not exhibit any particular trend: during the performance of this version the pianist tried to flatten timing without adding accelerations

(Figure 3). The other parabolas parameters, such as the vertex position, do not seem to be significant, at least in order to distinguish expressive intentions. They, in fact, show a close correlation to musical structure and therefore are difficult to modify without altering the correctness (i.e. the musical sense) of performance. The same consideration is applicable also for the last four notes (49-52) that are emphasized in all performances. From this result, it can be assumed that the performer varies the degree of accelerando-ritardando in relation to musical phrases in order to characterize each expressive intention. This supports the hypothesis that the performer may use the musical structure to convey his expressive intention.

Acoustic Performances

In De Poli et al. (1997) a professional musician was asked to perform an excerpt from Arcangelo

Figure 3. Least square regression of local tempo for the events 37-53 in Canzonetta. *The dashed line represents the local tempo profile observed, the solid lines indicates the regression curve on two (happiness, anger, no expression) or three (fear) levels.*

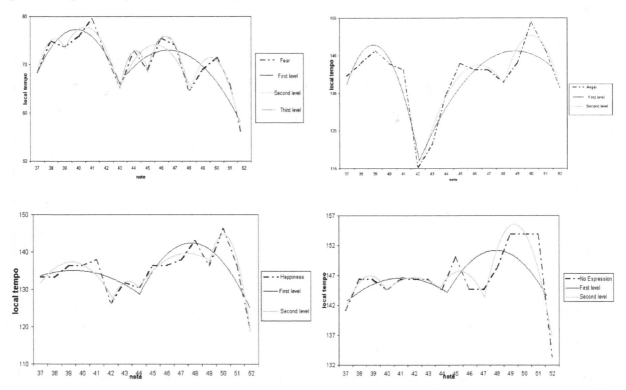

Corelli's Violin Sonata in A Major, V Op. (Figure 4) inspired by the following (Italian) adjectives: light (*leggero*), heavy (*pesante*), soft (*morbido*), hard (*duro*), bright (*brillante*), and dark (*duro*). The "flat" or literal performance, described by the adjective normal (*normale*), was also added and used as a standard measure of comparison in the acoustic analysis of the various interpretations. All the adjectives are related to sensorial experiences, in order to have a compact and coherent semantic space. Moreover, unconventional adjectives, in the musical field, were deliberately chosen in order to give the performer the greatest possible liberty of expression. The recordings were carried out in three cycles, each cycle consisting of the seven different interpretations. The musician then chose the performances that, in his opinion, best corresponded to the proposed adjectives. This procedure is intended to minimize the influence

Figure 4. Musical phrase used in the experiment

that the order of execution might have on the performer. The recordings were carried out at the Sound and Music Computing Laboratory of Padova University in the monophonic digital format at 16 bits and 44.1 kHz.

Choosing which parameters to measure and how to measure them is always a very critical moment in every acoustic analysis. In order to define and measure the principal parameters, it is necessary to make arbitrary choices, without any certainty that the choices are in any sense "correct." A method able to verify such choices is therefore needed. To this end, a first estimation of parameters is used to create synthesized performances. These are compared to the original performances to confirm the choices made in the previous measurement phase. This analysis-by-synthesis approach serves as a check that the data and results have meaning in human perceptual terms. This is always important in studies about performance. Seven parameters have been selected, related to timing (mean and local tempo), timbre (attack time, sustain, brightness, vibrato), dynamics, and articulation.

The first step is the segmentation of the audio signal, to separate each note from the successive one. After the segmentation, a set of parameters were defined to model the amplitude envelope of each note, calculated by means of a 4th-order Butterworth filter with a cut-off frequency $f_T = 100Hz$. In acoustic recordings of instruments like the violin, the amplitude envelopes have shapes and characteristics that vary considerably, both among the different performances and among different notes within the same interpretation. Some notes have an extremely rapid onset and the amplitude reaches a peak value almost immediately. Other notes, on the contrary, have a slow, gradually rising onset Figure 5 shows the parameters taken into consideration in relation to the envelopes.

The MA (end of attack) and MD (start of decay) points were manually determined by analyzing the envelope of each single note because of the

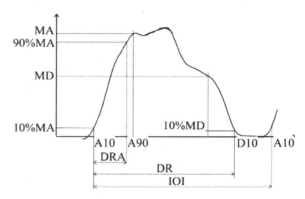

Figure 5. Definition of parameters used for time analysis

great variability in the shape. The Inter-Onset Interval (of n-th note) has been defined as $IOI(n) = A10(n + 1) - A10(n)$, while the note duration has been defined as $DR(n) = D10(n) - A10(n)$, given that the use of A10 and D10 is often assumed to better reflect the perceptual onset and offset of a tone. On the basis of these choices, articulation has been expressed by means of the legato parameter defined by $L(n) = DR(n) / IOI(n)$. Lastly, the attack duration (DRA) is defined as the time taken by the amplitude envelope to pass from 10 to 90% of the MA value, that is $DRA(n) = A90(n) - A10(n)$.

On the basis of the amplitude envelope model, many parameters can be analysed. For example Mean and Local Tempo (calculated by dividing $IOI(n)$ by the number of eighth-note beats in the n–th note. For example, the quarter note duration is divided by 2 and sixteenth note duration is multiplied by 2), the Articulation (defined by the ratio between the duration and IOI of the n-th note), Sustain Trend (ST), defined as the $MD-MA(n)$ difference in dB for the seven performances.

Figure 5 (right) shows the attack time values $DRA(n) = A90(n) - A10(n)$ measured for each note. All the performances had a double curve trend, reflecting the musical structure of the phrase, which can be divided into two half-phrases. In addition to this common trend, noticeable differences between individual performances can be identified. The attack times of the bright piece are generally shorter. It can be supposed that these variations depend on the expressive intentions of the musician. An analysis of variance (ANOVA) was made on the attack time values by intentions (light, heavy, etc.). It showed that these intentions had a significant effect on performance ($F(6,91) = 2.51$, $p < 0.03$).

The average attack duration for each performance was then calculated (Figure 5, left): the performances inspired by bright and hard adjectives have, on average, the lowest DRA, whereas the light and soft performances have the highest one.

The data presented suggest some considerations, in light of the results obtained by a similar analysis (Canazza, et al., 1997c). We intend to determine, at least at a general level, those common strategies used by different musicians to communicate their expressive intentions on the basis of an analysis at the signal (i.e. not symbolic) level.

Table 1 summarizes the tendencies of the statistically significant parameters on varying the expressive intentions. Each performance shows its own peculiarities. However, as we have already said, the musician has at his disposal more than one possibility to communicate the same content. Strategies of performance can therefore change in a significant manner. Besides, different musical instruments have different expressive means, which inevitably influence the musician's choices. In spite of this, comparison with previous studies shows some similarities in the way expressive intentions are transmitted.

Canazza et al. (1997c) carried out a study on clarinet performances, inspired by the same sensorial adjectives of Table 1, but with a different score. Not all the results can be compared as some of the parameters measured were defined differently in the two studies. Besides, quantitative comparisons are sometimes not very significant as the absolute values of parameters depend on the technical characteristics of the instrument used. Nevertheless, it is possible to make a qualitative comparison at least as far as the mean tempo (MM), legato (L), note attack time (DRA) and brightness (BR) of spectrum are concerned. Table 2 shows the tendencies of parameters measured in the clarinet performances. It can be seen how, notwithstanding some differences, the pieces referring to the various expressive intentions have a similar behaviour in the different experiments. For instance, the adjective *bright* induced the musicians to perform their piece with a quicker metronome, a lesser legato, and a shorter attack time. The main differences among the experiments have to do with a different choice in the expressive resources used, but not with a different use of these resources. In the soft version, for instance, the clarinet performer played with the values of the MM (low), DRA (high) and BR (low) parameters significantly different from the other versions. The violinist played in the same

Table 1. Behavior of statistically significant parameters on varying expressive intentions in violin performances

	N	Ha	S	He	L	B	D
MM		high		low	high	high	
L				high	low	low	
DRA		low			high	low	low
BR		high	low	high	low		low
UDR			low		high		
MD-MA			high		low		high
VR						high	low

Table 2. Behavior of statistically significant parameters on varying expressive intentions in clarinet performances (Canazza, et al., 1997c)

	N	Ha	S	He	L	B	D
MM			low	low	high	high	
L	high			low	low	low	
DRA		low	high	low		low	
BR		high	low	high	low		

way as far as the BR (low) parameter is concerned, but unlike the clarinetist, he modified the MD-MA (high) and UDR (low) parameters. It is worth noting that a high MD-MA value means an amplitude profile slowly raising, while a high DRA value in clarinet, together with a low MM, leads to an equivalent qualitative result. The only conflicting result regards the heavy piece performed by the clarinet player with a different use of the parameter L. In this case, it seems that the clarinetist used a quick note attack time and a slow metronome, causing in the listeners a sense of heavy locomotion; but the violinist tried to communicate a sense of effort in moving things.

Note-by-note analysis points out that the performer introduces some deviations that depend on the score. Different expressive intentions produce further deviations of certain parameters. Such deviations are not made to the same extent in each note because the score sets technical and structural limits that prevent the musical phrase from being distorted.

Perceptual studies proved how, generally speaking, it is possible to correlate the listeners' main appraisal categories and the acoustic parameters, which better characterize expressive intentions (Canazza, et al., 1997a, 1997c, 1997d). Analyses carried out on the clarinet performances (Canazza, et al., 1997b, 1997d) resulted in a two-dimensional semantic space. The two axes of this space were correlated to some acoustic parameters, determinants of a small number of expressive styles particularly evident in listening. The first axis was associated to the MM parameter, the second to the DRA parameter. The first axis also seemed to be correlated to the climax emphasis (principal/average accent), used in the clarinet experiments to highlight the principal note of the phrase. This finding was not confirmed in the violin analysis, but it is interesting to observe that the Tempo and the DRA arrange the violin performances in the same order observed in the perceptual studies, showing a possible generalization of these stylistic choices. More comparisons are possible with works analyzing the performers' expressive intentions using a different set of adjectives. Gabrielsson and co-workers (Gabrielsson & Juslin, 1996; Lindstrom, 1992; Juslin, 1993) carried out analyses on some flute, violin, electric guitar and singing voice recordings inspired by the adjectives happy, sad, angry, fearful, tender, solemn, no expression, and natural. The happy version was performed with a fast Tempo, a low legato value, a short attack time, a bright tone-colour, a greater contrast in dotted notes, and a high vibrato rate. Comparing it with violin analysis, it is possible to say that the violinist used the same strategies to perform the bright piece. This result can be considered the consequence of the semantic affinity of the two adjectives.

Relations among Different Expressive Spaces

Mion and De Poli (2008) addressed the question of whether expressive information can be communicated (and recognized) by means of features, which are not strictly related to the score. Thus, relevant musical attributes for differentiating expressions (such as articulation) can be replaced by more physical features (e.g. the attack time). With the aid of machine learning techniques, it is possible to find the most relevant audio features in the recognition of expressive intentions. Using these features as coordinates, the expression intentions could be placed on a features space to obtain an objective measure of physical similarity. In particular, Mion and De Poli (2008) extracted and selected a set of audio features from a set of expressive performances played by professional musicians on violin and flute. These features were tested and confirmed by the leave-one-out cross validation, and they can be grouped according to local audio features (using non-overlapping frames of 46ms length), and event features (using sliding windows with 4s duration and 3.5s overlap).

The windows size allows to include a reasonable number of events and it corresponds roughly to the size of the echoic memory. Among local features, the following were found to be relevant: Roughness, which is computed by the auditory model (Leman, 2000) and is considered to be a sensorial process highly related to sound texture perception; Spectral Ratio, which indicates the relative amount of energy for frequencies f < 1 kHz, and is related to brightness; Residual Energy, which describes the stochastic (noisy) energy in the high frequency band (f > 1.8 kHz), obtained by removing the sinusoidal components, and gives information on the quality of the perceived effort. Among event features, the following were found to be relevant: Peak Sound Level defined as $\max[RMS(t)]$, where $RMS(t)$ is the temporal envelope; Attack Time, as the time required to reach the $RMS(t)$ peak, starting from the onset instant; Notes per Second, which is computed by dividing the number of onsets by the window duration. For the computation of event features we segmented the signal by onset detection, based both on the derivative of the spectral magnitude and on pitch-tracking approach.

Principal Component Analysis on the recorded audio from violin, according to adjectives from both affective and sensorial spaces, put in evidence three main clusters emerged: (A) Hard/Heavy/Angry, (B) Sad/Calm/Soft, (C) Light/Happy. A very similar behaviour characterized the projection of the performances from other instruments. An interpretation of the clusters based on action and physical analogy can be devised. Using the physical analogy, force is often subjectively considered as the cause and movement as the effect. The cause-effect relation is represented by the admittance Y that mathematically describes the dynamic mapping and the qualitative behaviour from force to velocity by an integral-differential equation. The resistive admittance, which dissipates energy, can be distinguished by the reactive one, which stores energy. In linear mechanical systems, three elementary relations define the fundamental quantities friction, inertia, and elasticity. Ideal friction is a pure resistive admittance, and it acts as a scaling factor of the input force. Ideal inertia and elasticity are pure reactive admittances: in particular, inertia stores kinematics energy and it opposes changes in movement, while elasticity stores potential energy and opposes changes in forces. On the basis of this qualitative description of the behaviour of the three basic elements, Mion and De Poli (2008) hypothesize the association of Friction to the cluster Hard/Heavy/Angry, Inertia to cluster Sad/Calm/Soft, and Elasticity to cluster Light/Happy. In this sense, a relationship among different expressive spaces can be established.

Models for Music Performance

Researchers have applied findings from theory and fieldwork to develop new theories, methodologies, and innovative applications in the human-computer interaction area. An explosion of human interface technologies involving ecological interface designs, agents, virtual immersive workspaces, decision support systems, avatars, distributed architectures, and computer-supported

Figure 6. Attack duration values in the seven performances. Left: mean values of the parameter DRA in the seven performances. Right: DRA(n) measured for each note. Notes 6th and 12th were played legato to the preceding note. In these cases, it was not possible to determine an attack phase and therefore the DRA parameter was not measured.

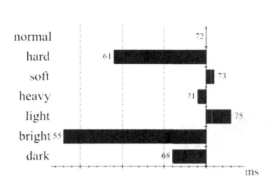
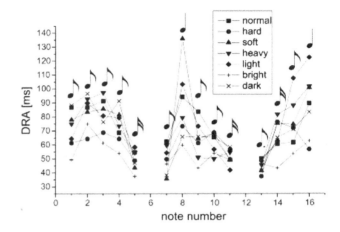

cooperative work, have appeared on the scene as means to address these complex problems. Yet an important facet of complexity has been missing: the role of expressiveness in human-computer interaction.

For the human-machine communication, we may distinguish two main classes of possible interfaces:

- Graphic panel dedicated to the control. The control variables are directly displayed on the panel and the user should learn how to use it.
- Multimodal, where the user interacts 'freely' through movements and non-verbal communication. Task of the interface is to analyze and to correctly identify human intention.

Humans communicate in a multimodal way. Multimodal signal processing is more than simply "putting together" text, audio, images, and video; it is the integration, interaction and the interpretation of these different media that creates new systems and new research challenges. According to Oviatt (2000), the "explicit goal [of multimodal

interaction is] to integrate complementary modalities in a manner that yields a synergistic blend such that each mode can be capitalized upon and used to overcome weaknesses in the other mode." This is not the same as fusion. The interactions complement each other, not necessarily fuse with each other.

By means of several experiments, Canazza et al. (2000b, 2003a) were able to devise an interpretation of an abstract space for expressive (multimodal) interaction in music performance. Therefore, a system to generate automatic expressive music performance were developed (Canazza, et al., 2000a, 2003b, 2004) and the abstract control space (obtained from the perceptual analyses) is employed as user interface to control, at an abstract level, generated performances. Analyses showed that to render a particular expressive intention, the performer uses different strategies depending on personal choices, on the musical excerpt structure, and on expressive controls offered by the instrument played. The system was developed using the results of perceptual and sonological analyses made of professional performances (see examples in subsection *Analysis of music performances)*. Canazza et al. (2004) defined a model for map-

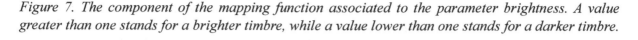

Figure 7. The component of the mapping function associated to the parameter brightness. A value greater than one stands for a brighter timbre, while a value lower than one stands for a darker timbre.

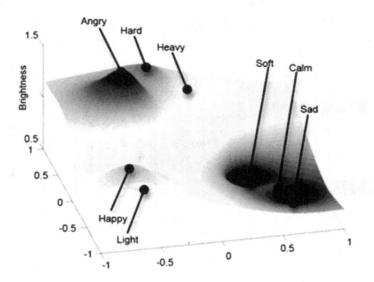

ping points in a two-dimensional space (named the Energy-Kinetics space) to deviations of the main expressive parameters as Tempo, Legato, Intensity, Brightness, Attack time. Thus, to render the expressive content, the model uses a reduced set of controls, which has been demonstrated to be more representative and independent of the instrument and of the musical excerpt. The system calculates these parameters and determines the deviations that must be applied to the score for reproducing a particular expressive intention. As an example, Figure 7 shows a mapping surface between points of the abstract control space and the parameter *Brightness*, related to the abstract control space defined in Canazza et al. (2004). On the basis of movements of the pointer on the x-y plane (Energy-Kinetics space), the variations of the parameter Brightness is applied to the performance and thus computed.

The model can be used in a directive way: the user selects an expressive intention, and the system plays all the score with the user's intention. Trajectories can also be characterized in this space, to study the dynamic aspects of expressive content. In fact, it results that by means a suitable choice of the internal parameters of the model, the performance, resulting from continuous movements in the abstract space, renders the intended intermediate expressive intention in a coherent and smooth way. Moreover, the continuous character of the space allows a conceptual interpretation of every point and trajectory in the abstract control space. In this way, the system can be used in an interactive way: the user draws a trajectory in the control space and the system plays the score modifying the expressive content accordingly, using musical excerpt morphing strategies in order to change the expressive content smoothly.

Music performance is an activity that is well suited as a target for multimodal concepts. Music is a nonverbal form of communication that requires both logical precision and intuitive expression. Researches carried out by the Sound and Computing Group (at Padua University, Italy) and by Infomus Laboratory (at Genova University, Italy) in the creative arts domain has focused on musical mapping of gestural input. In fact, since the control space works at an abstract level, it can be used as an interface between crossmodal signals. In particular, Camurri et al. (2001) developed an application allowing control of the expressive content of a pre-recorded music performance by means of dancer's movement as captured by a camera. Then, the features extracted by the dance are used as input for the abstract space, in conformity with a previous investigation.

In the entertainment area, Canazza et al. (2000a) built the application *Once upon the time*, released as an applet, for the fruition of fairytales in a remote multimedia environment. In this software, an expressive identity can be assigned to each character in the tale and to the different multimedia objects of the virtual environment. Starting from the storyboard of the tale, the different expressive intentions are located in synthetic control spaces defined for the specific contexts of the tale. The expressive content of audio is gradually modified with respect to the position and movements of the mouse pointer, using the abstract control space described above.

Encoding: The Representation of Music Performance Features

As discussed in the Background Section, the music content can be considered from different points of view (e.g. audio, symbolic, graphic), and can be expressed for different kinds of users (e.g. musician, musicologist, teachers, common people) with different aims. Therefore, depending on the specific task, the attention needs to be focused on one musical aspect, or a subset of all the possible aspects, as it is very difficult to satisfy all the requirements at the same time. As regards the symbolic representation, one of the less investigated aspect is the coding of information related to the music performance, i.e. all the information needed to allow a computer to play/perform a musical sheet in a non-mechanical (human-like) way (see Kuuskankare & Laurson, 2001, for an alternative non XML-based approach to this problem). This capability would be very useful in many contexts: the fruition of musical libraries, when an audio recordings is not available;

the educational field, in which computer generated performance can be a useful tool to study interpretative models Battel and Fimbianti (1997); the development of new interaction paradigm, based on the communication of emotions, that can be conveyed by means of music (Juslin, et al., 2002).

In the last years, several computational models for the automatic human-like performance of music were developed, using different strategies (see the section *Models for music performance*). Almost all these models, however, require extra information that normally are not coded in a musical sheet or in a MIDI file, such as a structural or an harmonic analysis of the score. This implies the need for developing a format to represent these information in a suitable and flexible way.

The authors based the XML representation on an existing expressiveness model (Canazza, et al., 1998) developed by the Sound and Music Computing Group of the Padova University (for a detailed description, see Canazza, et al., 1998). This model, focused on western tonal music, presents some interesting characteristics, that are very useful for the development of an automatic player:

1. It assumes that there isn't a unique "right" performance of a score, but the same score can be played with different expressive styles (called expressive intention); in this sense, the model makes a distinction between a neutral performance (i.e., a human performance of the score without any expressive intention or stylistic choice) and an expressive performance.

2. It is based on the hierarchical structure of the musical piece, i.e. the subdivision of the musical language in periods, phrases, and words.

3. It employs information that is expressed in an abstract way (closer to the musical language than to the physical one), i.e.

using the parameters intensity instead of key-velocity, or an accelerando instead of a duration expressed in *ms* or in *tick*, etc.

The item (1) implies that the system can change its performance following the user's expressive intentions, or depending on the user's actions. This capability makes possible a music fruition with different degrees of interaction (see Canazza, et al., 2000, for the description of a possible scenario). Many researches put in evidence that the musical structure, item (2), is one key aspect of musical language (at least for western music), and several interpretative models use this information to generate the performance (e.g., Todd, 1995; Friberg, 1991; De Poli, et al., 1998). Moreover, a musical structure description is very important for content retrieval applications, as the music segmentation plays the same role as word segmentation in textual retrieval engine. Finally, item (3) allows to face some common problems that arise when a computer plays a symbolic representation like MIDI. In this standard, in fact, the duration and the intensity of each note is exactly specified, by means of ticks and key-velocity. A MIDI file, therefore, is more similar to a (symbolic) *frozen* recording than a musical score that needs to be interpreted. As a consequence of it, if the instrument that plays the file is changed (e.g. in client-server applications, or when the file is shared with other users), the audio results are often not so god, because some parameters need to be changed to comply the requirements of the new instrument.

Moreover, the MIDI standard or equivalent representations do not codify a lot of information regarding timbre and articulation aspects such as spectrum, amplitude envelopes, vibrato, etc. Here is a list of the parameters taken into account by the expressiveness model, as reported in Canazza et al. (1998):

- **Time:** Starting moment of the event in tick, as specified in the score.

- **Duration:** Note duration in tick, or number of sub-events forming the event, as specified in the score.
- **Pitch:** e.g. a4 or e5.
- **Channel:** Number of the channel or track the events refers to.
- **Elasticity:** Degree of expressive elasticity of the event. It indicates when it is possible to work on the parameters of that group of notes (intensity, metronome, timbre characters) to reach a certain expressive intention without distorting the piece itself.
- **Dynamics:** Intensity curve that describes the profile of intensity deviations in the event.
- **Metronome:** Metronome curve that describes the profile of the metronome deviations in the event.
- **Expression:** Symbol of the adjective to be applied to the phrase + intention degree.
- **Attack Time:** Duration of the attack expressed in a perceptual scale.
- **Legato:** Legato-staccato degree expressed in a perceptual scale.
- **Intensity:** Perceptual loudness.
- **Brightness:** Perceptual measure of the high frequency spectral components.
- **Vibrato:** Rate and extent vibrato expressed in a perceptual scale.
- **Portamento:** Glissando speed degree in a perceptual scale.

The first four parameters represent the music information as noted in the score (metric position, duration, pitch, track). The dynamics and metronome parameters describe dynamics and timing deviations in term of profiles that reproduce different kinds of crescendo-decrescendo and accelerando-rallentando patterns. The last six parameters are expressed in a perceptual scale, in which the unit represents the difference between two perceptual levels (e.g. the difference between f and ff for loudness). Because of their (abstract) definition, these parameters are independent from

Figure 8. A section of the XML file representing a music score with expressive cues

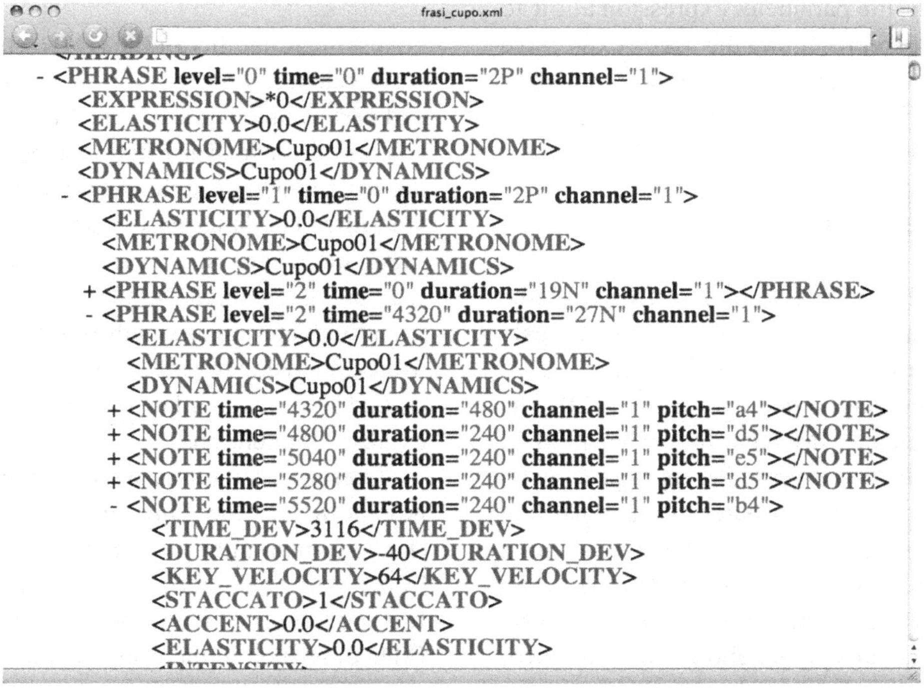

```
frasi_cupo.xml
- <PHRASE level="0" time="0" duration="2P" channel="1">
    <EXPRESSION>*0</EXPRESSION>
    <ELASTICITY>0.0</ELASTICITY>
    <METRONOME>Cupo01</METRONOME>
    <DYNAMICS>Cupo01</DYNAMICS>
  - <PHRASE level="1" time="0" duration="2P" channel="1">
      <ELASTICITY>0.0</ELASTICITY>
      <METRONOME>Cupo01</METRONOME>
      <DYNAMICS>Cupo01</DYNAMICS>
    + <PHRASE level="2" time="0" duration="19N" channel="1"></PHRASE>
    - <PHRASE level="2" time="4320" duration="27N" channel="1">
        <ELASTICITY>0.0</ELASTICITY>
        <METRONOME>Cupo01</METRONOME>
        <DYNAMICS>Cupo01</DYNAMICS>
      + <NOTE time="4320" duration="480" channel="1" pitch="a4"></NOTE>
      + <NOTE time="4800" duration="240" channel="1" pitch="d5"></NOTE>
      + <NOTE time="5040" duration="240" channel="1" pitch="e5"></NOTE>
      + <NOTE time="5280" duration="240" channel="1" pitch="d5"></NOTE>
      - <NOTE time="5520" duration="240" channel="1" pitch="b4">
          <TIME_DEV>3116</TIME_DEV>
          <DURATION_DEV>-40</DURATION_DEV>
          <KEY_VELOCITY>64</KEY_VELOCITY>
          <STACCATO>1</STACCATO>
          <ACCENT>0.0</ACCENT>
          <ELASTICITY>0.0</ELASTICITY>
```

Box 1.

```
The definition of the phrase event in the DTD.
<!-- event PHRASE -->
<!-- a PHRASE can be made with more phrases and/or chords and/or voice two's
in every combination -->
<!-- ELASTICITY is required -->
<!ELEMENT PHRASE ((ELASTICITY | EXPRESSION? | METRONOME? | DYNAMICS?)+,
(PHRASE* | NOTE* | VOICE_TWO* | CHORD*)+)>
<!ELEMENT EXPRESSION (#PCDATA)>
<!ELEMENT ELASTICITY (#PCDATA)>
<!-- curves -->
<!ELEMENT DYNAMICS (#PCDATA)>
<!-- METRONOME has been already declared -->
<!-- MIDI parameters are required and appear as attributes -->
<!ATTLIST PHRASE
        level CDATA ""
        duration CDATA ""
        channel CDATA ""
        time CDATA "">
```

the particular musical instrument that will play the score. Finally, the parameter expression allow to specify a label representing the user's expressive intention: up to now, the model supports a limited set of sensorial adjectives, but this list can be easily extended.

XML Representation

To develop an XML representation of the symbolic music information, it is necessary to rigorously define the structure of such information, i.e. to design a Document Type Definition (DTD). The first choice made was regarding what kind of information must be provided as tags (or elements) and what as attributes. Data regarding expressiveness are provided as elements since we focus our attention on this aspect. We also want to respect the logical structure of our score so we have events (phrase, note, chord and voice two) presented as tags. On the other hand information such as pitch or duration of a note, key velocity and others MIDI-like parameters are given as attributes of the events. Information about metronome, time-division, base-time and key-signature must appear at the beginning of the document in the section named <HEADING>.

Figure 8 shows a fragment of the DTD: we see how the event PHRASE is defined. A phrase can be made by sub phrases, notes, chords and voice two's in any order and quantity. We define also the attributes that represents MIDI parameters and tags regarding expressive curves.

Besides the existence of several tools for the parsing, the editing and the writing of XML files, the most evident advantage of this representation is its readable layout: in this way we have a clear vision on phrase division, duration and hierarchy, on what notes belong to a chord and so on. The self explicative labels for tags and attribute (e.g. <PHRASE> or <PORTAMENTO> make immediately accessible the data and the music structure (see Figure 8).

System Architecture

To test the reliability of the XML representation, we developed some tools for the creation, editing and performance of the XML file (see Figure 6). A score editor such as *Finale* can be used to write the score and to describe the musical structure of the score. The latter task is performed using the smart shape tool, so that each slur individuate a segment. The slurs can be hierarchically structured to individuate phrases, sub-phrases, and words. Moreover, using the text tool, it is possible to add textual labels that will be interpreted as the user's expressive intentions.

The score, completed with the expressive cues, is exported in the *Enigma Transportable File* (ETF) format and then automatically processed by the XML Creator tool. This tool parses the ETF file and translates the information following the DTD described in the previous section. In addition, when the routine finds a textual label that is supported by the expressiveness model, it automatically calculates the musical parameters and the dynamics and timing curves in order to render the desired expressive intention. As asserted in the previous section, XML file contains information at an abstract level, in order to allow an efficient rendering with many different synthesizer and synthesis techniques. However, another elaboration stage (called *Virtual Performer*), is necessary to specialize this information for a particular instrument. Ideally, a *Virtual Performer* would be necessary for each instrument (or each instrument family) that will be used. We developed a *Virtual Performer* to play an FM instrument, implemented in the CSound language. The output of the Virtual Performer, therefore, is a SCO file for CSound, that finally performs the audio rendering of the score (see Figure 9).

Figure 9. System architecture

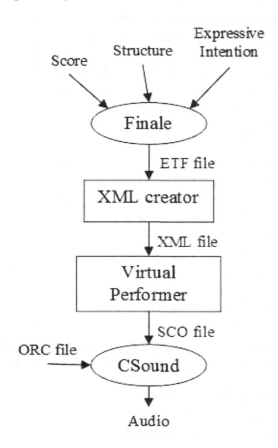

FUTURE TRENDS

Over the last few years, several services based on Web 2.0 technologies were developed, proposing new modalities of social interaction for music creation and fruition (Bernardini & De Poli, 2007). Most of these services are related to music fruition. For example, Pandora (2009), Last.fm (2009), and Soundpedia (2009) are automated music recommendation and Internet radio services. Users enter a song or artist that they enjoy, and the service responds by playing selections that are musically similar. Users provide feedback on approval or disapproval of individual songs, which will be taken into account for future selections. Another service for music recommendation, and that makes

use of ontologies and innovative algorithm for audio analysis, is Foafing the music (2009).

Jamendo (2009) is a music platform and community that allows emergent artists to broadcast their music in an environment integrated with a rating and recommendation system. All music on Jamendo is free to download and licensed through one of several Creative Commons licenses or the Free Art License, making it legal to copy and share. Other services are related to music creation. For example, Freesound Project (Freesound, 2009) is a collaborative database of Creative Commons licensed sounds. The Freesound Project aims to create a huge collaborative database of audio snippets, samples, recordings, bleeps, providing new ways of accessing these samples. While Freesound focuses only on sounds and not on songs, ccMixter (2009) is a community music site featuring remixes licensed under Creative Commons where you can listen to, sample, mash-up, or interact with music in whatever way you want.

Notwithstanding differences among the systems, all these services tend to divide users in two categories: on the one hand the large group of music listeners, which mainly have the job of evaluating and recommending music; on the other hand, the restricted group of the music content creators, which are required to have skills in the field of music composition or music performance. This partition limits the participation and interaction with the music content.

Rodà and Canazza (2009) conceived of a system that integrates a model of human expression by means of music and a Web 2.0 framework that allows for expressive processing, collaborative creativity and sharing of music content. The system architecture is composed by three layers: (1) Storage, (2) Access, and (3) User Layer.

(1) The Storage Layer contains (1a) a Music Content Base and (1b) a Knowledge Base (KB). (1a) is a repository of the original version of the music as well of the user-performed versions, which can be saved and published by the user. A music piece can be saved in a compressed audio

format (i.e. mp3, AAC, etc.) or in a symbolic music format (i.e. MIDI, MusicXML, etc.). (1b) contains the tags associated with each musical piece by the users, the definition of the human performance models (i.e. a set of feature vectors each associated to a performance style) and the control spaces (i.e. the position of the performance styles in the two-dimensional space). The creation and the managing of the KB is performed by means of (2).

(2) Access is composed by two tools. The first is an Authoring Tool (2a), that allows the users to associate tags to the musical pieces, to define human performance models, and to design customized abstract control spaces. Unlike other music fruition systems, which allow the user to freely choose the tags for a music piece, this system is focused on expressive characteristics of the music, so tags can be only chosen among a set of selected tags. This limitation allows a more consistent content description and retrieval and, in order to cover a sufficiently broad range of meanings, we are considering the adoption of ontology for emotion and affective states, such as presented in Benta et al. (2007). Besides using pre-defined human performance models and control spaces, users can define new models and spaces by means of an intuitive graphic interface, which allows to associate musical parameters to a performance style and to place the so-defined performance styles in the abstract control space. The user-defined models and spaces can be saved in the KB and employed by other users. The second tool is an Active Player (2b), by means of that the user can perform in an interactive way a musical piece, moving the mouse on the abstract control space. After loading the desired environment (i.e., the human performance model and the control space) and loading the music file, the user starts to play the file and the pointer is positioned at the center of the control space. Each time the user moves the pointer in a new position of the space the Active Player calculates the musical parameters that are used to control the synthesis

of the sound. Sounds can be generated by means of a commercial MIDI synthesizer or by a post-processing engine that modifies in real-time the loaded audio file. After playing the file, the user can save his performance in the Music Content Base and share it with other users. By means of RSS feed the users' performed music piece can be syndicate and access by other Web communities.

(3) The User Layer manages the user profiles (3a) and the social network (3b). (3a) stores the user music preference, takes trace of the user performances, and manages the rights authorization scheme. A user can access only to that music contents for which he is authorized. Access authorization can be bought as in a common online music store. The difference is that the user can access to music contents with different privileges: play only (the user can listen the piece as with a common music player), active play (the user can control in real time the musical parameter choosing one of the available control spaces and drawing on it the desired trajectory), active play and publish (after actively playing the musical piece, the user can tag his performance and publish it using the Authoring Tool). The access authorization can be also given by other users, which publish their music production. The social module manage users' groups that have common musical interests and that want to share their performance with the friends. A user can choose to keep his performances private, to reserve the access only to his friends, or to give access to everyone. Each shared performance can be commented and tagged by the other users.

CONCLUSION

The technologically mediated access to music requires new paradigms of interaction, based on a better understanding of music experience. The definition of models to represent music expressiveness can contribute to fill the gap between physical sound signal and cognition. In this chapter, we presented the state of the art in the research field of a computational approach to the study of music performance. First of all, we introduced a multi-layer approach to represent music contents at different level of abstraction, as well as several possible ways for representing high and mid level concepts by means of multidimensional spaces. Then, we presented different strategies—such as analysis-by-measurements, analysis-by-synthesis, machine learning, and case based reasoning—for studying and modeling human music performance. As case studies, we reported the results of several research works carried out by the Sound and Music Computing Group of the Padova University, that are focused on various aspects of music expressiveness, among them on suitable encoding structures for representing the music performance features. Finally, we presented a system that integrates a model for the automatic expressive performance of music in a multimodal interactive context.

Recently, new modalities of access are changing the user's relation with music contents. Musical games and social interaction music-based platform are getting always more users, which are attracted by tools to easily organize and retrieval the music contents, but overall, by an active participation in the fruition process. This change keeps up with the crisis of the traditional discography market, but at the same time offers new business opportunities related to the diffusion and sale of musical products. The authors described a system, focused on the expressive performance of music contents, aims to overcoming some limitations of the actual modalities of music fruition. The proposed system integrates an Active Player in a Web 2.0 framework. The Active Player is a software module that allows, by means of an intuitive interface, to apply a smooth morphing among different performance styles, adapting the audio-expressive character to their taste. The Web 2.0 framework allows to easily share the user's performances and to experience new modalities of collaborative creation, e.g. to compose and share music that others can play, modify and diffuse. This system could be integrated in the browser

engines of the music community services. In this way: (1) the databases keep track of the expressiveness of the songs played; (2) the users create/browse playlists based not only on the song title or the artist name, but also on the music expressiveness. This allows:

- In the rhythms games, the performance will be rated on the basis of the expressive intentions of the user, with obvious advantages for the educational skill and the user's involvement of the game;
- In the music community, the user will be able to search happy or sad music, accordingly to the user affective state or preferences.

This consideration seem be comforted by the success of projects like Music 3.0 (Serra, 2008) or SAME (funded by the European Commission under the 7th Framework Programme, Theme ICT-2007.1.5, Networked media—Camurri, et al., 2008).

A general conclusion that can be drawn from the literature reviewed in this work is that general computational frameworks for music performance processing hardly exist. The current state of the art is rather that many partial models exist for isolated tasks that have been evaluated with isolated empirical data.

Indeed, technology-mediated music access is more and more becoming an interactive process, involving non-linguistic communication and action based modalities. A better understanding of the musical experience and how this experience can be described is a crucial issue to render more effective and natural the interaction with musical contents. At the same time, the authors strongly believe that a computational approach to the study of music performance could lead to a better understanding of the music communication processes.

Adequate models of and for music performance are not just of intrinsic value. In fact, these are useful for understanding and solving applied problems such as: What are the significant similarities between different musical performance of the same score? (in the music information retrieval field); How do musical skills and competences develop? (music education); How can we predict the emotional and cognitive reaction of a listener? (emotion engineering). Furthermore, models for music performance can lead to the design of adaptive interfaces for music making. Expectation can be exploited for intelligent machine composition and improvisation explicitly controlling points of surprise. Context-driven expectation may improve accuracy of low-level descriptors compensating noise or uncertainty. Finally, the consideration of developmental issues can encourage the design of user-adaptive applications.

REFERENCES

Allmusic. (2009). *Website.* Retrieved July 5, 2009, from http://www.allmusic.com/

Arcos, J. L., & Lopez de Mantaras, R. (2001). An interactive case-based reasoning approach for generating expressive music. *Applied Intelligence, 14*(1), 115–119. doi:10.1023/A:1008311209823

Battel, G. U., & Fimbianti, R. (1997). Analisys of expressive intentions in pianistic performances. In *Proceedings of International Workshop on Kansei,* (pp. 128-133). Genova, Switzerland: Kansei.

Bellini, P., & Nesi, P. (2001). WEDELMUSIC format: An XML music notation format for emerging applications. In *Proceedings of WEDELMUSIC IEEE Conference,* (pp. 79-86). Florence, Italy: IEEE Press.

Benta, K., Rarău, A., & Cremene, M. (1997). Ontology based affective context representation. In *Proceedings of the Euro American Conference on Telematics and Information Systems.* Faro, Portugal: ACM.

Bernardini, N., & De Poli, G. (2007). The sound and music computing field: Present and future. *Journal of New Music Research, 36*(3), 143–148. doi:10.1080/09298210701862432

Bigand, E., Vieillard, S., Madurell, F., Marozeau, J., & Dacquet, A. (2005). Multidimensional scaling of emotional responses to music: The effect of musical expertise and of the duration of the excerpts. *Cognition and Emotion, 19*(8), 1113–1139. doi:10.1080/02699930500204250

Bonini, F., Rodà, A., & De Poli, G. (2006). Communicating expressive intentions with a single piano note. *Journal of New Music Research, 35*(3), 197–210. doi:10.1080/09298210601045575

Bresin, R. (1998). Artificial neural networks based models for automatic performance of musical scores. *Journal of New Music Research, 27*(3), 239–270. doi:10.1080/09298219808570748

Campbell, W., & Heller, J. (1981). Psychomusicology and psycholinguistics: Parallel paths or separate ways. *Psychomusicology, 1*(2), 3–14. doi:10.1037/h0094284

Camurri, A., Canepa, C., Coletta, P., Mazzarino, B., & Volpe, G. (2008). Mappe per affetti erranti: A multimodal system for social active listening and expressive performance. In *Proceedings NIME 2008 International Conference on New Interfaces for Musical Expression,* (pp. 134-139). Genova, Italy: NIME.

Camurri, A., De Poli, G., Leman, M., & Volpe, G. (2005). Toward communicating expressiveness and affect in multimodal interactive systems for performing arts and cultural applications. *IEEE MultiMedia, 12*(1), 43–53. doi:10.1109/MMUL.2005.2

Canazza, S., De Poli, G., Di Sanzo, G., & Vidolin, A. (1998). A model to add expressiveness to automatic musical performance. In *Proceedings of International Computer Music Conference,* (pp. 163-169). Ann Arbour, MI: ACM.

Canazza, S., De Poli, G., Drioli, C., Rodà, A., & Vidolin, A. (2000a). Audio morphing different expressive intentions for Multimedia Systems. *IEEE MultiMedia, 7*(3), 79–83.

Canazza, S., De Poli, G., Drioli, C., Rodà, A., & Vidolin, A. (2004). Modeling and control of expressiveness in music performance. *Proceedings of the IEEE, 92*(4), 686–701. doi:10.1109/JPROC.2004.825889

Canazza, S., De Poli, G., Drioli, C., Rodà, A., & Zamperini, F. (2000b). Real-time morphing among different expressive intentions in audio playback. In *Proceedings of ICMC,* (pp. 356-359). Berlin, Germany: ICMC.

Canazza, S., De Poli, G., Rinaldin, S., & Vidolin, A. (1997c). Sonological analysis of clarinet expressivity. In Leman, M. (Ed.), *Music, Gestalt, and Computing: Studies in Cognitive and Systematic Musicology* (pp. 431–440). Berlin, Germany: Springer-Verlag.

Canazza, S., De Poli, G., & Rodà, A. (2002). Analysis of expressive intentions in piano performance. *Journal of ITC Sangeet Research Academy, 16,* 23–62.

Canazza, S., De Poli, G., Rodà, A., & Vidolin, A. (1997d). Analysis and synthesis of expressive intentions in musical performance. In *Proceedings of the International Computer Music Conference 1997,* (pp. 113-120). Tessaloniki, Greece: International Computer Music Association.

Canazza, S., De Poli, G., Rodà, A., & Vidolin, A. (2003a). An abstract control space for communication of sensory expressive intentions in music performance. *Journal of New Music Research, 32*(3), 281–294. doi:10.1076/jnmr.32.3.281.16862

Canazza, S., De Poli, G., & Vidolin, A. (1997b). Perceptual analysis of the musical expressive intention in a clarinet performance. In Leman, M. (Ed.), *Music, Gestalt, and Computing: Studies in Cognitive and Systematic Musicology* (pp. 441–450). Berlin, Germany: Springer-Verlag. doi:10.1007/BFb0034132

Canazza, S., & Orio, N. (1997a). How are the players ideas perceived by listeners: Analysis of "How high the moon" theme. In *Proceedings of the International Kansei Workshop 1997,* (pp. 128-133). Genova, Switzerland: Associazione di Informatica Musicale Italiana.

Canazza, S., Rodà, A., Zanon, A., & Friberg, A. (2003b). Espressive director: A system for the real-time control of music performance synthesis. In *Proceedings of the Stockholm Music Acoustics Conference,* (pp. 521-524). Stockholm, Sweden: SMAC.

ccMixter. (2009). *Website.* Retrieved July 5, 2009, from http://ccmixter.org/

Cowie, R., Douglas-Cowie, E., Tsapatsoulis, N., Votsis, G., Kollias, S., Fellenz, W., & Taylor, J. G. (2001, January). Emotion recognition in human-computer interaction. *IEEE Signal Processing Magazine,* 32–80. doi:10.1109/79.911197

Dannenberg, R., & Bates, J. (1995). A model for interactive art. In *Proceedings of the Fifth Biennial Symposium for Arts and Technology,* (pp. 103-111). ACM.

De Poli, G., Rodà, A., & Vidolin, A. (1998). Note-by-note analysis of the influence of expressive intentions and musical structure in violin performance. *Journal of New Music Research, 27*(3), 293–321. doi:10.1080/09298219808570750

Drake, C., & Palmer, C. (1993). Accent structures in music performance. *Music Perception, 10,* 343–378. doi:10.2307/40285574

Ehresman, D., & Wessel, D. L. (1978). *Perception of timbral analogies. IRCAM Report 13/78.* Paris, France: Centre Georges Pompidou.

Foafing the Music. (2009). *Website.* Retrieved July 5, 2009, from http://foafing-the-music.iua.upf.edu/

Freesound. (2009). *Website.* Retrieved July 5, 2009, from http://www.freesound.org/

Friberg, A. (1991). Generative rules for music performance. *Computer Music Journal, 15*(2), 56–71. doi:10.2307/3680917

Friberg, A. (2004). A fuzzy analyzer of emotional expression in music performance and body motion. In Sundberg, J., & Brunson, B. (Eds.), *Proceedings of Music and Music Science*. Stockholm, Sweden: ACM.

Gabrielson, A., & Lindstrom, E. (2001). The influence of the musical structure on emotional expression. In Juslin, P. N., & Slodoba, J. A. (Eds.), *Music and Emotion: Theory and Research* (pp. 223–249). Oxford, UK: Oxford University Press.

Gabrielsson, A. (1995). Expressive intention and perfomance. In Steinberg, R. (Ed.), *Music and Mind Machine* (pp. 35–47). Berlin, Germany: Sprinter-Verlag. doi:10.1007/978-3-642-79327-1_4

Gabrielsson, A. (1999). The performance of music. In Deutsch, D. (Ed.), *The Psychology of Music* (pp. 501–602). Academic Press. doi:10.1016/B978-012213564-4/50015-9

Gabrielsson, A., & Juslin, P. N. (1996). Emotional expression in music performance: Between the performer's intention and the listener's experience. *Psychology of Music, 24*, 68–91. doi:10.1177/0305735696241007

Gazon, D., & Andriarin, X. (2001). XML as a means of control for audio processing, synthesis and analysis. In *Proceedings of MOSART, Workshop on Current Research Directions in Computer Music*, (pp. 85-91). Barcelona, Spain: MOSART.

Gracenote. (2009). *Website*. Retrieved July 5, 2009, from http://www.gracenote.com/

Hanslick, E. (1854). *Vom musikalisch-schönen*. Leipzig, Germany: Rudolph Weigel.

Hashimoto, S. (1997). KANSEI as the third target of information processing and related topics in Japan. In *Proceedings of the International Workshop on KANSEI: The Technology of Emotion*, (pp. 101-104). Genova, Switzerland: AIWA.

Haus, G., & Longari, M. (2002). Towards a symbolic/time-based music language based on XML. In *Proceedings of MAX 2002 International Conference*. Milan, Italy: MAX.

Jamendo. (2009). *Website*. Retrieved July 5, 2009, from http://www.jamendo.com/

Juslin, P. N. (1993). *The influence of expressive intention on electric guitar performance*. (Unpublished Thesis). Uppsala University. Uppsala, Sweden.

Juslin, P. N. (2000). Cue utilization in communication of emotion in music performance: Relating performance to perception. *Journal of Experimental Psychology. Human Perception and Performance, 26*(6), 1797–1813. doi:10.1037/0096-1523.26.6.1797

Juslin, P. N. (2001). Communicating emotion in music performance: A review and theoretical framework. In Juslin, P. N., & Slodoba, J. A. (Eds.), *Music and Emotion: Theory and Research* (pp. 279–309). Oxford, UK: Oxford University Press.

Juslin, P. N., Friberg, A., & Bresin, R. (2002). Toward a computational model of expression in performance: The GERM model. *Musicae Scientiae*, ▪▪▪, 63–122. Retrieved from http://www.speech.kth.se/prod/publications/files/847.pdf

Juslin, P. N., & Sloboda, J. A. (2001). *Music and emotion: Theory and research*. Oxford, UK: Oxford University Press.

Kalbach, J. (2002). Review: Classifying emotion for information retrieval: Three web sites. *Notes, 59*(2), 408–411. doi:10.1353/not.2002.0177

Krumhansl, C. L. (1996). A perceptual analysis of Mozart's piano sonata K.282: Segmentation, tension, and musical ideas. *Music Perception, 13*(3), 401–432. doi:10.2307/40286177

Kuuskankare, M., & Laurson, M. (2001). ENP, musical notation library based on common lisp and CLOS. In *Proceedings of ICMC 2001*. Havana, Cuba: ICMC.

Langner, J., & Goebl, W. (2002). Representing expressive performance in tempo-loudness space. In *Proceedings of the ESCOM 10th Anniversary Conference on Musical Creativity,* (pp. 109-113). Liege, Belgium: ESCOM.

Last.fm. (2009). *Website.* Retrieved July 5, 2009, from http://www.last.fm/

Leman, M. (2000). Visualization and calculation of the roughness of acoustical musical signals using the synchronization index model (sim). In *Proceedings of the COST G-6 Conference on Digital Audio Effects, DAFX 2000,* (pp. 125-130). Verona, Italy: DAFX.

Lerdahl, F., & Jackendoff, R. (1983). *A generative theory of tonal music.* Cambridge, MA: The MIT Press.

Lindstrom, E. (1992). *5 x oh my darling Clementine: The influence of expressive intention on music performance.* (Bachelor Thesis). Uppsala University. Uppsala, Sweden.

Mion, L. (2003). Application of Bayesian networks to automatic recognition of expressive content of piano improvisations. In *Proceedings of the Stockholm Music Acoustics Conference 2003,* (pp. 557-560). Stockholm, Sweden: Stockholm Music Acoustics Conference.

Mion, L., & De Poli, G. (2008). Score-independent audio features for description of music expression. *IEEE Transactions on Speech, Audio and Language Processing, 16*(2), 458–466. doi:10.1109/TASL.2007.913743

Muze. (2009). *Website.* Retrieved July 5, 2009, from http://www.muze.com/html/products/music/muzemusic/index.htm

Narmour, E. (1990). *The analysis and cognition of basic melodic structures: the implication-realization model.* Chicago, IL: University of Chicago Press.

Oviatt, S. L. (2000). Multimodal interface research: A science without borders. In B. Yuan Huang & X. Tang (Eds.), *Proceedings of the International Conference on Spoken Language Processing,* (vol 3, pp. 1-6). Beijing, China: ACM.

Pachet, F., Aucouturier, J. J., La Burthe, A., Zils, A., & Beurive, A. (2006). The cuidado music browser: An end-to-end electronic music distribution system. *Multimedia Tools and Applications, 30,* 331–349. doi:10.1007/s11042-006-0030-6

Palmer, C. (1997). Music performance. *Annual Review of Psychology, 48,* 115–138. doi:10.1146/annurev.psych.48.1.115

Pandora. (2009). *Website.* Retrieved July 5, 2009, from http://www.pandora.com/

Picard, R. W. (1997). *Affective computing.* Cambridge, MA: MIT Press.

Plutchik, R. (1980). *Emotion: A psychoevolutionary synthesis.* New York, NY: Harper & Row.

Plutchik, R. (1994). *The psychology and biology of emotions.* New York, NY: Harper-Collins.

Ramirez, R., Hazan, A., Gómez, E., Maestre, E., & Serra, X. (2005). Discovering expressive transformation rules from saxophone jazz performances. *Journal of New Music Research, 34,* 319–330. doi:10.1080/09298210600578097

Ramirez, R., Hazan, A., Maestre, E., & Serra, X. (2008). A genetic rule-based expressive performance model for jazz saxophone. *Computer Music Journal, 32*, 38–50. doi:10.1162/comj.2008.32.1.38

Repp, B. H. (1992). Diversity and commonality in music performance: An analysis of timing microstructure in Schumann's "Träumerei". *The Journal of the Acoustical Society of America, 92*, 2546–2568. doi:10.1121/1.404425

Repp, B. H. (1994). Relational invariance of expressive microstructure across global tempo changes in music performance: An exploratory study. *Psychological Research, 56*(4), 269–284. doi:10.1007/BF00419657

Repp, B. H. (1995). Expressive timing in Schumann's "Träumerei": An analysis of performances by graduate student pianists. *The Journal of the Acoustical Society of America, 98*, 2413–2427. doi:10.1121/1.413276

Repp, B. H. (1998). A microcosm of musical expression: Quantitative analysis of pianists' timing in the initial measures of Chopin's Etude in E major. *The Journal of the Acoustical Society of America, 104*, 1085–1100. doi:10.1121/1.423325

Repp, B. H. (1999). A microcosm of musical expression: Quantitative analysis of pianists' dynamics in the initial measures of Chopin's Etude in E major. *The Journal of the Acoustical Society of America, 105*, 1972–1988. doi:10.1121/1.426743

Rodà, A., & Canazza, S. (2009). A web 2.0 system for expressive performance of music contents. In *Proceedings of 2nd International Conference on Human System Interaction*. Catania, Italy: IEEE.

Rodà, A., & Canazza, S. (2009). Virtual performance, actual gesture: A web 2.0 system for expressive performance of music contents. In *Proceedings of Human System Interaction 2009*. Catania, Italy: IEEE. doi:10.1109/HSI.2009.5091025

Russell, J. A. (1980). A circumplex model of affect. *Journal of Personality and Social Psychology, 39*, 1161–1178. doi:10.1037/h0077714

Scherer, K. R. (1994). Affect bursts. In van Goozen, S., van de Poll, N. E., & Sergeant, J. A. (Eds.), *Emotions: Essays on Emotion Theory* (pp. 161–196). Hillsdale, NJ: Erlbaum.

Serra, X. (2008). *Technological development in the current social context: Who is really in control?* Paper presented at the 8th International Conference New Interfaces for Musical Expression. Genova, Italy.

Soundpedia. (2009). *Website*. Retrieved July 5, 2009, from http://www.soundpedia.com/

Swartz, A. (2002). MusicBrainz: A semantic web service. *IEEE Intelligent Systems, 17*(1), 76–77. doi:10.1109/5254.988466

Todd, N., & McAngus, P. (1995). The kinematics of musical expression. *The Journal of the Acoustical Society of America, 97*, 1940–1949. doi:10.1121/1.412067

Widmer, G. (1996). Learning expressive performance: The structure-level approach. *Journal of New Music Research, 25*(2), 179–205. doi:10.1080/09298219608570702

Chapter 9
MusicXML:
The First Decade

Michael D. Good
MakeMusic, Inc., USA

ABSTRACT

MusicXML is a universal interchange and distribution format for common Western music notation. MusicXML's design and development began in 2000, with the purpose to be the MP3 equivalent for digital sheet music. MusicXML was developed by Recordare and can represent music from the 17th century onwards, including guitar tablature and other music notations used to notate or transcribe contemporary popular music. MusicXML is supported by over 160 applications. The development and history of MusicXML is described in this chapter.

PURPOSE

MusicXML is a universal interchange and distribution format for common Western music notation. It is designed so that a single XML file can be used by a wide range of music software applications. These applications include the display and editing of music notation, the playback and editing of a performance of a musical score, musical analysis, and music retrieval.

MusicXML's design and development began in 2000, when Internet audio applications were coming into widespread use. Digital sheet music retail sites like Sunhawk were also starting to appear. However, there was no standard format for music notation that compared to the MP3 format

for audio. Instead, each application had its own proprietary format. The only way to share sheet music files between applications was with Standard MIDI Files. But MIDI loses a great deal of information when representing music notation (Selfridge-Field, 1997). MusicXML was designed to be the MP3 equivalent for digital sheet music.

MusicXML represents music from the 17th century onwards, including guitar tablature and other music notations used to notate or transcribe contemporary popular music. Since MusicXML was being developed by Recordare, a commercial company, the focus was relentlessly practical. The format needed to support a wide range of Western music of commercial and artistic interest, in a way that was practical for contemporary music notation applications to use.

DOI: 10.4018/978-1-4666-2497-9.ch009

MusicXML does not represent earlier Western music in its original notation, nor does it represent non-Western music. Most performers who read Western sheet music cannot read early or non-Western music. MusicXML reflects these commonalities and boundaries of musician experience. This makes the markup much more musician-friendly than is possible in more abstract, general-purpose languages. This is important for getting a format widely implemented, as most music notation software developers are musicians themselves (Good, 2006a). Over-abstraction was a fundamental reason why the earlier Standard Music Description Language (SMDL) format (Sloan, 1997) was never adopted.

DESIGN APPROACH

MusicXML models common Western music notation using concepts and vocabulary that are familiar to Western musicians. The basic organization of musical structure comes from the MuseData format (Hewlett, 1997), with additional ideas from the Humdrum format (Huron, 1997). MusicXML extended these designs to support popular as well as classical music, including tablature, guitar chord diagrams, and percussion notation.

Our initial implementations confirmed that MuseData was indeed a good starting point for MusicXML's design. The basic musical organization mapped smoothly to the music representation of popular music notation editors such as Finale and Sibelius. MusicXML's element and attribute names are based on the English-language musical terms used in the USA. This makes the format easier to read and understand than those that use either non-musical names or cryptic abbreviations, making the format better suited for archival use.

MusicXML primarily models a document—a musical score—rather than an abstraction of a document. Different aspects of music—the musical structure, the appearance of a particular score engraving, and the interpretive details of a particular musical performance—are all included in a single unified document, mirroring how contemporary music software works. The integration of appearance is especially important, since appearance conveys semantic meaning in musical scores. MusicXML places the musical data in XML elements, and places the visual and performance information (based on MuseData's print and sound suggestions) in XML attributes or special-purpose XML elements. This element/attribute distinction follows commonly accepted best practices for XML language design (Harold, 2004).

To illustrate, Box 1 shows how MusicXML can represent a staccato middle C. The formatting data assumes standard positioning in the treble clef, and the duration value assumes a definition of 4 divisions per quarter note.

Note how basic musical concepts are represented as elements, with print and sound suggestions represented as attributes. Since what is notated does not always match what is performed, MusicXML has separate elements to capture this duality. For instance, the <type> element represents what is notated, while the <duration> element represents what is performed. The default-y attribute for the stem element indicates that the upstem should end one and a half spaces below the top line of the staff. The release attribute for the note element indicates that the played duration should be one division shorter than indicated by the value in the duration element—equivalent to shortening by a sixteenth note in this example.

MusicXML's approach based on musical semantics differs dramatically from the approach of the earlier Notation Interchange File Format (NIFF—Grande, 1997). NIFF's graphical format primarily defines notes by their placement on the staff rather than by their musical pitch. This makes NIFF difficult to match to the data structures of contemporary notation programs, or any programs that need to play music as well as display it (Good, 2006b). NIFF's adoption was thus largely limited

Box 1.

```
<note release="-1">
  <pitch>
    <step>C</step>
    <octave>4</octave>
  </pitch>
  <duration>4</duration>
  <voice>1</voice>
  <type>quarter</type>
  <stem default-y="-15">up</stem>
  <notations>
    <articulations>
      <staccato placement="below"/>
    </articulations>
  </notations>
</note>
```

to export from music scanning programs, which could use the graphical approach more easily.

Iterative design and evolutionary delivery (Gilb, 1988; Gould & Lewis, 1985) were also critical components of MusicXML's design approach. MusicXML 1.0 was the 15th iteration of the format as delivered over an initial 4-year development period. MusicXML 1.1, 2.0, and 3.0 have provided further iterations since the version 1.0 release. The MusicXML format was designed in parallel with the software that used it, such as our Finale and Sibelius plug-ins. This continuous design, development, and testing ensured that MusicXML was a practical format to exchange music notation between leading notation applications like Finale and Sibelius, as well as a wide variety of music applications in other domains.

HISTORY

The design and development of the MusicXML format started with the founding of Recordare in January 2000. This design work was preceded by meetings with several experts in the area of computer music formats. Prof. Barry Vercoe of MIT recommended MuseData and Humdrum as starting points for developing a standard format for common Western music notation. Profs. Vercoe, Selfridge-Field, and Huron all provided important early guidance and encouragement in starting the MusicXML project.

MusicXML was introduced in Version 0.1 form at the first International Symposium on Music Information Retrieval (ISMIR—Good, 2000). This initial version was basically an XML version of the MuseData format. MusicXML's capabilities soon moved beyond MuseData and Humdrum, adding features to support notation of popular music more completely than was possible in either previous format.

MusicXML's design and development have always proceeded together with implementations to test and refine the language's design. As of IS-MIR 2000, the software included full import and export of MuseData files, partial import of NIFF files and Finale's Enigma Transportable Files, and partial export of Standard MIDI Files. However, we knew that the format had no chance of being adopted unless it could both read *and* write files from one of the two dominant music notation editors in the first decade of the 21st century: Finale and Sibelius.

Since creating a standard music notation interchange format would lower the barriers to entry in the music notation software market, these market leaders had little incentive to help Recordare with this project. We would need to create these initial implementations ourselves. Finale and Sibelius both provide plug-in development kits that allow third-party developers to create software for these applications. It quickly became apparent that only Finale's kit was sufficient for building a two-way MusicXML import/export plug-in, so that is where we focused our implementation efforts.

Once we had a working Finale plug-in ready to test outside of Recordare in May 2001, we started approaching third-party software developers. Graham Jones from *visiv* had particular incentive to support the MusicXML format. His SharpEye music scanning program was generally considered to be more accurate than the competition. However, since it could only communicate to Finale and Sibelius using MIDI files, much of that advantage was lost. By using the MusicXML format, Finale users could take full advantage of SharpEye's enhanced scanning capabilities.

In September 2001, SharpEye Music Reader became the first commercial program to support the MusicXML format, with SharpEye version 2.15 supporting MusicXML version 0.5. Recordare developed the Finale plug-in for MusicXML import and export that was first released in April 2002. The makers of Finale then saw that supporting the MusicXML format would improve how music scanning worked for their customers. Finale added MusicXML support in its Windows version in Finale 2003. Mac OS X support was added in Finale 2006, with Mac Universal Binary support added in Finale 2007. Recordare also developed a plug-in to export MusicXML files from Sibelius that was first released in August 2003.

Despite the initial successes with SharpEye and Finale, we waited to release a version 1.0 of the MusicXML format until we had enough experience with a variety of applications to be sure that we would not need to make incompatible changes later. Version 1.0 of the MusicXML format was released in January 2004. Version 1.1 added 70 new features, especially in the area of music formatting, and was released in May 2005. Version 2.0 added 95 further new features, included a compressed zip-based multimedia format, and was released in June 2007. These MusicXML definitions all used Document Type Definition (DTD) technology. A W3C XML Schema Definition (XSD) version of the MusicXML 2.0 format was released in September 2008. Version 3.0 includes improved virtual instrument support and was released in August 2011.

Figure 1 charts the status of MusicXML implementations as of October 2012. Applications on the left side of the chart are shipping; applications on the right side of the chart are in beta or prototype stage. Applications on the top of the chart both read and write MusicXML files; applications in the middle write MusicXML files, and applications on the bottom read MusicXML files.

As of October 2012, MusicXML is now supported by over 160 applications, including all the market leaders in music notation editing and music scanning; major players in music sequencing, electronic music stands, and Internet sheet music sales; and research applications in areas such as music analysis, automatic composition, and visualization.

The MusicXML developer community has been actively involved in the ongoing iterative design and development of the MusicXML format since we began a developer email list in 2001. Many of the best ideas that have moved MusicXML beyond its MuseData/Humdrum roots have come from other developers in the community. The design of Version 1.1's formatting

Figure 1. MusicXML implementations as of October 2012

features, for instance, benefited from the work of Curtis Morley and the musicRAIN team, as well as proposals by Doill Jung of AMuseTec. Other major contributors include Geri Actor, Don Byrd, Didier Guillion, Bernd Jungmann, Mark Maronde, Mark Olleson, and Christof Schardt.

Around 2000, many formats were proposed for representing common Western music notation in XML format. Only MusicXML is in widespread use by different software applications. Further information about the MusicXML format is available from MakeMusic, Inc. (2012). Recordare's MusicXML assets were acquired by MakeMusic in November 2011.

MusicXML has become the standard interchange file format for common Western music notation. It is also becoming more popular for distributing sheet music over the Internet, as shown by Wikifonia, Sheet Music Digital, and other websites. At the end of its first decade, MusicXML is well on its way to becoming the digital sheet music equivalent of the MP3 format.

REFERENCES

Gilb, T. (1988). *Principles of software engineering management*. Reading, MA: Addison-Wesley.

Good, M. (2000). Representing music using XML. In *Proceedings of Music IR 2000*. Retrieved January 11, 2010, from http://ismir2000. ismir.net/posters/good.pdf

Good, M. (2006a). Lessons from the adoption of MusicXML as an interchange standard. In D. Megginson (Ed.), *Proceedings of XML 2006*. Retrieved January 11, 2010, from http://2006. xmlconference.org/proceedings/46/presentation.pdf

Good, M. (2006b). MusicXML in commercial applications. In Hewlett, W. B., & Selfridge-Field, E. (Eds.), *Music Analysis East and West* (pp. 9–20). Cambridge, MA: The MIT Press.

Gould, J. D., & Lewis, C. (1985). Designing for usability: Key principles and what designers think. *Communications of the ACM, 28*(3), 300–311. doi:10.1145/3166.3170

Grande, C. (1997). The Notation Interchange File Format: A Windows-compliant approach. In Selfridge-Field, E. (Ed.), *Beyond MIDI: The Handbook of Musical Codes* (pp. 491–512). Cambridge, MA: The MIT Press.

Harold, E. R. (2004). *Effective XML*. Boston, MA: Addison-Wesley.

Hewlett, W. B. (1997). MuseData: Multipurpose representation. In Selfridge-Field, E. (Ed.), *Beyond MIDI: The Handbook of Musical Codes* (pp. 402–447). Cambridge, MA: The MIT Press.

Huron, D. (1997). Humdrum and kern: Selective feature encoding. In Selfridge-Field, E. (Ed.), *Beyond MIDI: The Handbook of Musical Codes* (pp. 375–401). Cambridge, MA: The MIT Press.

MakeMusic, Inc. (2012). MusicXML overview. Retrieved May 12, 2012, from http://www.makemusic.com/musicxml/

Selfridge-Field, E. (1997). Describing musical information. In Selfridge-Field, E. (Ed.), *Beyond MIDI: The Handbook of Musical Codes* (pp. 3–38). Cambridge, MA: The MIT Press.

Sloan, D. (1997). HyTime and Standard Music Description Language: A document-description approach. In Selfridge-Field, E. (Ed.), *Beyond MIDI: The Handbook of Musical Codes* (pp. 469–490). Cambridge, MA: The MIT Press.

Chapter 10
Universal Information Architecture of Acoustic Music Instruments

Jacques Steyn
Monash University, South Africa

ABSTRACT

The information architecture of acoustic music instruments is described. As contemporary acoustic research has not yet covered all the possible materials, shapes, designs, and other essential properties of possible acoustic instruments, the model proposed in this chapter serves as a high-level analysis with meta-level XML-based markup elements and attributes. The ultimate design goal of the proposed model is to be able to create a software synthesis application that could recreate the acoustic sounds of music instruments faithfully, as well as the ability to create novel acoustic sounds using virtual music instruments.

It is proposed that algorithms be created, which might lead to more realistically sounding instruments, as well as creating totally new sounds based on the properties of acoustic instruments, even the virtual creation of new types of acoustic instruments that would be impossible to build with real materials.

It is further proposed that the properties of different components serve as modifiers on a base soundwave. Modifiers include the materials used in the construction of instruments, energy sources, dimensions of 3D acoustic cavities, and relationships between instrument components are considered.

The properties of a wide range of musical instruments have been considered, ranging from ancient acoustic instruments to modern ones, as well as including the instruments of many music cultures. Following on a logical analysis and synthesis of previous research rather than acoustic lab results, a high-level generic and universal model of the information architecture of acoustic music instruments is constructed.

DOI: 10.4018/978-1-4666-2497-9.ch010

DEMARCATING THE FIELD

Music acoustics has been around for a long time, at least since Hermann von Helmholtz (1821-1894) invented the Helmholtz resonator in the 1860s, although his interest was more in the physics of perception. It could also be argued that the Ancient Greeks had some or other conceptualization of acoustics, given the observations of Pythagoras of Samos (ca. 570 – ca. 495 BCE) that the pitch of a string seems to be doubled at half its length. The Greek interest was more in the mathematical ratios of the music of the spheres (James, 1993) than understanding acoustics. In modern times, the acoustic properties of many artifacts have been researched, ranging from building spaces and the metal and concrete used in bridge construction to solids, liquids and many other phenomena. Although a lot is known, there is still a whole range of unknown properties, such as the acoustic behavior of different topographical shapes and thicknesses of many types of timber, metals, plastics, lacquers, and other materials used in the construction of acoustic music instruments. Before all the variants of acoustic behavior is known, a detailed model cannot be constructed. The model proposed here is thus a high-level tentative one, constructed on the basis of current available knowledge.

The first use of computers was for military purposes, and in large organizations, such as government and corporate environments. Almost simultaneously, music was also one of the first uses computers were put to. Much later, after the MIDI standard was introduced in the 1980s, as well as novel methods to create sound synthetically, there had been a boom in music technology, not only in the design of playback devices, but also in the design of sound and music creation devices. Strangely, despite the very long history of acoustics, as well as interest from music technologists in computers, there had not yet been a complete information architectural description of the acoustics of non-electronic music instruments. Extensive literature (such as the *Journal of the Acoustical Society of America*) exists describing the acoustic properties, but none in a format that computers could readily use in an information exchange environment. There is no formal approach to this description either. It is this gap that this chapter addresses.

The chapter on *The Architecture of Music* in this volume covers a brief discussion on ontology and related concepts. Here it suffices to state that an ontological analysis of music focuses on the information required for sound synthesis, and not on the engineering aspects of its physical synthesis or on synthesis models. Approaches to music synthesis is often more concerned with the hardware, the chip design, algorithms and on the methods to be used to generate sound. Relatively little attention is paid to the data structures that the system uses, except in the form of algorithms, or in the analysis of the final output sound. The focus seems to be on a sampled soundclip is a whole, and there is no interest in the intrinsic properties of the wholes. Most descriptions of sounds are about the physics of wave propagation and wave properties. Synthesizers typically use the sinusoidal wave as basic starting point. This wave is then modified and manipulated through filters and by adding other waves to serve as harmonics. Several waves are added together to obtain the required sound - hence called additive synthesis. The other main method, subtractive synthesis, starts off with a wave rich in harmonics, and by using for example filters, reduces the complexity of the wave. Wavetable synthesis is a variation of the additive synthesis method. The proposed model is not a synthesis model, but an information model of the architectural components of the acoustic music instrument. The approach is thus very different from approaches such as, for example, the parametric piano synthesizer of Rauhala *et al.* (2008).

The information architectural model in this chapter does not attempt to create a physical model from an algorithm perspective, but from the perspective of the information architecture of the physical music instrument. The proposed model assumes that the music instrument's information architecture can be described independently from algorithms or synthesis models, or even low-level characteristics of music instruments. In fact, the information architecture is algorithm ignorant, and various algorithms could be written for any component described by the information architecture.

An information architectural model is not to be confused with an information theory approach to music. Margulis and Beatty (2008) raises the problems why information theory has not found a solid way into music applications. Their definition of information concerns communication between composers and listeners. The information architectural model proposed here is concerned with the translation of the properties of acoustic music instruments into a generic format to be used in algorithm and synthesis design to recreate not only the sounds of acoustic instruments, but also to allow for the creation of new sounds. Here information is an interpreted data set, created by structuring knowledge about the acoustics of instruments, analyzing the components, and structuring that knowledge into a hierarchical and nodal markup language.

In this chapter, the common English generic word "sound" is used. In the context of electronic music instruments and software the word "patch" is often used, which is a term used in the early days of sound synthesis. Components such as oscillators, filters, and amplifiers were connected to one another with cables in different configurations to create different kinds of sound. A particular pattern of connections was called a patch, a term borrowed from early telephone exchanges. When a call was made, the operator plugged in the cable into a slot, thus patching up (i.e. connecting) the network in a specific pattern. The components of early synthesizers were connected in a similar way, hence *patched* together. Manufacturers of contemporary synthesizers still use the term "patch" for a sound, which is not really informative

to the average musician, therefore in this chapter the word "sound" will be used instead of patch.

The proposed model is derived from an analysis of how standard non-electronic acoustic music instruments produce sound with specific reference to the independent acoustic properties of the different components of these instruments. This does not include an analysis of soundwaves, but of the structural features of instruments, and their known acoustic effects on soundwaves. The description of a virtual flute in this proposed model, for example, is not similar to that of Ystad and Voinier's *Virtually Real Flute* (2001), which, although modeled physically, is more about interfacing the acoustic flute with a MIDI system. Bilbao's (2009) simulation of reed wind instruments, which covers the pipe (instrument body), the reed, the bell and the holes (tone-holes), is about algorithms for each of these components, not their information architecture.

Organology

For this project, a detailed acoustic analysis of all existing acoustic music instruments would be a near impossible task, so a standard music instrument classification system was used as starting point. The discipline of Organology originated within the discipline of Ethnomusicology. Apart from investigating how instruments are used in different cultures, Organology is also about the classification of instruments (Baines, 1960).

Classification systems of music instruments have been around for a long time. Buchner (1980) refers to the system of the ancient Chinese (more than 4000 years ago) based on the materials (stone, wood, silk) used in the construction of the instruments, the ancient Indian *Natya Shastra* (from the 500s BCE) using physical properties, and the system of the Frenchman Johannes de Muris from around the 1350s CE, which distinguished between *tensibilia* (strings), *inflatabilia* (pipes), and *percussibilia* (percussive) instruments, which is similar to the common contemporary classification system of Hornbostel-Sachs developed in the early 1900s.

Kartomi (2001) summarizes attempts at music instrument classification systems, and highlights the criticism of the Hornbostel-Sachs system especially from the 1930s onwards. Kassler (1995) argues for a revisiting of the Hornbostel-Sachs in the light of more recent research on acoustics, and this advise was followed. Discussion here is not about the philosophy of classification systems, as a practical decision needs to be made in order to design the desired artifact. This chapter is also not so much about the classification of music instruments, yet an ontological investigation would involve this discipline. As starting point then, the general framework of the Hornbostel-Sachs system was initially used, but tweaked based on the findings of research into acoustic properties of instruments. Interestingly enough, after the first few iterations of design, what emerged in typical grounded theory approach, results showed a system that confirmed Schaeffner's distinction between solids and air. In Schaeffner's system a distinction is made between solids and air, based on the vibrating substance of the instrument. This system will be used for high-level classification, while the broad categories of the Hornbostel-Sachs system will be used for lower level groups.

It is assumed that instruments within the same families (known as *consorts*) behave acoustically in similar ways, except for pitch. For example, there are many types of flutes: Alto flute, Bass flute, Contra-alto flute, Contrabass flute, Subcontrabass flute, Double contrabass flute, Hyperbass flute, Boehm flute with B foot, Boehm with C foot, Classical with C foot, Classical with D foot, Classical with flared foot, Baroque Flute, and so forth. Their basic sound generating mechanisms are assumed to be the same, and so are their structural components, except for dimensions. The different sounds they create are presumably due to the differences in the values of the distinguishable

properties they have. It is also assumed that other pipe instruments function on the same basis as the pipe drone, or when fingerholes are added, like a simple recorder or flute, and that differences could be described in terms of modifiers in the various sections of the pipe components. Described in this manner, other wind instruments, such as a saxophone, may be modeled on the flute as a pipe, but with different values to some properties, such as diameter, the addition of a flare and bell. In addition, of course, in the case of the saxophone, the reed in the mouthpiece is a crucial component, as this plays the role of a modifier on soundwaves created by the basic pipe construction.

Using the classification of music instruments is relevant for the sake of economy, as families of instruments presumably have similar properties. Any markup language should use as few as possible elements, which means that elements should cover a wide range as possible. Conversely, elements should be precise enough to enable an application program to use them adequately. By using the markup structure, an application must at least meet its design goals, which in the case of this chapter is the reproduction for the sounds of acoustic instruments. Classification systems depend on an ontological investigation. Due to space constraints, ontology will not be discussed in much detail here, as it is addressed in the chapter *The Architecture of Music* in this volume. For the sake of fast tracking then, only the following rudimentary remarks will be made before embarking on the purpose of this chapter.

MUSIC SYSTEMS

The approach to music instruments is as follows. The acoustic physics of the component parts of the music instrument is taken as point of departure. The prominent properties of the parts that influence the resulting soundwave are considered. The music instrument is thus deconstructed to arrive at the influencing parts. Their properties are described and labeled to create an architectural understanding of what is important in creating the unique sounds of each instrument. The markup language that results from this is the output of this chapter's investigation.

There are four distinguishable systems that contribute to the complexities of musical sounds and their perception: the musician, the instrument, the listener, and the environment (see Figure 1).

The proposed model only describes the general properties of the acoustic music instruments. The properties of the other systems, musician, listener and environment, will not be considered in this chapter. It suffices to state that the playing technique of the musician has an impact on the resulting texture of the soundwave, especially instruments that require more expertise than others, such as the bowing of a violin. This model also does not address the musician control system over sound generation - that is, the keys that need to be pressed, or strings that need to be energized. That would involve new musician interfaces such as proposed by Jordà (2002). It might eventually be possible to model every aspect of music-making, including breath control on the input side. One very complex modeling of human breathing was done for the Virtual Breath (2009) project at the University of Texas at Austin, which models airflow 23

generations of branches down the lung cavities. In the present description, modeling for breath is not considered. The model is generic enough to handle any such control by a virtual musician, provided such a system can be plugged in.

In the listener system it is not only the physiological perception subsystems that need to be considered (such as researched by psycho-acoustics), but also the ethnographic subsystem, as instrument design depends on cultural preferences, and so do the tuning systems used. The preferred sets of frequencies that make up scales are culturally determined, even though that might be guided by physical acoustics.

Due to different acoustic properties, the sound in a smoky jazz bar is very different to the sound in a large concert hall. The effects of the environment system have been implemented in popular devices over the past few decades. Pre-defined buttons for different types of room acoustics are nowadays available even on cheaper models of home entertainment systems. The focus here is on the acoustic instrument properties, and not so much on the details of the input energy or output consequences of the space into which the sound is released (i.e. room acoustic properties). The impact of room acoustics has been accounted for in research for quite some time. Such input and output contexts

Figure 1. Systems influencing music sound

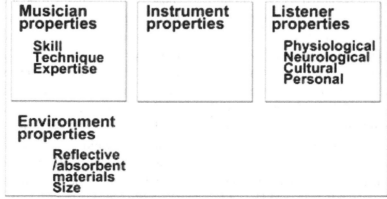

are acknowledged, but not described in the proposed model. The chapter of Pakarinen in this book pays some attention to room acoustics from an information architectural perspective.

Room and environmental acoustics are regarded to have extrinsic impact on the resulting soundwaves. The soundwave produced by the instrument itself is regarded to be intrinsic to the instrument. Environmental acoustics is very important for the sound of orchestras. No matter how many samples of virtual violins one duplicates, they never sound like the strings of an orchestra. That is because the intrinsic qualities of each individual instrument output interfere with one another extrinsically in the environment. In addition, subtle instrument differences and musician properties also influence the resulting soundwaves of each instrument so that even if the exact same instruments are used, their output soundwaves will differ, however subtly, while these different soundwaves interfere with one another in the room and result in richer harmonics. In order to model, for example, the strings section of an orchestra, small variations in musician and instrument properties need to be factored in, as well as the extrinsic contribution of the individual instruments to the section as a whole, and in addition to this also the behavior of waves in room spaces—such as halls.

All this is for another occasion. The focus here is on the most generic properties of acoustic music instruments only. In the abstract, a musical instrument within which energy is transferred to be perceived can be regarded as containing a trigger, generator, resonator, and amplifier. The trigger activates the mechanisms that create the sound (generator). This initial soundwave is modified by the various resonating materials of the instrument, ranging from the pipe cavity and its properties, to the body of the instrument, and even its immediate surroundings. The loudness of the soundwaves produced by many instruments, such as strings, is generally not enough to be audible beyond very small distances, so the loudness of these soundwaves are typically enhanced by add-

ing amplifiers, which are usually hollow objects ranging from naturally occurring dried gourds to artificially created chambers, such as the body of the guitar or piano.

Methodology

A design science approach is followed in this chapter. This approach merges theory and utility with the ultimate goal of designing an artifact that is constructed on the basis of solid theory (see e.g. Hevner, et al., 2004; Hevner & Chatterjee, 2010). Design Science is a relatively more recent scientific method, introduced as an addition to the positivist and constructivist (or interpretivist) approaches that dominated the science of Information Systems (Vaishnavi & Kuechler 2004). In Design Science, an artifact may be defined as a construct, a model, or methods and implementations (March & Smith, 1995). The model constructed in this chapter is a theoretical or virtual model, informed by theory. Being a virtual artifact, the content described here is thus one-step short of an actual, real artifact. The next step in realizing this theoretical model would be to build a working prototype as proof of concept.

Goal setting and the logical testing of goal achievement are criteria used to determine whether a proposed model conforms to the requirements of design as science. If the proposed model conforms to internal logic, and if the information (or knowledge) used is based on other scientific knowledge, those requirements will be met. The knowledge used in this chapter is firmly established in the physics and acoustics of sound, particularly with reference to musical instruments. It is thus my contention that even if the proposed model is virtual, and no physical synthesizer built to test the model, this is nevertheless a scientific approach.

The model is based on a set of postulates, which is a valid scientific approach. Einstein's General Theory of Relativity (Einstein, 1916) is an extension of the Special Theory of Relativity (Einstein, 1905). The General Theory postulated a gravitational redshift of the wavelength of light when it passes a strong gravitational field. This was only demonstrated a few years later in 1919 during an eclipse of the sun. On 29 May 1919, on the island of Sao Tome and Príncipe, west of Equatorial Guinea (Africa), Arthur Eddington (1882 – 1944) took photographs of a solar eclipse which clearly showed a bent light line. The validation of Einstein's postulates came several years after it had been proposed. Perhaps no one would today dispute the claim that Einstein's proposal was scientific. A theory or model is thus a valid scientific description. Einstein's primary logical tool was mathematics, which is a tool of very high-level logical abstraction, but that logic could also be expressed in natural language. Mathematics is an extremely concise symbolic system compared to natural human language. Formal mathematical formulae are not the only logical tools to use to construct scientifically based models. Einstein's approach was explanatory. The proposal in this chapter is explanatory and descriptive, using ordinary English and not mathematics.

The design purpose of the proposed model is to offer an information architecture of the components of acoustic music instruments based on an ontological description, that could be used in the construction of virtual instruments. The envisaged physical artifact is a synthesizer of some sort, although synthesis may not necessarily be the circuit or algorithmic methods used for generating the sound. The construction of such a synthesizer is aimed at a device that will enable end users to recreate the sounds of these acoustic instruments, as well as the ability to create new kinds of sounds. An application designed for such a virtual sound generator may also be useful for the analysis and classification of musical sounds by users, bearing in mind that the design phase of this model already classifies instruments. The application may also be useful for searching of sound types and specific sound instances, as well as for new ways in combining the different properties of musical sounds to create new

virtual instruments. It might be possible to create sounds that have some properties of horns, some of strings, and others of membranes for the same virtual "instrument."

As the properties of an instrument is described with reference to the instrument components, such a description might be useful for end-users to classify musical sounds according to their needs. Presently, the sound banks of music synthesizers that contain many thousands of different sounds, is very difficult to navigate as the names given by the designers of the sounds are not very helpful. For example, the Roland SonicCell contains names such as Funky Line, Over-D6, Crimson, Teethy Grit, Evangelized, Stimulation, Griggley, Brusky, Wet Atax, WaitnOutside, and many more similarly senseless names. When orchestrating it takes ages to scroll through such long lists of senseless names in order to find the sound texture one wants to use. A more careful description of the components of an instrument might make it easier to find suitable sounds, especially if artificial sounds are generated according to the acoustics of the components identified in this model. For example, the human sound creator may want a wind instrument type of sound with a slight percussive noise added. If an application follows the proposed model, the user could drag and drop the different components onto the design canvass and change the property values until the target sound is reached. Admittedly, the sounds labeled by the senseless names above were created by using standard synthesis models, and not by using the properties of acoustic instruments.

Models

In design science a model is an important output (see for example the summary table of possible outputs in Vaishnavi and Kuechler, 2004). Models are often interpreted to mean physical prototypes, or working algorithms. However, models could also refer to logical models, which are representations of entities, with relations between the components of entities explicated. Logic here does not necessarily need to be formal symbolic logic, but clear and grounded analysis and reasoning. Logic in this context refers to the coherence of arguments, based on some body of knowledge, and the translation of the entities and their relationships into symbolic formats such as illustrations, diagrams, or merely text. Textual models are relevant in the initial stages of a research project and in practice serve as project proposals for raising research funds. In the real world, this is often how science typically operates before funding is acquired to test the proposal. It is at this level where the model proposed in this chapter functions.

Different sound generation models have been used over the past decades to produce sound synthetically. The architectural model proposed here might impact on the design of sound producing generators, but it is not the sound producing model (in the sense of algorithm or chip design) that is in focus, but the structural information of the music instrument's acoustic properties. Synthesis models are usually designed for a specific instrument, such as the clavichord (Valimaki, Laurson, & Erkut, 2003), the parametric piano synthesizer synthesizer of Rauhala *et al.* (2008), and the virtual guitar of Pakarinen, Puputti, and Välimäki (2008). The clavichord and piano models are algorithmic models, not information models. The goal of the proposed model is to serve as a generic model of the architectural components of the instrument that could be applied to any acoustic instrument.

There are a host of sound generating methods that could be classified into families, and several different methods for turning algorithms into sounds. Chafe (2012) summarizes different methods used to create sound synthetically as follows. There are acoustical and physical models.

Acoustical Models

Acoustical models use Fourier analysis to resynthesize the properties of a soundwave.

- Subtractive acoustical models (beginning with source / filter vocal simulations)
- Additive acoustical models (recreating Fourier analyses)

Physical Models

Physical models analyze the vibrating mechanisms of sound sources.

- Impulsive linear physical models (beginning with plucked string simulations)
- Self-sustained physical models with acoustical feedback (electric guitar simulations with feedback)
- Self-sustained physical models with nonlinear excitation (beginning with simulations of bow, reed and air jet)

Smith (2006) summarizes sound generating models as follows:

- Wavetable (one period)
- Subtractive
- Additive
- Frequency Modulation (FM)
- Sampling
- Spectral Modeling
- Physical Modeling

As different methods are used to create the resulting sounds, different algorithms and different circuit and chip designs are used. These methods and algorithms used to create sounds are irrelevant. The proposed information architecture is algorithm agnostic, and could be used as data input into any of the models above. As the information architecture is not tied to a specific model, it is theoretically possible to use different methods for generating sound for each different component.

Sound generation through synthesis has several approaches: rule-based, model-based (physical and spectral) and sampling (see e.g. Smith, 2006). Sampling is very expensive if all the subtle nuances are captured. Smith concludes that to capture all the nuances (for example different velocities and pedal states) of timbre of a single piano note would amount to about a billion data bits. The standard piano has few parameters, while bowed instruments have several times more. For example, the bow movement alone has properties such as velocity, force, position, and angle, and there are other systems that also need to be considered. It is proposed that if the properties of the information architecture of those components are described, one would not need billions of bytes to reproduce a sound authentically. Such a detailed description belongs to another project. Here it is the high-level universal properties of acoustic instruments that are described.

Both rule-based and model-based synthesis are approaches for writing algorithms that could be used to create sounds similar to traditional musical instruments, but the sounds produced by present rule-based and model-based synthesizer systems are often unconvincing imitations of their acoustic counterparts. These approaches to sound indeed made it possible to generate previously unknown sounds, or manipulate sounds to have a tinge of the familiar, yet are different. In addition, so can the proposed architecture.

This should perhaps be clarified. Traditionally, since the first digital sound synthesis came into being, waveforms were in focus (e.g. Chafe, 2012). At first, the approach was typically to start with sinusoid, square, triangular and sawtooth waveforms and build sounds by combining these and by adding filters and other oscillations, such as Low Frequency Oscillation (LFO). Different modules were connected by plugging in cables into the modules to determine the flow of current through the system to create sound. A particular connected configuration was called a patch.

The next development saw the introduction of acoustical analysis, synthesis, and envelope control. Applications focused on the spectral decomposition of a waveform into its component frequencies. Acoustical analysis is informed by the properties of waveforms as a whole as they exit an instrument. In other words, the spectral components of the waveform of a saxophone as a whole is analyzed, and algorithm constructed to recreate that sound as a whole. The information of the waveform itself is not described. Neither are the acoustic properties of each component of an acoustic instrument described. The proposal differs in that the properties of the causes of the waveforms are described, an in addition to this, not the waveforms as the exit the instrument, but for each component as if it is a separate instrument. For example, the mouthpiece of a wind instrument can make a sound independently of the main instrument. The structures that play a role in creating this sound are described—their waveforms are considered. The structures are in focus, as it is assumed that waveforms will differ if the parameters of structures are changed - a pipe with a wider diameter outputs lower frequencies than a narrower pipe.

Thus, if the pipe properties are described and an algorithm designed around these, the same algorithm should be able to apply to all such pipes, while differences in resulting soundwaves would be because the values of the parameters have been changed. Each component of an acoustic instrument has its own soundwave properties. Change some attribute values, and the wave that ripples into another component impacts on the soundwave exiting that component, resulting in a different final sound. Different nuances in sound may be very subtle, or quite pronounced. The inputs into the waveform need to be considered and made explicit, rather than the final waveform itself. In the proposed model, each component of an instrument influencing the resulting soundwave is described. Once this description is complete, the next step would be to construct algorithms to generate just those properties of a particular component, but this chapter stops just short of that. It is thus not the sound of the whole instrument that is important here, but the sound of each component. The soundwave behavior of the mouthpiece of a trumpet can be measured, and its effect or contribution to the tube (the main structural component or body of a pipe instrument) of the trumpet can be calculated. The goal is of course also to create acoustic sounds synthetically, but the approach is different.

MUSIC INSTRUMENTS

Strictly speaking, no music instrument is natural. All music instruments found through all the aeons of human existence have been created artifacts. The oldest known still playable musical instruments are bone flutes excavated at Jiahu (Henan Province, China), dated between 7,000 and 9,000 years old. There are much older fragments of flutes. A flute made from a bone of a bird has been excavated at Hohle Fels cave (southern Germany) and dated to 35,000 years ago. None of these old instruments is natural, in the sense of naturally occurring as a music instrument. Although natural (or more precisely biological) substances were used, they are modified, thus recreated to serve a different function than their natural state. Music instruments are thus artifacts, and thus their design culturally determined. Older instruments might still lie waiting undiscovered. In addition, even older musical instruments might never be found as some materials do not preserve well for archaeologists to find. The bone flute is made of a biologically created natural substance. The holes were drilled with some technologically created artifact, and in previous ages possibly with a stone awl. All musical instruments are either made from existing, naturally occurring objects that are modified with some or other technology with varying degrees of modification. The holes in the bone flute, or in a piece of reed, are minimally invasive and result in a very simple instrument. A violin is created through the combination of many different artifacts and technologies, using much more complex tools, including the saw and the planer and is an extremely complex artifact compared to the bone flute. Contrary to the present common use of the term "music technology" reserved for electric and electronic music, all instruments are in fact created by some or other technology.

For most of human history, music instruments were constructed by combining naturally occurring substances as artifacts into a set that make up the complete instrument. Wood, metal, fiber, vellum, gourds, and so forth were used. It could be argued that the more recently constructed music instruments of the past few millennia are artificial recreations of more natural instruments. For example, the first flutes may have been made from the hollow stems of reeds, cane, or bamboo, while later models that used bird bones were merely somewhat more permanent versions of quickly decaying plant materials (see e.g. Grame, 1962). Contemporary metal and plastic flutes are merely modern variations of ancient designs. The amplifier boxes of violins and guitars may be regarded as variations of the calabash attached to the one-stringed bow used by hunter-gatherers, such as the San people.

The advent of electrically produced sounds introduced a whole new concept into music. A comparatively newly created artifact (given the long history of music), such as the Helmholz resonator, produces a sound through the electrical stimulation of the resonators, which in turn produce an audible frequency. Buchner lists the advent of electric instruments as far back as the 1700s, with examples such as Jean Baptiste Delaborde's electric harpsichord of 1761. Some of the first more modern electric musical instruments were the Theremin of 1917, Ondes-Martenot of 1928, and the Trautonium of 1928 (Hass, 1999; Doornbusch, 2009). Since the advent of electronically created synthetic music in the second half of the twentieth century, sound creation took on a different form. The 1958 Victor synthesizer (or more formally, the RCA Mark II Sound Synthesizer), used mainly by engineers and not musicians, was the first programmable sequencer. Synthesizers are constructed on the basis of the properties of soundwaves, not on the basis of the properties of traditional "natural" music instruments. For the average musician it is difficult to synthetically reconstruct the sounds of an acoustic instrument using concepts such as oscillators, low-frequency oscillators, filters, and waveforms. Knowledge of the physical structure of soundwaves is required. More technical musicians might be willing to take the plunge into such adventures, but the less technical musician might just want to get on with the job to create a sound similar to that of a flute, but with a slight bowing sound added. Understanding the components of musical instruments is much easier than understanding the physics of sounds. It is in this context that perhaps the information description of the components of musical instruments might make it easier to create the kinds of sounds a musician requires for a specific purpose.

The high-level Hornbostel-Sachs classification of music instruments is as follows - not using their numbering, but naming, and for this chapter only as starting point. For a more picturesque presentation of different kinds of instruments, see for example Buchner (1980).

- Aerophones (open and closed conduit, or tubular pipes)
- Chordophones (strings)
- Membranophones
- Membranes (such as plates, drum skins)
- Idiophones (vibrating rigid bars and solid pipes)
- Electrophones: Not useful for our discussion

Examples of "standard" music instruments within the Hornbostel-Sachs classification system are:

Aerophones

- Reed
  ◦ Single reed: clarinet, saxophone

  ◦ Double: bassoon, oboe, cor anglais, hecklephone
- Free reed: accordion, harmonium, harmonica
- Airjet: flute, piccolo
- Brass: tuba, trombone, horn, flugelhorn, trumpet, cornet, serpent, didjeridu

Chordophones

- Bowed: violin, viola, cello, double bass
- Plucked: Double bass, harp, harpsichord, guitar, mandolin, banjo
- Struck: Piano, dulcimer, cymbalum

Membranophones

- Membranes: Drums, timpani
- Idiophones: Sticks, bars, xylophone, marimba, plaques, tubes, vessels.

The Hornbostel-Sachs classification cannot apply universally. In the 1800s there were some bowed pianos, such as the *piano sostenente* patented by Isaac Mott in 1817, and a bowed piano called *wheel cymbals* in England (Buchner, 1980, p. 192). A bowed zither was invented in Bavaria. Plucking is only one method to activate a sound on a string instrument.

Based on the acoustic principles used for the proposed model, the present ontological model is more in line with Schaeffner's basic distinction between solids and air-based instruments. As will be explained below, membranophones could be collapsed into pipes (aerophones) and strings (chordophones). The vibrating string, rod or membrane could be non-tensed (open on both sides, such as the bars of a xylophone), completely tensed (on all or both ends, such as guitars and violins) or be open on one end (such as the "hand-piano," or *kalimba*). Membranophone instruments share such properties with the traditional aerophones and chordophones. Some membranes have resonating bodies attached to them. The cavities of the bodies share pipe-like properties, and thus behave like pipes. Membranophones can be analyzed as hybrids of pipes (Schaeffner's air) and strings (Schaeffner's solids).

Although the common contemporary Western music instruments were analyzed in the first design cycle of the model, if only because their acoustic properties have been studied more intensely in laboratories, in a later cycle a brief scan of music organology of both ethnomusicology and historical instruments resulted in no surprises, and the proposed model can easily account for such instruments. In addition, a brief informal and interpretative analysis of the historical music instruments of previous eras suggest that they could also be easily described by the proposed model. This would include pipes such as the gigantic three-meter long bass *bombard* and the *crumhorn* with its air chamber, to instruments such as the *hurdy-gurdy*, the single string *trumpet marine*, and the curved *black cornett* of the 1500s. The model would also be able to sufficiently describe instruments from non-western cultures. The Thai shawm (*pi nai*) is a typical pipe, and so are the Chinese shwam (*suo-na*) and multi-piped harmonica (*sheng*). The Burmese harp (*saung*) and violin (*turr*) are typical string instruments.

None of the observed possible properties are outside the descriptive power of the proposed model. The proposed model focuses on a high-level classification, to describe properties generically. On a lower level, it is assumed that it is the properties of different materials used in the construction of acoustic music instruments, as well as the structural relationships between component parts that result in different soundwave qualities among instruments that are within the same families (*consorts*). The Thai and Chinese pipes mentioned above would behave like any pipe instrument. If the sound producing qualities of each component of an instrument is known, it should be possible to recreate its sound, while instruments within the same families differ only with respect to the values of the properties.

Today only a small proportion of instrument types ever designed and constructed through the course of human history are in common use. Instruments went out of fashion for various reasons, one being the fashion of the day. Other reasons are such as that the instrument is too difficult to handle (e.g. the *contrabass trombone*), or its sound too soft to be heard among other instruments in an orchestra. Some instruments only gained popularity after technological advancements, such as the case of the double-action pedal for the harp, invented by Cousineau in the 1700s. The entire range of possibilities for new designs of instruments have not yet been exhausted, not even for acoustic instruments. The process of designing and prototyping a new instrument is a very expensive one. Although electronically generated sounds at this stage of technological development cannot mimic the sounds of acoustic instruments faithfully (except through sampling), a sufficiently detailed model should enable instrument designers to experiment with new instrument designs in virtual space, and at least have an approximate idea of what such an instrument might sound like. One aim of the model is to offer an information architecture of acoustic instruments that might be able to mimic real instruments better. The modular design of the model might make possible the design of new sounds, and thus new virtual instruments. It should also allow for the reconstruction of instruments from previous eras of which the specimens may only be available in museums. By recreating the sound virtually, perhaps some of the ancient instruments' popularity might make a comeback.

The proposed model does not attempt to describe all the finer nuances of effects on musical sounds. In its first version, it is a high-level generic model, while the finer detail should be addressed in later versions. The focus is only on the instruments themselves, which does not describe all the systems influencing the perception of music sound. Other factors will certainly need to be considered too.

The same instrument may sound differently in different spaces and times. For example, humidity levels differ during the course of a day and season.

On string instruments new strings have different results to old strings. The instruments of different manufacturers sound different. In the construction of instruments, the materials used influence the resulting sound. In Europe, the importance of lacquer was discovered in the 1600s through the construction of violins. That lacquer influences the tone quality is widely accepted, although I have not come across any research that compares the acoustic differences of different types of lacquer on different materials, or applied in variations of layers and thickness. The acoustic properties of lacquer might be unknown at this stage. Perhaps one day our analytical tools may enable us to account for all these variables and create algorithms for each. Ideally, it should be possible to describe the different effects of different thicknesses of lacquer, but that is far beyond our present reach. At this stage of technological development, it is not yet possible. The proposed model cannot account for all such variations, and because of the present state of research will need to be restricted to a fairly high level of description. This Version 1 is thus a general description, which might be extended in later versions as more knowledge is obtained through research of the acoustics of materials and spaces.

FORCE, VOLUME, VELOCITY, LEVEL, LOUDNESS

For the sake of clarity, the terms force, volume, velocity, level and loudness need to be explained. The force of a trigger shapes the wave. Although the fundamental of the sound spectrum of a certain instrument sound may remain unchanged, the force of the trigger determines the number of higher harmonics created. Force is measured in kPa, a useful measure for engineers, while for musicians Latin terminology (such as *piano*, *forte*) is usually used. For a computer process precise numbers are required, so technically kPa is the best method. An increase in higher harmonics introduces higher frequencies, which color the wave to sound brighter, while simultaneously increasing its loudness volume. Louder notes (i.e. bigger force on the trigger) sound brassier in wind instruments. Technically loudness is a subjective human perception. Factors that influence loudness are sound pressure level, sound duration, and sound frequency. Force is an essential property to be included in the information architecture of acoustic music instruments.

In the context of MIDI, novice users often suffer from confusion between *volume, velocity,* and *level.* When a sound engineer mixes the channels on the mixing device that blends many different sound tracks, the orchestral balance between different instruments (or tracks) is achieved by adjusting the different *volumes* of the different channels. Volume then means increasing the overall energy (i.e. amplification) of the sound reproduction. This "sound" is the sound as a canned whole artifact - the recorded product. Although this increase in volume does create new harmonics during the live playback, the effect is not the same as increasing the "volume" during the formulation of the soundwave by the instrument alone. No matter how much volume is added in the final mix, the recorded soundwave of a soft, mellow playing sax will not turn the sound texture into a fat, horny sax sound. In both cases it is increased energy that changes the shape of the sound, but the results are different, and thus important to distinguish. A musician changes the sound nuances of an instrument by applying force, either by blowing harder, strumming harder, or striking harder. The additional harmonics created by this certainly increase the instrument's loudness volume, but these are created within the instrument, so to speak. They are intrinsic to the instrument. Increasing the loudness volume of a recorded sound is an event of increasing loudness extrinsically. Different harmonics, induced by the room environment are the result. For the present analysis, intrinsic qualities are in focus.

Level typically refers to the position of the meter indicators that indicate the loudness volume of an instrument in a specific channel. The overall level can also be typically adjusted. In this sense level is synonymous to loudness, but emphasizing its measurement.

The English word *velocity* relates semantically to *speed*. When musicians talk about speed, the talk is typically about how quickly fingers can do some work on the instrument, and not on the force with which the action is performed. Alternatively, it could refer to the tempo of the song, as indicated by commands such as "We need to slow down/speed up this song." The MIDI term *velocity* will not be used in this chapter, as it typically refers to the "speed" with which a key is pressed, implying force. Velocity as "speed" does not equate force. It is possible to press a key down very, very quickly, but with soft force—a difference between *speed* or *velocity* and *force*. Speed/velocity seems to be irrelevant for an adequate description of generating sound synthetically, as it refers to playing technique. The degree of force imposed on a trigger, however, is crucial to the higher harmonics that are created.

In the proposed model, for element names, the name *Loudness* (volume) will be used for the role that amplitude plays in generating the sound—i.e. the loudness as it is leaving the instrument (extrinsic)—while the name *Force* will be used for the degree of energy intensity imposed on a trigger or modifier within the instrument, but before the final sound leaves the instrument (intrinsic). *Force* is thus restricted to the input side of the sequence, while *Loudness (volume)* to the characteristics that increase loudness on the output side. Sound volume is achieved through amplification, such as by a sound mixer, but could also be achieved by instrument body properties. In pipes, the flare increases loudness, while in strings the body of the soundbox size affects loudness. The volume of the space of resonating cavities of instruments also impact on the resulting soundwave. Volume

could thus refer to topological space as well as audio loudness. In acoustics, these properties should not be confused, so sound volume refers to loudness, while space volume refers to the internal dimensions of a cavity.

Force depends on playing technique, and thus a property of the musician system, which will not be described in this chapter. Yet, the result of force impacts on harmonics created in an instrument component, and will need to be considered. Although the musician system is not attended to, there will thus be reference to the properties of components that a musician uses. This also applies to modifiers, such as the tongue, which is an important modifier for wind-blown instruments. The possible properties of the tongue as modifier would belong to the instrument system. The actual properties used would be handled by the musician system.

VISUAL PRESENTATION

The content of this chapter is not merely a logical exercise, as the eventual goal is to create a software application based on the identified properties. Visual presentations of acoustic artifacts is problematic, especially when those objects are three dimensional, and require presentation on a coordinate system. The physical shapes of the components of a music instruments are also complex, and as the acoustic properties of each components need to be described, each component would require its own coordinate system. Moreover, the visual representation of acoustic music instruments often need to include the viewpoint of the musician. There are thus several sets of coordinate systems that need to be mapped onto one another, but some of these sets have no acoustic value, yet they have to be specified for the sake of the virtual representation.

For example, some instruments are held by the musician, while others are "independent" and the musician sits (as in the case of the piano) or stands (as in the case of large drums) in front of the instrument. To determine where the x-axis of an instrument is, the most efficient method seems to fix this with regard to the musician as human being's gaze along an x-axis that runs level and straight ahead form the face of the musician. Even so, there are many idiosyncratic variations that are difficult to capture generically. For example, some rock-n-rollers may stand instead of sit and play a piano. All instruments that are held in a similar position as the guitar (banjo, mandolin, zither, ukelele, etc.) belongs to the family *guitar*, as defined here. Defined from the musician's perspective, the table zither would be classified as a piano, but acoustically it is not.

In the case of the piano family, a distinction will need to be made between uprights and grand piano. This distinction only concerns their visual representation on a canvass. From an acoustic point of view, their string arrangement with respect to the resonating box is the same. In one case, the sound box is upright (vertical), in the other horizontal. It is not known to what extent this orientation influences the acoustics. Comparative experimentation will be required—such as turning the upright box into a horizontal position, and the soundbox of the grand piano into upright position, and perform an acoustic analysis of the soundwaves.

The dimensions of a rectangle and polygon are relatively simple to indicate visually. A spherical body is slightly more intricate, especially if it also bends into odd shapes, such a bean-like shape, and if not done mathematically. Describing a sphere on its own, such as the case of the *cabasa* or *güiro*, is relatively easy. When the spherical box is to be attached to a fretboard, as in the case of strings, the relationship with the fretboard needs to be accounted for. In this case, the midpoint of the instrument x-axis and of the width of the fretboard will be the anchor point. The sphere's x-axis would indicate the deviation of the x-point from this anchor point.

MEASUREMENTS AND AXES

Distance and Length Measurement

Soundwaves are measured by the distance traveled in time. Harmonics that are added to basic soundwaves depend on reflections within some space. When the dimensions of such a space change, different harmonics are the result. The distance property thus needs to be captured. For practical purposes, the dimensions of instruments are too small to use the meter as measurement standard; so the millimeter will be used as default measurement.

3D Description

A 3D description is important for two reasons. Soundwave behavior in 3D space needs to be described, while for user interface purposes such spaces need to be presented on the screens of computers, preferably in graphic format that mimic the outlines of the real instruments that are virtually represented. For example, the shape and dimensions of cavities impact on the output soundwave textures, so algorithms should be designed that can adapt when values are changed. The ideal interface will allow a user to drag the shape of a cavity into new values, while the algorithm produces a sound according to these new values. For this to be possible, the relations between all the different topographies need to be described and to be known, but a standard approach is required to ensure interaction between different applications. There is no convention for mapping different coordinate systems onto one another. Anchoring will thus need to be made explicit.

In this model length is plotted on an x-axis, but this is more complicated than at first glance as there are several different layers of orientation: the orientation of the instrument in relation to the musician; the orientation of the instrument's x-axis in relation to the other axes; the orientation of other components (e.g. soundbox) added to the "main" instrument orientation; the orientation of topological areas on these additions (e.g. sound-holes). The description of each of these requires its own 3D coordinate system. To map them onto one another requires some anchoring convention, but there is no such available convention.

When working on a virtual canvass on a computer screen, top-left usually has the coordinate values of 0,0, and the designer has the freedom to place a 3D object anywhere on the canvass in that virtual world. The placement is done through anchoring. However, modeling an acoustic music instrument visually as a 3D object on a computer screen is challenging, as there is no standard part of the music instrument that could serve as anchor point.

The standard Cartesian coordinate system is used here, but there are two superimposing sets. One set is from the musician's perspective (indicated in uppercase letters), the other from the instrument's perspective (indicated in lowercase letters). Which "direction" is used for each of x,y and z is a convention that seems to differ from discipline to discipline. Aircraft, wind tunnel studies, camera angles, and virtual worlds do not use the same conventions.

A music instrument has a certain orientation compared to the body of the musician. The point where the two sets of coordinates meet is the anchor point. To reference this point, the line of the musician's gaze straight ahead and level will be the X-axis. The anchor point for pipe-like instruments played by humans will be the mouthpiece, while for string-like instruments it will be the *nut*, which is the strip between the headstock and fretboard.

An instrument may have all kinds of curves and directions in 3D space. The instrument's zero coordinates will be at the anchor. The musician's coordinate perspective will be indicated in uppercase, and the instrument's in lowercase.

Here are the two primary coordinate systems of acoustic music instruments:

- **X-axis:** Left or right (*horizontal*) - looking left or right
- **Y-axis:** Pitch (elevation, not frequency; *vertical*) - looking up or down
- **Z-axis:** Tilt left or right (*roll*) - tilting head left or right
- **x-axis:** Left or right (*horizontal*) - from the anchor point along the body of the instrument
- **y-axis:** Pitch (elevation, not frequency; *vertical*) - looking up or down along the x-axis of the instrument
- **z-axis:** Tilt left or right (*roll*) - tilting head left or right along the x-axis
- **length:** The length from the anchor along the x-axis - this is used to determine the intervals where the values of the other axes change

An analysis of all possible physical orientation relationships between musicians and instruments is beyond the scope of this chapter. Personal playing styles vary. For example, some left-handed musicians use left-hand guitars. The anchor point of these two coordinate systems will be the zero value for the X and x axes. The side-flute is typically played to the right side of the musician, while the horizontal axis of the instrument is typically sloping downward. This is also described from the musician's point of view.

Independent from the musician, the instrument is described on a 3D coordinate system, with the instrument's x-axis running along the length of the body of the instrument, and the other axes used to describe the locations of body part orientation with respect to this axis. For example, the main body tube (such as of a *sousaphone*) may veer off in some direction away from the zero value, or the position of valves may be at an angle to the main orientation (see Figure 2).

Figure 2. Flute axes

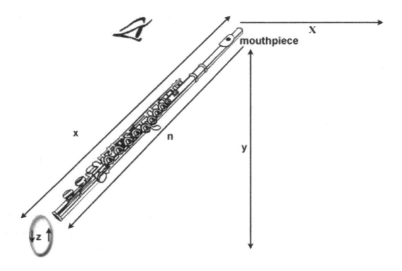

The guitar's own x-axis is also at an angle to the musician's X-axis. The soundbox body of the guitar is in a specific topographical relation to the x-axis of the main body of the guitar (see Figure 3).

Cross-Section of Pipes

The diameter of tubular shaped pipes are relatively easy to describe. For flaring pipes one would need the diameter values at different lengths along the x-axis of the instrument, bearing in mind that for the information architecture the area of the cross-section is not as important as describing the parameters. Not all pipes are circular, though. The chambers of the harmonica are rectangular, and it is logically possible for a "tube" to have odd interior shapes lengthwise, such as a triangular shape, or other polygon possibilities. The interior shape of the chamber, or pipe conduit, thus needs to be specified with cross-section dimensions.

For typical tube-like pipes, the center-point of the radius could serve as anchor point to the x-axis of the instrument. For such instruments, the center-point line along the instrument x-axis would serve as x-axis of

Figure 3. Guitar axes

the cross-section. For other shapes, the x-axis would still be the primary axis point, but the variations along the y- and z-axes will also need to be made explicit.

The polygon values for each variation of the polygon "pipe" will need to be mapped to the x-axis of the piped instrument, and at each interval along that axis where values change. This only if the cross-section polygon shape changes over the length of the pipe.

EXTENDING PROPERTIES WITH DESCRIPTORS

The high-level description of the properties of acoustic music instruments as presented in this chapter cannot account for the acoustic properties of specifics, as all acoustic properties of all materials and possibilities have not been done yet by acousticians. It is premature to attempt a description of the information architecture of the acoustic properties of different materials and their densities, yet such information would be important for the virtual rendering of acoustic music instruments. From a markup language perspective, there are various methods that can be used to incorporate such additional information. Stylistic features for an HTML document are captured in a CSS stylesheet, which lists the stylistic features of elements and attributes. Even the properties of the features in a style sheet could be further detailed with additional information contained as descriptors. For example, there are many thousands of fonts, yet their shape can be described with a common set of descriptors as a separate set. It is envisaged that the detailed properties of materials could be handled with a similar method. All the acoustic properties of a material such as mahogany at different sizes and thicknesses or densities might not be known yet. Once a complete description is known, the acoustic behaviors could be described and called upon from

a reference library to interpret the meaning of a markup attribute such as *material="mahogany."*

This method of Acoustic Property Descriptors could be used in other contexts too. The most common core of music notation symbols is represented in Unicode, but this does not allow for all the different symbols used by so many different cultures or by modern western composers. The set is just too larger. In order to cope with this problem, for the Notation system of the Music Markup Language system I developed, a Design Grid was proposed on which a user could design any possible shape for a written music symbol (Steyn, 2008). The Design Grid allows not only for the design of totally new symbols, but also to change the style of the conventional blob and stick notation symbols, such as making the stick extra long, at an angle, or changing the shape of the blob. Any new symbol designed on this grid is described with its own markup language that expresses all the relevant coordinate points on the grid with vector-like keywords and assigned a unique name. At implementation time the name is called when instantiated in a standard MML markup document. The interpretation of the symbol properties is handled programmatically. Damon O'Neill, a student of mine, wrote a Java-based application to test this with success. That Design Grid was for visual symbols. The same principal could be used for the information that describes the properties of different aspects of acoustics, ranging from materials to shapes. The properties of a material could be defined externally and included where needed. Ideally a library of such properties should be made available publically. For example, the different acoustic properties of a piece of wood with various thickness, area, topography, and so forth could be made available and plugged into specific applications.

This linked (or included) file method is very economical, as additional properties of some entity, phenomenon, or artifact could be declared once, and then called upon whenever required. The only challenge will be to create a standard list of required properties, which would be an extension of the model proposed in this chapter. Such a list will depend on the identified properties of the specific material (e.g. sprucewood, oak, or type of metal alloy, type of plastic, etc.), while the possible range might approach an infinite list of properties.

Other aspects that also require acoustic research in order to construct detailed property descriptors are such as the positions of the lips, tongue, and teeth, as well as vellum, fingers, and a host of other aspects involved in making music, but which presently lack proper acoustic descriptors.

At this point in history, it is far too early to offer guidelines for such properties with descriptors. The CSS font descriptors could only be designed because the font properties were known. At this stage, we do not know all the acoustic properties of many materials, or combinations of materials, or some of the acoustic properties of other aspects.

ABSTRACT MODEL OF A MUSIC INSTRUMENT

In broad terms the content of this chapter originated when I investigated the possibility of creating a markup language for birdsong (Steyn, 2007). In essence, birdsong, like the human voice, is created along the lines of an abstract pipe with several obstructions modifying the basic sound. The nature of these obstructions, and the characteristics of the pipe and where the obstructions (in humans, such as the glottis, tongue, teeth and lips) are located along the pipe influence the resulting soundwave. This is fairly easy to markup. The original idea for this chapter was to extend this concept in an attempt to make some progress on the notion of a virtual synthesizer, which I originally proposed in year 2000, but never found the time to develop any further. The physics of the soundwaves created by many music instruments is knowledge that is well-known and even available in public Web spaces (see e.g. Wolfe, 2010). The model

proposed in this chapter builds on this body of knowledge, but interprets the architecture of music instruments in categories of abstract data, and organizes it in a hierarchical model suitable for markup languages.

On the highest level of abstraction, all music is propagated by air. It is possible to hear underwater, with water as propagator, but the muffled sound will most likely never result in large underwater audiences listening to underwater music—except for the sake of novelty and experimentation. I cannot imagine audiences frequenting local pubs every Friday evening donning their snorkels, sipping beer through straws, listening to underwater blues! Even vibrating solids deliver soundwaves through air for normal humans to hear. The blind may feel vibrations through their bodies, but most people hear through vibrations captured by the ears. On a lower level of abstraction, acoustic music instruments can be divided into air and solids, a conclusion I came to independently from Schaeffner, having made this distinction before I stumbled upon references to his work. This of course does not make the present proposal true, but such a distinction is certainly the most economical manner to describe the information architecture of acoustic music instruments. In markup languages the term *class* is typically reserved for inheritance purposes, so to avoid confusion with that term, the word *genus* will rather be used for the most basic classes of instruments, namely *air* and *solid*.

Air instruments have air as a primary resonator, while solid instruments have some or other solid material is the primary resonator. The majority of solids also have some or other form of acoustic amplification chamber attached to them, as the loudness of the solid on its own is often not enough to be heard properly. Initiators (such as plucking a string or blowing a flute) are the generators of wave propagation. Initiators act as initial resonators, which set in motion much more complex waves within the body of the instrument. In pipes, the initial resonators are the tongue, lips and teeth, while in strings it is the string. Each of these components could make a sound independently from the instrument as a whole. Unattached to a body, a string would still make a sound, even if it is very faint. The mouth cavity used for pipes can still make a sound, such as whistling (using either the tongue, or the lips), or even just by blowing air using different lip shapes. The sound of the air rushing through the lips differ according to the lip shapes. An initiator could thus be abstractly described with the same terminology as the instrument as a whole.

The same kind of acoustic physics apply to the behavior of soundwaves in the cavity of the chambers of all kinds of air and solid instruments. The main difference is the force of air movement. In air instruments the force of air blown from the lungs of musicians, or from mechanical devices, cause the Bernoulli Effect either in the mouth cavity of the musician, and/or in the mouthpiece, which results in the base frequency, and which is then modified along its path within the cavity of the pipe or resonating body to include harmonics. The excitation level of air in the cavities of the boxes of solids is much less severe. There is no Bernoulli Effect, and it is the reflections of sound waves (as Helmholz Resonators), the effects of the materials and construction of the resonating chamber that contribute to the final sound of the instruments. Some solid materials are dense enough to produce a soundwave (such as solid bars). Each material influences the resulting soundwaves very subtly. See for example the subtle differences in the spectrograms between a brass tube and a glass tube slider on the sliding guitar (Pakarinen, Puputti, & Välimäki, 2008).

On the highest level of abstraction, an instrument could be described as:

```
<Instrument>
    <Part genus="air/solid" id="n">
        <Trigger>...
        <Initiator>...
        <Resonator>...
    </Part>
```

```
    <Part genus="air/solid" id="n">
        <Trigger>...
        <Initiator>...
        <Resonator>...
    </Part>
    <Part genus="air/solid" id="n">
        <Trigger>...
        <Initiator>...
        <Resonator>...
    </Part>
</Instrument>
```

An acoustic music instrument is here defined as an artifact that creates music sounds. The instrument consists of essential components for it to generate sound. The minimum components of an acoustic music instrument are the trigger that sets the soundwave in motion, an initiator that shapes the basic input soundwave, and a resonator that modifies the soundwave—Figure 4. Several different components of acoustic instruments conform to this basic model and can be linked in a series of causal chains where the output of one such three-part set feeds into the next set until the sound leaves the instrument as a whole. An instrument can be constructed of many instrument parts, and as defined in this model,

Figure 4. Abstract model of music sound

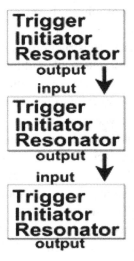

virtual components of different *geni* of instruments as well as the components of particular instruments could be mixed and matched at will, which is impossible with real instruments. One part could act as an air instrument, another as a solid, which is why this distinction is made on part-level, and not on instrument level. A set of these "instruments" could be connected either in series or in parallel, or with variations of both. The output of any such instrument component would serve as the input trigger for the next instrument in the series.

Propagation Medium

Sound propagates through pressure put onto air. To move the air, an energy source is required, and the energy source initiates the production of the soundwave by means of the force of some or other trigger. All instrumental sounds have some form of energy source. The energy source would thus serve as the parent node from which all other elements derive in the hierarchical tree of inheritance. Sequentially, the order for producing a soundwave would be as follows:

```
EventTrigger + EnergySource + [Propa-
gationMedium + PropagationChannel]
```

The EventTrigger may have different properties in different instruments. In a pipe instrument the initiator of the sound wave is a column of air puffed from the lungs and mouth of the musician, while the EnergySource is AirPressure. For pipe instruments, the EnergySource could also be WaterPressure, such as in the case of water organs, or SteamPressure, as in the case of steam whistles (such as those of ships, trains, or the fanfare organs of previous eras). When human lungs are the source of the airstream, the force initiating the air pressure is much smaller than when generated by mechanical devices. Generally speaking it is only the loudness that is affected, but the velocity of the airstream also impacts

on the kinds of harmonics that are generated by modifiers as Bernoulli Effects.

For string instruments the EventTrigger is typically the human finger (guitar), a plectrum (banjo), a bow (violin) or hammers (piano), but other methods could also be used. For membrane and bar instruments the most common EventTrigger is some kind of hammer—a drum stick can be regarded as a type of hammer. EventTrigger may be introduced into various components of the system of the musical instrument. In this sense, modifiers of the basic soundwave serve as trigger devices with their own properties that impact on the properties of the basic soundwave.

The EnergySource moves and propagates the soundwave. It could be either AirPressure (e.g. air in the pipe, air moved by the string), or WaterPressure. For example, in wind pipe instruments, air from the lungs serve as primary EnergySource, while the modifiers within the mouth (lips, teeth) trigger additional events. The holes (or valves) along the body of the main body of a pipe instrument trigger events that change the shape of the wave, and the flare and bell serve as triggers for further treatment of the wave. Trigger might not be the best term to use, as it implies an event, while the bell is not an event, but an artifact with certain properties. However, trigger is used not in the sense of agent, but as actor, which is an entity that influences and changes the shape of the wave, even if that actor is a passive and static physical shape.

The PropagationMedium could be either air (as in pipes) or some solid material, such as a string, as it is made of some solid substance (it is the solid that is the primary vibrating entity, not blown air). In pipes, right from the outset the soundwave is propagated through moving air. Although ultimately all sound depends on the movement of air, before a soundwave leaves a string (or bar or membrane) instrument the main propagation is firstly through a solid body (such as the string, the bridge and the materials of which the soundbox is made. Secondly, only in the case of instruments with resonant boxes attached to them (which might be considered as membranes of some sort), the air moves within the body cavity before it escapes to the air surrounding the instrument. For the purpose of the proposed model, PropagationMedium could be air or solids:

```
<PropagationMedium>
   <Air>...
   <Solid>...
</PropagationMedium>
```

Solids, such as strings, are themselves initial resonators, while the cavity of chamber boxes attached to them may be secondary in sequence, but are the main resonators with reference to the amplification of the soundwave. The main propagation channel of the soundwave in solids is typically the soundbox, but in some cases the solid itself (cymbals, solid wood blocks, etc.). In air instruments, the propagation channel is typically pipe-like. Within pipes the airflow is constrained within the walls of the tube; while for solids such as a string instrument, the string is attached to the body of the soundboard via the bridge. The vibration of the string sets in motion the vibration of the bridge, which in turn vibrates the box, which in turn sets in motion the air inside the box.

Standing waves within a tube, which is an enclosed cavity with holes, behave differently from those in a resonating box, due to a range of factors. When a soundbox is attached to solids, for both *geni* of instruments it is air in a cavity that impact on the soundwave. The outputs of the initial resonators are very different, not only because of the properties of the parts of instruments themselves, but also because of the position where the initial resonator is attached to the main resonator body. In pipes the flow of soundwave propagation follows the x-axis, in over-simplified terms. However, in strings the initial resonator is attached to the main resonator, and the line of soundwave propagation is not straight. Initially the vibration is along the x-axis, but then "jumps"

into the soundbox attached to the x-axis, whether this is acoustically significant is unknown.

Propagation Channel

The PropagationMedium is the substance through which the soundwave is propagated. It could be air or water, but it moves within the confinements of the PropagationChannel of the instrument. In string instruments, the string as PropagationChannel moves the air column around it, and the string is exposed to the air around it. Air is the PropagationMedium. The soundbox body of the string instrument serves to amplify the loudness of the sound, but also serves as PropagationChannel as its topological dimensions have harmonic impact on the base soundwave. The base soundwave should not be confused with a standing wave, as it refers to the virgin shape of the original soundwave when triggered at the InstrumentEntrance. This base soundwave, imagined as a very clean sine wave, is modified along its path through the PropagationChannel. More complexity is added along this path, until it leaves the instrument at the InstrumentExit to be heard as the unique instrument sound we are accustomed to.

PropagationChannel is the generic term used here for the cavity "material" that propagates the soundwave. This channel could be the pipe cavity, the body of the string or the membrane itself. The PropagationChannel could be exposed to the surrounding air (such as for strings and membranes) or enclosing the air inside the body (such as for pipes). In strings, the air is not contained. In pipes, the air is contained. Pipe instruments are tubes and the air as PropagationMedium is confined within the cavity of the tube, thus the conduit is enclosing the air. In membranes, the air is contained within the body of the drum, which functions like a pipe. The membrane itself is like a tensed string, with extended width, but the body to which the membrane is fixed (e.g. the drum tube) is a pipe, closed on the side of the membrane. The status (whether it is open or closed) of the conduit is important, particularly its properties where the soundwave starts. As there are so many different kinds of starting and ending points in acoustic music instruments, for this model different terms are used in different contexts to avoid confusion. For the starting position of the soundwave, where the wave begins, the term PropagationChannelEntrance is used, and PropagationChannelExit for the location where the wave leaves the PropagationChannel (or conduit).

The markup for the different PropagationChannel states is as follows.

```
<PropagationChannel genus="air/solid"
instrument="instrumentname"
type="exposed/enclosed"
entrance="open/closed" exit="open/
closed">...
```

The value *instrumentname* of the attribute *instrument* serves as identifier to be associated with the *instrumentname* as declared by *Instrument*. From a user application point of view, many standard instruments could be predefined, thus implying the values of attributes such as *type*, *entrance,* and *exit* without making them explicit. For example, if the instrument is declared a flute, the *type* would be "enclosed," and both *entrance* and *exit* would have the value "open." These values are the default values for standard flutes, while the application could make it possible for a user to change the properties of the flute to say, a closed exit value, while the system should be able to adapt to generate the appropriate sound.

A final set of attributes of instruments involves the Modifiers of the soundwave. The modifiers play an important role in not only distinguishing classes of instruments, but also in the more subtle differences in sound color within families of instruments.

TRIGGERS

Sound does not occur naturally, but some trigger must set the wave in motion. There is a very wide range of triggers used in acoustic music instruments, and they differ somewhat with respect to the two *geni*, if merely for the fact that in one genus a trigger moves air (in pipes), while in the other genus it moves a solid object (string, bar, etc.).

Pipes are channels and the air column, triggered within the pipe, moves through the conduit, which itself serves as amplifier. The trigger in pipes could be human lungs, or mechanical pumps, and even water pressure that moves air. The material of the trigger of air columns in pipes might not be as important as for strings. In pipes, the first modifiers of the basic air column are in the mouth of the musician—modifiers such as tongue, teeth, and lips. In the present model, the mouth itself is a pipe. In pipes, the impact of a trigger on the air column is important. Force thus needs to be described.

With string instruments the primary air column is outside the body of the instrument, while the body cavity of the attached resonating box serves as amplifier for the input soundwave. In the case of guitars and the violin families, the trigger is also outside the chamber cavity space. For the piano family the trigger is inside the piano body chamber. The fact that there is a complex mechanism from the keys to the hammers that hit the string in the piano family is irrelevant for the description of the properties of the trigger. Although the human finger (or in the case of piano rolls, the holes in the roll) is the initial "trigger," they should rather be described as actors, while the actual trigger of the soundwave in the case of pianos is the hammer. If the hammer is absent (such as when broken) there is no sound, no matter how hard the finger plays on a key. Hammers could be triggers through many different kinds of agents, ranging from humans and mechanical devices to electric and electronic actors. None of these impact on the resulting sound, as it is the trigger that instantiates the sound.

Triggering methods for strings are hammering (hitting), plucking and bowing, each resulting in different harmonics. The physical substance of which the trigger is made impacts on the resulting harmonics. Trigger materials may be plastic, wood, fingernail, fingertip, fiber, and so forth. The fingernail is hard, and its impact on sound would be similar to that of a plectrum. The fingertip consists of soft skin and flesh, and the sound would be more muffled and less bright. Some of the materials of which the trigger could be made are: finger (i.e. flesh), plectrum, felt metal, wood, fiber, plastic, etc.

Plucking could be singular (one note at a time), in very rapidly repeating (such as Spanish guitar *rasgueado*, or mandolin strumming), or continuous (such as bowing—the fibers' movement could be regarded as multiple soft pluckings on the strings as the strings begin to vibrate because of friction). Repeating triggers would be specified per played note, and as number of strokes per second. For example, *triggerrepeat="1"* would indicate a single stroke for a particular note, while *triggerrepeat="5"* would indicate five strokes per second on a particular note. For pipe instruments it is possible to interrupt the flow of air from the lungs into short rapid bursts of air, which is also described with this attribute. The diaphragm will be the trigger.

```
<Trigger genus="air" force="kPa"
triggerrepeat="n">...
```

Different positions where a string is triggered along its length cause different harmonics, and thus needs to be specified. The angle of touching the string does not seem to be important enough to specify. For bowed instruments, there are various techniques that result in different harmonics, and important properties are velocity, force, position, and angle of the approach of the bow fibers on the string. The position of the bow touching the string, as well as the force are important properties. Some of these techniques are: *col legno* (the wooden back of the bow is the trigger, not the fibers), *collé*, *spiccato*, *sul ponticello* (bowing the string on the bridge), *sul tasto* (bowing the string very far from the bridge on the fingerboard), and *tremolo* (bowing the string with rapid movements to and fro). The *pizzicato* technique does not use the bow, but the fingers, which thus require finger properties and not bow properties. Guitar strings can also be played very close the bridge, resulting in different harmonics. The same trigger properties apply to membranes such as drums.

```
<Trigger method="blow/pluck/hit/
bow" triggermaterial="keyword"
triggerrepeat="n"
triggerposition="x,y">...
```

Standard values for *triggermaterial* are "finger, plectrum, felt metal, wood, fiber, plastic, etc." The x-value for *triggerposition* would indicate the position on the length of the string where the trigger is applied, while y indicates the angle on the string, bar or membrane. The zero point of length is the *nut* (the strip between the headstock and fretboard) of the string instrument.

The properties of triggering methods are very complex and also depend on the unique properties of musicians. This requires more research. Here it suffices to say that instruments such as the *orchestrion* (Buchner, 1980) which uses real instruments that are triggered mechanically, cannot achieve the same sound textures as the same instruments played by human musicians. The *orchestrion* was manufactured in the earlier parts of the twentieth century. Perhaps with more refined property descriptions of trigger methods, and with finer mechanical handling, such as by robotic arms, more realistic sounds might be created mechanically in future. That would require a detailed property description of musician techniques.

Holes

Holes in chambers affect the resulting soundwave. In pipe-like air instruments, the major function of holes is to change frequency, while in solids with soundboxes attached to them the main function of holes is to allow amplified soundwaves to escape from the box, while the shape of the holes might affect the shape of the soundwave.

Pipe Holes

The most basic pipe instrument would be a tube with no holes, such as the Swiss *alp-horn,* the Uzbek *carnai/karnai,* Moldavian *bucium* and South African *vuvuzela.* Based on such a pipe, holes that are added to the pipe body serve as modifiers of the basic soundwave created by the basic pipe. For practical purposes, though, holes are such a common feature in pipes that for the description to be used for a markup language, holes will be regarded as an important distinguishable characteristic to warrant its own element. Holes could be in different shapes, with circular the dominant shape. The Italian folk pipe music instrument, the *launeddas*, has four square fingerholes (Buchner, 1980). In the pipe organ, holes are slit-shaped (rectangular) rather than circular. It is logically possible for holes to have any shapes. Different topological shapes of holes may have different acoustic results.

```
<Part id="n">
   <Hole genus="air" shape="circular/
square/poly">...
</Part>
```

A pipe has a fixed physical length, and should thus produce only one frequency, such as in the case of drones (e.g. the Tibetan *rag-dung*). However, in the distant past of human history an ingenious solution was found to artificially and rapidly change the length of the pipe temporarily by adding closeable holes along the body of the pipe. These holes in effect shorten the length of the pipe, thus increasing its frequency. More recently, the sliding mechanism was invented to change the length of a pipe (e.g. for the trombone).

The position of the valves along the cylinder of the pipe body is very important for creating the pitches required by a scale and tuning system. If the holes are positioned correctly, the pitches make up the notes of the desired scale.

For most of history, the open holes were blocked by closing them with fingers, thus lowering the frequency by this lengthening effect. As different hole sizes create different frequencies, the possible range was limited to the size of the hole a human finger could close, and the number of fingers that could close the holes. In more recent history, holes could be closed by mechanically operated valves that made much larger holes possible, and thus lower frequencies, and also more holes, as they could be closed by default and only need to be opened, requiring fewer fingers to manage all. The holes must have the same diameter as that of the main pipe body, which is why valves are used to close holes which would be too large for human fingers, such as in the case of instruments of flute size and larger. Valves also get larger as the diameter of the flare increases as there needs to be a correlation between pipe diameter and valve hole diameter.

The positioning of these holes determines which frequency pitches sound. Different positions will result in different frequencies. For proper tuning, whichever system is used, the position is important. The holes of popular modern instruments are made according to the requirements of the intervals of well-tempered tuning. This was not always the case, and more traditional instruments varied significantly in the frequencies and pitches they could make. For example, some pipes used by the Ancient Greeks had three-quarter tone distances (Sachs 2008, p. 224). Changing hole positions in physical instruments is not an easy task, but in the virtual world it is relatively easy as only the values of an algorithm generating the required sound need to be changed. An application should make it possible for users to specify the positions of the holes, and experiment with different possibilities. For the non-experimenting musician standard well-tempered tuning positions could be supplied by default.

The substance of human flesh and that of harder materials used as valves result in different reflected harmonics. Perhaps the initial effect is almost inaudible, but it might have a snowball effect along the length of the pipe, therefore the material of which the valve is made needs to be explicitly stated. The human finger, being flexible, can easily block a hole flush with the pipe outer body (such as recorder holes), unlike the mechanical valve that is more solid, and requires a ring raised above the body surface of the pipe in order to close tightly.

Acoustically the valve holes might be conceptualized as small pipes protruding from the main body pipe. The valve cavity also influences the soundwave, in effect extending the length of the pipe, however slightly. The cavity of these pipelets, however small, have pipe-like properties, serving as bypass filters. Open holes and valves sequentially following the first open hole and valve along the pipe body also influence the soundwave, and function as cut-off frequency modifiers. Low frequency waves are reflected at the first open hole, while high frequencies can bypass them.

The elements for holes are the following. The attributes are similar to the general pipe attributes, as the holes may be regarded as mini-pipes.

```
<Hole id="" valveheight="n"
interval="n" diameter="n"
valvematerial="x">...
```

The attribute *valveheight* describes the height of the valve cavity (which in the case of the recorder is practically zero); *interval* describes the position of the hole, measured in millimeter from the start of the main pipe body of the parent component (the mouthpiece), while *diameter* specifies the size of the hole. The attribute *valvematerial* has values such as *finger* (for human flesh) and *valve* (for standard valve construction material). If further research concludes that the properties of different types of valve material result in observable differences in sound texture, this list may be extended.

Soundbox Holes

Resonant boxes of string instruments and percussion instruments (such as *güiro*) also have holes. In the case of solids with soundboxes the function of these holes in not to change the frequency, as is the case with pipe holes. Soundbox holes serve as amplifier outlets. A pipe hole and a soundbox hole thus have different properties. The shapes of soundbox holes are varied, so the most economical method is to describe them with a topographical coordinate system. This would be a third coordinate system mapped onto the previous two already mentioned. However, the hole coordinate system would be a child-node of some parent element such as the frontplate, sideplates, or backplate.

```
<Hole plate="name"
holeposition="x,y,z"
holeshape="x,y,z">...
```

The *holeposition* would be its position on the plate, while the *holeshape* would describe the shape. The hole coordinate system needs to be anchored to the plate. The instrument x-axis seems to be the most logical anchor point, while the zero value of the plate as connected to the fret would perhaps be the best location for the anchor.

INSTRUMENT TYPES

The proposed model is based on the primary distinction between air and solid instruments. The most common air instruments are pipes, while the most common solid-based instruments are strings, bars, and membranes. The discussion will now turn to these most common major classes of instruments. The resonating soundboxes attached to membranes, such as drums, function like pipes, while the membranes themselves, as well as ideophone membranophones may be regarded as a sub-class of strings, as will be explained.

PIPES

The initiator of the sound wave (the EventTrigger) in pipe instruments is a column of air puffed from the lungs and mouth of the musician, but also through mechanical devices such as pumps. In earlier days the air required to drive an organ was supplied by a foot pump, while modern pipe organs have electric motors to do the job. That has influence on Force—e.g. the continuous flow of a steady, strong stream of air. The Bernoulli Effect is the method by which sound is generated by air, while the force of the air movement (in kPa) is a critical feature of the resulting soundwave.

General Pipe Properties

The simplest pipe instrument is a tube straight along its entire length. The next step up would be a simple pipe with a flare—the entire pipe in the shape of a stretched-out cone (such as the Swiss *alp-horn,* the Uzbek *carnai/karnai,* Moldavian *bucium* and South African *vuvuzela*), and its basic properties are easy to describe. Length (*pipelength*) and diameter of the tube (*diameter*) would be the two basic properties. To be able to play different pitches, different pipes with different lengths are used, such as is the case of the *panflute,* or pipe organ. The different pipes are played individually, so such instruments consist of a number of separate instruments that just happen to be played by the same musician. The soundwaves of one such pipe do not influence the soundwave intrinsically to the

instrument as a whole. Interference between pipes is "outside" the separate pipes and due to room acoustic properties, thus extrinsic to the instrument. Sometime in the history of music making, a major innovation came (at least about 35,000 years ago) when the same pipe was used to obtain different frequencies. To change frequencies the length of a pipe could be shortened temporarily. Holes are made along the pipe body, and are open by default, requiring fingers or valves to close them. Such pipes, when no holes are closed, thus start off with a high frequency as default. In the early Renaissance slide mechanisms came into use in Europe, with instruments such as the *sackbut* that later developed into the trombone. That era also saw the introduction of valves (or keys) to change the length of the pipe by opening or closing holes.

Both the diameter of a pipe and its shape are important properties. Regarding diameter, some instruments (e.g. the flute) are straight pipes (cylindrical), while others have bends of different degrees and complexities (e.g. trumpet, saxophone, and serpent). The diameter of a pipe, measured in the proposed model in millimeters, could remain constant along its body (assuming the pipe is circular), or it could change by gradually increasing the diameter along its length. This flaring out into a cone-like shape, is called PipeFlare. Although the word *flare* is usually used for the flaring at the end of the pipe, flaring could be present in section of the pipe instrument, including the mouthpiece (such as in the case of the saxophone). If the pipe is straight and if the angle of flaring is constant, only two values for the diameter of the pipe are required—where the flare begins and where it ends. However, flare could increase at different rates along the length of the pipe body, so new diameter values will need to be specified at regular intervals. If the instrument has a component with a pipe flare (indicated by Boolean values, with *No* as default), the diameter will need to take the following values: the intervals (measured in millimeters) at which the diameter values change, and the diameter value. The zero position of the interval is at the beginning (more precisely, at the mouthpiece) of the pipe, or if it is a pipe section, the midpoints where the sections meet. The cavity volume of the flute remains consistent at various length intervals, while the cavity volume increases the further one proceeds down the length of the conical tube of a clarinet. Frequencies and harmonics created by the cavities will thus be significantly different.

```
<Part type="cylinder/mouthpiece/
flare/bell/hole" pipelength="n"
interval="n" diameter="n">...
```

When the body of a pipe instrument is not straight, the description becomes more complex. Such instruments will need to be described as three-dimensional artifacts that can bend in any direction. The 3D Cartesian coordinate system will be used for such a description, as explained in the section on *3D description*. The element to describe the bending of the pipe will be called PipeShape. For pipes the connection between pipe sections serve as 0 anchor point for each of the pipe components, while the x-axis is for left or right (*horizontal*) direction along the body of the instrument, the y-axis for the pitch (elevation: up or down along the x-axis of the instrument) and the z-axis for left or right tilt (*roll*).

The format to indicate these attributes will be:

```
PipeShape = [bendlocation (at length
n) = x] + y + z + diameter
```

Example of long form:

```
<PipeShape x="33" y="30" z="35" diam-
eter="24">...
```

Example of short form, each set comma-separated:

```
<PipeShape shape="33 30 35 24, n n n
n ...">...
```

The above elements should be able to describe the shape of the complex form of an instrument such as the *sousaphone, compestating horn, cornophone, euphonium, sudrophone, serpent*, and similar complex shaped pipes. For example, the body pipe of the *sousaphone* consists of two large circular tubes, while the radius of the circles are constant. However, the PipeInlet of the InstrumentEntrance have several kinks, and the valve section has several curves. The orientation of the InstrumentEntrance PipeInlet in relation to that of the main instrument body is also different. The diameter of the PipeOutlet at the InstrumentExit is several times larger than the pipe diameter at the InstrumentEntrance side, and it has a huge bell at an angle to the general orientation of the instrument. Yet, the attributes of the PipeShape and PipeFlare elements should be sufficient to describe all these intricacies.

Pipe Components

Depending on the nature of the EnergySource (air, water, or steam), as well as the nature of the Trigger, a distinction can be made between classes of pipes. Properties also differ according to whether the source of the air is human or mechanical.

In pipe instruments, the physics of the mouthpiece, reed and embouchure, as well as the bell on the exit side operate on the same acoustic principles as the main pipe. In this sense, a pipe instrument may be regarded as consisting of a series of pipes, while each of these major components take on slightly different properties. The basic model for a pipe instrument is as follows—a pipe instrument consists of a series of pipes:

```
pipe1 + pipe2 + pipe3 ...
```

To distinguish between the types of input and output, for the input into the pipe as a whole instrument (e.g. the whole clarinet) InstrumentEntrance will be used, and for the output, InstrumentExit. For the input into a pipe component (e.g. the mouthpiece, or the bell) PipeInlet will be used, and for the output, PipeOutlet. The body of the main instrument will be called InstrumentBody, while the pipe shaped body of a component will be called PipeBody.

This description of a pipe instrument is modular, somewhat similar to that of Ducasse (2003), who distinguished between the pipe modules as mouthpiece, tube, hole, and bell. From the point of view of the proposed model, each of these modules is conceptualized as a pipe, which is modified in some or other way to give each component its unique properties. Even the valve hole could be conceptualized as a small pipe attached to the main body pipe.

The pipe instrument as a whole is described as consisting of:

```
InstrumentEntrance + InstrumentBody +
InstrumentExit
```

The component parts of a pipe instrument are:

```
[Initiator - lungs] + PipeInlet (e.g.
mouthpiece) + PipeBody (main body of
the component)
+ PipeOutlet (e.g. bell outlet)
```

An InstrumentEntrance, InstrumentBody and the InstrumentExit each consists of all three pipe parts: PipeInlet + PipeBody + PipeOutlet. There are several locations of inputs and outputs in pipes. To distinguish between these classes of inputs and outputs, and to avoid confusion, the inlet of air into a pipe instrument as a whole will be called an entrance (InstrumentEntrance or PipeEntrance), while the input of a component of the instrument, will be called an inlet (PipeInlet). Similarly, the output from a pipe instrument will be called PipeExit (or InstrumentExit), while the output of a component will be called PipeOutlet (see Figure 6).

The element *Instrument* takes the attributes *instrumententrance*, *instrumentbody* and *instrumentexit*, while Air (or pipe) and Solid are its children. The element Pipe is parent to PipeInlet, PipeBody, and PipeOutlet.

Each distinguishable pipe in the series of a pipe instrument's construction has typical pipe properties. The properties of each pipe component (i.e. pipelets) modifies the standing wave uniquely. Each of the identified pipelets has an input, a body and an output, defined in terms of airflow. The soundwave produced as output of one pipelets feeds into the next pipelets in the series as its input wave, where it is further modified by the properties of that pipelets. For example, when played by itself, the mouthpiece of a pipe makes its own unique sound. This output sound feeds (as input) into the next pipe in the series (as standard into the body of the main pipe). In the body of the main pipe, the soundwave is further manipulated, and the output soundwave may be even further modified by the flare and bell, which function as pipes in their own right.

The human mouth cavity, as well as lips may be regarded as some kind of pipe—a conduit through which air flows. In lip reed instruments, for example, the lips act as a vibrating valve (Ber-

Figure 6. Components of a pipe instrument

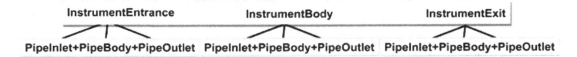

noulli Effect) modifying the characteristics of air from the lungs. The lips act as a control oscillator, or a modifier on the resonants impacting the air in the instrument. The next pipe in line (the mouthpiece) has its own Bernoulli Effect. Playing just the mouthpiece will result in one kind of soundwave. Mouthpieces lower the frequency of the highest resonances, while reinforcing some frequencies. Playing just the pipe body results in a different kind of sound—although some kind of vibrator would be required (e.g. lips). Together all these separate soundwaves created by different pipe components create the characteristic sound of a reed instrument. The properties of each pipe component differ. The characteristics of the input pipe (i.e. mouthpiece) differ depending on lip movements ("lip up" or "lip down"), single reed or double reed. Even the last pipe (e.g. the bell) in the series of pipes further modifies the soundwaves as it generally increases the resonants of the soundwave in frequency, as well as increases loudness. The mouthpiece (lowering frequency) and flare and bell (increasing frequency) thus have opposite effects on the main soundwave, but apart from that, as they function in separate components of the instrument, their contributions to the final soundwave differ.

The type of pipe component needs to be specified, and the keywords below would serve as the short form for the type of pipe.

```
<Part type="cylinder / mouthpiece /
flare / bell">...
```

The generic properties of the different components of pipe air instruments will now be discussed.

PipeInlet

The PipeInlet is the area at the beginning of a pipe cavity of a particular pipe in the pipe series. Various kinds of inputs are received here. Typical inputs into the pipe inlet are the mouthpiece, the lips, and tongue, while the latter two play a role in the mouth cavity as a pipe. The tongue and lips

(embouchure) of a player influence the harmonics of the airflow that produce a soundwave, which means that even before the airflow reaches the opening into the pipe, the soundwave has been generated uniquely. Add a reed to the pipe inlet, the instrument becomes perhaps a saxophone, and the sound texture is very different from that of a flute. Pipelets further down the series of pipes have as input waves the output of previous pipes. The output of one inputs into the following one.

Mouthpiece

The mouthpiece decreases the frequency of the higher modes, as well as increasing the prominence of particular frequencies. The basic properties of the mouthpiece are the same as for any pipe. The mouthpiece of a *clarinet* or *saxophone* might not easily be regarded as pipes, but consider the mouthpieces of the *bassoon* and *cor anglais*, which on observation alone look like pipes. Acoustically, though, all kinds of mouthpieces influence the soundwaves. The mouthpiece typically has open ends, and modifiers act on the wave coming into the mouthpiece from the mouth of the musician, or from a mechanical device, such as bellows. The diameter of the mouthpiece as well as its length play a role. The outlet end of a mouthpiece is usually flared, or the entire mouthpiece could be flared along its length, so all the characteristics of a flared pipe would apply to the mouthpiece as well. The mouthpiece, as an earlier pipe in the sequence of pipes of the instrument, impacts on the input wave into the main body pipe.

Embouchure (shaping of the lips and facial muscles) is important. For example, a trumpet player must "lip up" or "lip down." For proper tuning subtle lip changes need to be made to be in tune with some tuning system, such as equal temperament. At the input end of the mouthpiece, the player's lips close the tube. Lips, single reeds and double reeds all have the same function, which is interrupting airflow (Bernoulli Effect), and thus they serve as modifiers on the air column triggered by the lungs.

All the elements of a typical pipe apply to the mouthpiece. Default values for the mouthpiece would of course differ from those of the main body pipe or the outlet pipe. A mouthpiece as inlet to the instrument is not always straight, but could be bent, and thus takes on the element PipeShape and the attributes of flare.

```
<Part type="mouthpiece">...
   <PipeShape x="33" y="30" z="35"
diameter="24">...
</Part>
```

The X-axis orientation (i.e. that of the musician) of the mouthpiece will be with reference to the gaze of the musician straight ahead, while the instrument x-axis will be at an angle from this anchor point. For example, the side flute is typically held to the right of the musician at a slight downward angle, while the saxophone is held frontwards. Musicians of course are not statues and move around, especially those in more entertaining genres. However, such movements do not influence the intrinsic properties of the soundwaves created by the instrument. Anchoring the instrument orientation to that of the musician only serves a purpose for the visual representation of the instrument on a computer screen.

PipeBody

The bore of a pipe is quantified as diameter, and the wider it is, the lower the resulting frequency. It is thus important to specify the pipe diameter, which is a general pipe property. As the PipeBody could be of many types, the generic element that applies is:

```
<Part type="cylinder / mouthpiece /
flare / bell / hole">...
```

The diameter of the body of most pipe instruments does not remain constant over its length (as in the case of the flute as cylinder), but flares (is conical, as in the case of the clarinet). This general pipe element would thus apply:

```
<Pipe type="flare" pipelength="n"
interval="n" diameter="n">...
```

The PipeBody is the main tube of a pipe instrument, and that part of a pipe on which frequency changers such as finger holes and valves are typically installed. Several properties of the tube of the pipe body influence the generated soundwave. The length of the pipe (pipelength) determines which frequency is the easiest to produce. The length of the pipe can be manipulated artificially through the use of a slider or valves or fingerholes (discussed separately). The volume of space inside the pipe determines the kind of wave that could be formed. Narrow pipes create higher frequencies than wider pipes.

The bore of the body of a pipe could be open on both ends, or closed at either end. Each of these positions have an effect on the soundwave. The *flute* can be regarded as open on both ends as the musician's lips cover only a small portion of the embouchure hole. The *bassoon*, *oboe*, *saxophone* are closed on the end where the sound is triggered—at the Inlet. The Outlet of a *bottle* into which one blows is closed, so the air blown into the bottle must escape at the Inlet, which is open. The bottle mouth serves as embouchure hole, and the blowing style is the same as for the flute. The main body pipe of many wind instruments (including the *saxophone*) is open on both ends. A mouthpiece (as a pipe, which is closed on the inlet side) and bell (as an additional pipe at the outlet side) are attached to the main body.

The different states of the PropagationChannel, as per Figure 5, apply here. Airflow is enclosed within the body channel of pipes. Cross-section topological properties need to be described as they determine the interior shape of the tube, which will reflect soundwaves in different ways. Sets of cross-section values change at different length spots (x-axis) if the body is flared (i.e. conical). The instrument x-axis serves as cross-section anchor.

```
<PropagationChannel
instrument="instrumentname"
type="enclosed" entrance="open/
closed" exit="open/closed"
bodyshape="circular, rectangular,
polygon"
x="n" cross-section="x y,x y,x
y...n">...
```

It should theoretically be possible to string together a series of any number of pipes, while the order of pipe components could be any order. For example, a particular pipe instrument configuration may have a pipe with outlet properties as first pipe (InstrumentEntrance), and as InstrumentExit a pipe with mouthpiece properties. The properties of soundwave modification of the standard outlet may thus be used as inlet into the pipe body.

Parallel Pipes

Parallel pipes serve as individual pipes and do not deserve separate attention. Examples of such pipes are the pipes of an *organ*, the *dual flute* (which some authors call *dual shawm*) of the ancient Egyptians and Greeks, the *panflute*, the double English *flageolet*, the *harmonica* and *accordion*. Acoustically the organ is a pipe, or more precisely, a collection of many different pipes of fixed pitches. The Wanamaker Grand Court Organ (Philadelphia, Pennsylvania, originally built in 1904) has 28,543 independent pipes in 462 ranks. Each of these pipes is an individual instrument of the *genus* "air," linked in parallel. Soundwave influences of one pipe on the others are outside the body of the individual pipes (extrinsic), and occur in the air surrounding the pipes, not inside the pipes. Inside each of the pipes modifiers (such as flue) influence the soundwave inside the pipe.

PipeOutlet

The properties of the PipeOutlet could be exactly the same shape as the main PipeBody, as the case of the cylindrical flute. The minute bell at the end of a cylindrical flute probably does not make enough of a difference to the sound texture, which I could not verify. For many other pipe instruments the outlet consists of a flared section as well as a bell. The PipeOutlet is, however, not necessarily circular, and neither is it necessarily at the end of the cylindrical pipe (*frontal*). In the pipe organ, the flue gap is on the side (*lateral*) of the body of the pipe, and the hole is slit-shaped rather than circular. The outlets of the harmonica or mouth organ are also not round, but rectangular. The position of the outlet with respect to the pipe body, as well as its shape thus need to be made explicit. As most pipes have circular outlets at the end of the pipe body, those attributes will be the default values.

If the outletshape is rectangular, its dimensions need to be described. The outlet may also take on different shapes, even the shape of a polygon.

Figure 5. Properties of the PropagationChannel

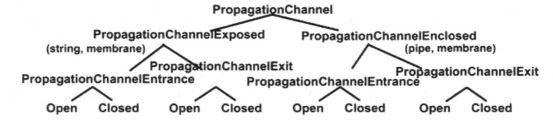

An outlet of a pipe may not necessarily be at the instrument exit position. The shape of the outlet of a pipe that feeds into another pipe may take on any form, and thus the shape of the input wave into the next pipe in the sequence may be different to the shape of the wave produced by a pipe outlet of a different shape.

Indicating a fixed position on a tubular shaped object is challenging as there is no fixed reference point such as an angle, as discussed in an earlier section. The bell cannot be taken as endpoint along the instrument's x-axis, as the bell could be mounted laterally, as in the case of the *sousaphone*. The orientation of the outlet pipe might differ from that of the instrument in general. Whether this makes acoustic difference needs to be further investigated.

```
<Pipe outletposition="frontal/
lateral" outletshape="circular/
rectangular/polygon"
outletorientation=""length, x, y,
z">...
```

Flare

In pipe instruments, the flare is the pipe section typically at the outlet end of the pipe that flares out in diameter from an earlier section of the pipe. Flare, in the sense of increasing diameter across the length of the pipe is, however, not restricted to the pipe section at the instrument exit. Any pipe component can have flare. Mouthpieces typically have flare. The *clarinet* could abstractly be regarded as a flute with a flare and bell. The flare raises the frequencies of the standing wave of the pipe, thus increasing the volume of body cavity space, leading to a louder sound. This increase in amplitude is due to the increasing space along the pipe body of the flare, hence an increase in cavity space volume.

The Flare can be described with the general pipe properties, and can apply to any pipe instrument part:

```
<Part type="flare" pipelength="n"
interval="n" diameter="n">...
```

Bell

The bell is located right at the exit end of pipe instruments. It is possible to add a bell to a pipe that has a consistent diameter throughout its length (cylinder), but it is typically added to the end of a flare (conical instruments). The shape of the bell, its curve along its body, has an influence on the soundwave. If the distance of the bell along the pipe body is small, long waves cannot create enough resonance (there is nothing to reflect against) while shorter waves can. The bell increases the frequency of the lower modes. The result is that higher pitches have more harmonics, and sound louder and richer in texture, or brighter. The Bell may be regarded as a pipe in its own right, and can thus be described by the general pipe properties.

```
<Part type="bell" pipelength="n"
interval="n" diameter="n">...
```

Pipe Modifiers

The tubular characteristics of pipes have been described above. Various instruments require the addition of soundwave modifiers at various stages in the sequence of creating their unique sound. If a tube with no obstacles could be regarded as the "pure" pipe instrument, with the simplest soundwave (a pure sine wave), all objects introduced to the pipe system can be regarded as modifiers of that basic soundwave. This would even include modifiers right at the outset of activating the soundwave on the instrument entrance side.

The general markup for modifiers consists of the Modifier element, while attributes could be generic, following known modifier types.

The following classes of general modifiers in pipe instruments can be distinguished. The term *reed* used traditionally is misleading, but will nevertheless be used here. It is used for an object that vibrates because of the strong movement of an air column, and the resulting sound is because of the Bernoulli Effect that creates a frequency.

- Lip reed modifiers, in instruments such as the *flute* and *bugle*, where the lips are the modifiers.
- Single reed modifiers, in instruments such as the *clarinet* and *saxophone*.
- Double reed modifiers, in instruments such as the *oboe* and *bassoon*.
- Free reed modifiers, in instruments such as the *harmonica, accordion* and *harmonium*.

The precise acoustic properties of these different modifiers could be described in external Acoustic Property Descriptors files.

Lips, Tongue, Teeth as Modifiers

The degree of tightness of lips determines the frequency with which the air escapes through the lips in instruments such as trumpets. Lips serve as modifiers on the steady stream of air coming from the lungs, while the mouth cavity may be also regarded as a pipe. For lip reed instruments, lips also serve as yet another pipe in series of pipes that are strung together to form the pipe instrument.

In reed instruments the reeds act like control oscillators. There is a feedback loop between the reed and the mouthpiece. The resonances in the pipe body of a reed instrument such as a *clarinet* cause the reed to vibrate, but the air coming into the reed from the player's mouth also vibrates the reed. When these two columns are out of phase, a squeak sound is the result. Avoiding squeak requires precise control by the musician.

At the instrument entrance, the tongue and teeth could also act as modifiers. For example, a flute could be played with a trilling tongue, or while playing the tongue could be moved into different positions, influencing the resulting harmonics.

```
<Modifier type="lips, tongue,
teeth...">...
```

This description of Modifier captures only the most generic properties. Details could be handled by Acoustic Property Descriptors. The shape of the lips is important, as the positions of the two lips vary between instruments. Bottles and flutes are played with similar lip positions, while trumpets have a different set of positions. More research is required to be able to describe all the possible lip positions adequately.

The shape and position of the tongue are important. The mouth as a whole could be envisaged as a pipe, while the tongue would be a subordinate instrument in its own right, moving around in the 3D cavity of the mouth. The PipeShape attributes would thus apply here, even if the tongue is not a pipe. It may be regarded as a solid pipe with length and 3D diameter values. Air does not flow through the tongue, but around it. The x-axis of the tongue would be along its length, with the zero value at its root on the floor of the mouth. The mouth cavity could be described with the same properties as the cross-section of a pipe.

The mouth as cavity would function similarly to any other cavity, such as the soundbox of a guitar. The differences are the volume of the cavity, the shape, and of course the material of the "box" (in one case human flesh; in the other most commonly wood). The biggest difference, however, is the force of the moving air column. Air is blown through the mouth as pipe, while in a guitar soundbox air is moved because of the vibrations of the materials of which it is made, triggered by the strings.

Modifiers on the Mouthpiece

The diameter of a mouthpiece determines the pitch of the soundwave, while its shape determines the harmonics. Larger diameters lower the pitch, because the volume of space inside the mouthpiece is larger. Technically the space volume operates as a Helmholtz resonator. The mouthpiece itself is a type of pipe, and can be described with typical Pipe elements. The frequencies of the highest resonances are lowered in the mouthpiece.

The most common modifiers added to the mouthpiece pipe are reeds. The possible values of the types of Modifiers can thus be extended to:

```
<Modifier type="lips, tongue, teeth,
reed, reeds">...
```

Modifiers on an Outlet Pipe

Mute

When a Mute is added to a bell, the radiating effectiveness for most frequencies is reduced. The result is reduced loudness, but harmonics are also reduced,. The resulting sound is not so bright, thus less brassy. The color of the sound is changed by the mute.

The shape of the mute has an influence on the base frequency. In *French horns* adding a hand as a mute changes the pitch by as much as a semitone. Details of the properties of mutes could be handled by Acoustic Property Descriptors. Material, shape and position are the most likely properties.

```
<Modifier type="mute" material'""
shape="" position="">...
```

Application Development for Pipes

The ideal virtual music instrument should allow a user to choose how many pipe sections to add to build an instrument. The properties of each component should be user-defined, while factory default settings could be based on popular well-tempered requirements. An example for this approach to synthesis is found in Bruyns (2006). In her model "The parameters that the user can control, corresponding to the sliders at the top the plug-in, are as follows: the size of object; its material (from precomputed solutions); damping parameters a1 and a2; resolution of the mesh (from precomputed solutions); number of modes used for the computation; and the base impulse applied to the object (that the triggering MIDI note-on velocity then scales)" (2006, p. 35). The user should be able to control all values of all element attributes. Ideally, the user interface should show a virtual visual replica of the acoustic instrument on the computer screen, while also making it possible to design totally novel instruments by dragging and dropping shapes and parts by choice.

An application developed to cater for the description above of pipe attributes will make possible the generation of many different kinds of pipe sounds. Not all musicians might want so many degrees of freedom. Product developers might wish to create default instruments based on the existing set of popular acoustic instruments, while allowing end-users to be able to tweak any of the properties according to their liking, even moving pipe components around.

Given the properties of a virtual tube or pipe, an application should offer the functionality to a user to use, for example, the virtual flute's basic properties, and create different instances of it, ranging from the baroque flute (with fewer keys) to the modern flute. By stipulating other properties, such as whether the pipe is open or closed, on which end (inlet or outlet), whether a bell is attached or not, and so forth, it should be possible to create all the possible variations of wind instruments. In addition, by mixing the properties of different instruments, it should be theoretically possible to create novel instruments. Ducasse (2003) mentions the transverse saxophone, which has a mouthpiece volume of zero, obviously impossible with a real acoustic instrument. The mouthpiece as input pipe into the tube influences the resulting soundwave. If the values of such pipe components could be user adjusted, and if components could be sequentially attached in any order and any number, there is a wide scope for creating novel virtual instruments based on the acoustics of real instruments.

STRINGS

Strings are one of the three most commonly used groups of solids, in addition to membranes and bars. The three main component parts of string instruments are the strings themselves, the soundbox body (as resonators and amplifiers), and manner in which the strings are activated (triggered). The number of strings range from one, such as the bowed single string instrument of the San people, the Chinese *erh-hu*, and the Yugoslavian *gusle* (Buchner, 1980) to almost two hundred strings (as in the case of the piano). The proposed description properties of the body of string instruments should allow for the virtual construction of string instruments ranging from the *walking stick violin* with its very narrow body (Buchner, 1980, p. 172) and the San single string bow with calabash resonator, to the *orphica* (Buchner, 1980, p. 169), Russian *balalaika*, the Ukranian *gusli*, the Japanese violin (*rebab*), and so forth.

For sound production purposes, a string may be regarded conceptually as being "closed" on both ends—as closed "pipes," so to speak. If open on any side, there would not be enough tension for the string to produce a sound. The only "string" that is open on one end would be the whip, in which case the backlash makes the cracking sound, and it is not continuously vibrating. The basic defining property of a string is that tension is required in order for it to vibrate. Unlike for pipe instruments, it would thus be redundant to explicitly state that strings are closed on both ends. The degree of tension influences the harmonics, while the preferred degree of tension is determined by the tuning system and scale used.

The String

Properties of a string include length, mass (or density), and tension. The mass of a string (linear mass density) may affect its wave velocity. Guitar strings are used as an example here. For nylon guitar string mass is important, while for steel strings the diameter of a string determines the base frequency, only of course once tension is applied. For nylon acoustic guitars, the lower nylon strings (E, A, D) are wire-wound. That diameter impacts on the harmonics is easily observed by tuning a lower range string an octave higher than it is supposed to be tuned - provided it does not snap. The base frequency may be the same as the string designed for that tuning, but the harmonics will be subtly different.

The thicker a string, the lower the base frequency. Frequency increases as tension is increased. Fingering down a string on the fingerboard also increases tension, thus raising the pitch. Once a string is tensed, frequency is increased by shortening the string through the firm placement of the finger (or other object, such as a bottle or similar hard object) on the instrument neck.

The tension to which a string is stretched is measured in *newton* (N). For the technical description of tension, Newton suffices, but of course the desired tension for each string would depend on its relations to other strings, which in turn depends on the tuning system.

```
<Part genus="solid" type="string"
length="n" diameter="n" mass="n"
tension="N"
material="wood, metal,
plastic,vellum, paper, nylon, catgut,
horsehair, etc."
dimensions="x,y,z"
material="name">...
```

For the *dimensions* attribute, x is the length of the string, y is height (or diameter) and z is width (also diameter). In the case of proper strings, which are circular, y and z are collapsed into a single diameter measure. Separating these values would only be applicable to membrane-like "strings" (solids), as explained below. These "strings" (bars and membranes) can be described with exactly the same properties as string, except that y an z have much larger values, and values that might differ from one another. While for the strings of string instruments length, diameter and mass are important, for bars and membranes (viewed as strings) width is also important.

In order to specify sets of strings, *stringset* is used while interval differences need to be made explicit. Strings typically run along the length of a finger- or fretboard for fingered strings, while for hammered strings they can run in any direction. For fretboard strings (e.g. guitar, violin) the location of strings can easily be indicated with reference to the musician's X-axis, where *stringid* numbers increase with increasing distance from the musician's gaze. For other instruments, such as piano and harp, it is more tricky, and a formal convention is required. Such a convention might be debated, but for the sake of praxis I will use a left-to-right direction, for no apparent reason but to get on with the job. So on instruments such as the piano, stringid="1" will be the string furthest left from the zero value of the X-axis of the musician's gaze. To account for double strings (such as 12-string guitar and the double strings of piano), and for the triple strings of piano, an attribute called *number* is required. The interval ratio between strings is required. Intervals imply a starting and end point, so an interval implies a from-to relationship between two items. For the sake of economy both items do not need to be made explicit, so an interval value will be from the lower number to the higher number, where "lower" is either from the musician's gaze, or from left to right. The first string's value will be zero.

```
<Part genus="solid" type="string"
   <Stringset stringid="n" number="n"
interval="320">...
</Part>
```

Example

```
<Stringset stringid="3" number="2"
interval="320">
```

This stringset consists of two strings at 320 cent value from the previous string. The two strings are the second group of strings in the set.

Body of String Instrument

For string instruments, the body is essential to increase the loudness of the sound. Without the body, the sounds are very soft, and inaudible among other instruments. The bridge is regarded acoustically as part of the body, even though its position may be shifted in many string instruments. Fixed bridges are fixed to make life easier for the musician, who certainly does not want to spend unnecessary time trying to find the right spot during each tuning event. The body (soundbox) of strings instruments serve as resonator. The cavity inside the body (if there is a cavity, which does not apply to the body of electric guitars) can be described with reference to volume of space, as well as shape (coordinates in three dimensions). Both these properties have an impact on changing the wave shapes of the fundamental. The solid body of an electric guitar does not serve as an acoustic resonator, and soundwaves are amplified electrically. As this sound amplification is outside the instrument, and created by an additional system external to the electric guitar instrument, this will not be addressed in this chapter.

To indicate that an acoustic soundbox is attached to the string(s), the following properties need to be included. String instruments such as guitars and violins have necks to which the soundbox is attached, but the orientation of the soundbox may be different on other types of string instruments. On some instruments the strings are mounted on the soundboard, as in the case of the *pointed harp* and *nail violin* (Buchner, 1980), *zither,* and the *dulcimer*. On the *zither* the entire fretboard is installed on top of the soundboard. Perhaps these locations of the fretboards with respect to the soundboxes have no acoustic impact, in which case the description is required for the visual representation of the instruments in order to be rendered on a computer screen—keeping in mind that a user can design any virtual instrument by assigning values to the different attributes.

The soundbox could run parallel to the entire length of the string(s), or could be attached toward one side. The position where the box starts thus needs to be stated, measured from the furthest point where the string can vibrate, such as the *nut* of a guitar (that strip between the headstock and fretboard). On a guitar, the x-axis is the length from the *nut* to the position under the fretboard where the soundboard starts. The position where the soundbox begins with reference to the x-axis, will be called its anchor point.

```
<Part boxattached="yes/no"
boxposition="x,y,z">...
```

The x value of the instrument part would thus be 0 and serve as anchor. The y and z values would be for different topological orientations of the box with respect to the upper surface of the neck or fretboard, even if a real instrument with high values here would be awkward to play by a human musician—in the virtual world awkward shapes and dimensions do not matter.

The shape of the body cavity will amplify some harmonics and suppress others. The shape thus influences the soundwave reflections inside the body cavity, and would thus be important to describe. It should be obvious that the larger the body, the better it would be at amplifying lower frequencies, which have longer standing waves. The body box of a string instrument might be rectangular, such as the case of the Ancient Greek *kithara* (Politis, et al., 2008), bean shaped, acoustic guitar shaped, and in fact any possible shape as virtual instrument. The bodies of most modern string instruments are oddly shape and can only be described as 3 dimensional polygons. Oddly shaped bodies do influence acoustic properties (e.g. Bruyns, 2006) and thus need to be accounted for. Several layers of anchored x,y,z sets are required to make this possible.

The front plate of the body of string instruments is usually made of softer wood that could vibrate more easily, and thus contributes to the generation of specific harmonics. Both the front and back plates may be curved or arched. This would require a topographical description, and a fixed viewpoint is required from the perspective of a complete instrument to make the description possible. The front-plate would be the side of the soundbox that points in the same direction of the x-axis of the instrument. For a guitar, the front-plate would be that side showing upwards when the instrument is placed down horizontally. An upper body plate might bulge upwards as a topographical peak, while the bottom body plate might be depressed downwards as a valley. Cross-beams inside the body cavity influence reflections and need to be described (crossbeam="x,y,z"). The inside body cavity of a virtual instrument might be as complex as having many stalactites and stalagmites. Too many will dampen the sound though. A cave with those features is one of the best recording studios one could find as there is almost zero reflection.

In order to specify the fixed anchor point for virtual representation, the same method as used for pipe instruments cannot be used. For pipe instruments the musician's viewpoint is used. However, the viewpoint of a musician with respect to each for a guitar, a piano, a harp, a violin, and a lap or board zither is very different. In addition, different musicians have different styles of holding instruments such as guitars. The orientation also differs for left-handed musicians who string their instruments differently. It seems that different layered sets of x,y,z axes would do the job of describing oddly shaped soundboxes. Unfortunately it also seems that the anchor between these sets arbitrarily differ between different instruments. At the time of writing, we have not yet found an efficient method for a generic description that would serve as anchor point for all string instruments. A computer screen canvass requires an explicit anchor position, while the orientation of the playing of real acoustic instruments is almost random, especially between the different classes of instruments. It seems that until a more generic method is created, positions will need to be specific by instrument class, while leaving open an option to extend possible classes of instruments. Note that the musician system is not in focus in the proposed model, but that for a generic system the musician needs to be considered for the sake of finding an anchor point on the virtual screen.

The *instrument* attribute for a string instrument is used to describe the classes (or families) of instruments. From the musician's viewpoint, many instruments have the same playing style. For example, the piano-family would include all instruments where the musician sits in front of a keyboard playing on a bed of keys, thus including the *organ*, *harpsichord*, *spinett*, *clavichord*, *virginal*, etc. Note that this refers to the playing style, and the orientation of the instrument with respect to the musician, and not to the acoustics of the instrument. Regarding playing style the organ is like a piano; but regarding acoustics the organ is a pipe (i.e. not the electronic organ!). This viewpoint is idealized, as idiosyncratic positions of musicians in relation to instruments are too indeterminable for economic description. Some rock-n-rollers may even stand and play a piano. All instruments (banjo, mandolin, zither, ukelele, etc.) that are held in a similar position

as the guitar belongs to the family *guitar*, as defined here. The table zither would have a similar instrument-musician orientation description as a piano, but recall that this is only for the purpose of visual representation.

The names selected here for generic families of string instruments reflect the contemporary popularity of instruments. In a previous era *zither* might have been used for guitar-like instruments, as was done in the Hornbostel-Sachs system. Their system is also not useful for determining the anchor position of a virtual instrument on a computer canvass. For example, some zithers are held like the modern guitar, while others are held on the lap (like the slide guitar). These positions do not influence acoustics to an important degree, but as said, description is required for anchoring purposes on computer canvasses for virtual instruments. The basic markup for a string instrument as a solid, is as follows.

```
<Part type="solid"
instrument="guitar/piano/violin/..."
frontplatedimensions="x,y,z"
frontplatethickness="x,y,z"
backplatedimensions="x,y,z"
backplatethickness="x,y,z"
sideheight="x,y"
crossbeam="x,y,z">...
```

As *sideheight* may vary along length, different heights need to be stipulated at different lengths. Created virtually, any number of sides are possible, ranging from rectangular and hexagon to totally irregular, indicated by polygons. For the sake of economical markup, the frontplate will be taken as basis from which the distance at regular intervals are measured for the height between it and the backplate. Here y measures inverted height—that is depth—and x the *boxposition* distance along the x-axis at the point where a y value applies.

The backplate of the body of some string instruments is spherical (such as the *mandolin*), and the description would thus differ from rectangular or the guitar or violin family shapes. The sideplates could slope up or down, meaning that its height is not constant. Here *shape* refers to the shape of the soundbox.

```
<Part shape="rectangular/polygon/
sphere">...
```

String Modifiers

The acoustic properties of the soundbox body of a string instrument serve as modifiers to the basic soundwave created by the string itself. The acoustic properties of the string's soundwave is in its turn influenced by the properties of the Trigger material properties, which thus also serve as modifiers. Finally, the presence of other strings may influence acoustics, however faintly, as they might vibrate along with the played string. Such additional harmonics will need to be specified, but a general description is still required. As mentioned above, some Trigger properties are:

```
<Trigger method="blow/pluck/hit/
bow" triggermaterial="keyword"
triggerrepeat="n"
triggerposition="x,y">...
```

Although properties of the musician system, such as the playing style, are not addressed, it needs to be noted that modifiers such as vibrato change the basic soundwave. Vibrato causes a cyclical variation in pitch, impacting on the harmonics. Vibrato is described with reference to its intensity, measured numerically as the number of finger movements (finger oscillations, not frequency oscillations) over time, and which slightly changes length of the string at the finger placement position. Vibrato will need to be a child of Trigger:

```
<Trigger>
    <Vibrato intensity="n"...>...
</Trigger>
```

BARS

The length of the rod or bar is essential for the frequency of the base soundwave. The longer the rod, the lower the frequency. Some instruments consist just of the rods (solid wood bar), while others are mounted on boxes that serve as resonating bodies. In this sense, the rods function in a very similar manner than the strings of stringed instruments that also require bodies to amplify the sound. The hollow wood block could be described with the same properties as pipes, even though their body shape is square and not tubular. The "membrane" in the case of the hollow wood block is its body. The material density of a bar instrument is also important. Higher density materials have higher base frequencies.

In a very abstract sense, a bar may be regarded as a string. While the bar is intrinsically stressed due to the nature of its material substance, a string is tensed extrinsically by stretching it. The bar is thus naturally tensed, while a string is artificially tensed. Yet both a bar and a string are 3D artifacts with two of the dimensions very small compared to the third one—the long one. The body of both the strings and the bar activate the movement of air surrounding it. Due to the much smaller dimensions of strings—on the two collapsed dimensions only—and the elasticity of the materials of their construction, the resulting sounds differ from those of bars. Bars are naturally louder than strings—because of both their density and much greater length along the width axis—while strings require an attached resonating body to be heard adequately. This can be observed easily. The string of a bow and arrow makes a very faint sound. Add a resonator, such as a hollow calabash, to it and it is much easier to hear. Construct a body box with chambers that enable soundwaves to enhance one another, and the sound is even louder. Some bar instruments also function like strings as they typically have a soundbox body attached to them. This body cavity serves to increase the loudness of the soundwave. Some bars, such as the solid wood block, do not have an attached resonating body, in which case the bar body itself is the main resonator.

A bar with ends free to vibrate (*marimba*, *glockenspiel*) creates a standing wave when struck, with both ends being anti-nodes. A bar with one end clamped (*kalimba* or *thumb piano*) creates a standing wave in which the clamped end is a node, and the free end an antinode. On an abstract level of description, bars and strings thus share properties.

```
<Part type="solid" type="bar"
length="n" width="n" height="n"
material="wood, metal,
plastic,vellum, paper, nylon, catgut,
horsehair, etc."
boxattached="yes/no">...
```

Bars are not only struck, but can also be bowed. Instruments that fall in the category of bowed bars are the *musical saw*, *glass harmonica*, *Tibetan singing bowl*, *cymbals*, and *glass rubbing* (Essl, et al., 2004b). From an information architecture point of view the difference between a bowed string and bowed bar would be extrinsic and intrinsic tenseness, as well as mass.

MEMBRANES

Membranes are typically struck, and are thus percussive. As Cook (1997) points out, the definition of instruments classified as percussive is vague. When a violin is struck with the backside of a bow, does the violin now become a percussive instrument, or is this to be described as musician playing technique? Cook designed the PhISEM algorithm for the synthesis of percussive sounds. Aramaki *et al.* (2006) go one step further than Cook by also considering the perceptual aspects in their algorithm. Such algorithms are not described here, but the information architecture of membranes.

A string of string instruments could be visualized on a coordinate system as a line along the length of an x-axis, while the width of strings could be indicated on the y-axis. On an abstract level, the value of the y-axis of a string could be gradually increased until it reaches a critical point at which a phase shift occurs and the string becomes a membrane. The location of that phase shift is unclear, and probably definitional, which is why strings and membranes are on the highest level rather described as solids, while for the sake of economy only, a distinction is made on a lower level. In practice, there is not a range of different instruments along the different intervals on the y-axis between strings and membranes. Even the thickest string of a string instrument is manifold times thinner than the narrowest membrane or bar. However, of when the acoustic properties of different thicknesses of materials are fully known, it might be possible to design a virtual system that could indeed gradually increase the width of a tensed string into becoming a bar or membrane.

Membranes are thus, abstractly speaking, strings that are extended along the y-axis (width). Conversely, strings could be conceptualized as membranes with extremely reduced values along some axis. Another perspective is that membranes attached to pipe-like soundboxes move a column of air within the PropagationChannel. From this point of view, the actual membrane acts as Trigger to move air in a contained tubular shaped soundbox. Property-wise this is very similar to a pipe instrument, where the lungs act as Trigger of the air column. However, the trigger mechanism of membranes is different. In the case of pipes, it is air itself that is the PropagationMedium, while for membranes, bars and strings (i.e. the solids) it is the solid material that is the initial PropagationMedium, while a soundbox is an optional additional PropagationMedium.

Membrane instrument characteristics are as follows. The body of the membrane itself is described with the Strings properties. The soundbox attached to membranes is described with Pipe properties. For percussive pipes it is the air within the pipe body that is moved, while the movement is initiated either by a membrane on the inlet side (such as drums), or by the movement of the body itself—no matter how rigid it is (e.g. the *hollow wood block*)—or by objects within the body cavity (such as beads, in the case of the *calabash*), or objects attached to the outer body (such as the *cabasa*).

The actual membrane (e.g. drums with vellum-like membrane surfaces) needs to be distinguished from its soundbox. For the actual membrane, the term *membraneplate* will be used. A membraneplate has its own body and properties; the membrane soundbox has its own body and properties.

The *membraneplate* of extrinsically tensed membrane instruments is never used on its own. It would be impossible, because for it to sound it needs to be tensed, which is only possible by stretching it over some rigid framework. The most commonly used framework is cylindrical, thus a pipe. When described from this perspective, the Hornbostel-Sachs category for a separate class for membranophones is redundant. The *membraneplate* of membranophones and strings behave acoustically in the same manner, while the soundboxes of membranophones and pipes behave the same.

The *membraneplate* itself can be described as follows. The shape of the membraneplate, the material of which the membraneplate is manufactured, as well as the thickness (in millimeter) are the most important distinguishable characteristics. If the bodyshape of the membraneplate is a polygon, the coordinate values need to be specified as x and y pairs. The exact orientation of the 0,0 values are user defined, and would only be important when linked within virtual space. On the design canvas of a computer, the top left corner would serve as 0,0.

```
<Part membrane="membraneplate"
bodyshape="circular, rectangular,
polygon" thickness="n"
```

```
material="plastic, vellum, pa-
per, etc" coordinates="n n, n n, n
n...">...
```

Membrane instruments are typically circular, in which case this property needs to be described in terms of radius. However, they could be rectangular, or even in polygon shape (Essl, et al., 2004a). Apart from the planar topography that is important, the thickness of the membrane needs to be stipulated, as well as additional modifying objects that modify the basic soundwave, such as the springs on snare drums. It might be possible in future to create algorithms that would be able to generate sound on any shape of membrane, so the option of polygon values for the shape of membranes will need to be planned for.

The output of the *membraneplate* would serve as input to the pipe component of the membrane instrument. However, some membrane soundboxes are not tubular, but rectangular, as in the case of tea boxes (of which the cavity is cubicle) that are used as drums. The acoustic properties of rectangular and cubicle cavities are different enough from tubular cavities, so the different shapes need to be specified. The keyword *soundbox* for a membrane identifies the list of properties as applying to the soundbox of a membrane.

```
<Part membrane="soundbox"
pipelength="n" interval="n"
diameter="n">...
```

The attribute *diameter* only applies to circular pipes. For rectangular membrane soundboxes, measurements of *length* (x-axis) and *width* (y-axis) would also apply.

Some additional modifying objects are subcomponents of *composite instruments*, which can be regarded as instruments by themselves. Such additional components are child instruments of their composite parent instruments. The parent-child notion should not be confused with its use for inheritance classes. Child instruments as described here are independent with their own unique sounds, but in composite instruments attached to their parent instruments. A child instrument would make its own unique sound when detached from the parent, and the parent would also still make a sound. By sounding together as one instrument, the child contributes to the main sound created by the parent.

For example, the sound created by the springs on a snaredrum, or the sound of the "bangles" or small "cymbals" on a *tambourine*, have their own characteristics and can sound independently of parent instruments. They are not dominant, but add harmonics to the base soundwave of the main parent instrument to which they are attached. It is possible for a double bass player to wear handbells which sound every time he strikes a string. However, in such cases the *handbells* do not impact on the source instrument. The double bass would still sound like a double bass, and the handbells like handbells. In composite instruments though, the subcomponent (or secondary/subordinate "instrument") is integral to creating the unique sound of the instrument. In a sense, the sound-sources of such parent-child instrument relationships are extrinsic, similarly to the many pipes of a pipe organ. They do not contribute to the soundwave intrinsically to the instrument as would, for example, the mouthpiece of a *saxophone* do.

To indicate explicitly that the two instruments form a single instrument, the attribute *compositeinstrument* is used, while the value would be the identifiers, where the first identifier will be the main instrument, and the following identifier(s) the secondary instruments. Further subinstruments may be added to the series.

```
compositeinstrument="mydrum, myshaker..."
```

This would make possible interesting sound combinations from different instruments, to create new composite instruments. The application should allow a user to adjust the comparative loudness of composite instruments, and also modifying the interference of the different soundwaves.

Triggering Membranes

The position where a membrane is struck (triggered) results in different harmonics (see e.g. Bruyns, 2006). Further from the attached side of the membrane, lower frequencies are created, while closer to the attached side overtones of higher frequencies result. This needs to be indicated. The attribute *triggerposition* is used. The coordinate positions are important to indicate this. For circular membranes the center of the membrane will be the radius center point, while for rectangles and polygons the particular area within the larger membrane surface needs to be marked.

The same markup is used as for strings:

```
<Trigger method="pluck/hit/
bow" triggermaterial="keyword"
triggerrepeat="n"
triggerposition="x,y">...
```

EXAMPLES OF SOME INSTRUMENTS

At first glance, one might wonder whether the proposed attributes are sufficient to describe the extremely wide range of traditional acoustic musical instruments from all historical eras and cultures. A detailed analysis has not been made, but a quick overview of traditional instruments confirms that all seem to fit the model. Here are some examples of instruments that might at first sight appear tricky to fit into the proposed model.

The *harmonica*'s reeds (typically made of metal) are fixed at one end, but they vibrate in small, typically rectangular channels open on both ends, although strictly speaking closed on the players mouth end as soundwaves that are reflected back into the mouth disappear. The channels may be regarded as small rectangular pipes, with the fixed ends of the reeds serving as resonators. The harmonica can thus be described with typical pipe properties, consisting of several independent pipes within the set. The harmonics that arise from two notes being played simultaneously may be described on the same principles of separate pipe instruments that play different notes together—e.g. several saxophones that play the different notes. Of course, the environments will be different, as the "room" of the pipes (the resonating chamber) of the harmonica is within its own body, while the room of the saxophones is massively larger. The space volumes differ significantly.

The *music box* consists of a series of small rods that are triggered mechanically, while on instruments such as the *kalimba* (which Buchner 1980 calls *sansas*), the trigger is by human fingers. The music box and kalimba are thus very similar. The range of the music box is just typically much wider than the kalimba.

Shakers are pipes of which the body is closed on all ends. The shape of the body is oval-like and can be marked as spheres, while the inner surfaces of the body trigger the beads to move the air column inside the body. The body itself is thus the trigger. For example, the body of a *maracas* is hollow, filled with beads that collide and resonate with each other. Although no air is blown into shakers, their impact against the inner body wall propagates the soundwave created inside the cavity. Recall that for string instruments, the body act as amplifiers of the air surrounding the string, while for pipes the air moves inside the pipe body. Shakers thus behave more like pipes than like strings, although their body sides are solid, and thus behave like membranes. However, the force of air movement in pipes is much more pronounced than in solids. From that perspective, shakers behave more like string soundboxes. Shakers are hybrids, and as the different component parts of acoustic music

instruments of both the air and solid *geni* can be mixed, the description of shakers does not fall outside the scope of the model.

Xylophones and *marimbas* consist of sets of bars. Their sound is amplified by boxes attached to them similarly to the soundboxes attached to string instruments. The proposed high-level markup can deal with these instruments.

The *güiro* could be described as a closed pipe with typically one hole on the body although more holes may be used to modify the sound by, for example, opening or closing the additional hole with the hand. The Trigger is typically a piece of wood stroked across the notches on the body. The EnergySource is not air, but the vibrations of the body itself. The güiro functions in the same way as a series bottles that are hit by some or other object. The sound texture differences are due to the mass of the materials of which the bodies are made. Bottles are typically glass or plastic, while güiros are hollow gourds (a dried natural plant), or nowadays also made of plastic. The mass of glass bottles is much more than the mass of gourds or plastic (at least the types of plastics commonly used in the manufacturing of these güiros).

The *cabasa* is a closed pipe with small balls strung together around the body. The body of the cabasa was traditionally gourd-like, while the small balls were hard seeds of plants or trees. Today all these components are artificially made, typically using plastics, although the balls are sometimes made of some or other metal. The difference between a traditional and modern cabasa would thus be the material, particularly density and mass. A single ball makes a faint sound. The more balls that are added, the louder the sound as they reinforce the individual balls' soundwaves. It is impossible to play a cabasa softly, so for small acoustic ensembles, players usually remove some of the balls. The balls are the triggers, while the body amplifies the soundwave.

A *bell* is a pipe closed at one end. Instead of air that is blown, a small hard object inside the body of the bell hammers against the pipe body to create the sound. The bell flares out towards the outlet. Muffling occurs as modifier on the body by touching it with various degrees of intensity or mass of materials. It is much easier to muffle the sound of a small bell that for larger bells (such as the huge bells of clock towers). The principles of their sound creation are exactly the same.

Steelpans are constructed by tensing a steel plate mounted in a drum pipe. The plate is thus a tensed membraneplate, while the drum acts like a pipe. However, to obtain different tones, sections of the tensed steel plate are tensed even further. The steelpan produces sound in much the same way as a drum, such as a snare drum, creates subtle difference in the resulting soundwave when struck on different areas of the membrane surface. The uniqueness of the steelpan is that the areas for impact are predefined and pre-tuned. To achieve different pitches, oval areas of different sizes are hammered out to tense those areas more than the overall area of the steel plate. The unique sound results from the harmonics that arise from all these other pitches when a particular pitch is struck. The basic architecture of the steelpan is thus that of a membrane and pipe, while the modifiers are the interfering areas surrounding the spot for a particular pitch.

The *cymbal* is a membrane that is not stretched over a body, but tensed during the metal manufacturing process. The cymbal as membrane is tensed by its nature, and does not require to be tensed over a pipe-like body. The y-axis shape of a cymbal is not a flat surface (not zero). At its center is flares rapidly, but at the end of its bell, the angle is dramatically reduced and slowly slopes over the remainder of its body. In a certain sense, a cymbal is an extremely short pipe, although the properties relate more to those of a membrane. For the purpose of the proposed model, a cymbal is a flat membrane, with the pipe-like flare and bell serving as modifiers of the soundwave that would have been created if the cymbal had zero vertical coordinates. Secondary instruments may be added to a cymbal. Some drummers add thin strings of metal beads to increase the resonance and sustain. In Asia, some "cymbals" are bowl shaped, which can be easily described as a pipe. The Tibetan singing bowl might be regarded as a bowl shaped cymbal.

Non-Standard Modifiers

Musicians often experiment with novel sound textures, trying to modify the soundwaves created by standard music instruments. Some non-standard methods are such as placing newspaper between the strings of a piano and the hammers, or use a non-standard plectrum on a guitar. From the perspective of this proposed model, all these non-standard methods can be described as modifiers on the base wave, while the properties of the materials might be decisive. The property set for modifiers stated above seem to be sufficient enough to describe these possible modifiers.

CONCLUSION

The proposed model of the information architecture of acoustic music instrument presented here is a high-level meta-description of the model—a Version 1.0. The markup presented in this chapter serve as meta-language. For many aspects the acoustics is unknown, and research in such and other areas covered still need to be undertaken before lower-level markup can be designed.

A universal model of an acoustic instrument is as follows. In essence, an instrument may be regarded as consisting of an InstrumentEntrance (the entry point of energy into the instrument), InstrumentBody, and InstrumentExit (where the energy leaves the instrument). The InstrumentBody consists of any number of components, each with its own inlet and outlet. Inlet refers to the soundwave that enters the component, while outlet refers to the soundwave exiting the component. In the component body modifiers of various kinds impact on the basic soundwave, so that the properties of the output wave differ from those of the input wave.

On the energy input side inlet modifiers such as airflow, embouchure (lip positions), initiation action or trigger (e.g. blowing, striking, plucking), and so forth are described. The properties of each of these are different. For example, for striking, the properties of the striking mechanism (e.g. fingertip, fingernail, wooden plectrum, steel plectrum, plastic plectrum) result in different harmonics. For the body system, different music instrument body types (e.g. membrane, string, tube, etc.), body material (e.g. wood, steel), body shape (e.g. cylinder, polygon, rectangular, box, etc.) are important properties. The properties of each of these can be described in more detail. For example, for a pipe (or tube or cylinder) the following properties are important: radius, length, shape (straight, conical, polygon), flare, and bell. Various modifiers of the basic soundwave can also be described. By describing the information architecture of musical instruments more clearly, it will be possible to recreate these sounds more authentically using synthetic processes, and also makes it possible to create novel sounds by recombining the subsystems of instruments in different relational configurations. Algorithms can be designed for each of the sets of described properties, thus fine-tuning the capabilities of synthetic music much more than presently possible. Imagine the characteristics of the attacking lips of a trumpet player released on the properties of a piano string, but instead of a box body, it is linked to a flute pipe, with a saxophone flare. As the sound properties of each of these components are unique, created by different algorithms, the resulting sound should be very different too.

A more realistic rendering of the sounds of acoustic music instruments would make it possible for musicians to explore instruments that are now only available in museums and instruments from other cultures too difficult to obtain easily. Today sound samples are indeed available for an astonishingly wide range of instruments, but the samples are wholes, and intrinsic properties cannot be manipulated. The proposed model allows for the intrinsic manipulation of component properties.

This chapter presents an abstract and ideal initial model for the description of the properties of different music sounds, particularly as created by acoustic instruments. The validity of this model can be tested by analyzing the sound spectrum of each of the components. Sound generating algorithms could then be created for each of these components. It is very probable that even if some variations are required to the proposed model, this model would fall within expectations, making it possible for musicians to recreate the sounds of acoustic instruments more faithfully, as well as to create totally novel sounds.

NOTES

- The markup in this chapter is based on conceptualization. It is not complete.
- Images of the instruments mentioned can be viewed at www.musicmarkup.info/musicinstruments/

REFERENCES

Aramaki, M., Kronland-Martinet, R., Voinier, T., & Ystad, S. (2006). A percussive sound synthesizer based on physical and perceptual attributes. *Computer Music Journal*, *30*(2), 32–41. doi:10.1162/comj.2006.30.2.32

Baines, A. (1960). Organology and European folk music instruments. *Journal of the International Folk Music Council*, *12*, 10–13. doi:10.2307/835418

Bilbao, S. (2009). Direct simulation of reed wind instruments. *Computer Music Journal, 33*(4), 43–55. doi:10.1162/comj.2009.33.4.43

Bos, B., Lie, H. W., Lilley, C., & Jacobs, I. (2008). *Cascading style sheets, level 2: CSS2 specification W3C recommendation*. Retrieved from http://www.w3.org/TR/2008/REC-CSS2-20080411/

Bruyns, C. (2006). Modal synthesis for arbitrarily shaped objects. *Computer Music Journal, 30*(3), 22–37. doi:10.1162/comj.2006.30.3.22

Buchner, A. (1980). *Colour encyclopedia of musical instruments*. New York, NY: Hamlyn.

Chafe, C. (2012). *A short history of digital sound synthesis by composers in the U.S.A.* Retrieved from https://ccrma.stanford.edu/~cc/lyon/historyFinal.pdf

Cook, P. R. (1997). Physically informed sonic modeling (PhISM): Synthesis of percussive sounds. *Computer Music Journal, 21*(3), 38–49. doi:10.2307/3681012

Dannenburg, R. B., & Goto, M. (2005). *Music structure analysis from acoustic signals*. Retrieved from http://repository.cmu.edu/compsci/494

Doornbusch, P. (2009). *A chronology of computer music and related events 1906 - 2009*. Retrieved from http://www.doornbusch.net/chronology/

Ducasse, E. (2003). A physical model of a single-reed wind instrument, including actions of the player. *Computer Music Journal, 27*(1), 59–70. doi:10.1162/01489260360613344

Einstein, A. (1905). On the electrodynamics of moving bodies. *Analen der Physik, 17*.

Einstein, A. (1916). The foundations of the general theory of relativity. *Annalen der Physik, 49*.

Essl, G., Serafin, S., Cook, P. R., & Smith, J. O. (2004a). Theory of banded waveguides. *Computer Music Journal, 28*(1), 37–50. doi:10.1162/014892604322970634

Essl, G., Serafin, S., Cook, P. R., & Smith, J. O. (2004b). Musical applications of banded waveguides. *Computer Music Journal, 28*(1), 51–63. doi:10.1162/014892604322970643

Goldfarb, C. F., & Prescod, P. (1998). *The XML handbook*. Upper Saddle River, NJ: Prentice Hall.

Grame, T. C. (1962). Bamboo and music: a new approach to organology. *Ethnomusicology, 6*(1), 8–14. doi:10.2307/924243

Hass, J. (1999). *Electronic music historical overview*. Retrieved from http://www.indiana.edu/~emusic/elechist.htm

Hevner, A. R., & Chatterjee, S. (2010). Design research in information systems. *Integrated Series in Information Systems, 22*.

Hevner, A. R., March, S. T., Park, J., & Ram, S. (2004). Design science in information systems research. *Management Information Systems Quarterly, 28*, 75–105.

James, J. (1993). *The music of the spheres: Music, science, and the natural order of the universe*. London, UK: Abacus. doi:10.1119/1.18443

Jordà, S. (2002). FMOL: Toward user-friendly, sophisticated new musical instruments. *Computer Music Journal, 26*(3), 23–39. doi:10.1162/014892602320582954

Kartomi, M. (2001). The classification of musical instruments: Changing trends in research from the late nineteenth century, with special reference to the 1990s. *Ethnomusicology, 45*(2), 283–314. doi:10.2307/852676

Kassler, J. (1995). *Inner music: Hobbes, Hooke and North on internal character*. London, UK: Farleigh Dickinson University Press.

March, S. T., & Smith, G. F. (1995). Design and natural science research on information technology. *Decision Support Systems, 15*, 251–266. doi:10.1016/0167-9236(94)00041-2

Margulis, E. H., & Beatty, A. P. (2008). Musical style, psychoaesthetics, and prospects for entropy as an analytic tool. *Computer Music Journal, 32*(4), 64–78. doi:10.1162/comj.2008.32.4.64

McGurk, H., & MacDonald, J. (1976). Hearing lips and seeing voices. *Nature, 264*(5588), 746–748. doi:10.1038/264746a0

Pakarinen, J., Puputti, T., & Välimäki, V. (2008). Virtual slide guitar. *Computer Music Journal, 32*(3), 42–54. doi:10.1162/comj.2008.32.3.42

Politis, D., Margounakis, D., Lazaropoulos, S., & Papaleontiou, L. (2008). Emulation of ancient Greek music using sound synthesis and historical notation. *Computer Music Journal, 32*(4), 48–63. doi:10.1162/comj.2008.32.4.48

Rauhala, J., Laurson, M., Välimäki, V., Lehtonen, H., & Norilo, V. (2008). A parametric piano synthesizer. *Computer Music Journal, 32*(4), 17–30. doi:10.1162/comj.2008.32.4.17

Sachs, C. (2008). *The rise of music in the ancient world: East and west.* New York, NY: Dover.

Smith, J. (2006). *History and practice of digital sound synthesis.* Retrieved from http://www.aes.org/technical/heyser/ downloads/AES121heyser-Smith.pdf

Steyn, J. (2007). *Working notes on a markup language for birdsong.* Unpublished.

Steyn, J. (2008). Challenges of designing a markup language for music . In Ng, K., & Nesi, P. (Eds.), *Interactive Multimedia Music Technologies* (pp. 111–132). Hershey, PA: IGI Global. doi:10.4018/978-1-59904-150-6.ch006

Vaishnavi, V., & Kuechler, B. (2004). *Design science research in information systems.* Retrieved from http://desrist.org/desrist

Valimaki, V., Laurson, M., & Erkut, C. (2003). Commuted waveguide synthesis of the clavichord. *Computer Music Journal, 27*(1), 71–82. doi:10.1162/01489260360613353

Virtual Breath. (2009). *Press release.* Retrieved from http://www.tacc.utexas.edu/documents/13601/137149/CS_Virtual_Breath.pdf

Wolfe, J. (2010). *Music acoustics.* Retrieved from http://www.phys.unsw.edu.au/music/

Ystad, S., & Voinier, T. (2001). A virtually real flute. *Computer Music Journal, 25*(2), 13–24. doi:10.1162/014892601750302552

Compilation of References

Allen, J. F. (1983). Maintaining knowledge about temporal interval. *Communications of the ACM, 26*(11), 832–843. doi:10.1145/182.358434

Allen, J. F. (1984). Towards a general theory of action and time. *Artificial Intelligence, 23*, 123–154. doi:10.1016/0004-3702(84)90008-0

Allmusic. (2009). *Website.* Retrieved July 5, 2009, from http://www.allmusic.com/

Allombert, A., Assayag, G., & Desainte-Catherine, M. (2007). A system of interactive scores based on petri nets. In *Proceedings of the 4th Sound and Music Computing Conference.* Lefkada, Greece: ACM.

Amatrain, X., Arumi, P., & Ramirez, M. (2002). CLAM: Yet another library for audio and music processing? In *Proceedings of the ACM Conference on Object Oriented Programming, Systems, and Applications,* (pp. 22–23). ACM Press.

Ames, C. (1989). The Markov process as a compositional model: A survey and tutorial. *Leonardo Music Journal, 22*(2). doi:10.2307/1575226

Aramaki, M., Kronland-Martinet, R., Voinier, T., & Ystad, S. (2006). A percussive sound synthesizer based on physical and perceptual attributes. *Computer Music Journal, 30*(2), 32–41. doi:10.1162/comj.2006.30.2.32

Arcos, J. L., & Lopez de Mantaras, R. (2001). An interactive case-based reasoning approach for generating expressive music. *Applied Intelligence, 14*(1), 115–119. doi:10.1023/A:1008311209823

Arfib, D., Couturier, J.-M., Kessours, L., & Verfaille, V. (2002). Strategies of mapping between gesture data and synthesis model parameters using perceptual spaces. *Organised Sound, 7*(2), 135–152. doi:10.1017/S1355771802002054

Assayag, G., Rueda, C., Laurson, M., Agon, C., & Delerue, O. (1999). Computer assisted composition at IRCAM: From PatchWork to OpenMusic. *Computer Music Journal.* Retrieved from http://recherche.ircam.fr/equipes/repmus/RMPapers/CMJ98/

Austin, J. L. (1975). *How to do things with words.* Cambridge, MA: Harvard University Press. doi:10.1093/acprof:oso/9780198245537.001.0001

Baines, A. (1960). Organology and European folk music instruments. *Journal of the International Folk Music Council, 12*, 10–13. doi:10.2307/835418

Barron, M. (2008). Raising the roof. *Nature, 453*(12), 859–860. doi:10.1038/453859a

Battel, G. U., & Fimbianti, R. (1997). Analisys of expressive intentions in pianistic performances. In *Proceedings of International Workshop on Kansei,* (pp. 128-133). Genova, Switzerland: Kansei.

Bavu, E., Smith, J., & Wolfe, J. (2005). Torsional waves in a bowed string. *Acta Acustica united with Acustica, 91,* 241-246.

Beard, S., & Reid, D. (2002). MetaFace and VHML: A first implementation of the virtual human markup language. In *Proceedings of the AAMAS Workshop on Embodied Conversational Agents-Let's Specify and Evaluate Them.* AAMAS.

Bellini, P., & Nesi, P. (2001). WEDELMUSIC format: An XML music notation format for emerging applications. In *Proceedings of the First International Conference on Web Delivering of Music*. Florence, Italy: ACM.

Benade, A. H. (1960). On the mathematical theory of woodwind finger holes. *The Journal of the Acoustical Society of America, 32*(12), 1591–1608. doi:10.1121/1.1907968

Benta, K., Rarău, A., & Cremene, M. (1997). Ontology based affective context representation. In *Proceedings of the Euro American Conference on Telematics and Information Systems*. Faro, Portugal: ACM.

Bernardini, N., & De Poli, G. (2007). The sound and music computing field: Present and future. *Journal of New Music Research, 36*(3), 143–148. doi:10.1080/09298210701862432

Beurivé, A. (2000). Un logiciel de composition musicale combinant un modèle spectral, des structures hiérarchiques et des contraintes. In *Proceedings of the 5th Journées d'Informatique Musicale (JIM 2000)*. Bordeaux, France: JIM.

Bigand, E., Vieillard, S., Madurell, F., Marozeau, J., & Dacquet, A. (2005). Multidimensional scaling of emotional responses to music: The effect of musical expertise and of the duration of the excerpts. *Cognition and Emotion, 19*(8), 1113–1139. doi:10.1080/02699930500204250

Bilbao, S. (2009). Direct simulation of reed wind instruments. *Computer Music Journal, 33*(4), 43–55. doi:10.1162/comj.2009.33.4.43

Blauert, J., & Xiang, N. (2009). *Acoustics for engineers: Troy lectures* (2nd ed.). Berlin, Germany: Springer-Verlag.

Boll, S., Klas, U., & Westermann, W. (1999). *A comparison of multimedia document models concerning advanced requirements. Technical Report – Ulmer Informatik-Berichte No 99-01*. Ulm, Germany: University of Ulm.

Bonini, F., Rodà, A., & De Poli, G. (2006). Communicating expressive intentions with a single piano note. *Journal of New Music Research, 35*(3), 197–210. doi:10.1080/09298210601045575

Bos, B., Lie, H. W., Lilley, C., & Jacobs, I. (2008). *Cascading style sheets, level 2: CSS2 specification W3C recommendation*. Retrieved from http://www.w3.org/TR/2008/REC-CSS2-20080411/

Bresin, R. (1998). Artificial neural networks based models for automatic performance of musical scores. *Journal of New Music Research, 27*(3), 239–270. doi:10.1080/09298219808570748

Bresin, R., & Friberg, A. (2000). Emotional coloring of computer-controlled music performances. *Computer Music Journal, 24*(4), 44–63. doi:10.1162/014892600559515

Bruyns, C. (2006). Modal synthesis for arbitrarily shaped objects. *Computer Music Journal, 30*(3), 22–37. doi:10.1162/comj.2006.30.3.22

Buchner, A. (1980). *Colour encyclopedia of musical instruments*. New York, NY: Hamlyn.

Buitelaar, P., et al. (2006). *LingInfo: Design and applications of a model for the integration of linguistic information in ontologies*. Retrieved from http://www.dfki.de/~romanell/OntoLex2006.pdf

Bulterman, D., Jansen, J., Cesar, P., Mullender, S., Hyche, E., & DeMeglio, M. … Michel, T. (Eds.). (2008). *Synchronized multimedia integration language (SMIL 3.0)*. Retrieved July 6, 2009, from http://www.w3.org/TR/2008/REC-SMIL3-20081201/

Campbell, W., & Heller, J. (1981). Psychomusicology and psycholinguistics: Parallel paths or separate ways. *Psychomusicology, 1*(2), 3–14. doi:10.1037/h0094284

Camurri, A., Canepa, C., Coletta, P., Mazzarino, B., & Volpe, G. (2008). Mappe per affetti erranti: A multimodal system for social active listening and expressive performance. In *Proceedings NIME 2008 International Conference on New Interfaces for Musical Expression*, (pp. 134-139). Genova, Italy: NIME.

Camurri, A., De Poli, G., Leman, M., & Volpe, G. (2005). Toward communicating expressiveness and affect in multimodal interactive systems for performing arts and cultural applications. *IEEE MultiMedia, 12*(1), 43–53. doi:10.1109/MMUL.2005.2

Camurri, A., Lagerlof, I., & Volpe, G. (2003). Recognizing emotion from dance movement: Comparison of spectator recognition and automated techniques. *International Journal of Human-Computer Studies, 59*(1-2), 213–225. doi:10.1016/S1071-5819(03)00050-8

Canazza, S., & Orio, N. (1997). How are the players ideas perceived by listeners: Analysis of "How high the moon" theme. In *Proceedings of the International Kansei Workshop 1997*, (pp. 128-133). Genova, Switzerland: Associazione di Informatica Musicale Italiana.

Canazza, S., De Poli, G., Di Sanzo, G., & Vidolin, A. (1998). A model to add expressiveness to automatic musical performance. In *Proceedings of International Computer Music Conference*, (pp. 163-169). Ann Arbour, MI: ACM.

Canazza, S., De Poli, G., Drioli, C., Rodà, A., & Zamperini, F. (2000). Real-time morphing among different expressive intentions in audio playback. In *Proceedings of ICMC*, (pp. 356-359). Berlin, Germany: ICMC.

Canazza, S., De Poli, G., Rodà, A., & Vidolin, A. (1997). Analysis and synthesis of expressive intentions in musical performance. In *Proceedings of the International Computer Music Conference 1997*, (pp. 113-120). Tessaloniki, Greece: International Computer Music Association.

Canazza, S., Rodà, A., Zanon, A., & Friberg, A. (2003). Espressive director: A system for the real-time control of music performance synthesis. In *Proceedings of the Stockholm Music Acoustics Conference*, (pp. 521-524). Stockholm, Sweden: SMAC.

Canazza, S., De Poli, G., Drioli, C., Rodà, A., & Vidolin, A. (2000). Audio morphing different expressive intentions for Multimedia Systems. *IEEE MultiMedia, 7*(3), 79–83.

Canazza, S., De Poli, G., Drioli, C., Rodà, A., & Vidolin, A. (2004). Modeling and control of expressiveness in music performance. *Proceedings of the IEEE, 92*(4), 686–701. doi:10.1109/JPROC.2004.825889

Canazza, S., De Poli, G., Rinaldin, S., & Vidolin, A. (1997). Sonological analysis of clarinet expressivity. In Leman, M. (Ed.), *Music, Gestalt, and Computing: Studies in Cognitive and Systematic Musicology* (pp. 431–440). Berlin, Germany: Springer-Verlag.

Canazza, S., De Poli, G., & Rodà, A. (2002). Analysis of expressive intentions in piano performance. *Journal of ITC Sangeet Research Academy, 16*, 23–62.

Canazza, S., De Poli, G., Rodà, A., & Vidolin, A. (2003). An abstract control space for communication of sensory expressive intentions in music performance. *Journal of New Music Research, 32*(3), 281–294. doi:10.1076/jnmr.32.3.281.16862

Canazza, S., De Poli, G., & Vidolin, A. (1997). Perceptual analysis of the musical expressive intention in a clarinet performance. In Leman, M. (Ed.), *Music, Gestalt, and Computing: Studies in Cognitive and Systematic Musicology* (pp. 441–450). Berlin, Germany: Springer-Verlag. doi:10.1007/BFb0034132

Cannam, C., Landone, C., Sandler, M., & Bello, J. P. (2006). The sonic visualiser: A visualization platform for semantic descriptors from musical signals. In *Proceedings of the International Conference on Music Information Retrieval*, (pp. 324–327). ACM.

Casey, M. (2005). Acoustic lexemes for organizing internet audio. *Contemporary Music Review, 24*(6). doi:10.1080/07494460500296169

ccMixter. (2009). *Website*. Retrieved July 5, 2009, from http://ccmixter.org/

Chafe, C. (2012). *A short history of digital sound synthesis by composers in the U.S.A.* Retrieved from https://ccrma.stanford.edu/~cc/lyon/historyFinal.pdf

Chandrasekaran, B., Josephson, J. R., & Benjamins, V. R. (1999). What are ontologies, and why do we need them? *IEEE Intelligent Systems, 14*(1), 20–26. doi:10.1109/5254.747902

Chion, M. (1983). *Guide des objets sonores*. Paris, France: Buchet/Chastel.

Chomsky, N. (1957). *Syntactic structures*. The Hague, The Netherlands: Mouton.

Chung, H., & Lee, Y. (2004). MCML: Motion capture markup language for integration of heterogeneous motion capture data. *Computer Standards & Interfaces, 26*(2), 113–130. doi:10.1016/S0920-5489(03)00071-0

Conklin, H. A. (1999). Generation of partials due to nonlinear mixing in a stringed instrument. *The Journal of the Acoustical Society of America, 105*(1), 536–545. doi:10.1121/1.424589

Cook, D., & Holder, L. B. (2000). Graph data mining. *IEEE Intelligent Systems, 15*(2). doi:10.1109/5254.850825

Cook, P. R. (1997). Physically informed sonic modeling (PhISM): Synthesis of percussive sounds. *Computer Music Journal, 21*(3), 38–49. doi:10.2307/3681012

Cover, R. (Ed.). (2006). *XML and music*. Retrieved July 6, 2009 from http://xml.coverpages.org/xmlMusic.html

Cowie, R., Douglas-Cowie, E., Tsapatsoulis, N., Votsis, G., Kollias, S., Fellenz, W., & Taylor, J. G. (2001, January). Emotion recognition in human-computer interaction. *IEEE Signal Processing Magazine*, 32–80. doi:10.1109/79.911197

Cox, C., & Warner, D. (Eds.). (2004). *Audio culture: Readings in modern music*. New York, NY: Continuum.

Dahan, K., & Laliberté, M. (2008). Réflexions autour de la notion d'interprétation de la musique électroacoustique. In *Proceedings of the 13th Journées d'Informatique Musicale (JIM 2008)*. Albi, France: JIM.

Dannenberg, R., & Bates, J. (1995). A model for interactive art. In *Proceedings of the Fifth Biennial Symposium for Arts and Technology,* (pp. 103-111). ACM.

Dannenburg, R. B., & Goto, M. (2005). *Music structure analysis from acoustic signals*. Retrieved from http://repository.cmu.edu/compsci/494

Dattorro, J. (1997). Effect design, part 1: Reverberator and other filters. *Journal of the Audio Engineering Society. Audio Engineering Society, 45*(9), 660–684.

De Carolis, B., Pelachaud, C., Poggi, I., & Steedman, M. (2004). APML: A mark-up language for believable behavior generation. In Prendinger, H., & Ishizuka, M. (Eds.), *Life-Like Characters: Tools, Affective Functions and Applications* (pp. 65–85). Berlin, Germany: Springer-Verlag.

De Poli, G., Rodà, A., & Vidolin, A. (1998). Note-by-note analysis of the influence of expressive intentions and musical structure in violin performance. *Journal of New Music Research, 27*(3), 293–321. doi:10.1080/09298219808570750

de Saussure, F. (1990). *Course in general linguitsics* (Harris, R., Trans.). London, UK: Duckworth.

Diaz, M. (2008). *Petri nets: Fundamental models, verification and applications*. Oxford, UK: Wiley-Blackwell.

Doornbusch, P. (2009). *A chronology of computer music and related events 1906 - 2009*. Retrieved from http://www.doornbusch.net/chronology/

Downie, S. (2003). Music information retrieval. In Cronin, B. (Ed.), *Annual Review of Information Science and Technology* (*Vol. 37*, pp. 295–340). Medford, NJ: Information Today.

Drake, C., & Palmer, C. (1993). Accent structures in music performance. *Music Perception, 10*, 343–378. doi:10.2307/40285574

Ducasse, E. (2003). A physical model of a single-reed wind instrument, including actions of the player. *Computer Music Journal, 27*(1), 59–70. doi:10.1162/01489260360613344

Duda, R. O., Hart, P. E., & Stork, D. G. (2001). *Pattern classification*. New York, NY: John Wiley & Sons Inc.

Ehresman, D., & Wessel, D. L. (1978). *Perception of timbral analogies. IRCAM Report 13/78*. Paris, France: Centre Georges Pompidou.

Einstein, A. (1905). On the electrodynamics of moving bodies. *Analen der Physik, 17*.

Einstein, A. (1916). The foundations of the general theory of relativity. *Annalen der Physik, 49*.

Elliott, R., Glauert, J. R. W., Kennaway, J. R., & Marshall, I. (2000). The development of language processing support for the visicast project. In *Proceedings of the Fourth International ACM Conference on Assistive Technologies,* (pp. 101–108). New York, NY: ACM Press.

Engelfriet, J., & Rozenberg, G. (1990). Graph grammars based on node rewriting: An introduction to nlc graph grammars. In *Graph-Grammars and Their Application to Computer Science* (pp. 12–23). Bremen, Germany: Springer-Verlag. doi:10.1007/BFb0017374

Engelfriet, J., & Rozenberg, G. (1997). Node replacement graph grammars. In Rozenberg, G. (Ed.), *Handbook of Graph Grammars and Computing by Graph Transformation* (pp. 1–94). Singapore, Singapore: World Scientific Publishing Co.doi:10.1142/9789812384720_0001

Erfle, R. (1993). Specification of temporal constraints in multimedia documents using HyTime. *Electronic Publishing*, *6*(4), 397–411.

Essl, G., Serafin, S., Cook, P. R., & Smith, J. O. (2004). Theory of banded waveguides. *Computer Music Journal*, *28*(1), 37–50. doi:10.1162/014892604322970634

Essl, G., Serafin, S., Cook, P. R., & Smith, J. O. (2004). Musical applications of banded waveguides. *Computer Music Journal*, *28*(1), 51–63.doi:10.1162/014892604322970643

Evrard, M., Couroussé, D., Castagné, N., Cadoz, C., Florens, J.-L., & Luciani, A. (2006). *The GMS file format: Specifications of the version 0.1 of the format*. Technical report. Grenoble, France: INPG, ACROE/ICA.

Fahy, F. (2001). *Foundations of engineering acoustics*. London, UK: Academic Press.

Fletcher, N. H. (1999). The nonlinear physics of musical instruments. *Reports on Progress in Physics*, *62*, 723–761. doi:10.1088/0034-4885/62/5/202

Fletcher, N. H., Blackham, E. D., & Stratton, R. (1962). Quality of piano tones. *The Journal of the Acoustical Society of America*, *34*(6), 749–761.doi:10.1121/1.1918192

Fletcher, N. H., & Rossing, T. D. (1991). *The physics of musical instruments*. New York, NY: Springer. doi:10.1007/978-1-4612-2980-3

Foafing the Music. (2009). *Website*. Retrieved July 5, 2009, from http://foafing-the-music.iua.upf.edu/

Fong, S. (2002). On the ontological basis for logical metonomy: Telic roles and WORDNET. [Ontolex.]. *Proceedings of Ontolex*, *2002*, 37–41.

Fonseca, F. (2007). The double role of ontologies in information science research. *Journal of the American Society for Information Science and Technology*, *58*(6), 786–793. doi:10.1002/asi.20565

Freesound. (2009). *Website*. Retrieved July 5, 2009, from http://www.freesound.org/

Friberg, A. (1991). Generative rules for music performance. *Computer Music Journal*, *15*(2), 56–71. doi:10.2307/3680917

Friberg, A. (2004). A fuzzy analyzer of emotional expression in music performance and body motion. In Sundberg, J., & Brunson, B. (Eds.), *Proceedings of Music and Music Science*. Stockholm, Sweden: ACM.

Gabrielson, A., & Lindstrom, E. (2001). The influence of the musical structure on emotional expression. In Juslin, P. N., & Slodoba, J. A. (Eds.), *Music and Emotion: Theory and Research* (pp. 223–249). Oxford, UK: Oxford University Press.

Gabrielsson, A. (1995). Expressive intention and perfomance. In Steinberg, R. (Ed.), *Music and Mind Machine* (pp. 35–47). Berlin, Germany: Sprinter-Verlag. doi:10.1007/978-3-642-79327-1_4

Gabrielsson, A. (1999). The performance of music. In Deutsch, D. (Ed.), *The Psychology of Music* (pp. 501–602). Academic Press. doi:10.1016/B978-012213564-4/50015-9

Gabrielsson, A., & Juslin, P. N. (1996). Emotional expression in music performance: Between the performer's intention and the listener's experience. *Psychology of Music*, *24*, 68–91. doi:10.1177/0305735696241007

Gaudrain, E., & Orlarey, Y. (2003). *A Faust manual*. GRAME.

Gazon, D., & Andriarin, X. (2001). XML as a means of control for audio processing, synthesis and analysis. In *Proceedings of MOSART, Workshop on Current Research Directions in Computer Music*, (pp. 85-91). Barcelona, Spain: MOSART.

Gilb, T. (1988). *Principles of software engineering management*. Reading, MA: Addison-Wesley.

Godøy, R. I., Jensenius, A. R., & Nymoen, K. (2008). *Production and perception of goal-points and coarticulations in music*. Paper presented at the ASA-EAA Conference. Paris, France.

Godøy, R. I. (2004). Gestural imagery in the service of musical imagery. *Lecture Notes in Artificial Intelligence, 2915*, 55–62.

Godøy, R. I. (2006). Gestural-sonorous objects: Embodied extensions of schaeffer's conceptual apparatus. *Organised Sound, 11*(2), 149–157. doi:10.1017/S1355771806001439

Godøy, R. I., & Leman, M. (2009). *Musical gestures - Sound, movement, and meaning*. New York, NY: Routledge.

Goldfarb, C. (1991). Standards: HyTime: A standard for structured hypermedia interchange. *IEEE Computer Magazine, 24*(8).

Goldfarb, C. F., & Prescod, P. (1998). *The XML handbook*. Upper Saddle River, NJ: Prentice Hall.

Good, M. (2000). Representing music using XML. In *Proceedings of Music IR 2000*. Retrieved January 11, 2010, from http://ismir2000.ismir.net/posters/good.pdf

Good, M. (2001). MusicXML: An internet-friendly format for sheet music. In *Proceedings of XML 2001*. Orlando, FL: XML.

Good, M. (2006). Lessons from the adoption of MusicXML as an interchange standard. In D. Megginson (Ed.), *Proceedings of XML 2006*. Retrieved January 11, 2010, from http://2006.xmlconference.org/proceedings/46/presentation.pdf

Good, M. (2006). MusicXML in commercial applications. In Hewlett, W. B., & Selfridge-Field, E. (Eds.), *Music Analysis East and West* (pp. 9–20). Cambridge, MA: MIT Press.

Gould, J. D., & Lewis, C. (1985). Designing for usability: Key principles and what designers think. *Communications of the ACM, 28*(3), 300–311. doi:10.1145/3166.3170

Gracenote. (2009). *Website*. Retrieved July 5, 2009, from http://www.gracenote.com/

Grame, T. C. (1962). Bamboo and music: a new approach to organology. *Ethnomusicology, 6*(1), 8–14. doi:10.2307/924243

Grande, C. (1997). The notation interchange file format: A windows-compliant approach. In Selfridge-Field, E. (Ed.), *Beyond MIDI: The Handbook of Musical Codes* (pp. 491–512). Cambridge, MA: The MIT Press.

Gruber, T. R. (1992). *What is an ontology?* Retrieved from http://www-ksl.stanford.edu/kst/what-is-an-ontology.html

Hall, D. E. (1986). Piano string excitation in the case of small hammer mass. *The Journal of the Acoustical Society of America, 79*(1), 141–147. doi:10.1121/1.393637

Hanslick, E. (1854). *Vom musikalisch-schönen*. Leipzig, Germany: Rudolph Weigel.

Harold, E. R. (2004). *Effective XML: 50 specific ways to improve your XML*. Boston, MA: Addison Wesley.

Hartmann, B., Mancini, M., & Pelachaud, C. (2002). Formational parameters and adaptive prototype instantiation for MPEG-4 compliant gesture synthesis. [Computer Animation.]. *Proceedings of Computer Animation, 2002*, 111–119.

Hashimoto, S. (1997). KANSEI as the third target of information processing and related topics in Japan. In *Proceedings of the International Workshop on KANSEI: The Technology of Emotion*, (pp. 101-104). Genova, Switzerland: AIWA.

Hass, J. (1999). *Electronic music historical overview*. Retrieved from http://www.indiana.edu/~emusic/elechist.htm

Haury, J. (2012). *La grammaire de l'exécution musicale au clavier et le mouvement des touches*. Unpublished.

Haus, G., & Longari, M. (2002). Towards a symbolic/time-based music language based on XML. In Haus & Longari (Eds.), *MAX 2002: Musical Applications using XML: Proceedings First International Conference Laboratoria di Informatica Musicale*, (pp. 38-46). Milan, Italy: State University of Milan.

Haus, G., & Longari, M. (2005). A multi-layered, time-based music description approach based on XML. *Computer Music Journal, 29*(1), 70–85. doi:10.1162/comj.2005.29.1.70

Hevner, A. R., & Chatterjee, S. (2010). Design research in information systems. *Integrated Series in Information Systems, 22*.

Hevner, A. R., March, S. T., Park, J., & Ram, S. (2004). Design science in information systems research. *Management Information Systems Quarterly, 28*, 75–105.

Hewlett, W. B. (1997). MuseData: Multipurpose representation. In Selfridge-Field, E. (Ed.), *Beyond MIDI: The Handbook of Musical Codes* (pp. 402–447). Cambridge, MA: The MIT Press.

Hofmann, P. (1996). *MHEG-5 and MHEG-6: Multimedia standards for minimal resource systems. Technical Report.* Berlin, Germany: Technische Universitat.

Houtsma, A. J. M., & Smurzynksi, J. (1990). Pitch identification and discrimination for complex tones with many harmonies. *The Journal of the Acoustical Society of America, 87*(1), 304–310. doi:10.1121/1.399297

Hunt, A., & Wanderley, M. M. (2002). Mapping performer parameters to synthesis engines. *Organised Sound, 7*(2), 97–108. doi:10.1017/S1355771802002030

Huron, D. (1997). Humdrum and kern: Selective feature encoding. In Selfridge-Field, E. (Ed.), *Beyond MIDI: The Handbook of Musical Codes* (pp. 375–401). Cambridge, MA: The MIT Press.

Huron, D. (1999). *Music research using humdrum: A user's guide*. Stanford, CA: Center for Computer Assisted Research in the Humanities.

HyTime. (1992). *HyTime: Information technology - Hypermedia/time-based structuring language (HyTime). ISO/IEC DIS 10744, 8*. HyTime.

Ingram, J. (2004). *A survey of the world's music notations with special emphasis on early, contemporary and non-European notations*. MusicNetwork.

Jackendoff, R., & Lehrdal, F. (1981). Generative music theory and its relationship to psychology. *Journal of Music Therapy, 25*(1).

Jain, A. K., & Dubes, R. C. (1988). *Algorithms for clustering data*. Upper Saddle River, NJ: Prentice Hall.

Jamendo. (2009). *Website*. Retrieved July 5, 2009, from http://www.jamendo.com/

James, J. (1993). *The music of the spheres: Music, science, and the natural order of the universe*. London, UK: Abacus. doi:10.1119/1.18443

Jazzmutant. (2006). *Extension and enchancement of the OSC protocol*. Paper presented at the OSC-meeting at NIME 2006, IRCAM. Paris, France.

Jensenius, A. R., Camurri, A., Castagne, N., Maestre, E., Malloch, J., & McGilvray, D. … Wright, M. (2007). Panel: The need of formats for streaming and storing music-related movement and gesture data. In *Proceedings of the 2007 International Computer Music Conference*, (pp. 13–16). Copenhagen, Denmark: International Music Conference.

Jensenius, A. R., Kvifte, T., & Godøy, R. I. (2006). Towards a gesture description interchange format. In N. Schnell, F. Bevilacqua, M. Lyons, & A. Tanaka (Eds.), In *Proceedings of the 2006 International Conference on New Interfaces for Musical Expression*, (pp. 176–179). Paris, France: IRCAM – Centre Pompidou.

Jensenius, A. R., Nymoen, K., & Godøy, R. I. (2008). A multilayered GDIF-based setup for studying coarticulation in the movements of musicians. In *Proceedings of the 2008 International Computer Music Conference*, (pp. 743–746). Belfast, Ireland: ACM.

Jordà, S. (2002). FMOL: Toward user-friendly, sophisticated new musical instruments. *Computer Music Journal, 26*(3), 23–39. doi:10.1162/014892602320582954

Juslin, P. N. (1993). *The influence of expressive intention on electric guitar performance*. (Unpublished Thesis). Uppsala University. Uppsala, Sweden.

Juslin, P. N. (2000). Cue utilization in communication of emotion in music performance: Relating performance to perception. *Journal of Experimental Psychology. Human Perception and Performance, 26*(6), 1797–1813. doi:10.1037/0096-1523.26.6.1797

Juslin, P. N. (2001). Communicating emotion in music performance: A review and theoretical framework. In Juslin, P. N., & Slodoba, J. A. (Eds.), *Music and Emotion: Theory and Research* (pp. 279–309). Oxford, UK: Oxford University Press.

Juslin, P. N., Friberg, A., & Bresin, R. (2002). Toward a computational model of expression in performance: The GERM model. *Musicae Scientiae*, •••, 63–122. Retrieved from http://www.speech.kth.se/prod/publications/files/847.pdf

Juslin, P. N., & Sloboda, J. A. (2001). *Music and emotion: Theory and research*. Oxford, UK: Oxford University Press.

Kalbach, J. (2002). Review: Classifying emotion for information retrieval: Three web sites. *Notes*, *59*(2), 408–411. doi:10.1353/not.2002.0177

Kania, A. (2007). The philosophy of music. *Stanford Encyclopedia of Philosophy*. Retrieved from http://plato.stanford.edu/entries/music/

Kartomi, M. (2001). The classification of musical instruments: Changing trends in research from the late nineteenth century, with special reference to the 1990s. *Ethnomusicology*, *45*(2), 283–314. doi:10.2307/852676

Kassler, J. (1995). *Inner music: Hobbes, Hooke and North on internal character*. London, UK: Farleigh Dickinson University Press.

Kim, H., Moreau, N., & Sikora, T. (2006). *MPEG-7 audio and beyond: audio content indexing and retrieval*. Hoboken, NJ: Wiley and Sons.

Kitahara, T. (2008). *A unified and extensible framework for developing music information processing systems*. Unpublished Manuscript.

Kranstedt, A., Kopp, S., & Wachsmuth, I. (2002). MURML: A multimodal utterance representation markup language for conversational agents. In *Proceedings of the AAMAS Workshop on Embodied Conversational Agents – Let's Specify and Evaluate Them*. AAMAS.

Krumhansl, C. L. (1996). A perceptual analysis of Mozart's piano sonata K.282: Segmentation, tension, and musical ideas. *Music Perception*, *13*(3), 401–432. doi:10.2307/40286177

Kshirsagar, S., Magnenat-Thalmann, N., Guye-Vuillome, A., Thalmann, D., Kamyab, K., & Mamdani, E. (2002). Avatar markup language. In *Proceedings of the Workshop on Virtual Environments 2002*, (pp. 169–177). Aire-la-Ville, Switzerland: Eurographics Association.

Kuhn, T. S. (1962). *The structure of scientific revolutions*. Chicago, IL: University of Chicago Press.

Kuuskankare, M., & Laurson, M. (2001). ENP, musical notation library based on common lisp and CLOS. In *Proceedings of ICMC 2001*. Havana, Cuba: ICMC.

Laban, R. V. (1980). *Mastery of movement* (4th ed.). Plymouth, MA: MacDonald & Evans Ltd.

Lacy, L. W. (2005). *OWL: Representing information using the web ontology language*. Victoria, Canada: Trafford Publishing.

Lander, J. (1998, January). Working with motion capture file formats. *Game Developer*, 30–37.

Langner, J., & Goebl, W. (2002). Representing expressive performance in tempo-loudness space. In *Proceedings of the ESCOM 10th Anniversary Conference on Musical Creativity*, (pp. 109-113). Liege, Belgium: ESCOM.

Last.fm. (2009). *Website*. Retrieved July 5, 2009, from http://www.last.fm/

Lattard, J. (1993). Influence of inharmonicity on the tuning of a piano—Measurements and mathematical simulation. *The Journal of the Acoustical Society of America*, *94*(1), 46–53. doi:10.1121/1.407059

Legge, K. A., & Fletcher, N. H. (1984). Nonlinear generation of missing modes on a vibrating string. *The Journal of the Acoustical Society of America*, *76*(1), 5–12. doi:10.1121/1.391007

Leman, M. (2000). Visualization and calculation of the roughness of acoustical musical signals using the synchronization index model (sim). In *Proceedings of the COST G-6 Conference on Digital Audio Effects, DAFX 2000*, (pp. 125-130). Verona, Italy: DAFX.

Lenci, A. (2010). The life cycle of knowledge. In Huang, C., Calzolari, N., Gangemi, A., & Lenci, A. (Eds.), *Ontology and the Lexicon: A Natural Language Processing Perspective* (pp. 241–257). Cambridge, UK: Cambridge University Press. doi:10.1017/CBO9780511676536.015

Lerdahl, F., & Jackendoff, R. (1983). *A generative theory of tonal music*. Cambridge, MA: MIT Press.

Lindstrom, E. (1992). *5 x oh my darling Clementine: The influence of expressive intention on music performance.* (Bachelor Thesis). Uppsala University. Uppsala, Sweden.

Luciani, A., Evrard, M., Castagné, N., Couroussé, D., Florens, J.-L., & Cadoz, C. (2006). A basic gesture and motion format for virtual reality multisensory applications. In *Proceedings of the 1st International Conference on Computer Graphics Theory and Applications.* Setubal, Portugal: ACM.

Luciani, A., Evrard, M., Courousse, D., Castagne, N., Summers, I., Brady, A., ... Pirro, D. (2006). *Report on gesture format: State of the art.* Partners' propositions. Deliverable 1 D.RD3.3.1, IST-2004-002114-ENACTIVE Network of Excellence.

Lucidovo, L. (2009). IEEE 1599: A multi-layer approach to music description. *Journal of Multimedia, 4*(1).

Madsen, S. T. (2003). Automatic discovery of parallelism and hierarchy in music. (Master Thesis). University of Arhus. Arhus, Denmark.

Maestre, E., Janer, J., Blaauw, M., Pérez, A., & Guaus, E. (2007). Acquisition of violin instrumental gestures using a commercial EMF tracking device. In *Proceedings of the 2007 International Computer Music Conference.* Copenhagen, Denmark: ICMA.

Malloch, J., Sinclair, S., & Wanderley, M. M. (2007). From controller to sound: Tools for collaborative development of digital musical instruments. In *Proceedings of the 2007 International Computer Music Conference.* Copenhagen, Denmark: ICMA.

Manjunath, B., Salembier, P., & Sikora, T. (2002). *Introduction to MPEG-7: Multimedia content description interface.* New York, NY: John Wiley and Sons.

March, S. T., & Smith, G. F. (1995). Design and natural science research on information technology. *Decision Support Systems, 15,* 251–266. doi:10.1016/0167-9236(94)00041-2

Margulis, E. H., & Beatty, A. P. (2008). Musical style, psychoaesthetics, and prospects for entropy as an analytic tool. *Computer Music Journal, 32*(4), 64–78. doi:10.1162/comj.2008.32.4.64

Marshall, M. T., Peters, N., Jensenius, A. R., Boissinot, J., Wanderley, M. M., & Braasch, J. (2006). On the development of a system for gesture control of spatialization. In *Proceedings of the International Computer Music Conference,* (pp. 360–366). New Orleans, LA: ICMA.

Martinez, J., Koenen, R., & Pereira, F. (2002). MPEG-7: The generic multimedia content description standard, part. *IEEE MultiMedia, 9*(2), 78–87. doi:10.1109/93.998074

McGilvray, D. (2007). *On the analysis of musical performance by computer.* (PhD Thesis). University of Glasgow. Glasgow, UK.

McGurk, H., & MacDonald, J. (1976). Hearing lips and seeing voices. *Nature, 264*(5588), 746–748. doi:10.1038/264746a0

McKay, C. (2004). *Automatic genre classification of MIDI recordings.* (M.A. Thesis). McGill University. Montreal, Canada.

McKay, C., & Fujinaga, I. (2012). jMIR: Tools for automatic music classification. In *Proceedings of the International Computer Music Conference.* ACM.

McKay, C., Fiebrink, R., McEnnis, D., Li, B., & Fujinaga, I. (2005). ACE: A framework for optimizing music classification. In *Proceedings of the International Conference on Music Information Retrieval,* (pp. 42–49). ACM.

Merker, B. (2006). Layered constraints on the multiple creativities of music. In Deliège, I., & Wiggins, G. (Eds.), *Musical Creativity: Multidisciplinary Research in Theory and Practice.* New York, NY: Psychology Press.

Mierswa, I., Wurst, M., Klinkenberg, R., Scholzn, M., & Euler, T. (2006). YALE: Rapid prototyping for complex data mining tasks. In *Proceedings of the ACM SIGKDD International Conference on Knowledge Discovery and Data Mining,* (pp. 935–940). ACM Press.

Mion, L. (2003). Application of Bayesian networks to automatic recognition of expressive content of piano improvisations. In *Proceedings of the Stockholm Music Acoustics Conference 2003,* (pp. 557-560). Stockholm, Sweden: Stockholm Music Acoustics Conference.

Mion, L., & De Poli, G. (2008). Score-independent audio features for description of music expression. *IEEE Transactions on Speech. Audio and Language Processing, 16*(2), 458–466. doi:10.1109/TASL.2007.913743

Music Ontology Specification. (2010). *Specification document*. Retrieved from http://www.musicontology.com/

Muze. (2009). *Website*. Retrieved July 5, 2009, from http://www.muze.com/html/products/music/muzemusic/index.htm

Narmour, E. (1990). *The analysis and cognition of basic melodic structures: the implication-realization model*. Chicago, IL: University of Chicago Press.

Ng, K., & Nesi, P. (Eds.). (2007). *Interactive multimedia music technologies*. Hershey, PA: IGI Global. doi:10.4018/978-1-59904-150-6

Oviatt, S. L. (2000). Multimodal interface research: A science without borders. In B. Yuan Huang & X. Tang (Eds.), *Proceedings of the International Conference on Spoken Language Processing*, (vol 3, pp. 1-6). Beijing, China: ACM.

Pachet, F., Aucouturier, J. J., La Burthe, A., Zils, A., & Beurive, A. (2006). The cuidado music browser: An end-to-end electronic music distribution system. *Multimedia Tools and Applications*, *30*, 331–349. doi:10.1007/s11042-006-0030-6

Pakarinen, J., Puputti, T., & Välimäki, V. (2008). Virtual slide guitar. *Computer Music Journal*, *32*(3), 42–54. doi:10.1162/comj.2008.32.3.42

Pakarinen, J., & Yeh, D. T. (2009). A review of digital techniques for modeling vacuum-tube guitar amplifiers. *Computer Music Journal*, *33*(2), 85–100. doi:10.1162/comj.2009.33.2.85

Palmer, C. (1996). On the assignment of structure in music performance. *Music Perception*, *14*, 23–56. doi:10.2307/40285708

Palmer, C. (1997). Music performance. *Annual Review of Psychology*, *48*, 115–138. doi:10.1146/annurev.psych.48.1.115

Pandora. (2009). *Website*. Retrieved July 5, 2009, from http://www.pandora.com/

Peeters, G., McAdams, S., & Herrera, P. (2000). Instrument sound description in the context of MPEG-7. In *Proceedings of ICMC*. ICMC.

Perry, R. (2002). The music encoding initiative (MEI). In Proceedings of the First International Conference MAX 2002: Musical Application Using XML. Milan, Italy: MAX.

Peters, N. (2008). Proposing spatdif - The spatial sound description interchange format. In *Proceedings of the 2008 International Computer Music Conference*. Belfast, Ireland: ACM.

Pfaltz, J., & Rosenfeld, A. (1967). *Web grammars*. Paper presented at the Joint International Conference on Artificial Intelligence. Washington, DC.

Picard, R. W. (1997). *Affective computing*. Cambridge, MA: MIT Press.

Place, T., & Lossius, T. (2006). Jamoma: A modular standard for structuring patches in max. In *Proceedings of the 2006 International Computer Music Conference*, (pp. 143–146). New Orleans, LA: ICMA.

Plutchik, R. (1980). *Emotion: A psychoevolutionary synthesis*. New York, NY: Harper & Row.

Plutchik, R. (1994). *The psychology and biology of emotions*. New York, NY: Harper-Collins.

Politis, D., Margounakis, D., Lazaropoulos, S., & Papaleontiou, L. (2008). Emulation of ancient Greek music using sound synthesis and historical notation. *Computer Music Journal*, *32*(4), 48–63. doi:10.1162/comj.2008.32.4.48

Powers, S. (2003). *Practical RDF*. Sebastopol, CA: O'Reilly Media.

Prendinger, H., Descamps, S., & Ishizuka, M. (2004). MPML: A markup language for controlling the behavior of life-like characters. *Journal of Visual Languages and Computing*, *15*(2), 183–203. doi:10.1016/j.jvlc.2004.01.001

Pullinger, S., McGilvray, D., & Bailey, N. (2008). Music and gesture file: Performance visualisation, analysis, storage and exchange. In *Proceedings of the 2008 International Computer Music Conference*. Belfast, Ireland: ACM.

QuickTime. (1991). *QuickTime developer's guide*. QuickTime.

Raimond, Y., & Giasson, F. (Eds.). (2010). *Music ontology specification*. Retrieved from http://musicontology.com/

Raimond, Y., Abdallah, S., Sandler, M., & Giasson, F. (2007). The music ontology. *Austrian Computer Society*. Retrieved from http://fgiasson.com/articles/ismir2007.pdf

Ramirez, R., Hazan, A., Gómez, E., Maestre, E., & Serra, X. (2005). Discovering expressive transformation rules from saxophone jazz performances. *Journal of New Music Research, 34*, 319–330. doi:10.1080/09298210600578097

Ramirez, R., Hazan, A., Maestre, E., & Serra, X. (2008). A genetic rule-based expressive performance model for jazz saxophone. *Computer Music Journal, 32*, 38–50. doi:10.1162/comj.2008.32.1.38

Rank, E., & Kubin, G. (1997). A waveguide model for slapbass synthesis. In *Proceedings of the IEEE International Conference on Acoustics, Speech, and Signal Processing*, (pp. 444-446). IEEE Press.

Rauhala, J., Laurson, M., Välimäki, V., Lehtonen, H., & Norilo, V. (2008). A parametric piano synthesizer. *Computer Music Journal, 32*(4), 17–30. doi:10.1162/comj.2008.32.4.17

Ray, E. T. (2003). *Learning XML*. Sebastopol, CA: O'Reilly Media.

Recordare, L. L. C. (2011). *MusicXML overview*. Retrieved May 12, 2011, from http://www.recordare.com/musicxml/

Repp, B. H. (1992). Diversity and commonality in music performance: An analysis of timing microstructure in Schumann's "Träumerei". *The Journal of the Acoustical Society of America, 92*, 2546–2568. doi:10.1121/1.404425

Repp, B. H. (1994). Relational invariance of expressive microstructure across global tempo changes in music performance: An exploratory study. *Psychological Research, 56*(4), 269–284. doi:10.1007/BF00419657

Repp, B. H. (1995). Expressive timing in Schumann's "Träumerei": An analysis of performances by graduate student pianists. *The Journal of the Acoustical Society of America, 98*, 2413–2427. doi:10.1121/1.413276

Repp, B. H. (1998). A microcosm of musical expression: Quantitative analysis of pianists' timing in the initial measures of Chopin's Etude in E major. *The Journal of the Acoustical Society of America, 104*, 1085–1100. doi:10.1121/1.423325

Repp, B. H. (1999). A microcosm of musical expression: Quantitative analysis of pianists' dynamics in the initial measures of Chopin's Etude in E major. *The Journal of the Acoustical Society of America, 105*, 1972–1988. doi:10.1121/1.426743

Reynolds, D. D. (1981). *Engineering principles of acoustics*. Boston, MA: Allyn and Bacon Inc.

Ridley, A. (2003). Against musical ontology. *The Journal of Philosophy, 100*(4), 203–220.

Roads, C. (1978). Composing grammars. In *Proceedings of the 1977 International Computer Music Conference*. San Francisco, CA: ACM.

Roads, C. (1979). Grammars as a representation for music. *Computer Music Journal, 3*(1). doi:10.2307/3679756

Roads, C. (1982). An overview of music representations. In Baroni, M., & Callegari, L. (Eds.), *Musical Grammars and Computer Analysis*. Firenze, Italy: Leo S. Olschi.

Rodà, A., & Canazza, S. (2009). A web 2.0 system for expressive performance of music contents. In *Proceedings of 2nd International Conference on Human System Interaction*. Catania, Italy: IEEE.

Rodà, A., & Canazza, S. (2009). Virtual performance, actual gesture: A web 2.0 system for expressive performance of music contents. In *Proceedings of Human System Interaction 2009*. Catania, Italy: IEEE. doi:10.1109/HSI.2009.5091025

Roland, P. (2002). The music encoding initiative (MEI). In *Proceedings of the First International Conference on Musical Applications Using XML*, (pp. 55–59). ACM.

Roma, G. (2008). Freesound radio: Supporting collective organization of sounds. (Master Thesis). Universitat Pompeu Fabra. Barcelona, Spain.

Roma, G., & Herrera, P. (2010). Graph grammar representation for collaborative sample-based music creation. In *Proceedings of the 5th Audio Mostly Conference*. Audio Mostly.

Roma, G., Herrera, P., & Serra, X. (2009). *Freesound radio: Supporting music creation by exploration of a sound database*. Paper presented at the Computational Creativity Support Workshop (CHI 2009). Boston, MA.

Rossing, T. D. (1990). *The science of sound* (2nd ed.). Boston, MA: Addison-Wesley.

Rozenberg, G. (Ed.). (1997). Handbook of graph grammars and computing by graph transformation. Singapore, Sinapore: World Scientific Publishing Co.

Russell, J. A. (1980). A circumplex model of affect. *Journal of Personality and Social Psychology, 39*, 1161–1178. doi:10.1037/h0077714

Ryle, G. (1965). *The concept of mind.* New York, NY: Barnes and Noble.

Sachs, C. (2008). *The rise of music in the ancient world: East and west.* New York, NY: Dover.

Schaeffer, P. (1966). *Traité des objets musicaux.* Paris, France: Editions du Seuil.

Scherer, K. R. (1994). Affect bursts. In van Goozen, S., van de Poll, N. E., & Sergeant, J. A. (Eds.), *Emotions: Essays on Emotion Theory* (pp. 161–196). Hillsdale, NJ: Erlbaum.

Schnell, N., Borghesi, R., Schwarz, D., Bevilacqua, F., & Muller, R. (2005). FTM – Complex data structures for Max. In *Proceedings of the 2005 International Computer Music Conference,* (pp. 9–12). Barcelona, Spain: ICMA.

Schulte, C., & Tack, G. (2005). Views and iterators for generic constraint implementations. In *Proceedings of the Fifth International Colloquium on Implementation of Constraint and Logic Programming Systems, CICLOPS 2005.* CICLOPS.

Schwarz, D., & Wright, M. (2000). Extensions and applications of the SDIF sound description interchange format. In *Proceedings of the 2000 International Computer Music Conference,* (pp. 481–484). Berlin, Germany: ICMA.

Selfridge-Field, E. (1997). Describing musical information. In Selfridge-Field, E. (Ed.), *Beyond MIDI: The Handbook of Musical Codes* (pp. 3–38). Cambridge, MA: The MIT Press.

Selfridge-Field, E. (Ed.). (1997). *Beyond MIDI: The handbook of musical codes.* Cambridge, MA: MIT Press.

Serra, X. (2008). *Technological development in the current social context: Who is really in control?* Paper presented at the 8th International Conference New Interfaces for Musical Expression. Genova, Italy.

Sinclair, S., & Wanderley, M. M. (2007). Defining a control standard for easily integrating haptic virtual environments with existing audio/visual systems. In *Proceedings of the 2007 Conference on New Interfaces for Musical Expression.* New York, NY: NIME.

Sloan, D. (1993). Aspects of music representation in HyTime SMDL. *Computer Music Journal, 17,* 51–59. doi:10.2307/3680544

Sloan, D. (1997). HyTime and standard music description language: A document-description approach. In Selfridge-Field, E. (Ed.), *Beyond MIDI: The Handbook of Musical Codes* (pp. 469–490). Cambridge, MA: The MIT Press.

SMIL. (2008). *SMIL 3.0 W3C recommendation.* Retrieved from http://www.w3c.org

Smith, J. (2006). *History and practice of digital sound synthesis.* Retrieved from http://www.aes.org/technical/heyser/downloads/AES121heyser-Smith.pdf

Soundpedia. (2009). *Website.* Retrieved July 5, 2009, from http://www.soundpedia.com/

Steinberger, R., Hagman, J., & Scheer, S. (2000). *Using thesauri for automatic indexing and for the visualisation of multilingual document collections.* Paper presented at OntoLex 2000 – Workshop on Ontologies and Lexical Knowledge Bases. Sozopol, Bulgaria.

Steyn, J. (1999). *MML (music markup language).* Retrieved from http://www.musicmarkup.info/

Steyn, J. (2002). Framework for a music markup language. In *Proceedings of the First International Conference MAX 2002: Musical Application Using XML.* Milan, Italy: MAX.

Steyn, J. (2004). Introducing music space. In *Proceedings of the 4th Open Workshop of MUSICNETWORK: Integration of Music in Multimedia Applications.* Barcelona, Spain: MUSICNETWORK.

Steyn, J. (2007). *Working notes on a markup language for birdsong.* Unpublished.

Steyn, J. (2007). Challenges of designing a markup language for music. In Ng, K., & Nesi, P. (Eds.), *Interactive Multimedia Music Technologies*. Hershey, PA: IGI Global. doi:10.4018/978-1-59904-150-6.ch006

Steyn, J. (2008). Challenges of designing a markup language for music. In Ng, K., & Nesi, P. (Eds.), *Interactive Multimedia Music Technologies* (pp. 111–132). Hershey, PA: IGI Global. doi:10.4018/978-1-59904-150-6.ch006

Swartz, A. (2002). MusicBrainz: A semantic web service. *IEEE Intelligent Systems*, *17*(1), 76–77. doi:10.1109/5254.988466

Tervaniemi, M., Just, V., Koelsch, S., Widmann, A., & Schröger, E. (2005). Pitch discrimination accuracy in musicians vs nonmusicians: An event-related potential and behavioral study. *Experimental Brain Research*, *161*, 1–10. doi:10.1007/s00221-004-2044-5

Todd, N., & McAngus, P. (1995). The kinematics of musical expression. *The Journal of the Acoustical Society of America*, *97*, 1940–1949. doi:10.1121/1.412067

Tzanetakis, G., & Cook, P. (2000). Marsyas: A framework for audio analysis. *Organized Sound*, *4*(3), 169–175. doi:10.1017/S1355771800003071

Vaggione, H. (2001). Some ontological remarks about music composition processes. *Computer Music Journal*, *25*(1), 54–61. doi:10.1162/014892601300126115

Vaishnavi, V., & Kuechler, B. (2004). *Design science research in information systems*. Retrieved from http://desrist.org/desrist

Valimaki, V., Laurson, M., & Erkut, C. (2003). Commuted waveguide synthesis of the clavichord. *Computer Music Journal*, *27*(1), 71–82. doi:10.1162/01489260360613353

Välimäki, V., Pakarinen, J., Erkut, C., & Karjalainen, M. (2006). Discrete-time modelling of musical instruments. *Reports on Progress in Physics*, *69*(1), 1–78. doi:10.1088/0034-4885/69/1/R01

Virtual Breath. (2009). *Press release*. Retrieved from http://www.tacc.utexas.edu/documents/13601/137149/CS_Virtual_Breath.pdf

Vuorimaa, P., Bulterman, D., & Cesar, P. (Eds.). (2008). *SMIL timesheets 1.0 - W3C working draft*. Retrieved July 6, 2009, from http://www.w3.org/TR/2008/WD-timesheets-20080110/

Walker, R. (2007). *Music education: Cultural values, social change and innovation*. New York, NY: Charles C Thomas Pub Ltd.

Wanderley, M. M., Schnell, N., & Rovan, J. B. (1998). Escher-modeling and performing composed instruments in real-time. In *Proceedings of the 1998 IEEE International Conference on Systems, Man, and Cybernetics*, (vol. 2, pp. 1080–1084). San Diego, CA: IEEE Press.

Wand, Y., & Weber, R. (1990). An ontological model of an information system. *IEEE Transactions on Software Engineering*, *16*(11). doi:10.1109/32.60316

Wand, Y., & Weber, R. (1993). On the ontological expressiveness of information systems analysis and design grammars. *Journal of Info Systems*, *3*, 217–237. doi:10.1111/j.1365-2575.1993.tb00127.x

Whitehead, A. N. (1960). *Process and reality*. New York, NY: MacMillan.

Widmer, G. (1996). Learning expressive performance: The structure-level approach. *Journal of New Music Research*, *25*(2), 179–205. doi:10.1080/09298219608570702

Wiggins, G. (2009). Computer-representation of music in the research environment. In Crawford & Gibson (Eds.), *Modern Methods for Musicology: Prospects, Proposals and Realities*. Oxford, UK: Ashgate.

Wiggins, G., Miranda, E., Smaill, A., & Harris, M. (1993). A framework for the evaluation of music representation systems. *Computer Music Journal*, *17*, 31–42. doi:10.2307/3680941

Wirag, S., Rothermel, K., & Wahl, T. (1995). Modelling interaction with HyTime. In *Proceedings of the GI/ITG Kommunikation in Verteilten Systemen*, (pp. 188-202). GI/ITG.

Witten, I. H., & Frank, E. (2005). *Data mining: Practical machine learning tools and techniques*. New York, NY: Morgan Kaufman.

Wittgenstein, L. (1953). *Philosophical investigations* (Anscombe, G. E. M., Trans.). New York, NY: Macmillan.

Wolfe, J. (2010). *Music acoustics*. Retrieved from http://www.phys.unsw.edu.au/music/

Woods, W. A. (1970). Transition network grammars for natural language analysis. *Communications of the ACM*, *13*(10). doi:10.1145/355598.362773

Wright, M., Chaudhary, A., Freed, A., Wessel, D., Rodet, X., & Virolle, D. … Serra, X. (1998). New applications of the sound description interchange format. In *Proceedings of the 1998 International Computer Music Conference*, (pp. 276–279). Ann Arbor, MI: ICMA.

Wright, M., Freed, A., Lee, A., Madden, T., & Momeni, A. (2001). Managing complexity with explicit mapping of gestures to sound control with OSC. In *Proceedings of the 2001 International Computer Music Conference*, (pp. 314–317). La Habana, Cuba: ICMA.

Wuyssusek, B. (2004). Ontology and ontologies in information systems analysis and design: A critique. In *Proceedings of the Tenth Americas Conference on Information Systems*, (pp. 4303-4308). New York, NY: Americas Conference.

Ystad, S., & Voinier, T. (2001). A virtually real flute. *Computer Music Journal*, *25*(2), 13–24. doi:10.1162/014892601750302552

Zhang, T., & Kuo, C.-C. J. (1999). Hierarchical classification of audio data for archiving and retrieving. Paper presented at the IEEE International Conference on Acoustics, Speech, and Signal Processing. Phoenix, AZ.

Zuniga, G. L. (2001). Ontology: Its transformation from philosophy to information systems. In *Proceedings of the International Conference on Formal Ontology in Information Systems*, (pp. 187-197). ACM Press.

About the Contributors

Jacques Steyn is the Head of School of IT at Monash University's South African campus, and member of ACM, AIS, IEEE, and Director of IDIA. He currently works in the fields of Development Informatics and Music Informatics. Previously, he was Associate Professor in Multimedia at the University of Pretoria. In 1999, he developed a generic XML-based markup language for music (MML). He was also member of the ISO/MPEG-4 extension workgroup for music notation (i.e. symbolic music representation). In the field of development informatics, he was editor-in-chief of a book set on theory and practice. He composed and performed in various genres ranging from blues, rock, and jazz to musical theatre.

* * *

Antoine Allombert studied Computer Sciences in ENSEIRB, a school of Engineering in Bordeaux, France. After that, he started a PHD thesis under the direction of Myriam Desainte-Catherine. The subject of this thesis was the formalization of a scores system for composition and interpretation in the context of electro-acoustic music. His work focused on the temporal issues of such a system. During this period, he was partly involved in the team "Représentations Musicales" of Gerard Assayag at Ircam. This thesis was defended in 2009. In addition, Antoine Allombert was part of the Virage Project. This project was funded by the French National Agency for Research, and it aimed to adapt the musical concepts developed in the thesis to the context of living shows. This project produced a software system based on these concepts, and it carried on tests during real situations of show production. After having taught in university, he is now a teacher in an elementary school near Paris.

Sergio Canazza received a Master's degree in Electronic Engineering from the University of Padova, Italy. He is Assistant Research Professor ("Professore Aggregato") at the Department of Information Engineering, University of Padova, where he is responsible for the course of Computer Science, and Lecturer for the courses of Sound and Music Computing. He is also a Board Member of the Centro di Sonologia Computazionale (CSC), University of Padova. He is with the Sound and Music Computing Group, and his main research interests involve 1) expressive information processing, 2) auditory displays, and 3) audio documents preservation and restoration. He is advisory editor in *Journal of New Music Research* (Taylor & Francis Group). He is author or co-author of more than 100 publications in international journals and refereed international conferences. He has been general chairman and member of technical committees at several conferences and project manager in European projects.

Giovanni De Poli (Member, IEEE) received the Master's degree in Electronic Engineering from the University of Padova, Italy. He is currently Full Professor of Computer Science at the Department of Information Engineering, University of Padova, Italy, where he teaches classes on the fundamentals of informatics and processing systems for music. He is also the Director of the Centro di Sonologia Computazionale (CSC), University of Padova. He is author of several scientific international publications, served on the scientific committees of international conferences, and is Associate Editor of the *Journal of New Music Research*. He is owner of patents on digital music instruments. His main research interests are in algorithms for sound synthesis and analysis, models for expressiveness in music, multimedia systems and human-computer interaction, and preservation and restoration of audio documents. He is/was involved with several European research projects. Systems and research developed in his lab have been exploited in collaboration with the digital musical instruments industry (GeneralMusic, IK Multimedia).

Myriam Desainte-Catherine is Professor in Computer Science at IPB, University of Bordeaux. She is the Scientific Director of the SCRIME (Studio for Research and Creation in Computer Science and Electracoustic Music), which she created with Christian Eloy, Professor in Electroacoustic Music Composition at the Music Institute of Bordeaux. She is the head of the research team "Sound and Music Modeling" at LaBRI (CNRS UMR 5800). The research applications of which are mainly oriented towards musical creation and pedagogy.

Ichiro Fujinaga is an Associate Professor and the Chair of the Music Technology Area at the Schulich School of Music at McGill University. He has Bachelor's degrees in Music/Percussion and Mathematics from University of Alberta, and a Master's degree in Music Theory, and a Ph.D. in Music Technology from McGill University. In 2003-4, he was the Acting Director of the Center for Interdisciplinary Research in Music Media and Technology (CIRMMT) at McGill. In 2002-3, he was the Chair of the Music Technology Area at the School of Music. Before that, he was a faculty member of the Computer Music Department at the Peabody Conservatory of Music of the Johns Hopkins University. Research interests include music theory, machine learning, music perception, digital signal processing, genetic algorithms, and music information acquisition, preservation, and retrieval.

Michael Good is the inventor of the MusicXML format for exchanging digital sheet music between computer applications. MusicXML is now supported by over 160 music applications on Windows, Mac, Linux, and iOS, including Finale, Sibelius, and Cubase. It has become the most widely used symbolic music format since MIDI. Michael founded Recordare in 2000 to grow the market for digital sheet music through the creation of a standard notation format. In 2011, Recordare's MusicXML assets were acquired by MakeMusic, Inc., where Michael is now Director of Digital Sheet Music. Prior to starting Recordare, Michael held technical leadership roles in computer-human interaction at SAP Labs, Xtensory, and Digital Equipment Corporation. He received his B.S. and M.S. degrees in Computer Science from MIT, with his B.S. thesis work conducted at the MIT Experimental Music Studio. Michael sings tenor with the San Francisco Symphony Chorus and the West Bay Opera Chorus.

Perfecto Herrera received the degree in Psychology from the University of Barcelona, Barcelona, Spain, in 1987. He was with the University of Barcelona as a Software Developer and as Assistant Professor. His further studies focused on Sound Engineering, Audio Postproduction, and Computer

Music. Now he is finishing his PhD on Music Content Processing in the Universitat Pompeu Fabra (UPF), Barcelona. He has been working with the Music Technology Group (UPF) since its inception in 1996, first responsible for the sound laboratory/studio, then as a researcher. He worked in the MPEG-7 standardization initiative from 1999 to 2001. Then, he collaborated in the EU-IST-funded CUIDADO project, contributing to the research and development of tools for indexing and retrieving music and sound collections. This work was continued and expanded as Scientific Coordinator for the Semantic Interaction with Music Audio Contents (SIMAC) project, again funded by the EU-IST. He is currently the Head of the Department of Sonology, Higher Music School of Catalonia (ESMUC), where he teaches Music Technology and Psychoacoustics. His main research interests are music content processing, classification, and music perception and cognition.

Alexander Refsum Jensenius (BA, MA, MSc, PhD) is a Music Researcher and Research Musician working in the fields of embodied music cognition and new instruments for musical expression at the University of Oslo and Norwegian Academy of Music.

Marc Leman is Professor in Systematic Musicology at Ghent University (UGent). He is Head of the Department of Art, Music, and Theater Sciences and Director of IPEM. His research activities deal with questions related to musical meaning formation, the effect of music on human cognition and emotion, the description of musical content, and the understanding of gestures, musical imitation, and corporeal resonance. His research is focused on finding regularities in human sensory, perceptive, cognitive, synaesthetic/kinaesthetic, social and emotional/affective information processing, using methods that bridge the gap between natural and cultural sciences.

Cory McKay is a Professor at Marianopolis College and a Lecturer at McGill University in Montréal, Canada. He holds a B.Sc. in Physics from McGill University; a double honours B.A. in Music and Computer Science from the University of Guelph; and both an M.A. and a Ph.D. in Music Technology from McGill University. His research focuses on extracting and representing information from music using machine learning applied to audio recordings, symbolic musical representations, lyrical transcriptions, general information available on the Internet, and, most recently, images. Creative interests include the design and use of automatic music accompaniment systems and live electronic music performance software. Dr. McKay is the Founder and Music Director of MLOrk, the Marianopolis College Laptop Computer Orchestra.

Jyri Pakarinen was born in Lappeenranta, Finland, in 1979. He received the M.Sc. and D. Sc. (Tech.) degrees in Acoustics and Audio Signal Processing from the Helsinki University of Technology, in 2004 and 2008, respectively. He has been working since 2002 in the Audio Signal Processing Group in Espoo, Finland, currently known as the Department of Signal Processing and Acoustics, Aalto University School of Electrical Engineering, where he presently works as a Postdoctoral Researcher and Lecturer. His main research interests are digital emulation of electric audio circuits, sound synthesis through physical modeling, and vibro- and electroacoustic measurements. As a semiprofessional guitar player, he is also interested and involved in music activities.

Antonio Rodà (1971, Verona, Italy) received a Master's degree in Electronic Engineering from the University of Padua (1996), and a PhD degree in Audiovisual Studies from the University of Udine (2007). Since 1997, he has been working as a Researcher at the "Centro di Sonologia Computazionale" of Padova, a research center on computer music founded in 1976. His main research interests are in models for expressiveness in music, multimedia systems, preservation and restoration of audio documents. He is currently Assistant Research Professor at the Department of Information Engineering, University of Padova.

Gerard Roma received a degree in Philosophy from Universitat Autònoma de Barcelona (UAB) in Barcelona, Spain, in 1997. After several years working as a Software Developer, he went back to the university and obtained a Master in Information and Communication Technologies from Universitat Pompeu Fabra (UPF) in 2008. He is currently a PhD candidate at the Music Technology Group in UPF, were his research focuses on computational models and applications for supporting collective musical creativity.

Wijnand Schepens did a PhD in Physics at the Department of Mathematical Physics and Astronomy at Ghent University (Belgium) but switched to Computer Science. He is currently in Informatica at the University College Ghent (Hogeschool Gent). His current research interest is about the representation and manipulation of complex time structures, particularly in the domain of symbolical music, as well as visual programming. He participates in renaissance music choirs.

Alvise Vidolin (1949, Padova, Italy) received a Master's degree in Electronic Engineering from the University of Padova, Italy. He is Cofounder and Staff Member with the Centro di Sonologia Computazionale (CSC), University of Padova, Padova, where he is also teaching Computer Music as an Invited Professor and conducting his research activity in the field of computer-assisted composition and real-time performance. He was Professor of Electronic Music at B. Marcello Conservatory of Music, Venezia, Italy. Since 1977, he has often worked with La Biennale di Venezia, Venezia. He has also given his services to several important Italian and foreign institutions, and he worked with several composers, such as C. Ambrosini, G. Battistelli, L. Berio, A. Guarnieri, L. Nono, and S. Sciarrino, on the electronic realization and performance of their works. Vidolin is Cofounder of the Italian Computer Music Association (AIMI), where he was President from 1988 to 1990, and SaMPL Laboratory (at Conservatory "C. Pollini", Padova.

Index